P9-DVU-413

Hot Gimmick

vol.9

MIKI AIHARA

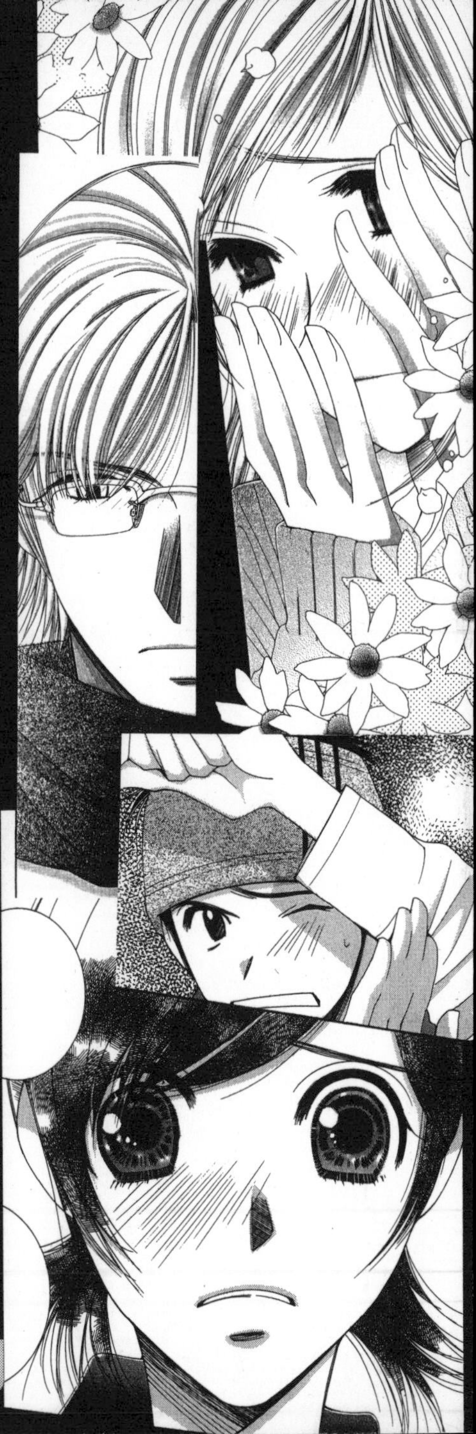

HOT GIMMICK
CONTENTS

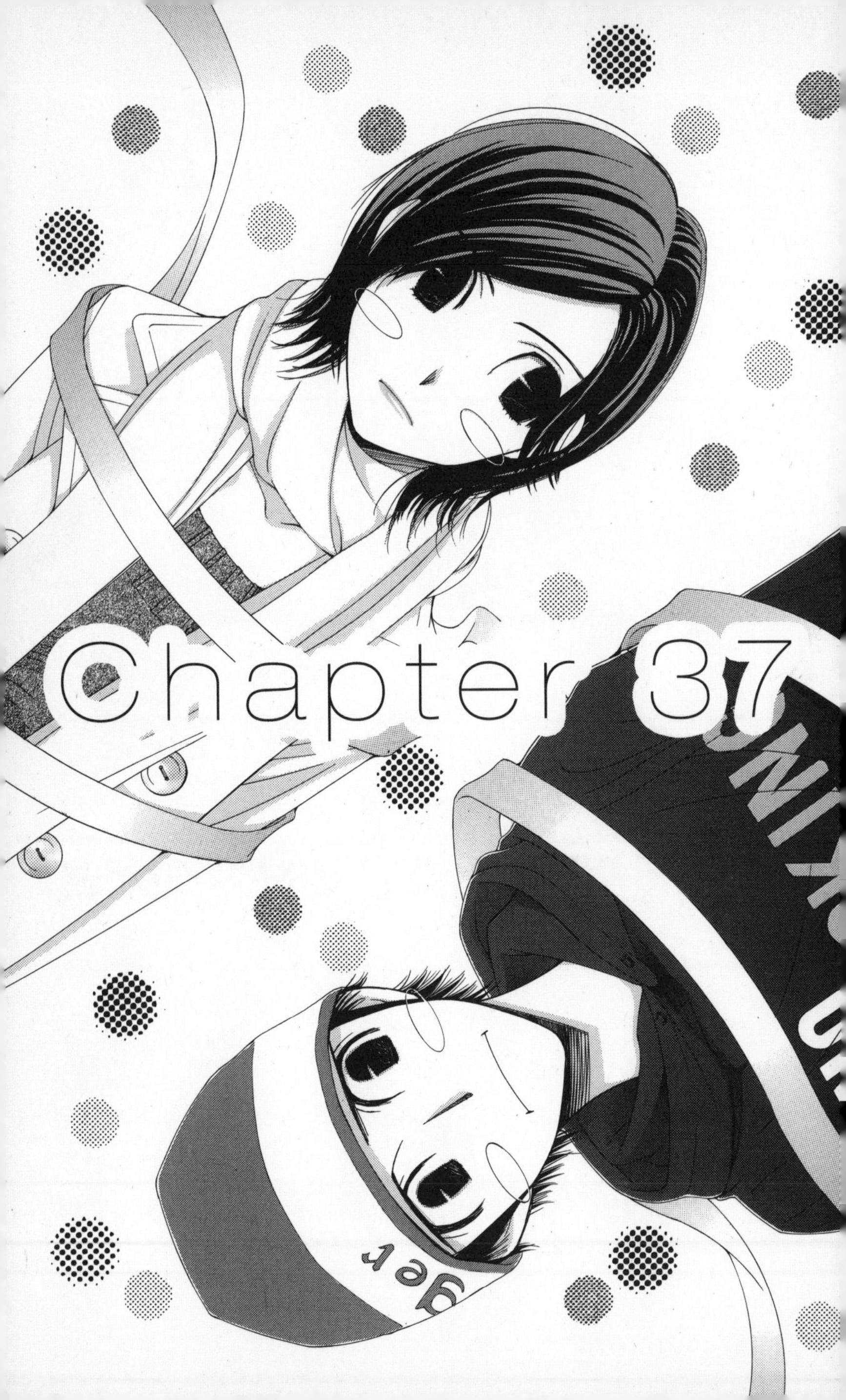
Chapter 37

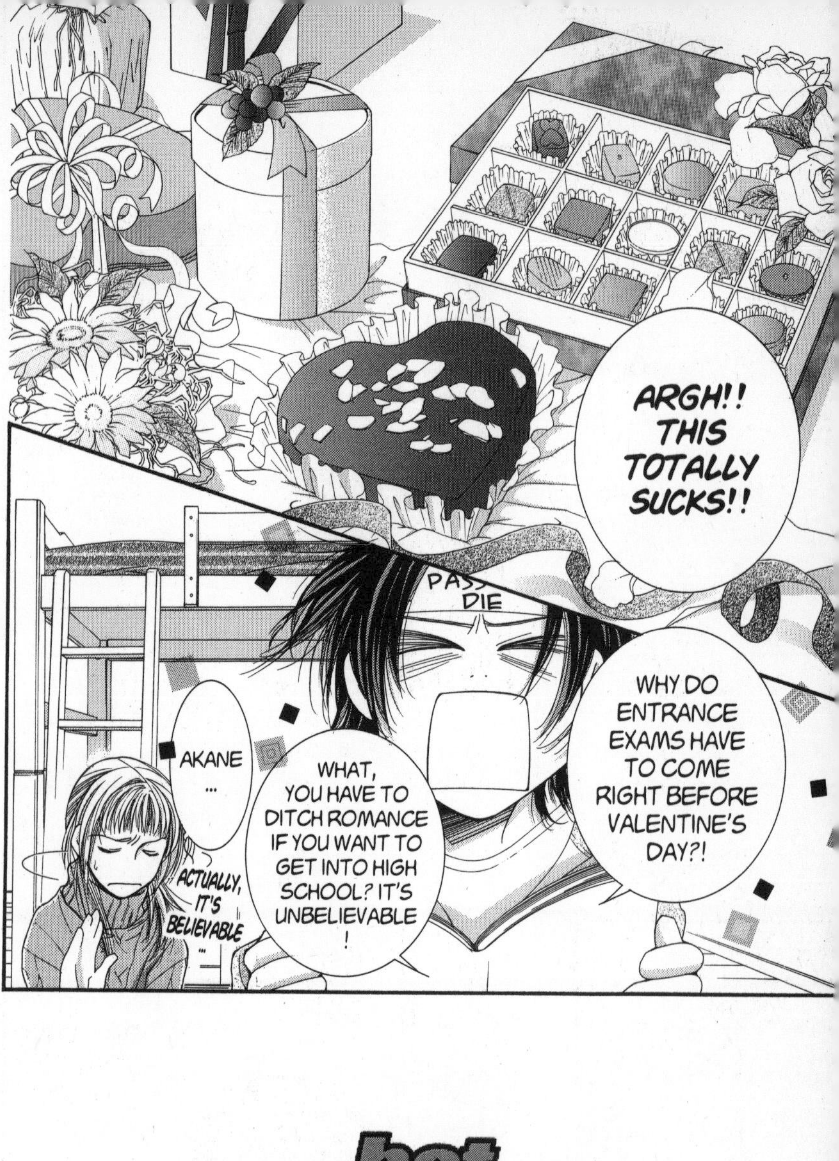
ARGH!! THIS TOTALLY SUCKS!!
DIE
WHY DO ENTRANCE EXAMS HAVE TO COME RIGHT BEFORE VALENTINE'S DAY?!
WHAT, YOU HAVE TO DITCH ROMANCE IF YOU WANT TO GET INTO HIGH SCHOOL? IT'S UNBELIEVABLE!
AKANE...
ACTUALLY, IT'S BELIEVABLE...

hot gimmick

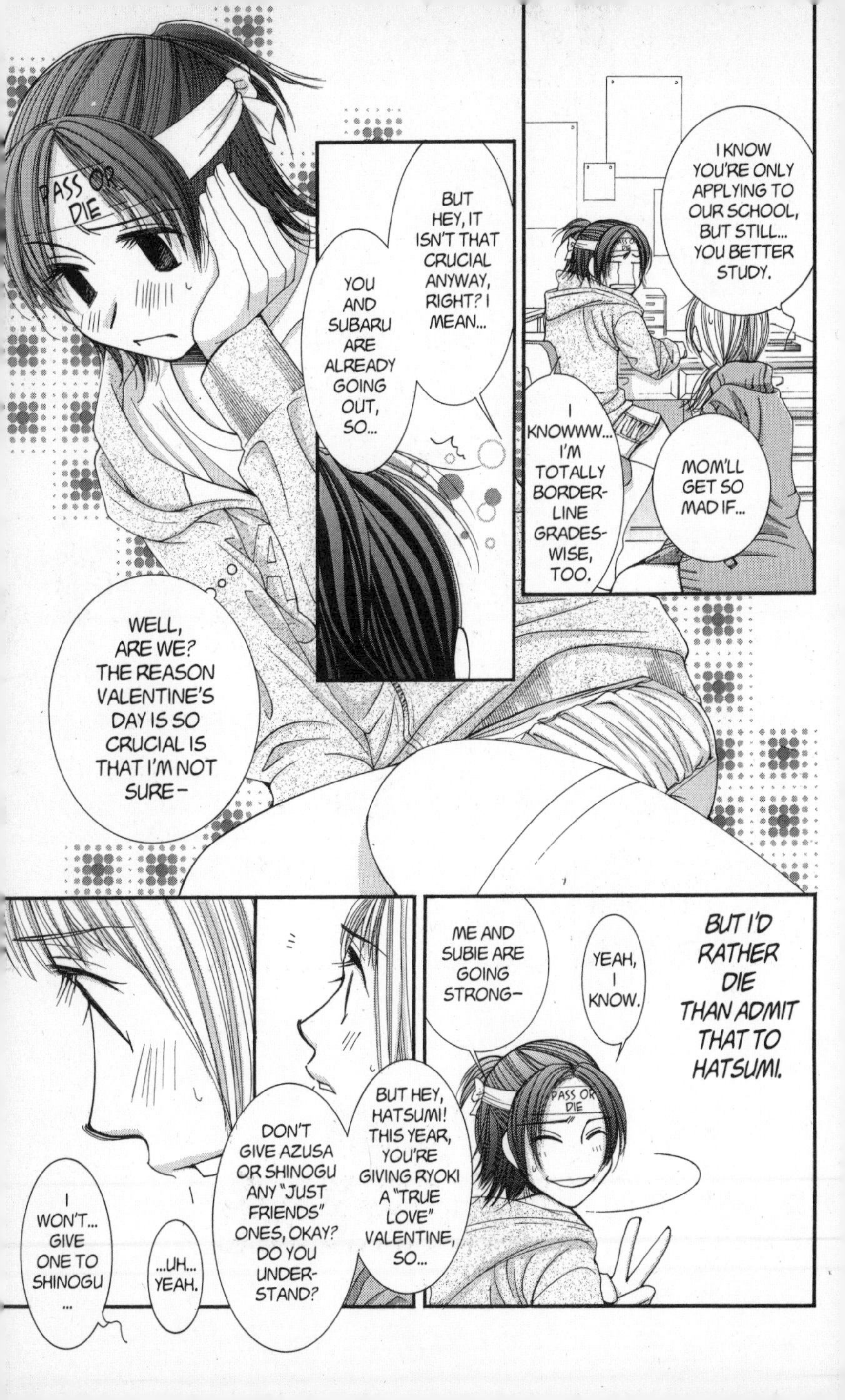
I KNOW YOU'RE ONLY APPLYING TO OUR SCHOOL, BUT STILL... YOU BETTER STUDY.
PASS OR DIE
MOM'LL GET SO MAD IF...
I KNOWWW... I'M TOTALLY BORDER-LINE GRADES-WISE, TOO.
BUT HEY, IT ISN'T THAT CRUCIAL ANYWAY, RIGHT? I MEAN...
YOU AND SUBARU ARE ALREADY GOING OUT, SO...
PASS OR DIE
WELL, ARE WE? THE REASON VALENTINE'S DAY IS SO CRUCIAL IS THAT I'M NOT SURE–
BUT I'D RATHER DIE THAN ADMIT THAT TO HATSUMI.
YEAH, I KNOW.
ME AND SUBIE ARE GOING STRONG–
PASS OR DIE
BUT HEY, HATSUMI! THIS YEAR, YOU'RE GIVING RYOKI A "TRUE LOVE" VALENTINE, SO...
DON'T GIVE AZUSA OR SHINOGU ANY "JUST FRIENDS" ONES, OKAY? DO YOU UNDER-STAND?
...UH... YEAH.
I WON'T... GIVE ONE TO SHINOGU ...

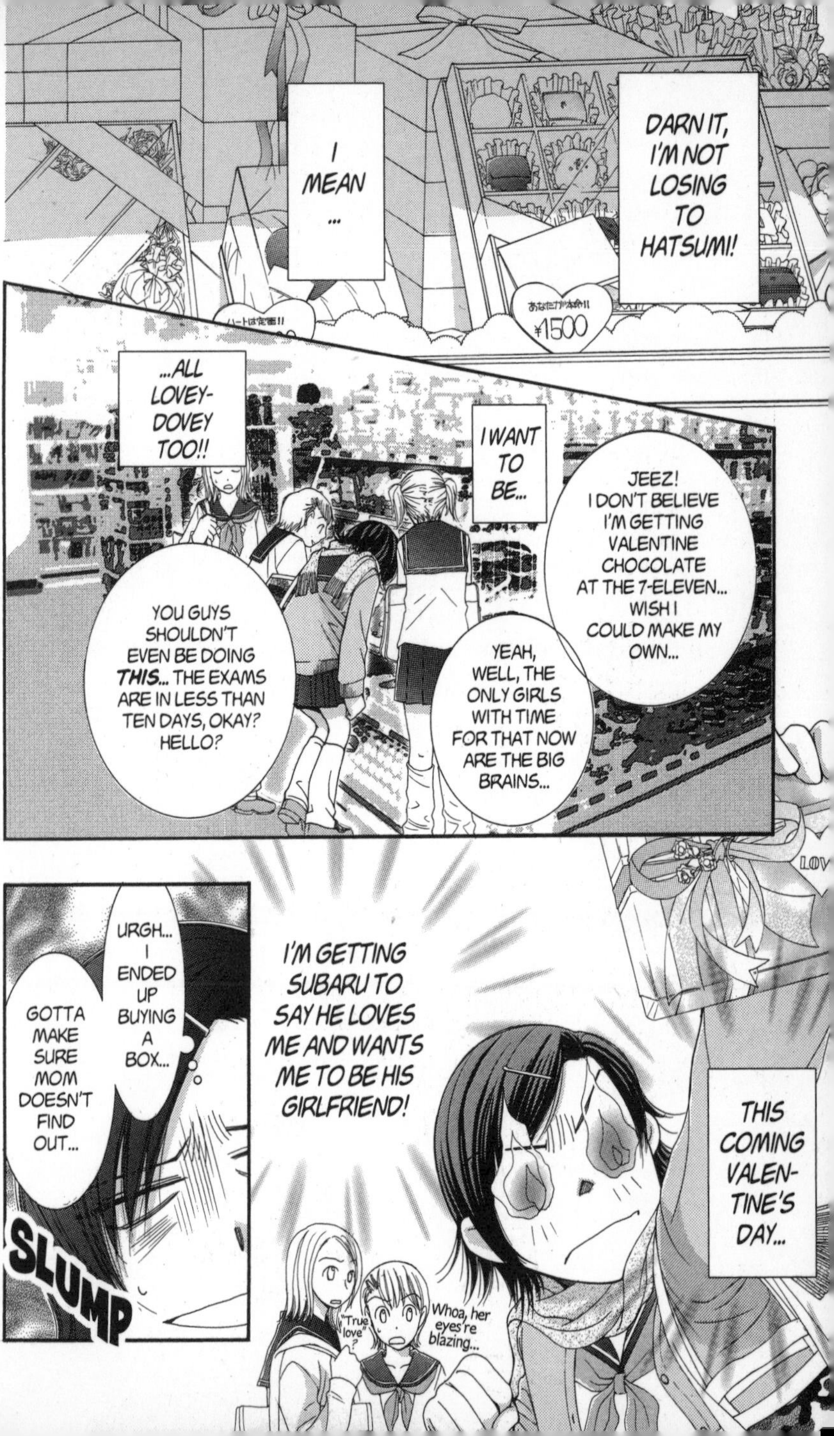
DARN IT, I'M NOT LOSING TO HATSUMI!
I MEAN ...
あなたが本命!!
¥1500
ハートは定番!!
JEEZ! I DON'T BELIEVE I'M GETTING VALENTINE CHOCOLATE AT THE 7-ELEVEN... WISH I COULD MAKE MY OWN...
I WANT TO BE...
...ALL LOVEY-DOVEY TOO!!
YEAH, WELL, THE ONLY GIRLS WITH TIME FOR THAT NOW ARE THE BIG BRAINS...
YOU GUYS SHOULDN'T EVEN BE DOING **THIS**... THE EXAMS ARE IN LESS THAN TEN DAYS, OKAY? HELLO?
THIS COMING VALENTINE'S DAY...
I'M GETTING SUBARU TO SAY HE LOVES ME AND WANTS ME TO BE HIS GIRLFRIEND!
Whoa, her eyes're blazing...
"True love"?
URGH... I ENDED UP BUYING A BOX...
GOTTA MAKE SURE MOM DOESN'T FIND OUT...
SLUMP

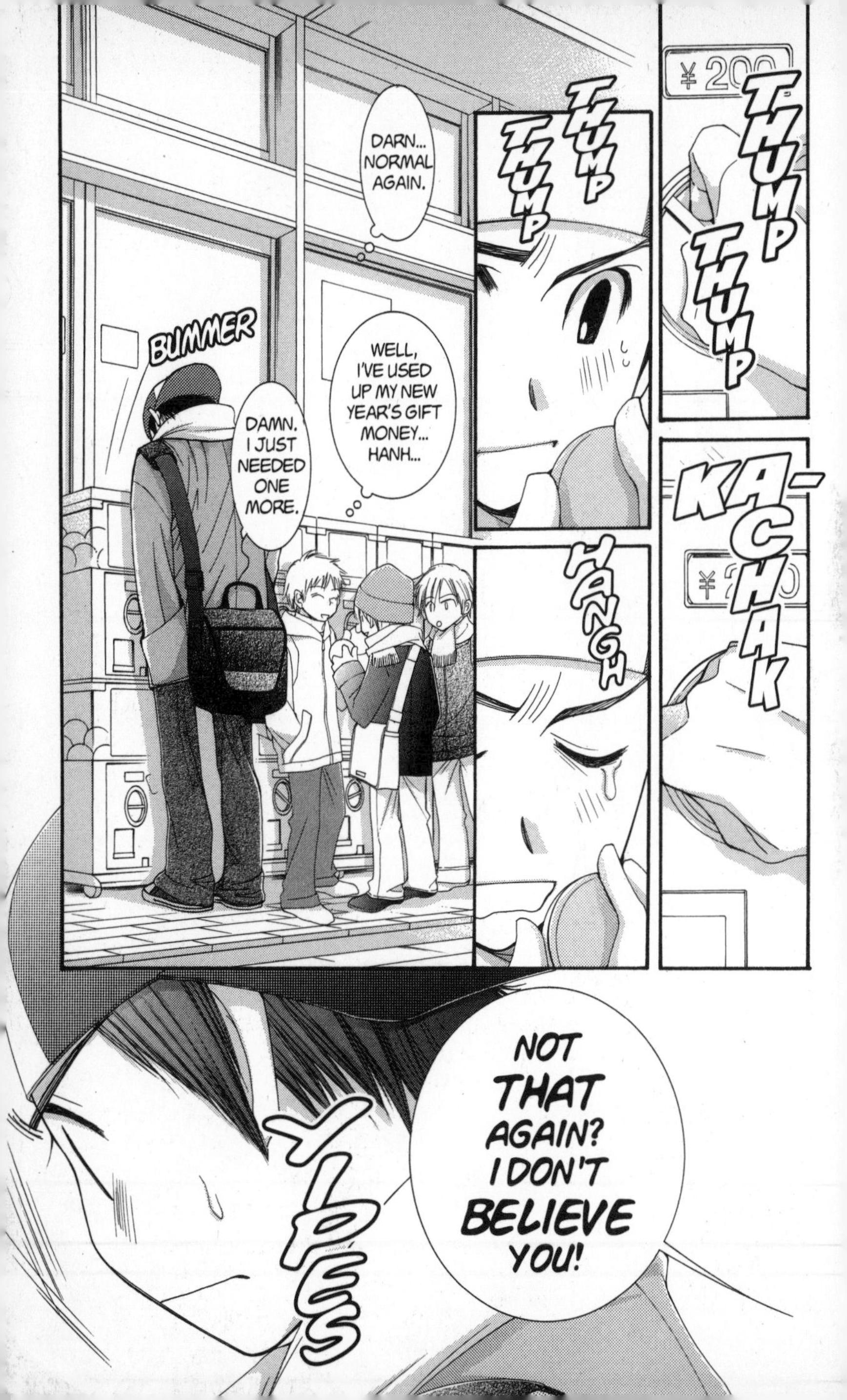

¥200
THUMP THUMP
KA-CHAK
THUMP THUMP
HANGH
DARN... NORMAL AGAIN.
WELL, I'VE USED UP MY NEW YEAR'S GIFT MONEY... HANH...
BUMMER
DAMN. I JUST NEEDED ONE MORE.
NOT THAT AGAIN? I DON'T BELIEVE YOU!
YIPES

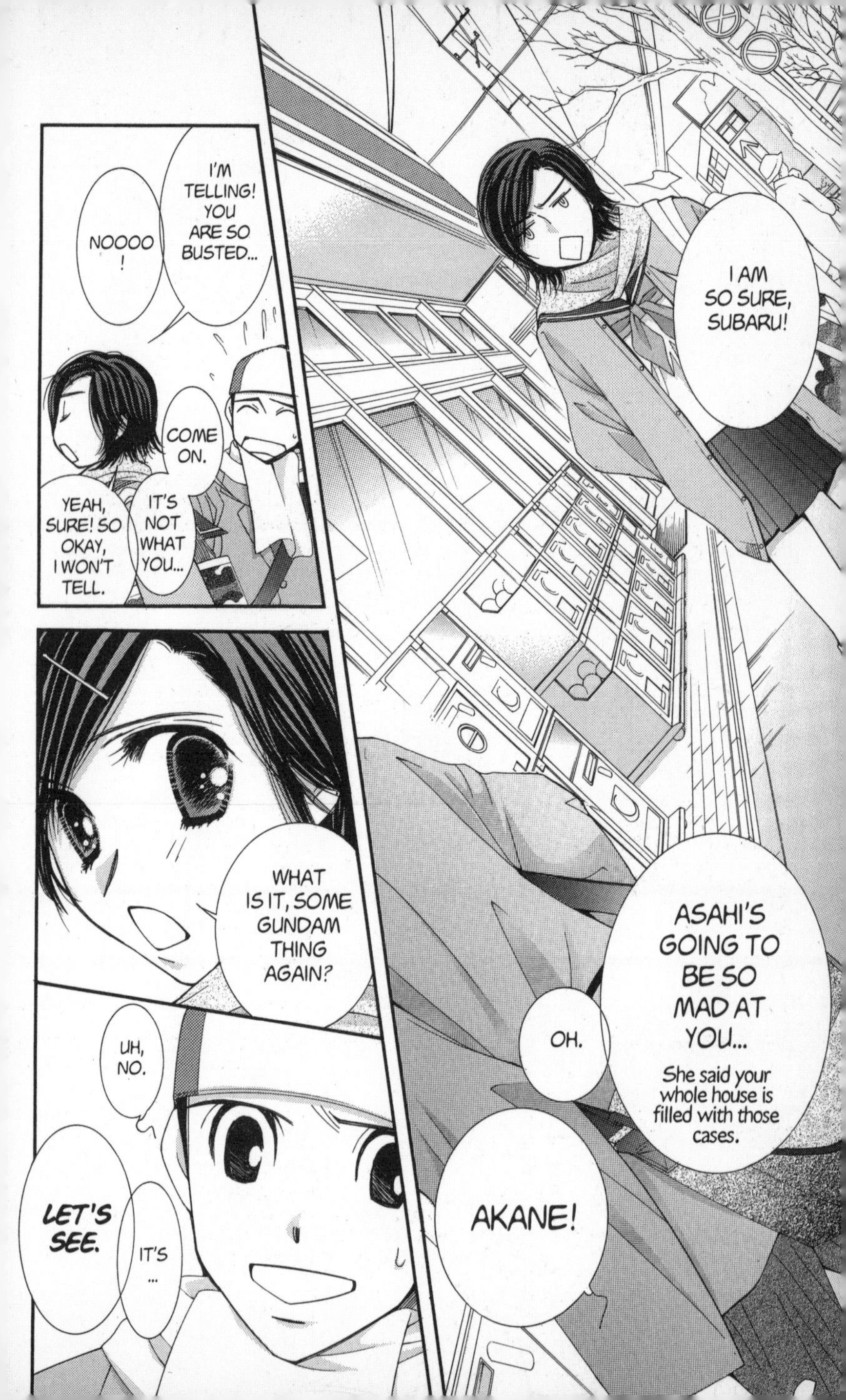
I AM SO SURE, SUBARU!
ASAHI'S GOING TO BE SO MAD AT YOU...
She said your whole house is filled with those cases.
OH.
AKANE!
I'M TELLING! YOU ARE SO BUSTED...
NOOOO!
COME ON.
IT'S NOT WHAT YOU...
YEAH, SURE! SO OKAY, I WON'T TELL.
WHAT IS IT, SOME GUNDAM THING AGAIN?
UH, NO.
IT'S ...
LET'S SEE.

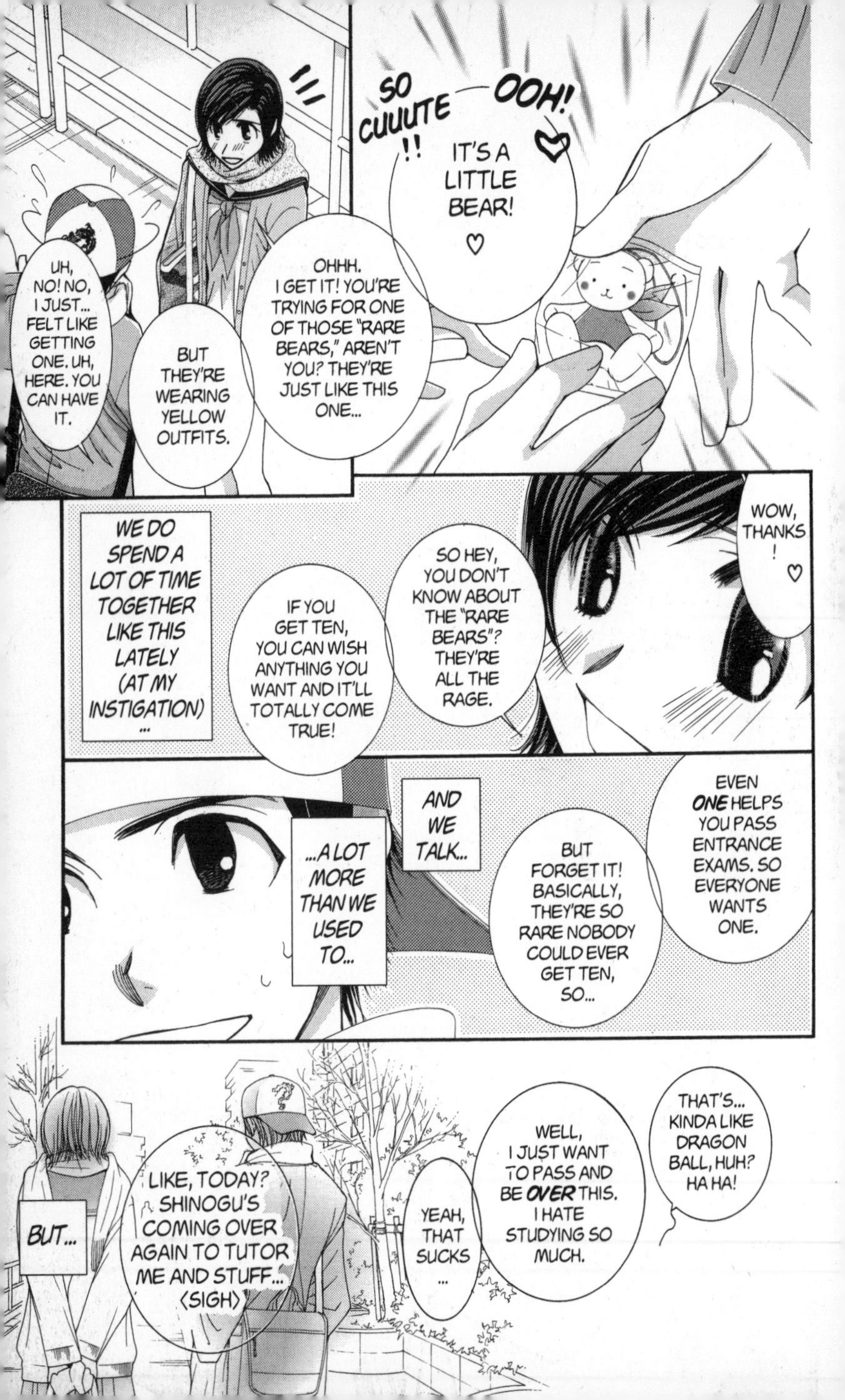

SO CUUUTE!!—OOH!♡
IT'S A LITTLE BEAR! ♡
OHHH. I GET IT! YOU'RE TRYING FOR ONE OF THOSE "RARE BEARS," AREN'T YOU? THEY'RE JUST LIKE THIS ONE...
BUT THEY'RE WEARING YELLOW OUTFITS.
UH, NO! NO, I JUST... FELT LIKE GETTING ONE. UH, HERE. YOU CAN HAVE IT.
WOW, THANKS! ♡
SO HEY, YOU DON'T KNOW ABOUT THE "RARE BEARS"? THEY'RE ALL THE RAGE.
IF YOU GET TEN, YOU CAN WISH ANYTHING YOU WANT AND IT'LL TOTALLY COME TRUE!
WE DO SPEND A LOT OF TIME TOGETHER LIKE THIS LATELY (AT MY INSTIGATION) ...
EVEN ONE HELPS YOU PASS ENTRANCE EXAMS. SO EVERYONE WANTS ONE.
BUT FORGET IT! BASICALLY, THEY'RE SO RARE NOBODY COULD EVER GET TEN, SO...
AND WE TALK...
...A LOT MORE THAN WE USED TO...
THAT'S... KINDA LIKE DRAGON BALL, HUH? HA HA!
WELL, I JUST WANT TO PASS AND BE OVER THIS. I HATE STUDYING SO MUCH.
YEAH, THAT SUCKS ...
LIKE, TODAY? SHINOGU'S COMING OVER AGAIN TO TUTOR ME AND STUFF... 〈SIGH〉
BUT...

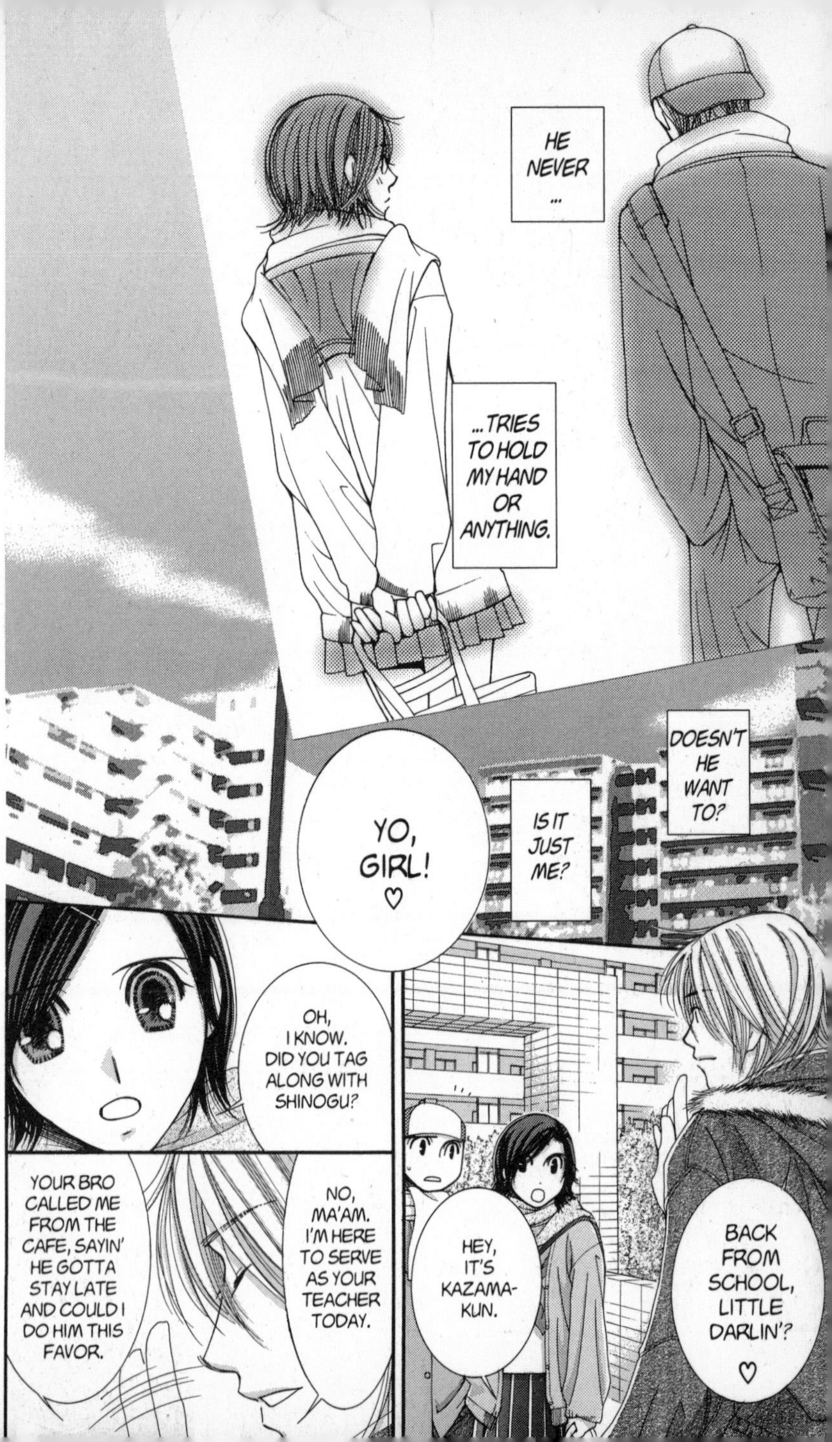
HE NEVER ...
...TRIES TO HOLD MY HAND OR ANYTHING.
DOESN'T HE WANT TO?
IS IT JUST ME?
YO, GIRL! ♡
BACK FROM SCHOOL, LITTLE DARLIN'? ♡
HEY, IT'S KAZAMA-KUN.
OH, I KNOW. DID YOU TAG ALONG WITH SHINOGU?
NO, MA'AM. I'M HERE TO SERVE AS YOUR TEACHER TODAY.
YOUR BRO CALLED ME FROM THE CAFE, SAYIN' HE GOTTA STAY LATE AND COULD I DO HIM THIS FAVOR.

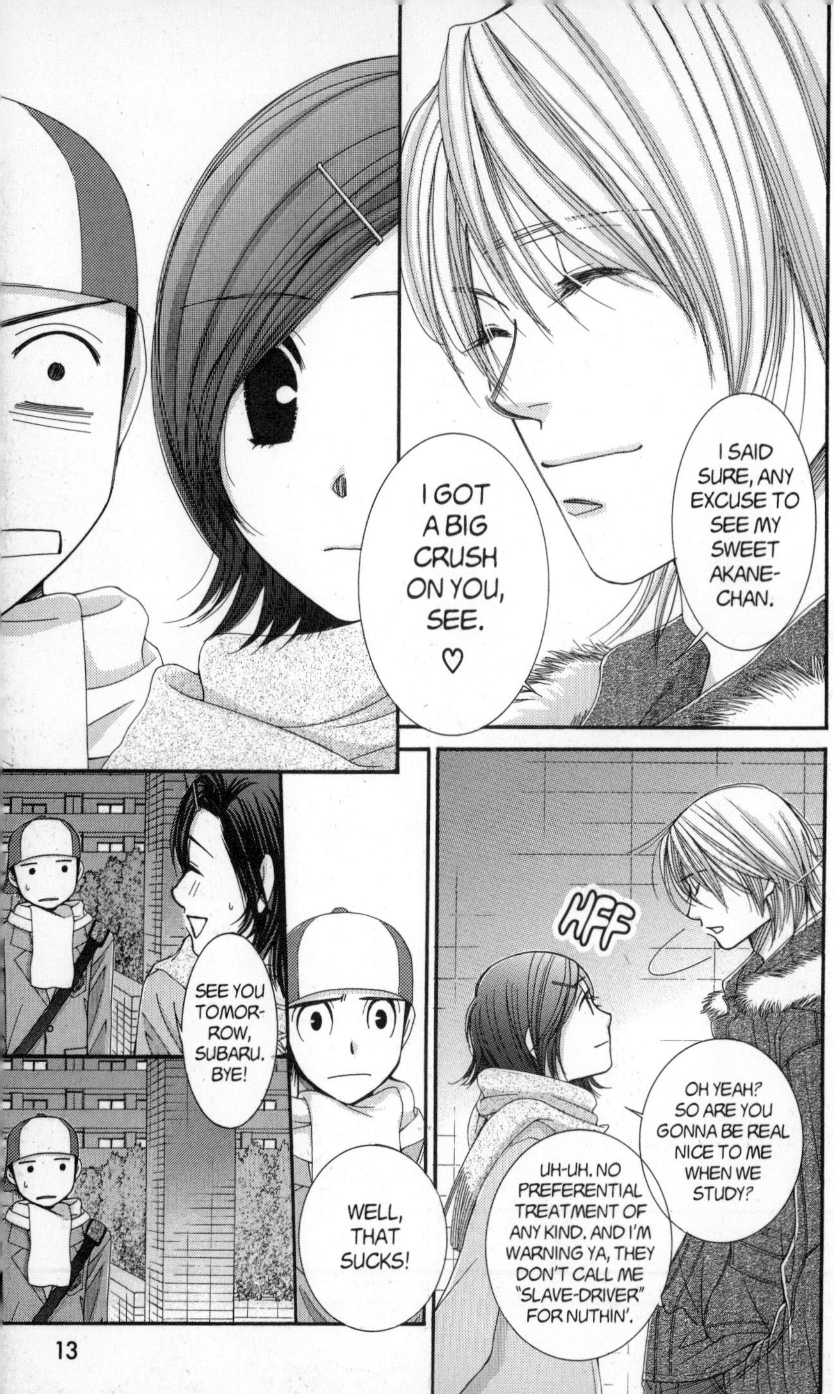
I SAID SURE, ANY EXCUSE TO SEE MY SWEET AKANE-CHAN.
I GOT A BIG CRUSH ON YOU, SEE. ♡
HFF
OH YEAH? SO ARE YOU GONNA BE REAL NICE TO ME WHEN WE STUDY?
UH-UH. NO PREFERENTIAL TREATMENT OF ANY KIND. AND I'M WARNING YA, THEY DON'T CALL ME "SLAVE-DRIVER" FOR NUTHIN'.
SEE YOU TOMOR-ROW, SUBARU. BYE!
WELL, THAT SUCKS!

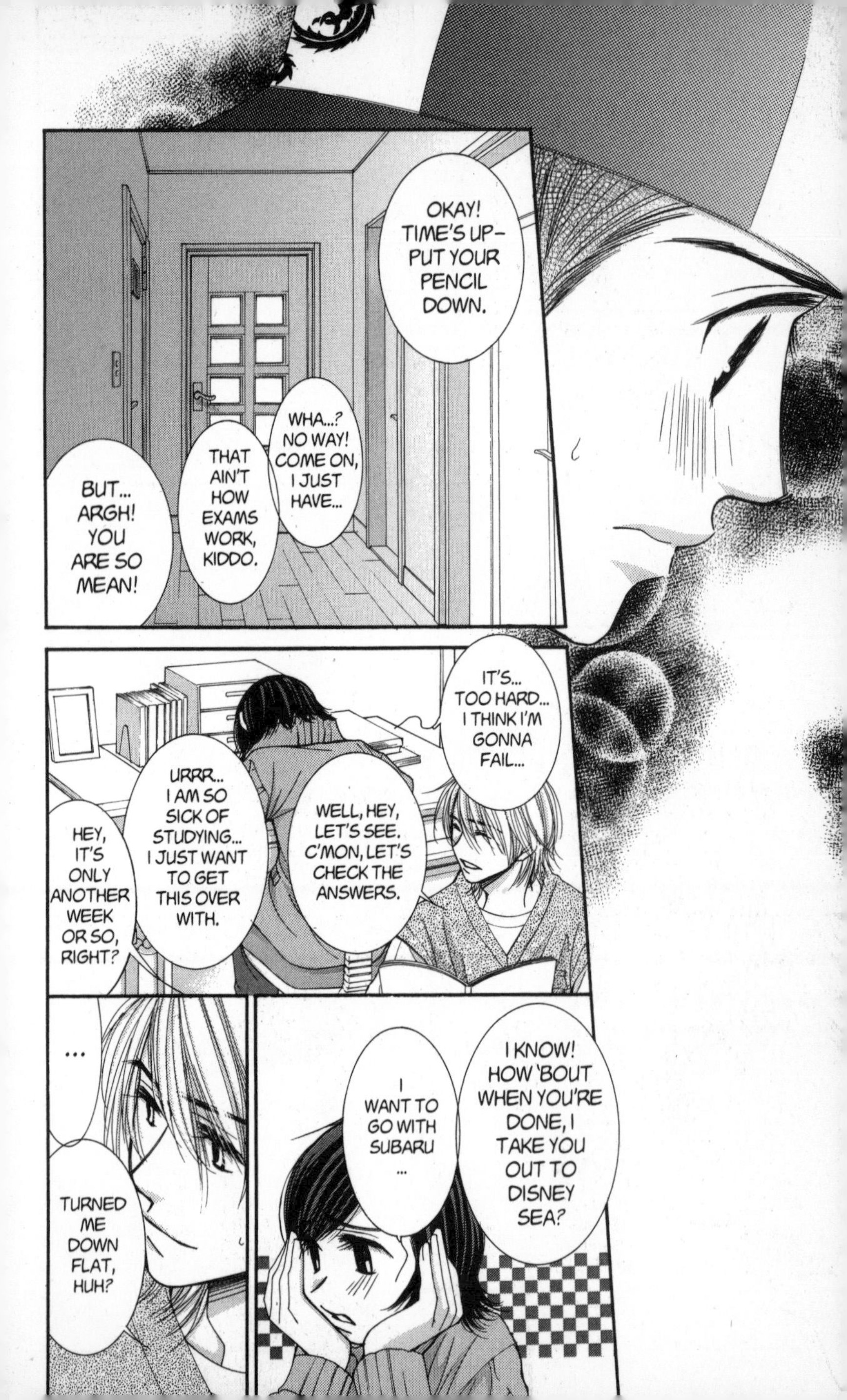
OKAY! TIME'S UP– PUT YOUR PENCIL DOWN.
WHA...? NO WAY! COME ON, I JUST HAVE...
THAT AIN'T HOW EXAMS WORK, KIDDO.
BUT... ARGH! YOU ARE SO MEAN!
IT'S... TOO HARD... I THINK I'M GONNA FAIL...
WELL, HEY, LET'S SEE. C'MON, LET'S CHECK THE ANSWERS.
URRR... I AM SO SICK OF STUDYING... I JUST WANT TO GET THIS OVER WITH.
HEY, IT'S ONLY ANOTHER WEEK OR SO, RIGHT?
I KNOW! HOW 'BOUT WHEN YOU'RE DONE, I TAKE YOU OUT TO DISNEY SEA?
I WANT TO GO WITH SUBARU...
...
TURNED ME DOWN FLAT, HUH?

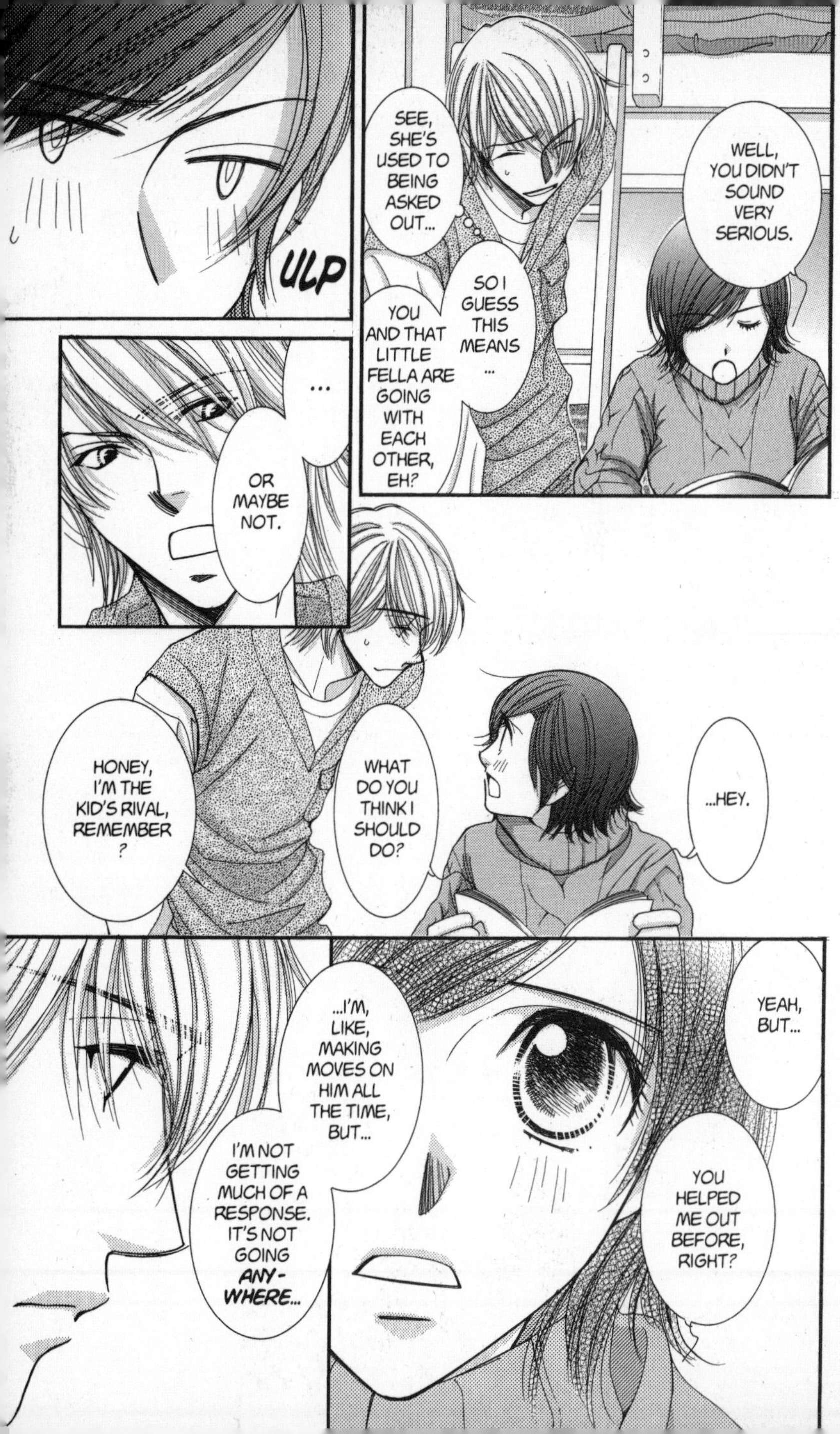
WELL, YOU DIDN'T SOUND VERY SERIOUS.
SEE, SHE'S USED TO BEING ASKED OUT...
SO I GUESS THIS MEANS ...
YOU AND THAT LITTLE FELLA ARE GOING WITH EACH OTHER, EH?
ULP
...
OR MAYBE NOT.
...HEY.
WHAT DO YOU THINK I SHOULD DO?
HONEY, I'M THE KID'S RIVAL, REMEMBER?
YEAH, BUT...
YOU HELPED ME OUT BEFORE, RIGHT?
...I'M, LIKE, MAKING MOVES ON HIM ALL THE TIME, BUT...
I'M NOT GETTING MUCH OF A RESPONSE. IT'S NOT GOING ANY-WHERE...

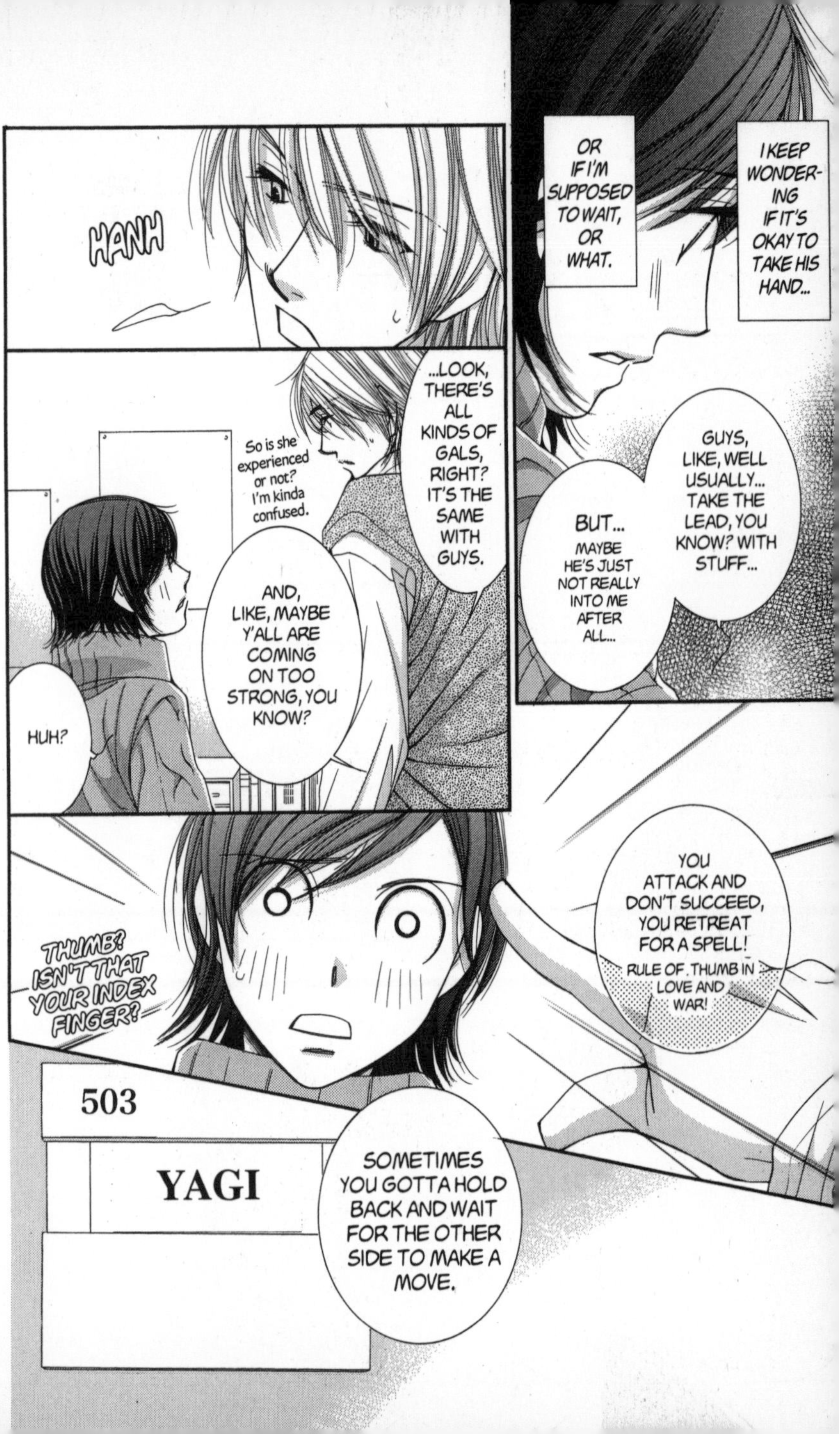
I KEEP WONDERING IF IT'S OKAY TO TAKE HIS HAND...
OR IF I'M SUPPOSED TO WAIT, OR WHAT.
GUYS, LIKE, WELL USUALLY... TAKE THE LEAD, YOU KNOW? WITH STUFF...
BUT... MAYBE HE'S JUST NOT REALLY INTO ME AFTER ALL...
HANH
...LOOK, THERE'S ALL KINDS OF GALS, RIGHT? IT'S THE SAME WITH GUYS.
So is she experienced or not? I'm kinda confused.
AND, LIKE, MAYBE Y'ALL ARE COMING ON TOO STRONG, YOU KNOW?
HUH?
YOU ATTACK AND DON'T SUCCEED, YOU RETREAT FOR A SPELL!
RULE OF THUMB IN LOVE AND WAR!
THUMB? ISN'T THAT YOUR INDEX FINGER?
SOMETIMES YOU GOTTA HOLD BACK AND WAIT FOR THE OTHER SIDE TO MAKE A MOVE.
503
YAGI

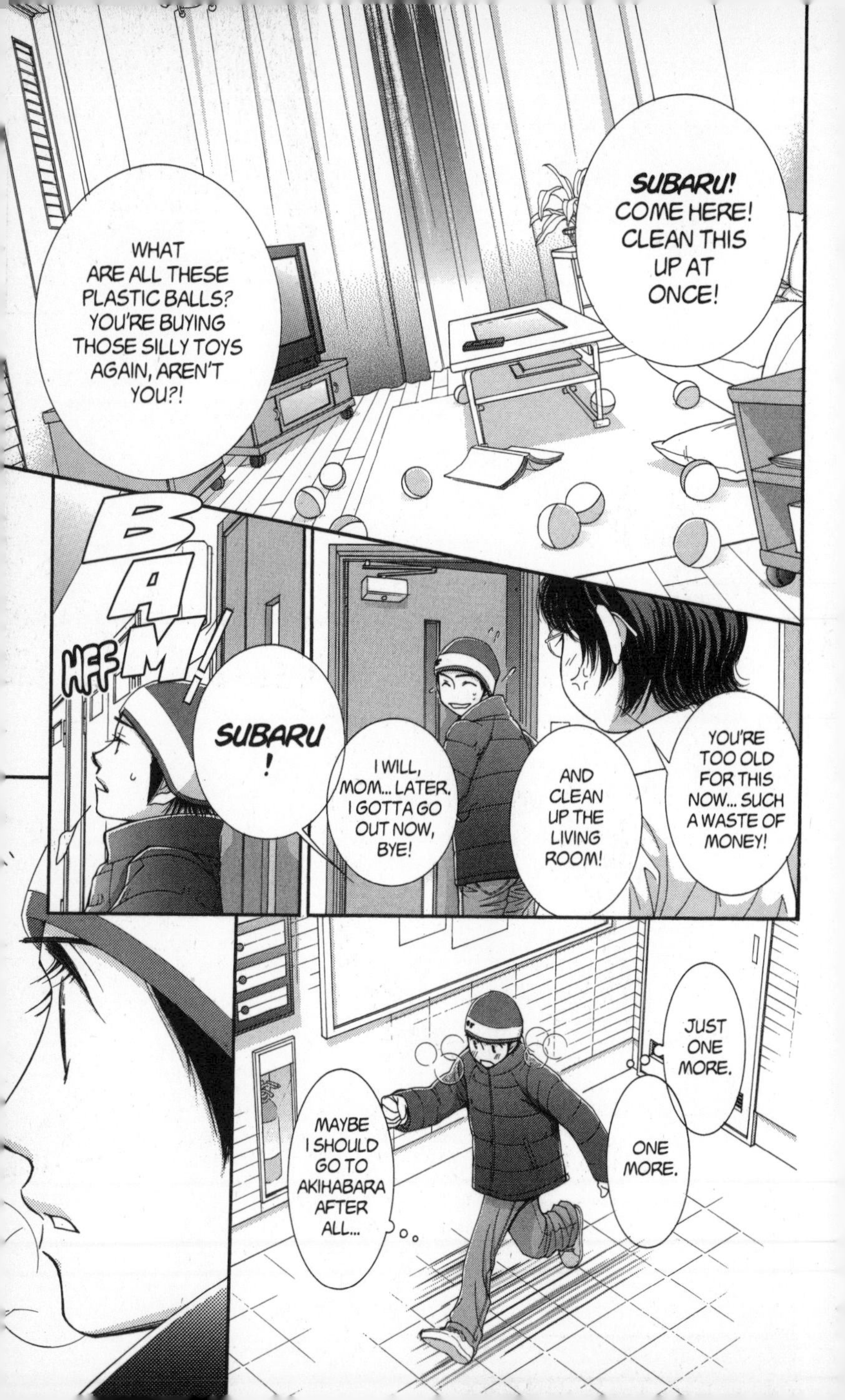
SUBARU! COME HERE! CLEAN THIS UP AT ONCE!
WHAT ARE ALL THESE PLASTIC BALLS? YOU'RE BUYING THOSE SILLY TOYS AGAIN, AREN'T YOU?!
YOU'RE TOO OLD FOR THIS NOW... SUCH A WASTE OF MONEY!
AND CLEAN UP THE LIVING ROOM!
I WILL, MOM... LATER. I GOTTA GO OUT NOW, BYE!
BAM
SUBARU!
HFF
JUST ONE MORE.
ONE MORE.
MAYBE I SHOULD GO TO AKIHABARA AFTER ALL...

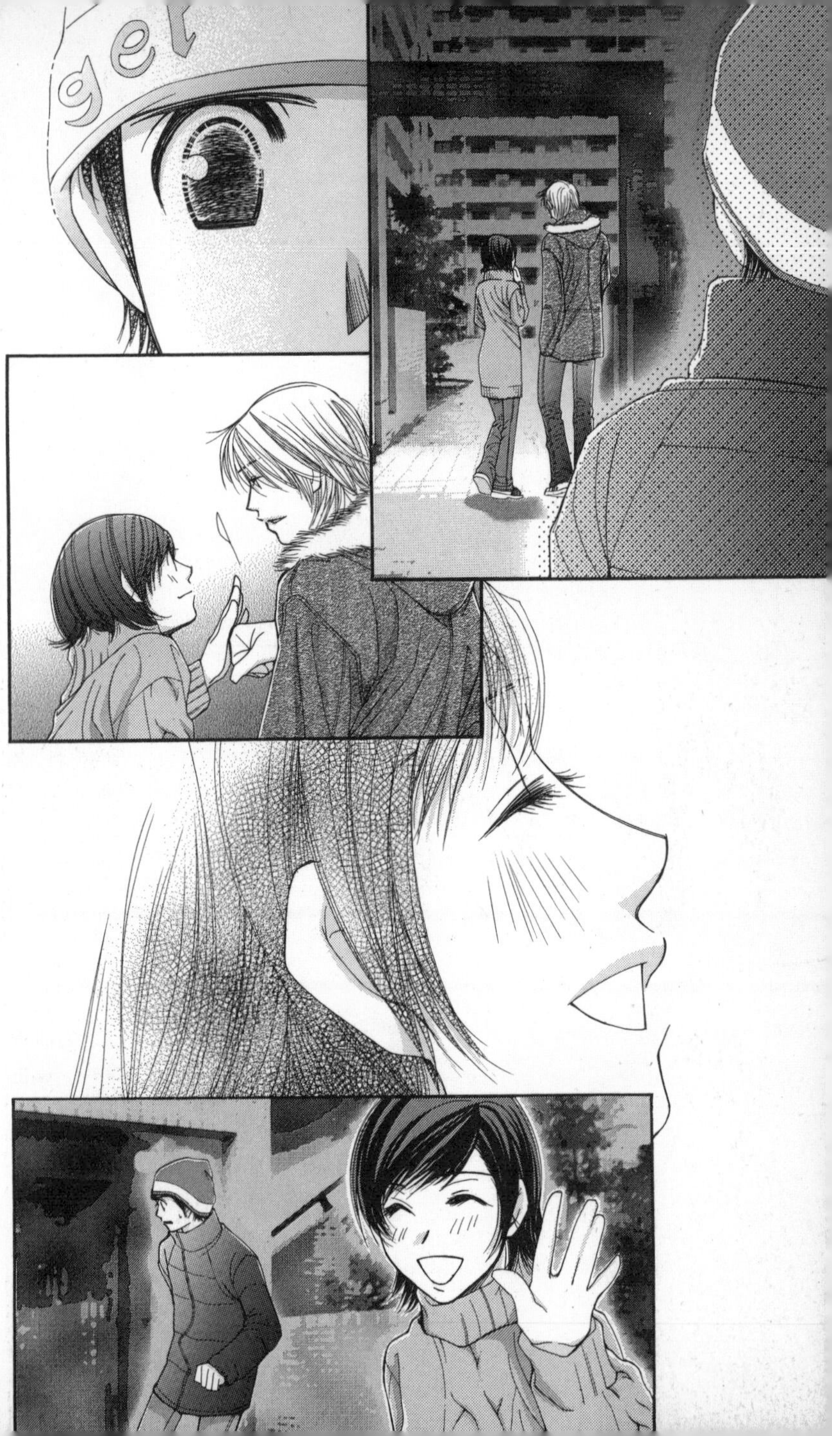

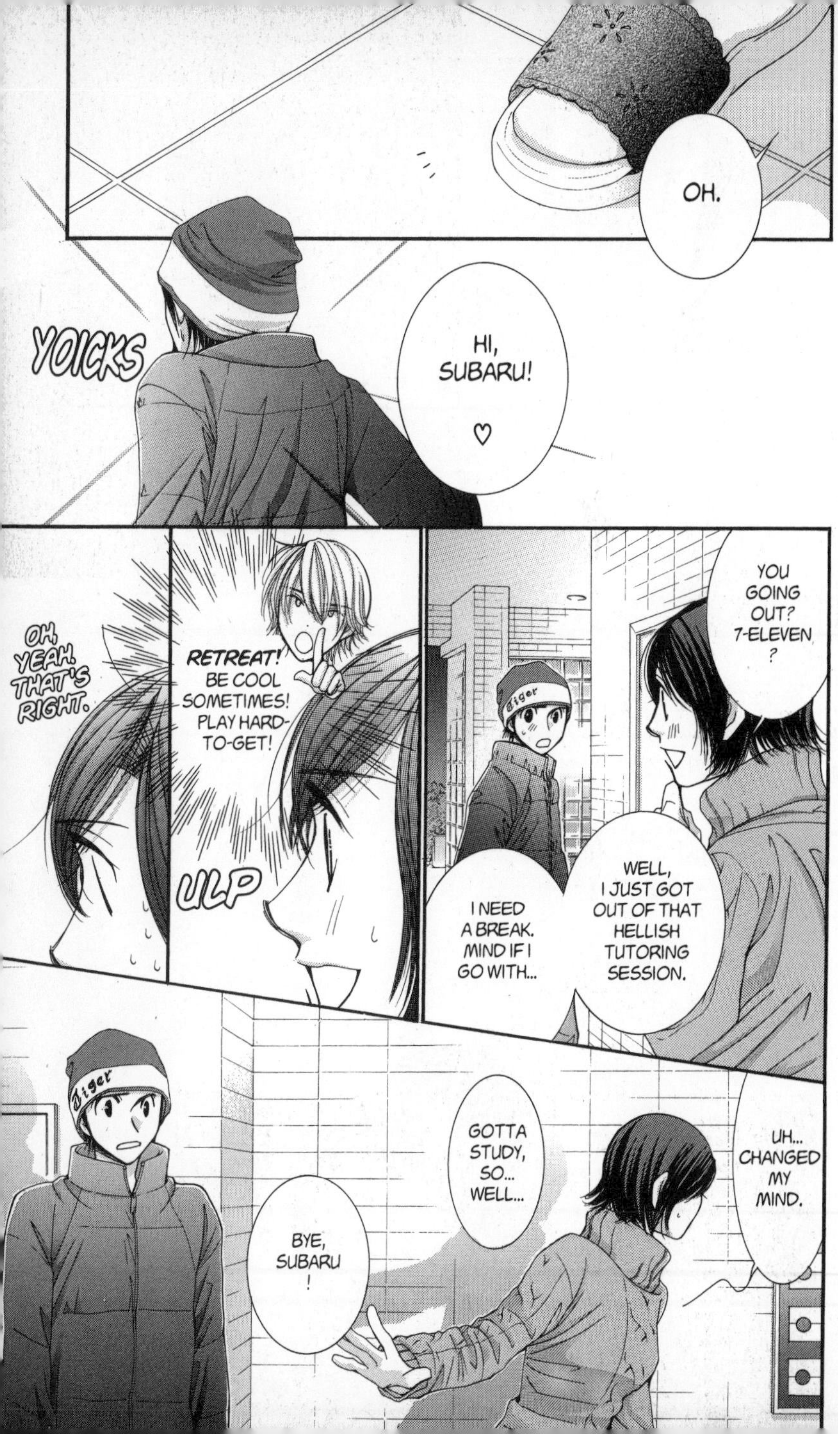
OH.
HI, SUBARU! ♡
YOICKS
YOU GOING OUT? 7-ELEVEN?
WELL, I JUST GOT OUT OF THAT HELLISH TUTORING SESSION.
I NEED A BREAK. MIND IF I GO WITH...
RETREAT! BE COOL SOMETIMES! PLAY HARD-TO-GET!
ULP
OH, YEAH. THAT'S RIGHT.
UH... CHANGED MY MIND.
GOTTA STUDY, SO... WELL...
BYE, SUBARU!

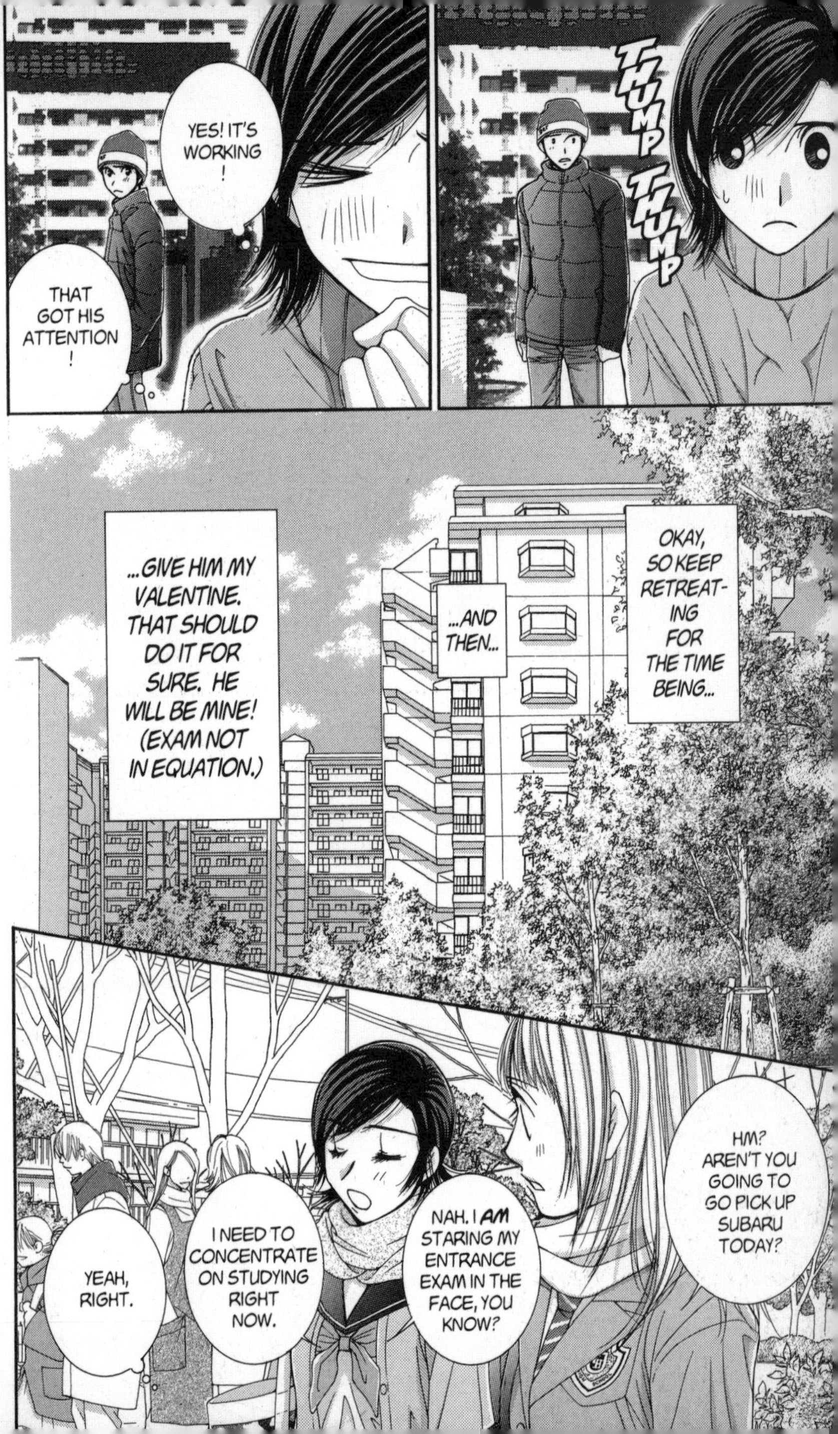
THUMP THUMP THUMP
YES! IT'S WORKING!
THAT GOT HIS ATTENTION!
OKAY, SO KEEP RETREAT-ING FOR THE TIME BEING...
...AND THEN...
...GIVE HIM MY VALENTINE. THAT SHOULD DO IT FOR SURE. HE WILL BE MINE! (EXAM NOT IN EQUATION.)
HM? AREN'T YOU GOING TO GO PICK UP SUBARU TODAY?
NAH. I AM STARING MY ENTRANCE EXAM IN THE FACE, YOU KNOW?
I NEED TO CONCENTRATE ON STUDYING RIGHT NOW.
YEAH, RIGHT.

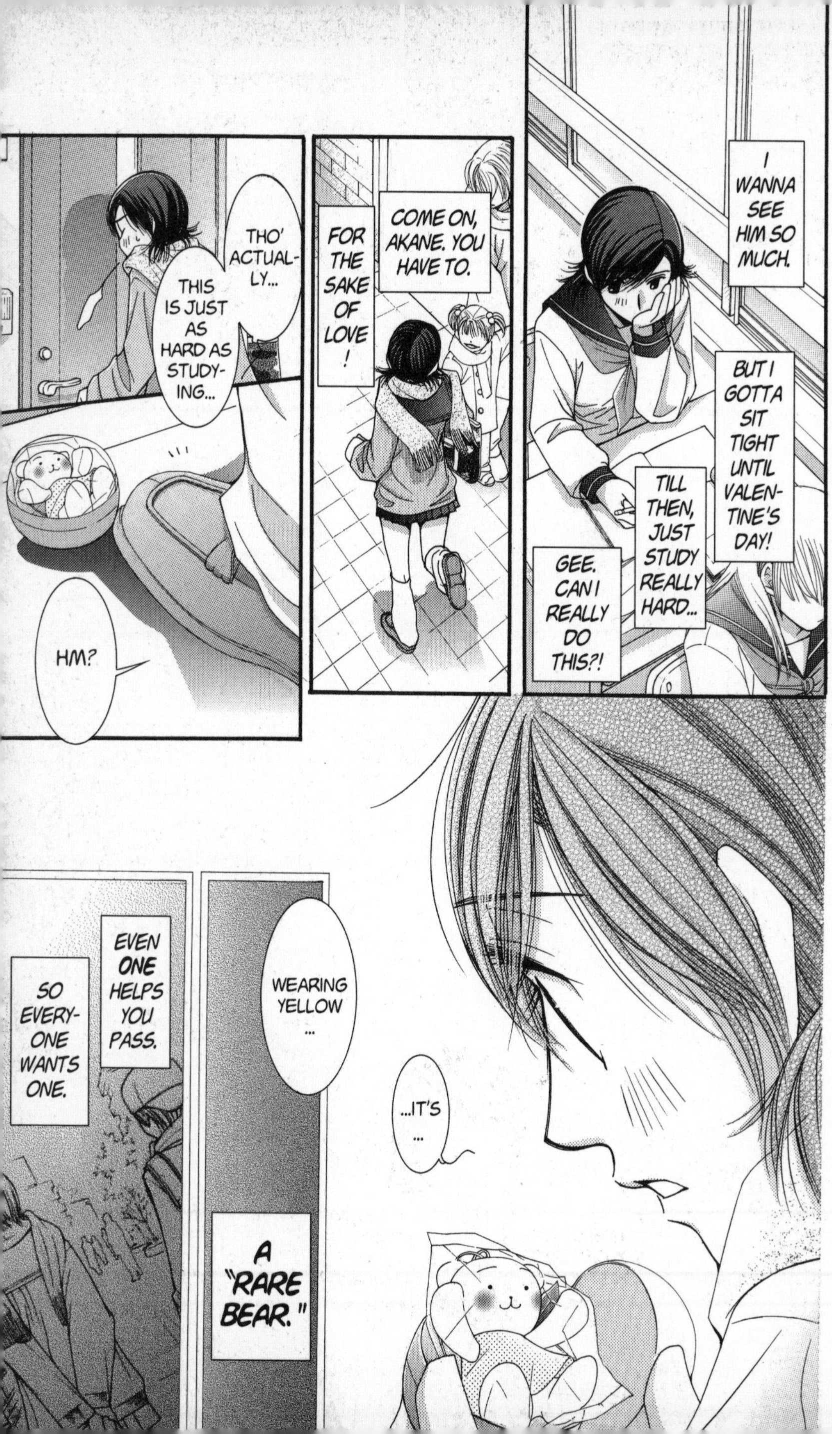
I WANNA SEE HIM SO MUCH.
BUT I GOTTA SIT TIGHT UNTIL VALEN-TINE'S DAY!
TILL THEN, JUST STUDY REALLY HARD...
GEE. CAN I REALLY DO THIS?!
COME ON, AKANE. YOU HAVE TO.
FOR THE SAKE OF LOVE!
THO' ACTUAL-LY...
THIS IS JUST AS HARD AS STUDY-ING...
HM?
...IT'S...
WEARING YELLOW...
A "RARE BEAR."
EVEN ONE HELPS YOU PASS.
SO EVERY-ONE WANTS ONE.

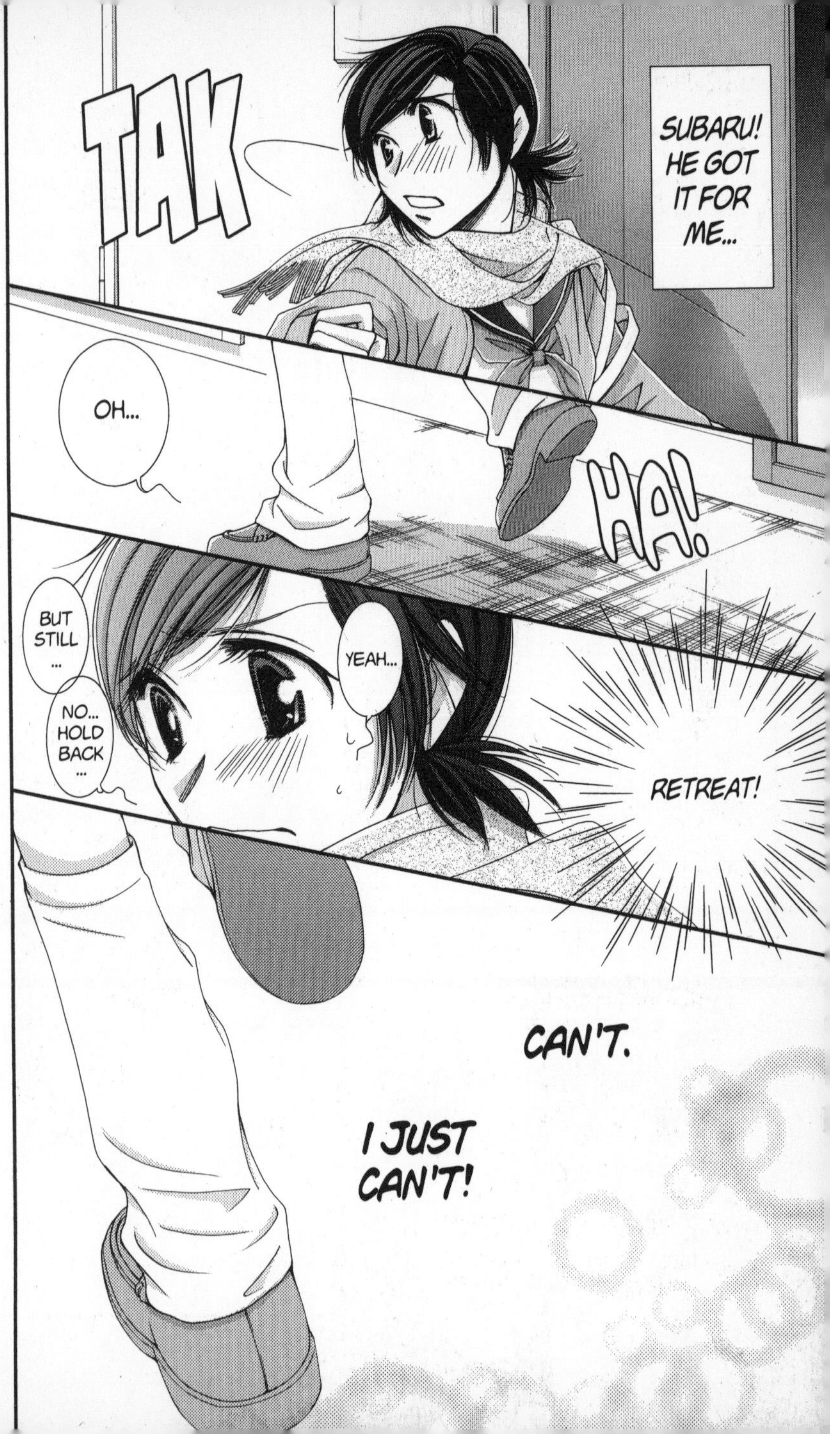
SUBARU! HE GOT IT FOR ME...
TAK
HA!
OH...
RETREAT!
YEAH...
BUT STILL...
NO... HOLD BACK...
CAN'T.
I JUST CAN'T!

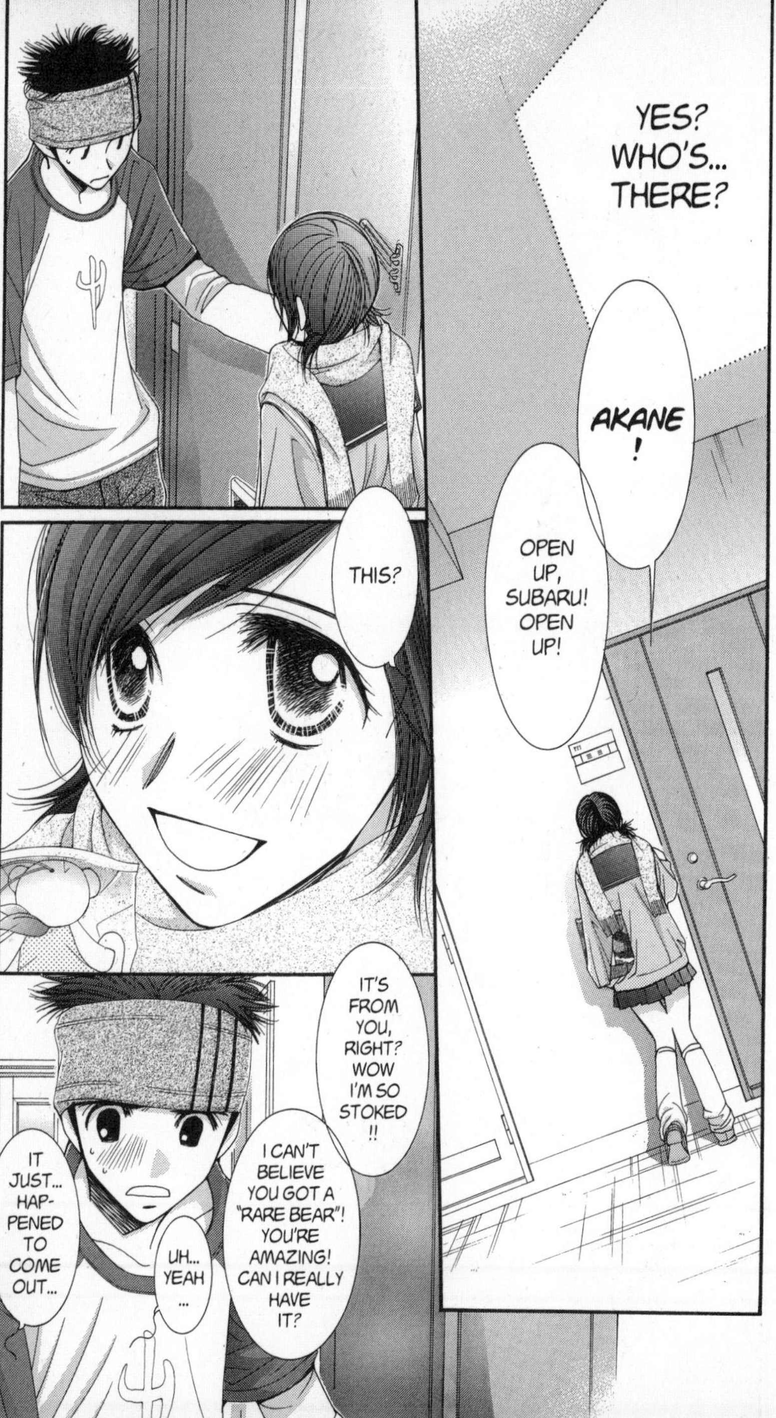
YES? WHO'S... THERE?
AKANE!
OPEN UP, SUBARU! OPEN UP!
THIS?
IT'S FROM YOU, RIGHT? WOW I'M SO STOKED!!
I CAN'T BELIEVE YOU GOT A "RARE BEAR"! YOU'RE AMAZING! CAN I REALLY HAVE IT?
UH... YEAH...
IT JUST... HAP-PENED TO COME OUT...

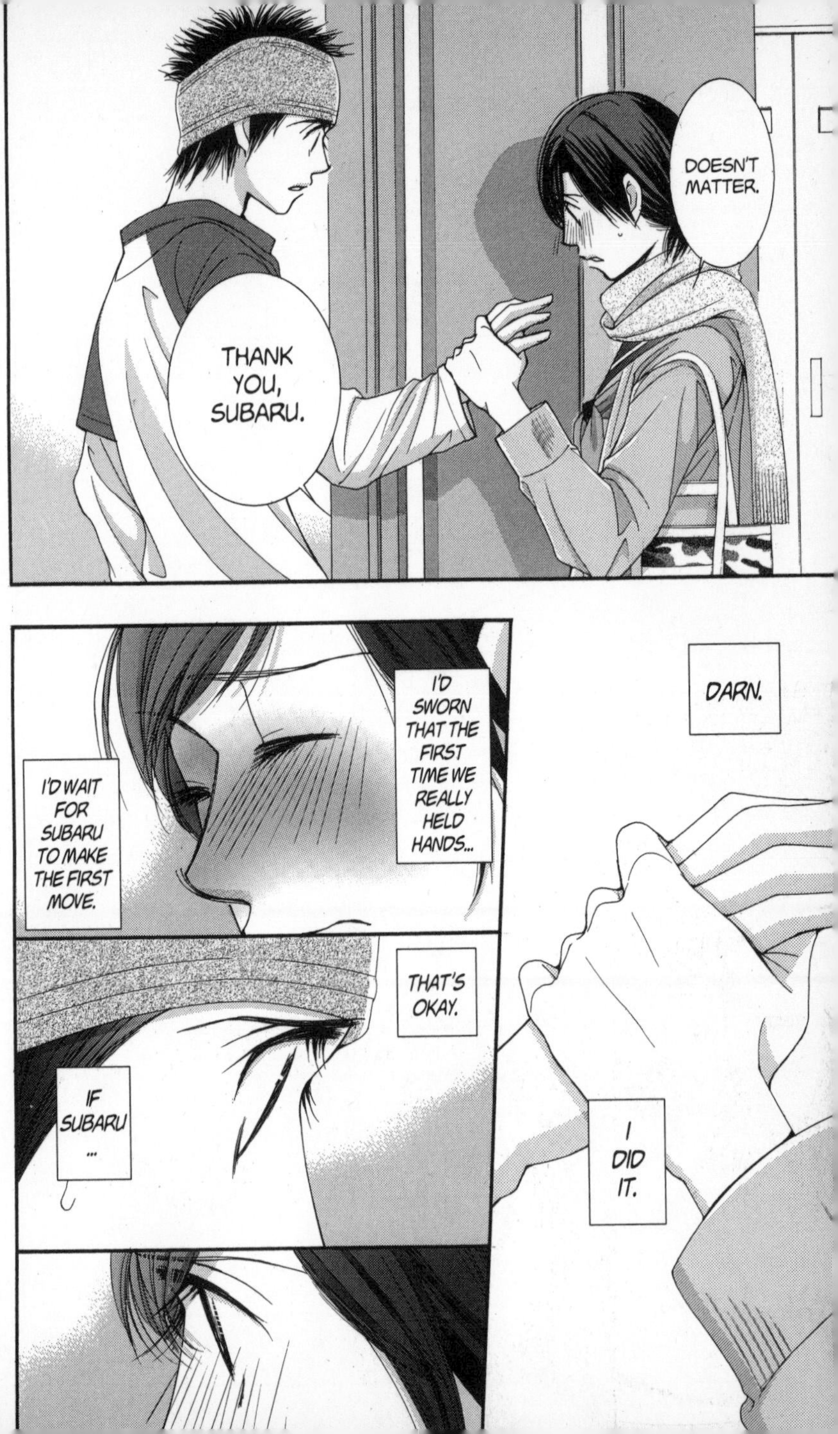
DOESN'T MATTER.
THANK YOU, SUBARU.
DARN.
I DID IT.
I'D SWORN THAT THE FIRST TIME WE REALLY HELD HANDS...
I'D WAIT FOR SUBARU TO MAKE THE FIRST MOVE.
THAT'S OKAY.
IF SUBARU...

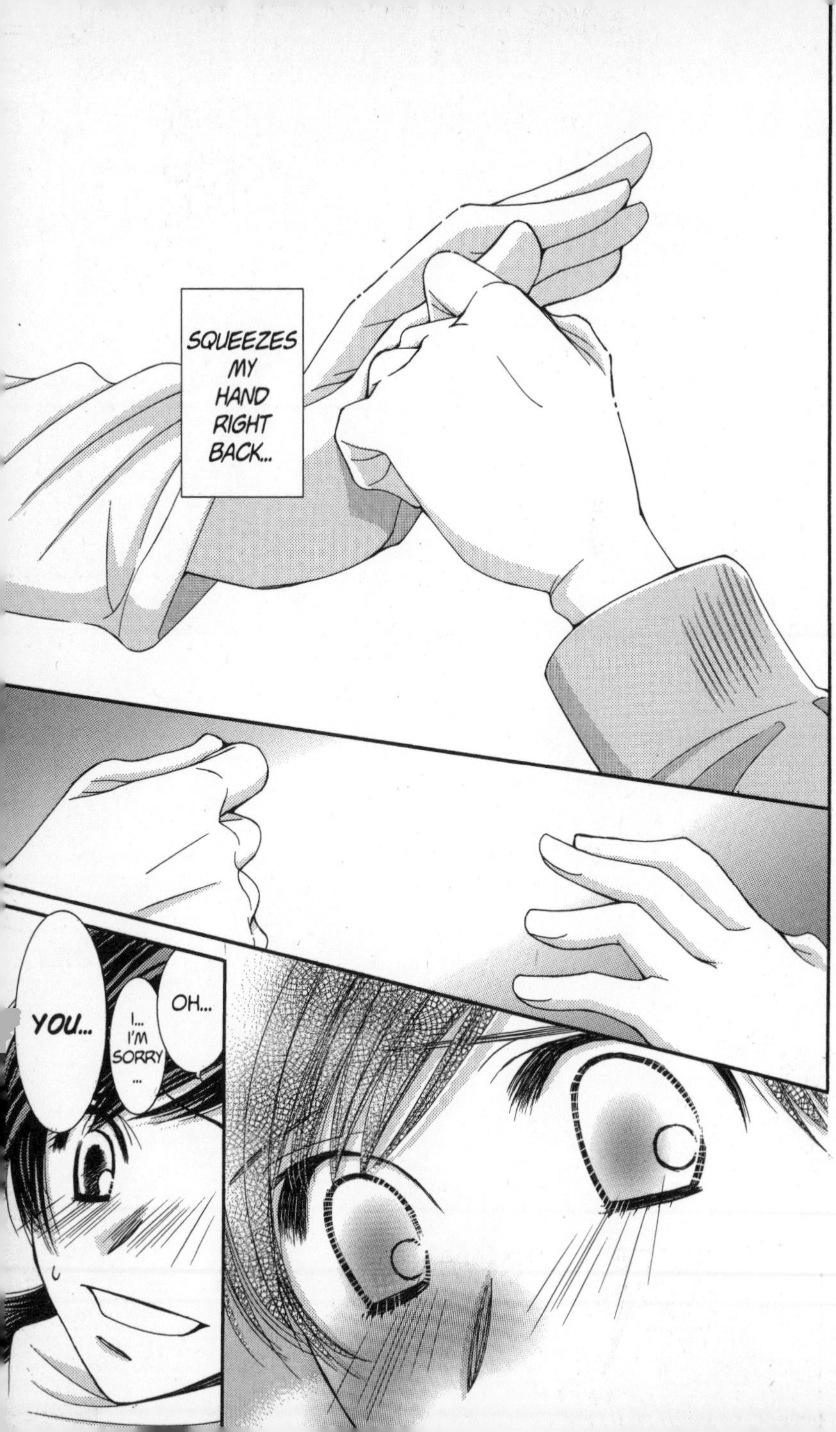
SQUEEZES MY HAND RIGHT BACK...
OH...
I... I'M SORRY...
YOU...

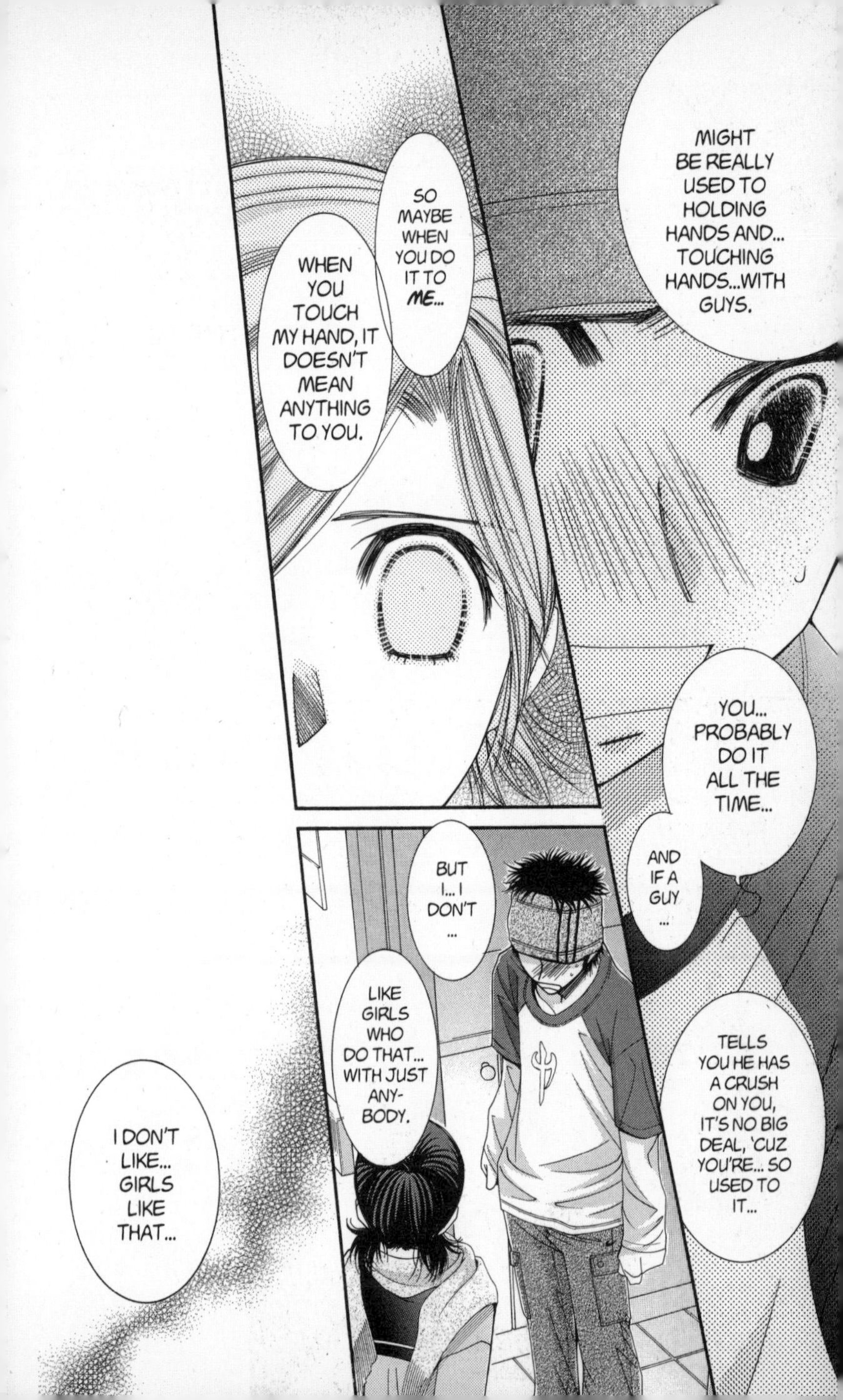

MIGHT BE REALLY USED TO HOLDING HANDS AND... TOUCHING HANDS...WITH GUYS.
YOU... PROBABLY DO IT ALL THE TIME...
AND IF A GUY ...
TELLS YOU HE HAS A CRUSH ON YOU, IT'S NO BIG DEAL, 'CUZ YOU'RE... SO USED TO IT...
SO MAYBE WHEN YOU DO IT TO *ME*...
WHEN YOU TOUCH MY HAND, IT DOESN'T MEAN ANYTHING TO YOU.
BUT I... I DON'T ...
LIKE GIRLS WHO DO THAT... WITH JUST ANY-BODY.
I DON'T LIKE... GIRLS LIKE THAT...

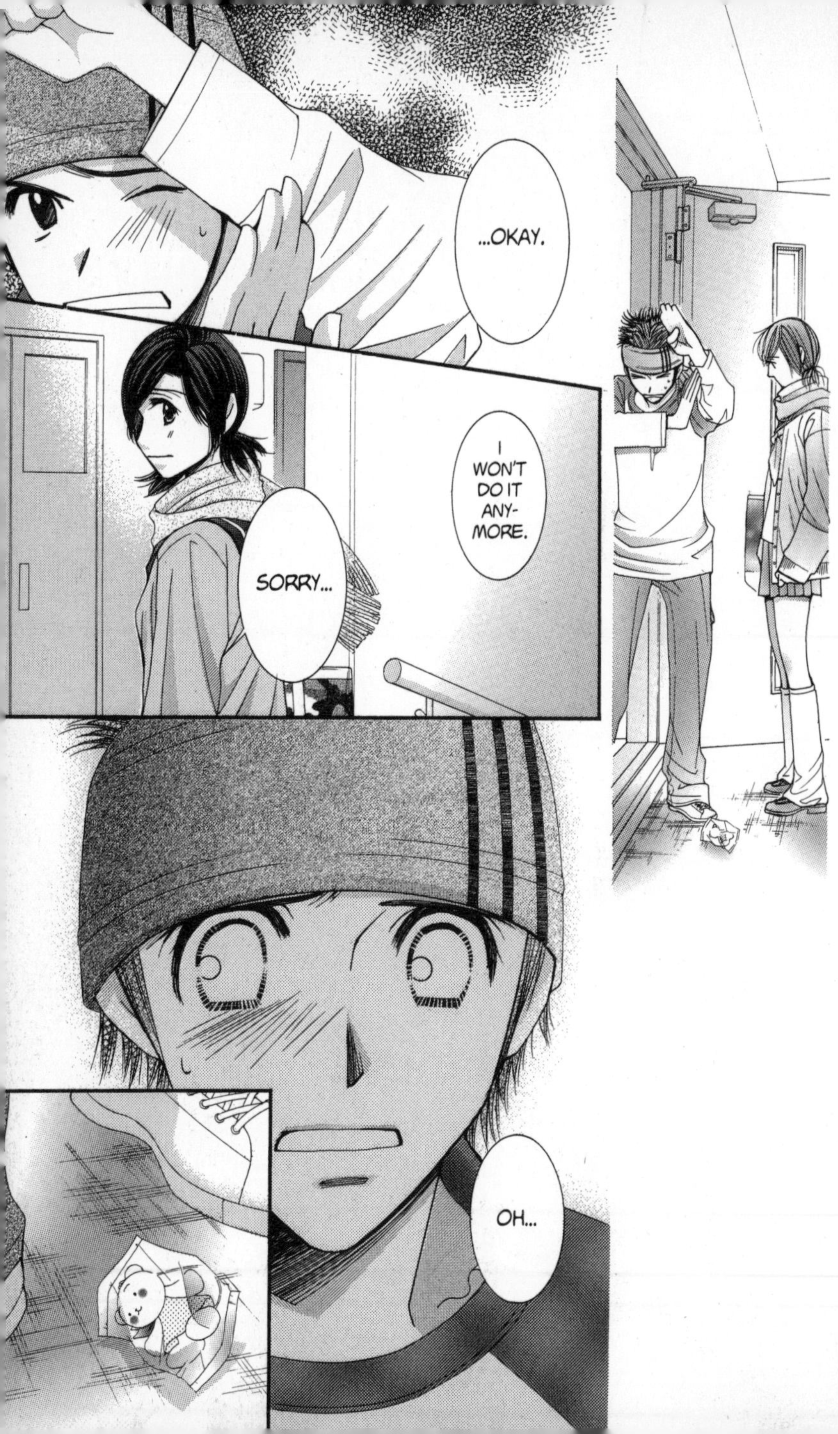
...OKAY.
I WON'T DO IT ANY-MORE.
SORRY...
OH...

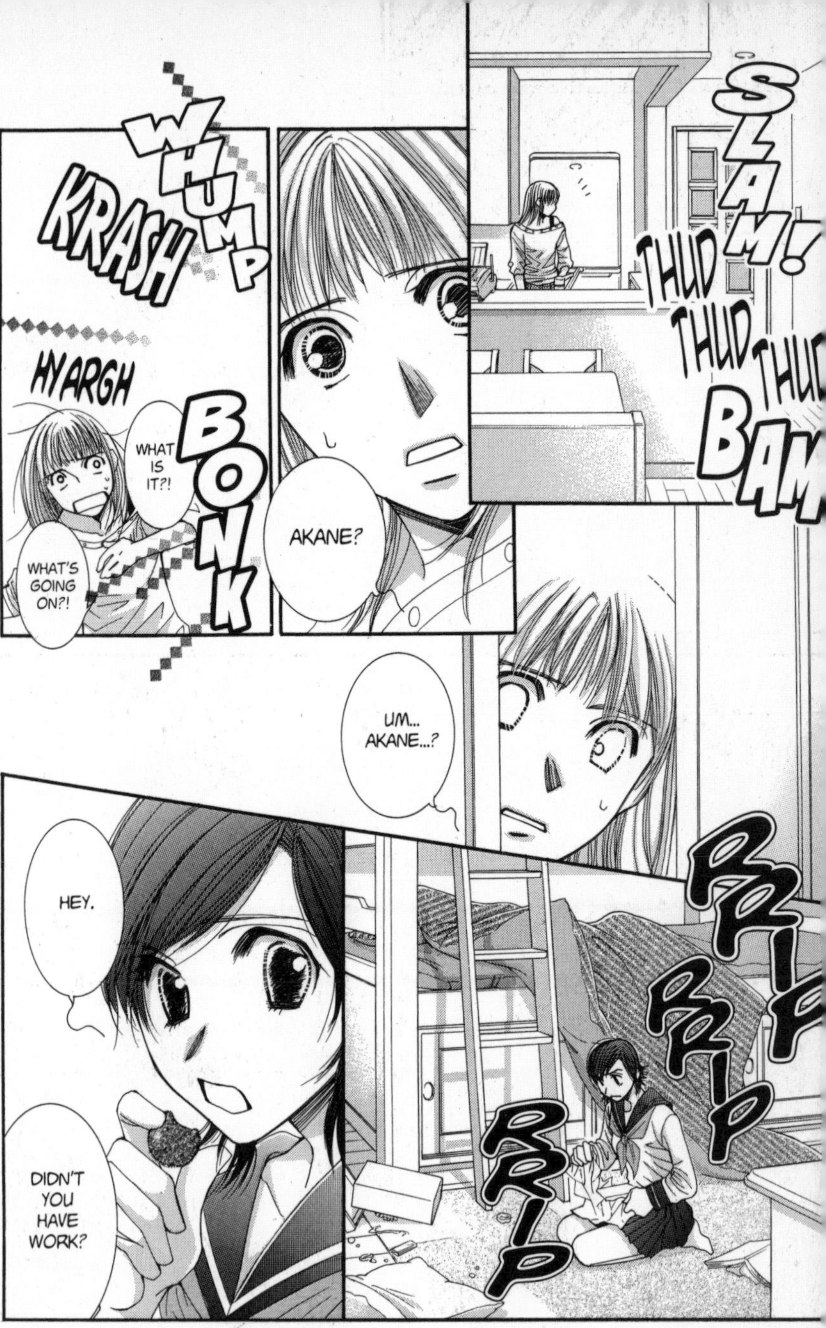
SLAM!
THUD
THUD
THUD
BAM
AKANE?
WHUMP
KRASH
HYARGH
WHAT IS IT?!
WHAT'S GOING ON?!
BONK
UM... AKANE...?
RRIP
RRIP
RRIP
HEY.
DIDN'T YOU HAVE WORK?

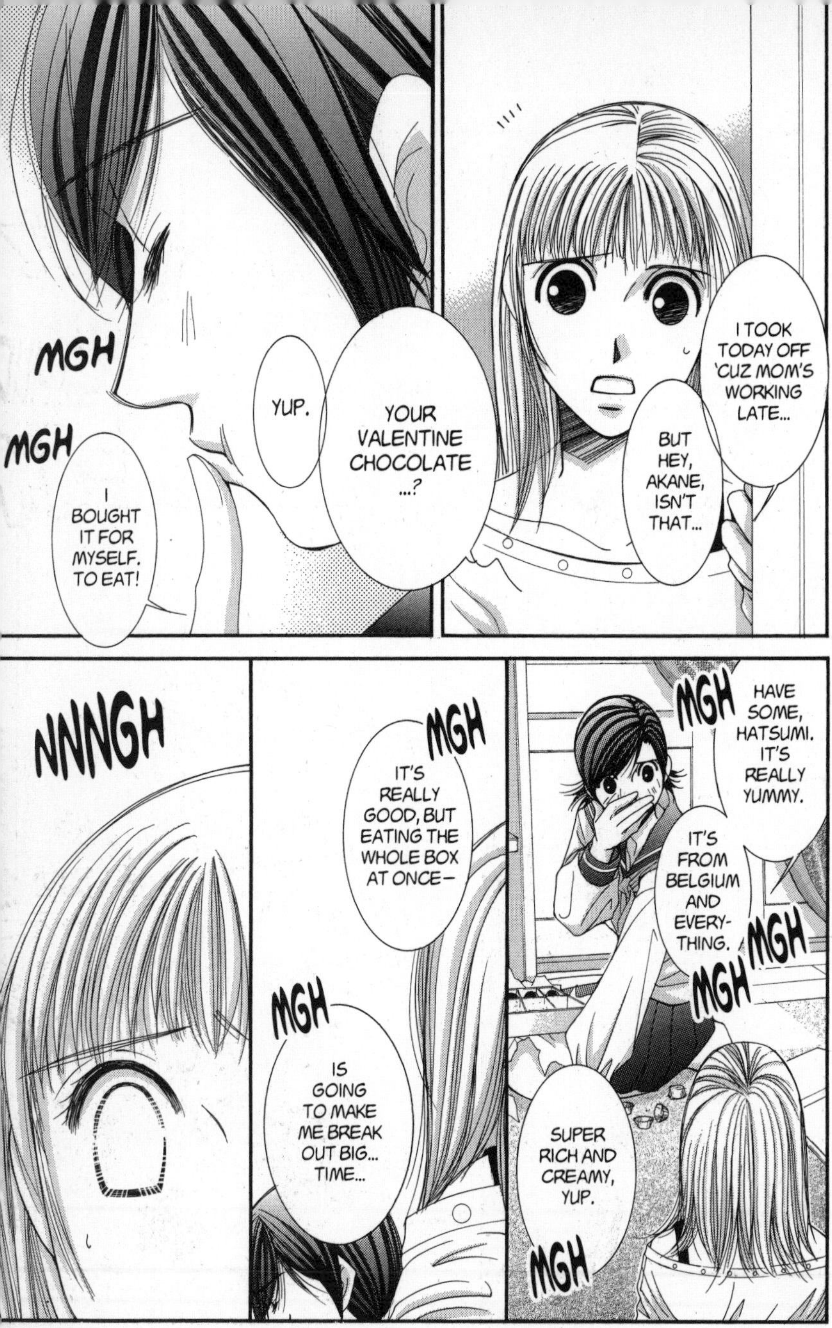
I TOOK TODAY OFF 'CUZ MOM'S WORKING LATE...
BUT HEY, AKANE, ISN'T THAT...
YOUR VALENTINE CHOCOLATE ...?
YUP.
MGH
MGH
I BOUGHT IT FOR MYSELF. TO EAT!
MGH
HAVE SOME, HATSUMI. IT'S REALLY YUMMY.
IT'S FROM BELGIUM AND EVERY- THING.
MGH
MGH
SUPER RICH AND CREAMY, YUP.
MGH
MGH
IT'S REALLY GOOD, BUT EATING THE WHOLE BOX AT ONCE—
MGH
IS GOING TO MAKE ME BREAK OUT BIG... TIME...
NNNGH

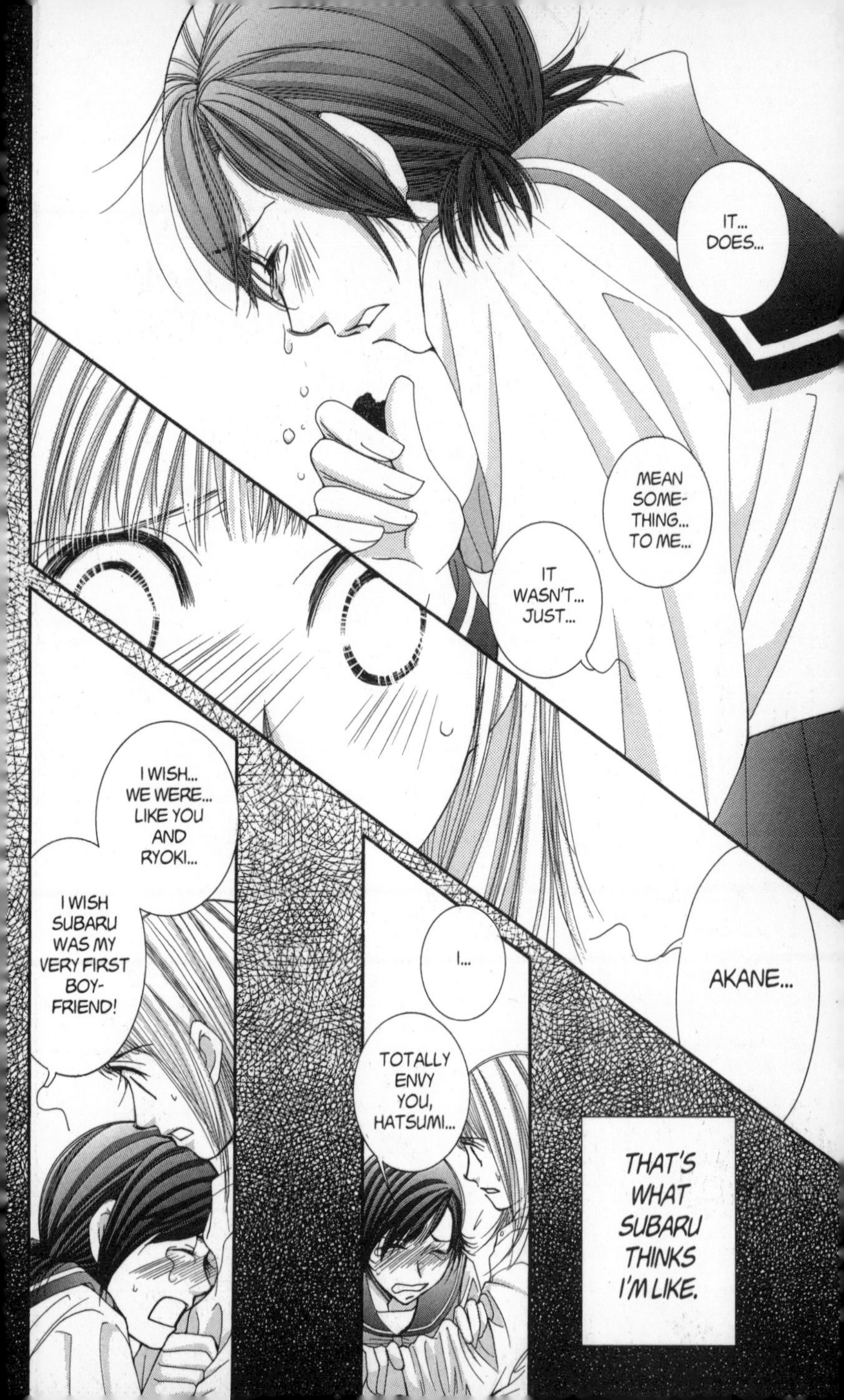
IT... DOES...
MEAN SOME-THING... TO ME...
IT WASN'T... JUST...
AKANE...
THAT'S WHAT SUBARU THINKS I'M LIKE.
I...
TOTALLY ENVY YOU, HATSUMI...
I WISH... WE WERE... LIKE YOU AND RYOKI...
I WISH SUBARU WAS MY VERY FIRST BOY-FRIEND!

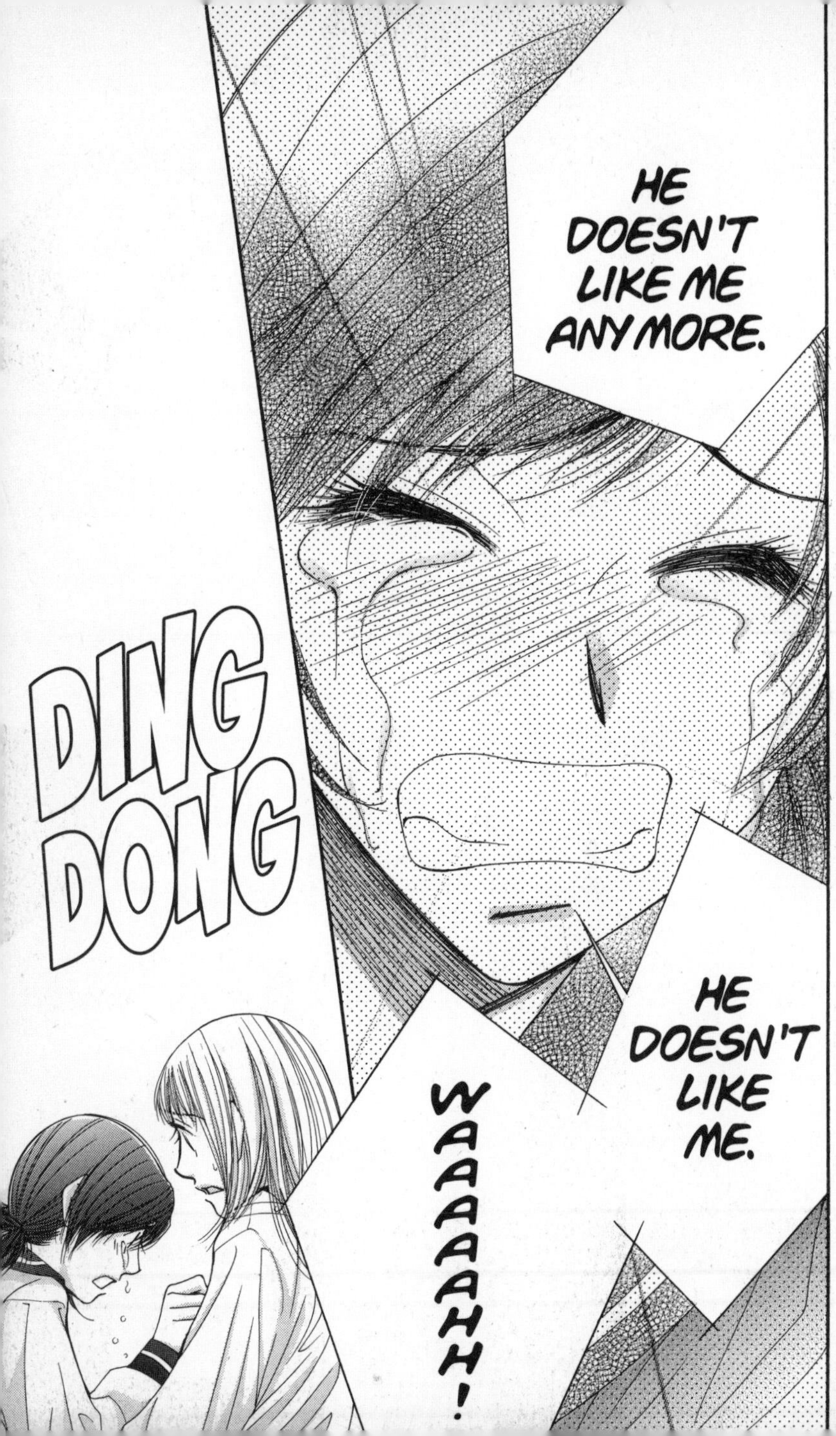
HE DOESN'T LIKE ME ANYMORE.
HE DOESN'T LIKE ME.
WAAAAAAH!
DING DONG

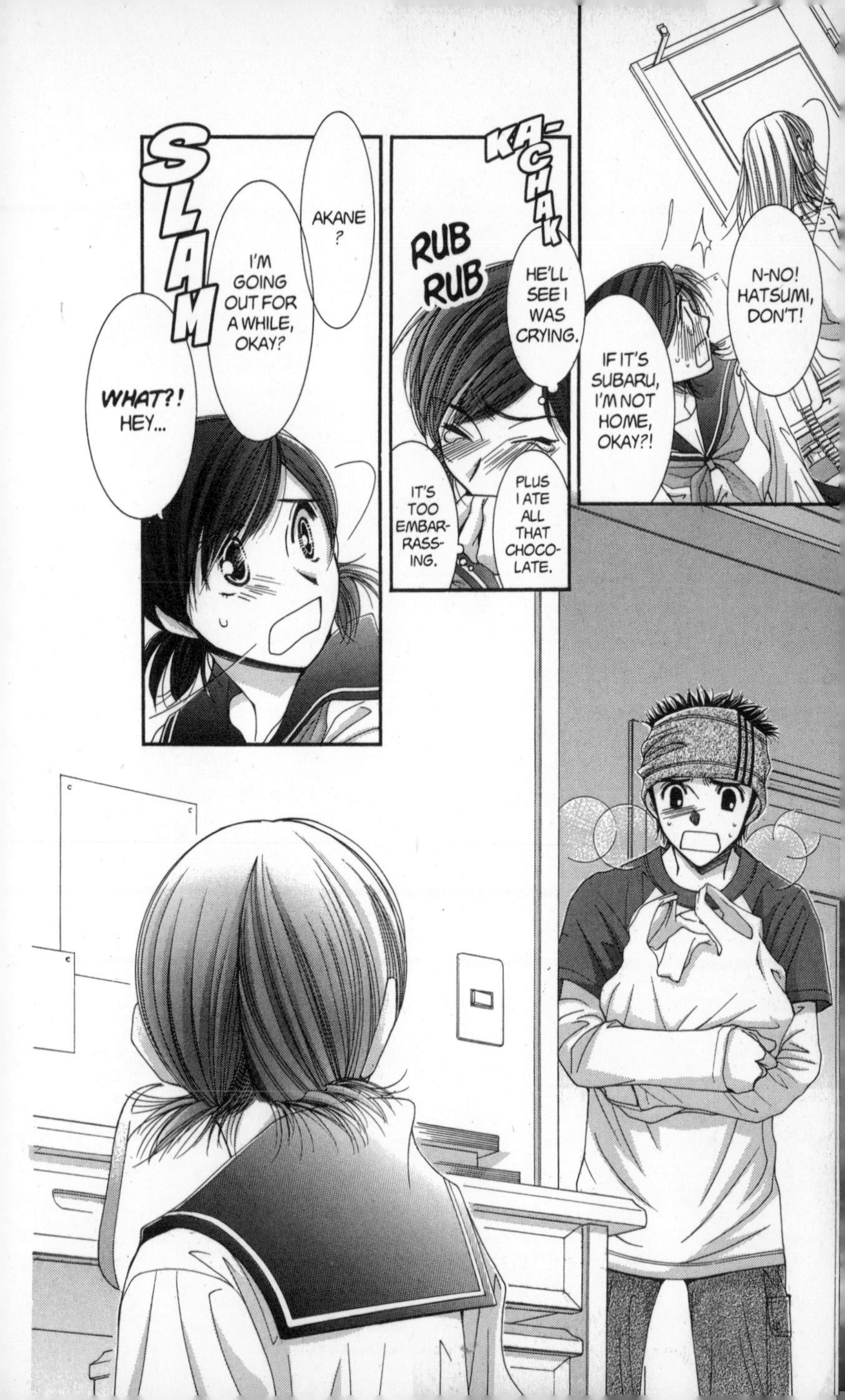
N-NO! HATSUMI, DON'T!
IF IT'S SUBARU, I'M NOT HOME, OKAY?!
KA-CHAK
HE'LL SEE I WAS CRYING.
RUB RUB
PLUS I ATE ALL THAT CHOCOLATE.
IT'S TOO EMBARRASSING.
AKANE?
I'M GOING OUT FOR A WHILE, OKAY?
SLAM
WHAT?! HEY...

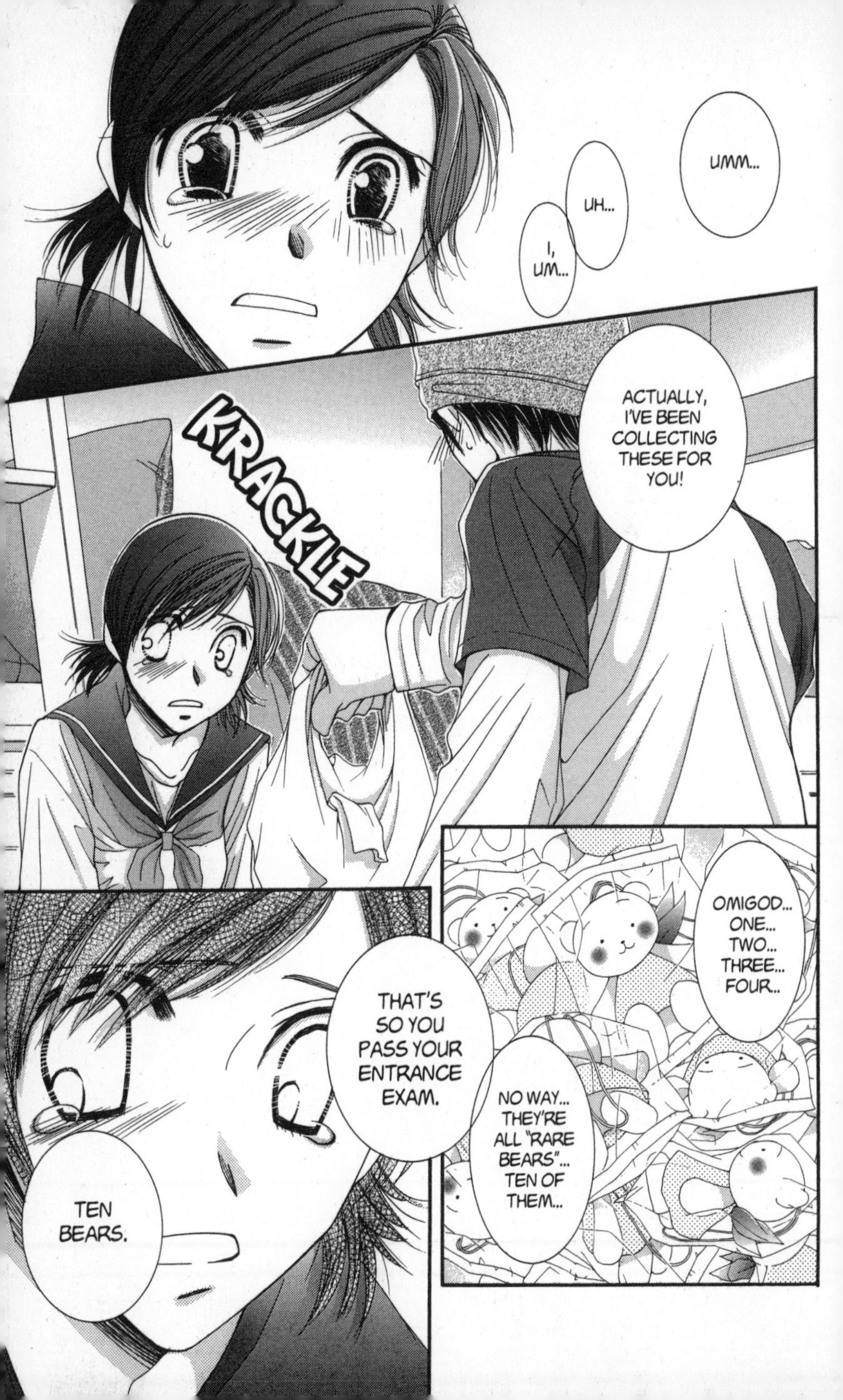
UMM...
UH...
I, UM...
ACTUALLY, I'VE BEEN COLLECTING THESE FOR YOU!
KRACKLE
OMIGOD... ONE... TWO... THREE... FOUR...
NO WAY... THEY'RE ALL "RARE BEARS"... TEN OF THEM...
THAT'S SO YOU PASS YOUR ENTRANCE EXAM.
TEN BEARS.

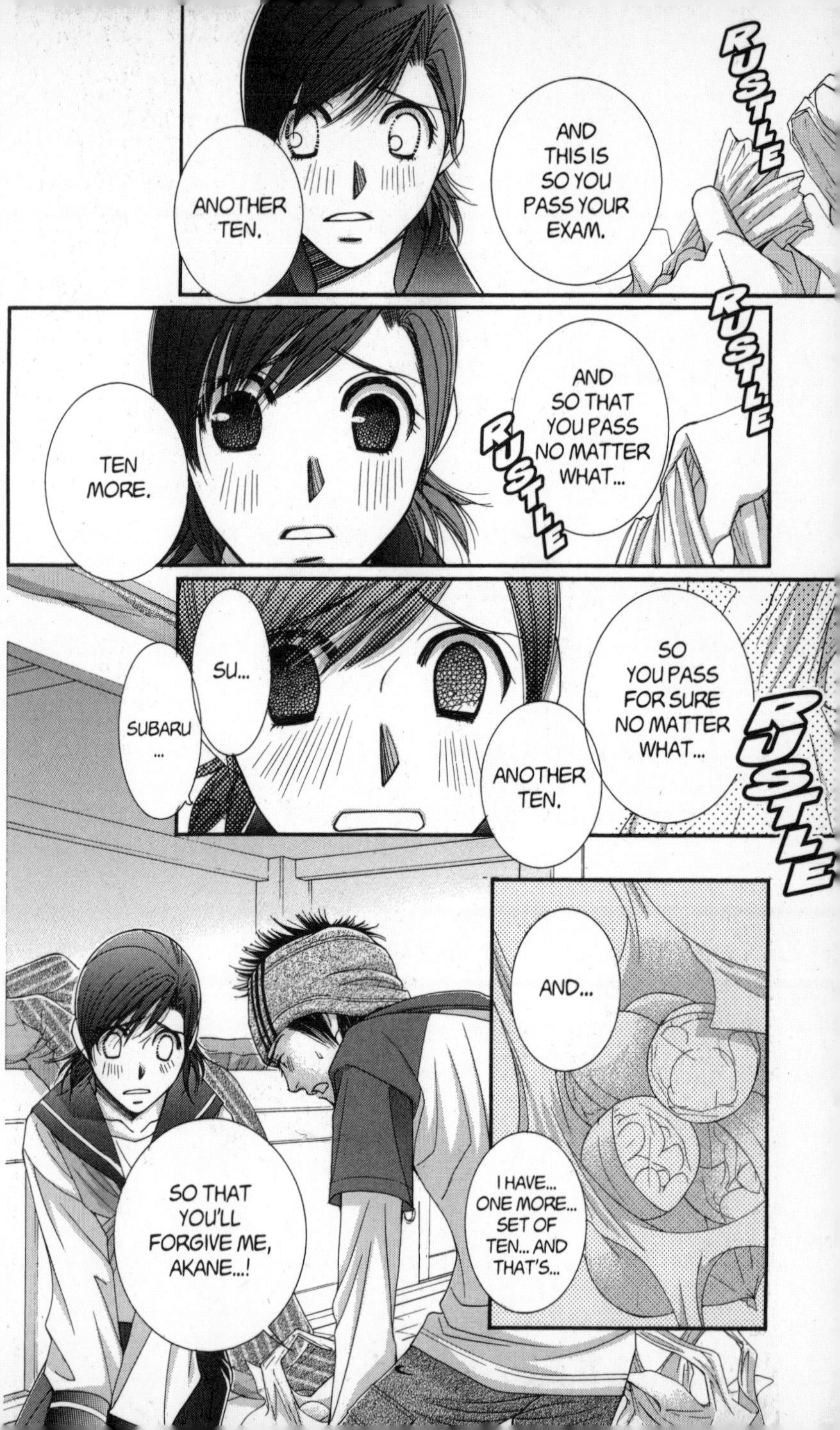
RUSTLE
AND THIS IS SO YOU PASS YOUR EXAM.
ANOTHER TEN.
RUSTLE
AND SO THAT YOU PASS NO MATTER WHAT...
RUSTLE
TEN MORE.
RUSTLE
SO YOU PASS FOR SURE NO MATTER WHAT...
ANOTHER TEN.
SU...
SUBARU...
AND...
I HAVE... ONE MORE... SET OF TEN... AND THAT'S...
SO THAT YOU'LL FORGIVE ME, AKANE...!

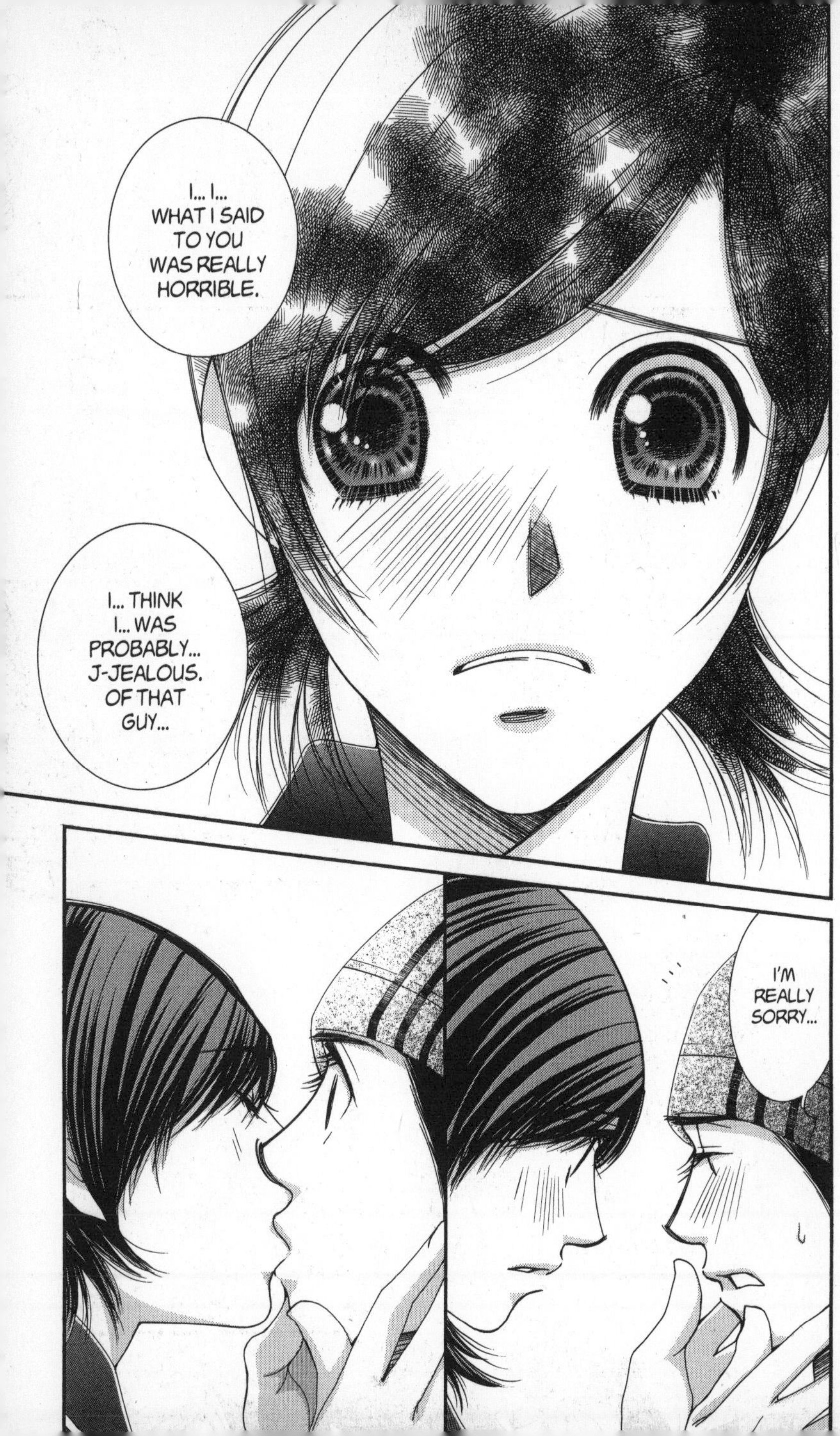
I... I... WHAT I SAID TO YOU WAS REALLY HORRIBLE.
I... THINK I... WAS PROBABLY... J-JEALOUS. OF THAT GUY...
I'M REALLY SORRY...

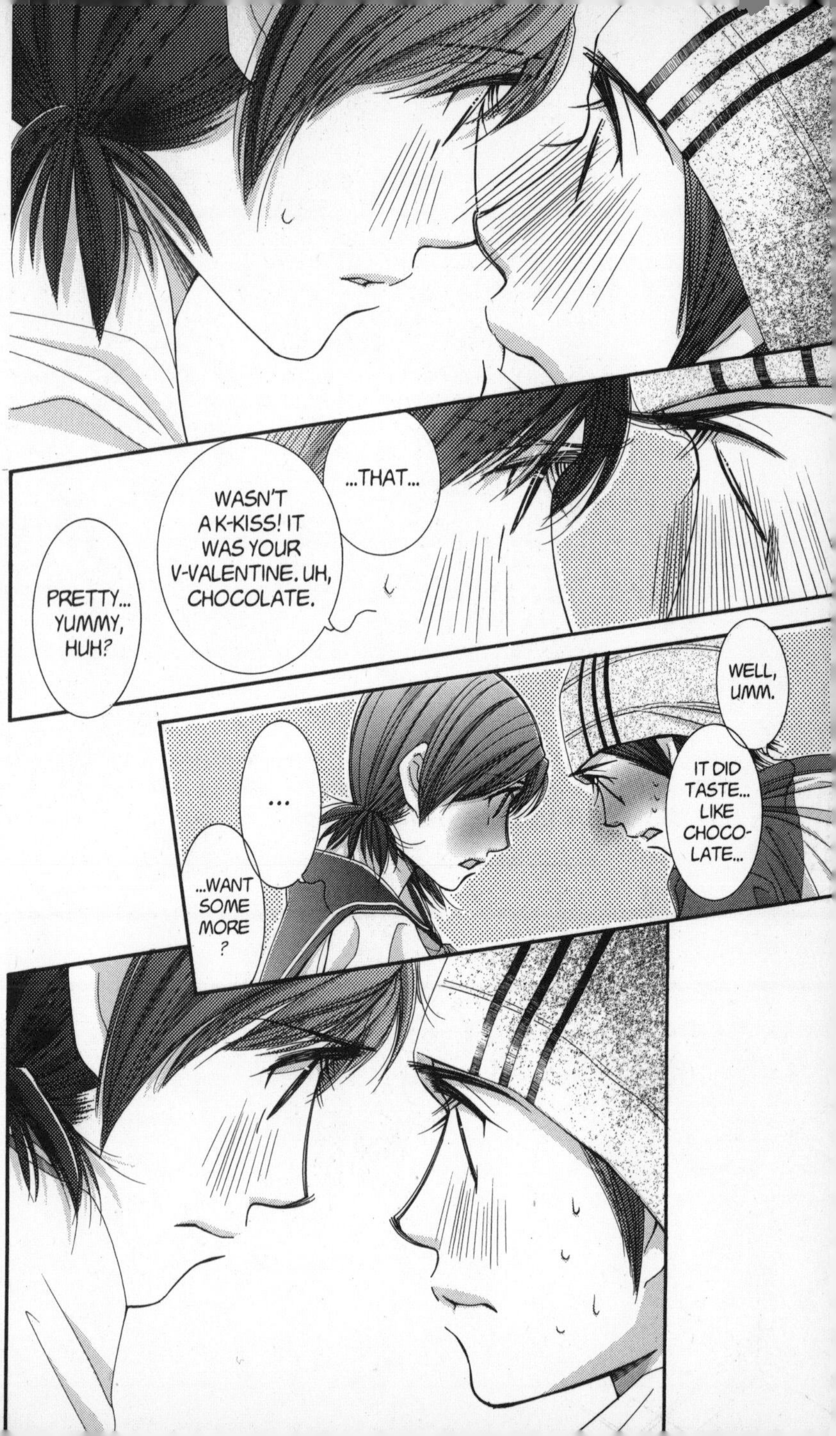
...THAT...
WASN'T A K-KISS! IT WAS YOUR V-VALENTINE. UH, CHOCOLATE.
PRETTY... YUMMY, HUH?
WELL, UMM.
IT DID TASTE... LIKE CHOCO-LATE...
...
...WANT SOME MORE?

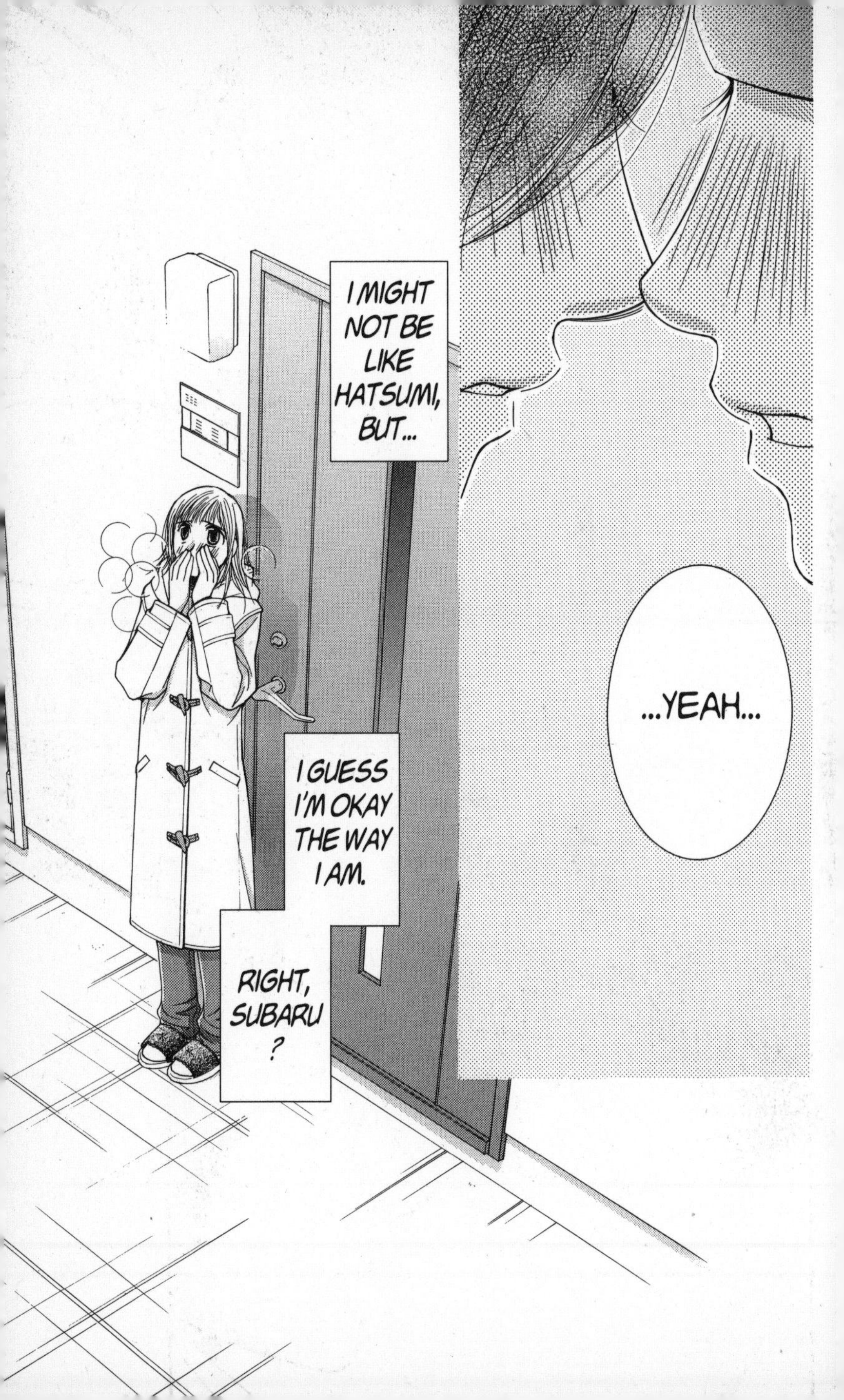
I MIGHT NOT BE LIKE HATSUMI, BUT...
I GUESS I'M OKAY THE WAY I AM.
RIGHT, SUBARU?
...YEAH...

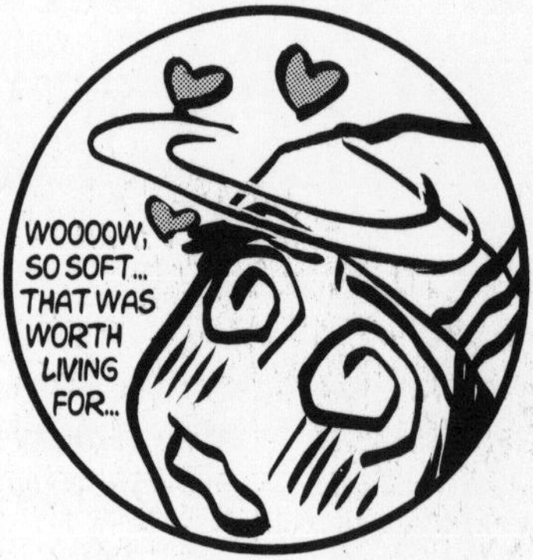
WOOOOW, SO SOFT... THAT WAS WORTH LIVING FOR...

Chapter 38

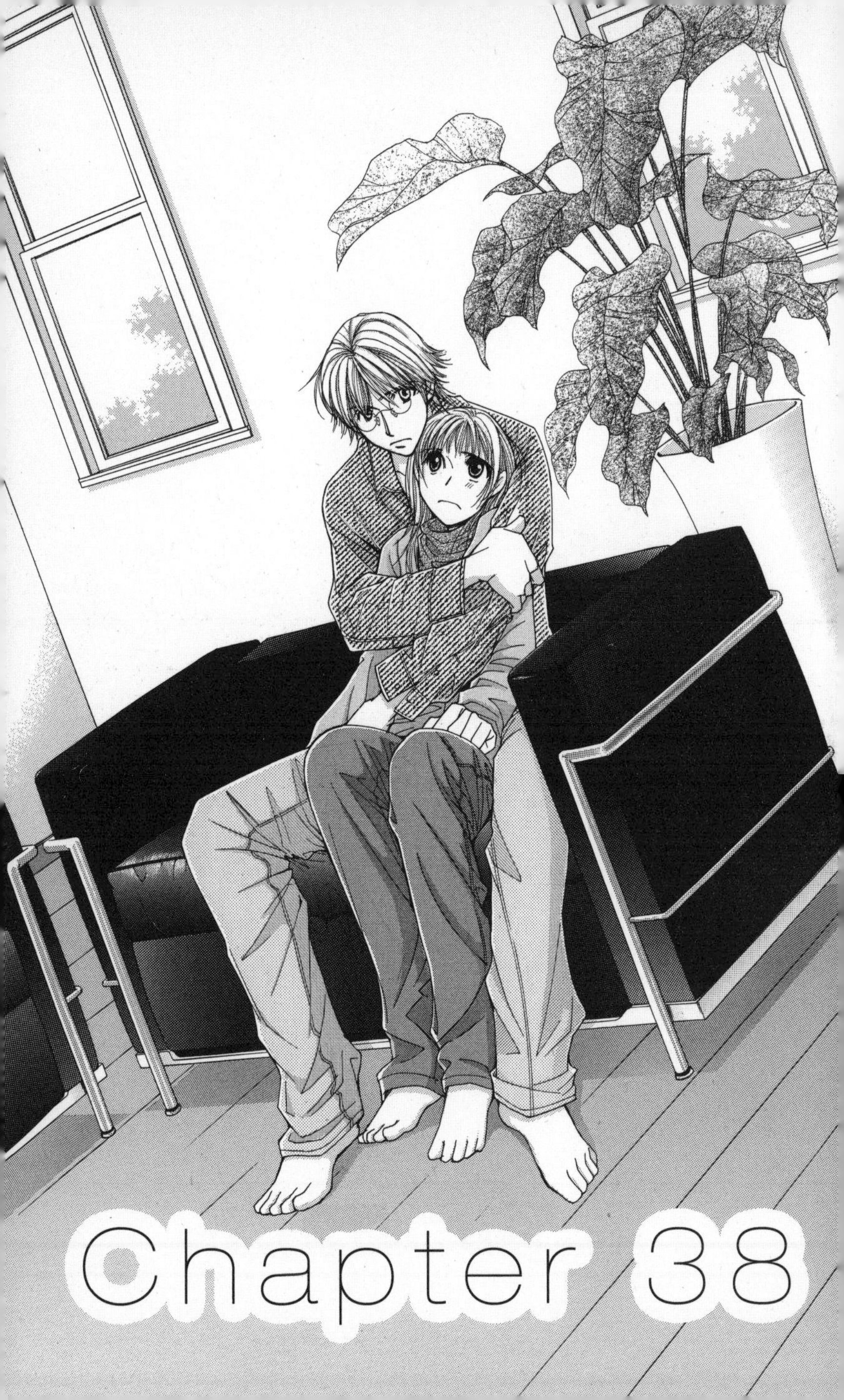

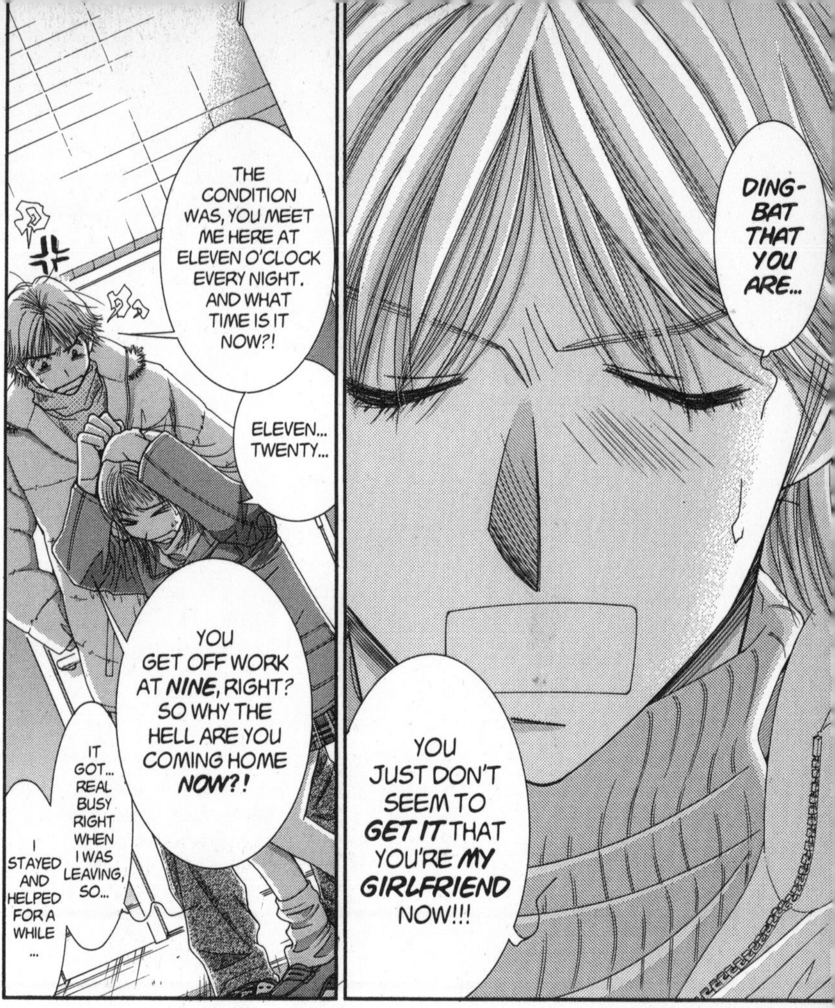
DING-BAT THAT YOU ARE...
YOU JUST DON'T SEEM TO **GET IT** THAT YOU'RE **MY GIRLFRIEND** NOW!!!
THE CONDITION WAS, YOU MEET ME HERE AT ELEVEN O'CLOCK EVERY NIGHT. AND WHAT TIME IS IT NOW?!
ELEVEN... TWENTY...
YOU GET OFF WORK AT **NINE**, RIGHT? SO WHY THE HELL ARE YOU COMING HOME **NOW?!**
IT GOT... REAL BUSY RIGHT WHEN I WAS LEAVING, SO...
I STAYED AND HELPED FOR A WHILE ...

hot gimmick

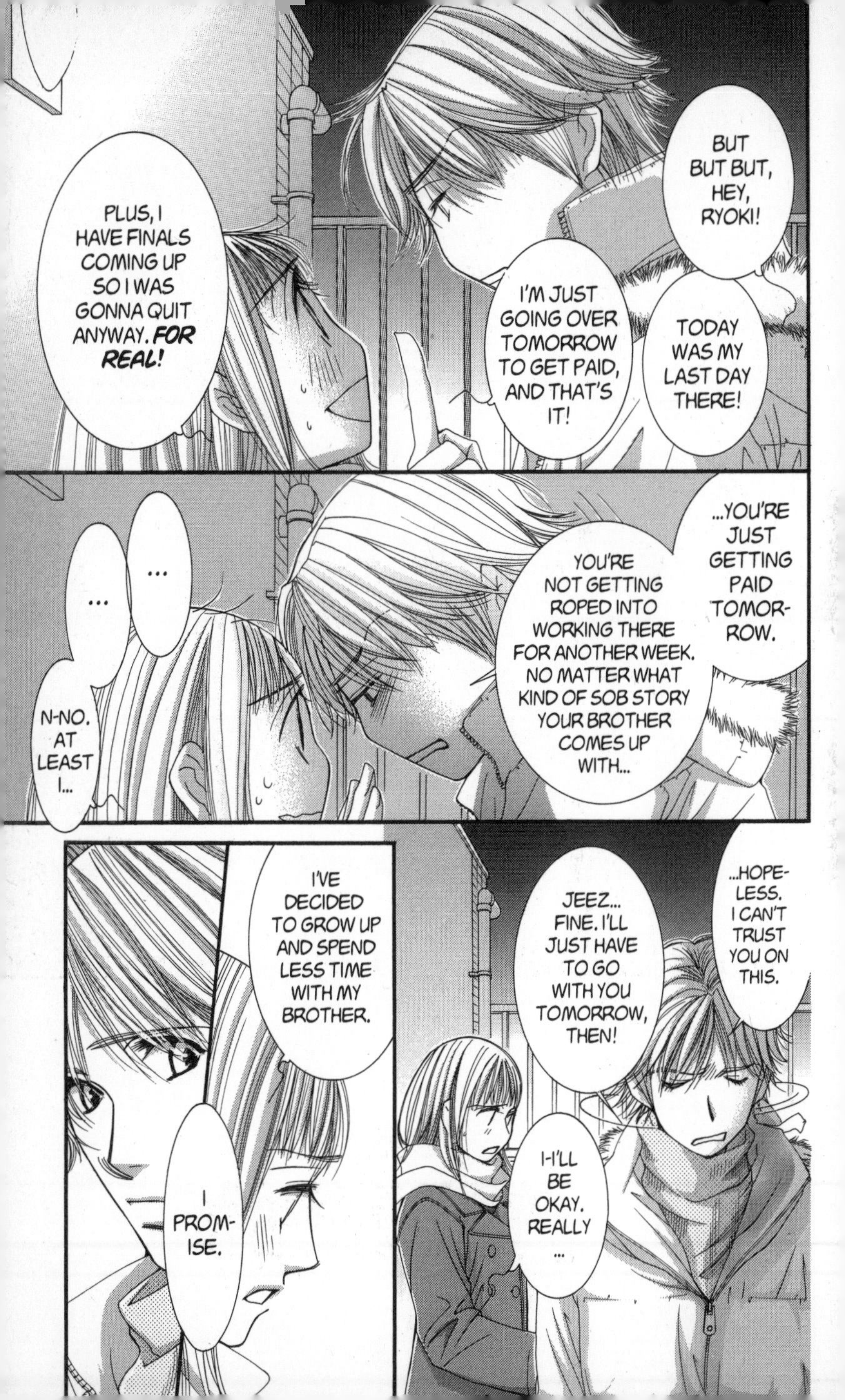
BUT BUT BUT, HEY, RYOKI!
TODAY WAS MY LAST DAY THERE!
I'M JUST GOING OVER TOMORROW TO GET PAID, AND THAT'S IT!
PLUS, I HAVE FINALS COMING UP SO I WAS GONNA QUIT ANYWAY. FOR REAL!
...YOU'RE JUST GETTING PAID TOMORROW.
YOU'RE NOT GETTING ROPED INTO WORKING THERE FOR ANOTHER WEEK. NO MATTER WHAT KIND OF SOB STORY YOUR BROTHER COMES UP WITH...
...
...
N-NO. AT LEAST I...
...HOPE-LESS. I CAN'T TRUST YOU ON THIS.
JEEZ... FINE. I'LL JUST HAVE TO GO WITH YOU TOMORROW, THEN!
I-I'LL BE OKAY. REALLY ...
I'VE DECIDED TO GROW UP AND SPEND LESS TIME WITH MY BROTHER.
I PROM-ISE.

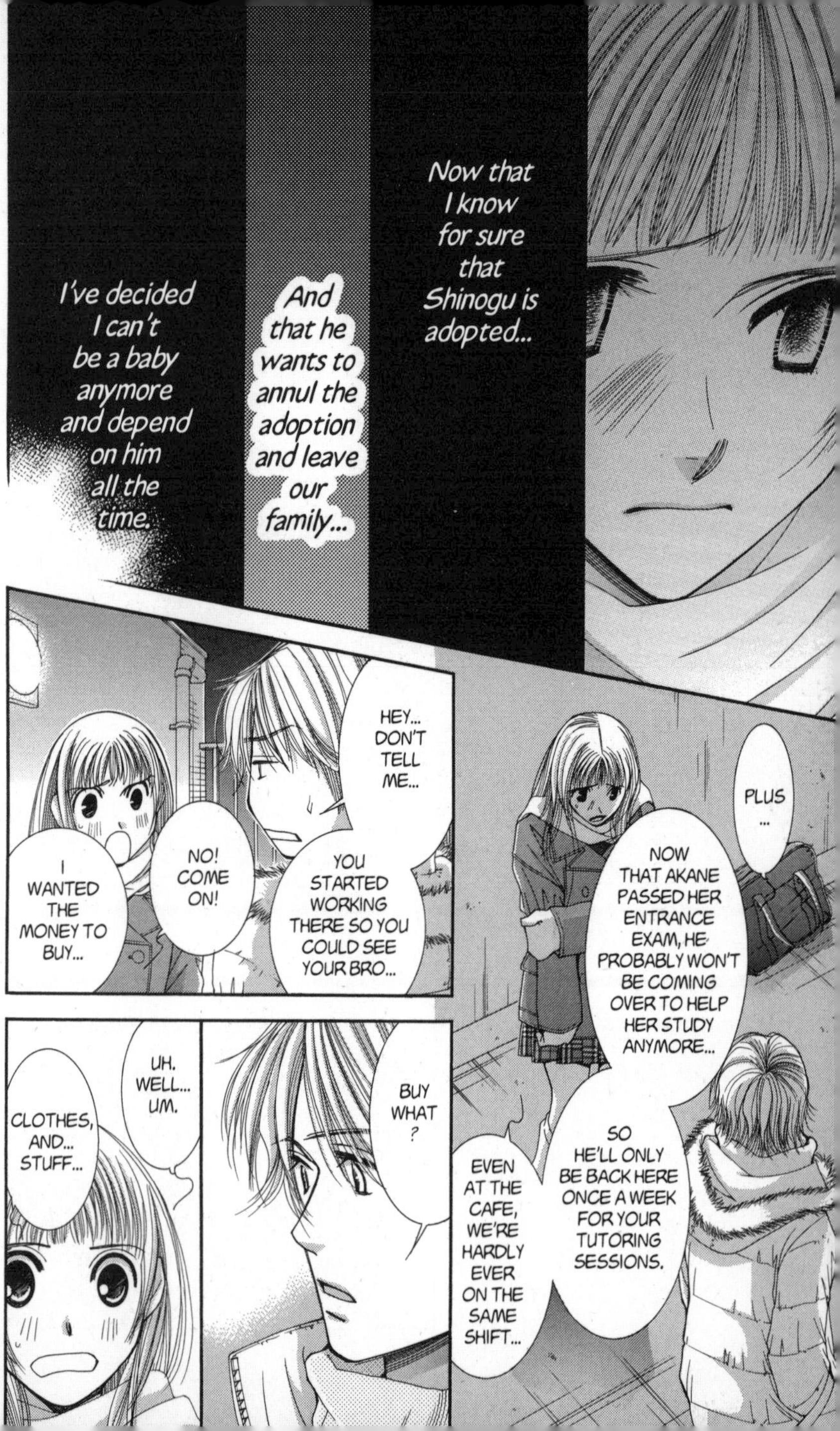

Now that I know for sure that Shinogu is adopted...
And that he wants to annul the adoption and leave our family...
I've decided I can't be a baby anymore and depend on him all the time.
PLUS...
NOW THAT AKANE PASSED HER ENTRANCE EXAM, HE PROBABLY WON'T BE COMING OVER TO HELP HER STUDY ANYMORE...
SO HE'LL ONLY BE BACK HERE ONCE A WEEK FOR YOUR TUTORING SESSIONS.
EVEN AT THE CAFE, WE'RE HARDLY EVER ON THE SAME SHIFT...
HEY... DON'T TELL ME...
YOU STARTED WORKING THERE SO YOU COULD SEE YOUR BRO...
NO! COME ON!
I WANTED THE MONEY TO BUY...
BUY WHAT?
UH. WELL... UM.
CLOTHES, AND... STUFF...

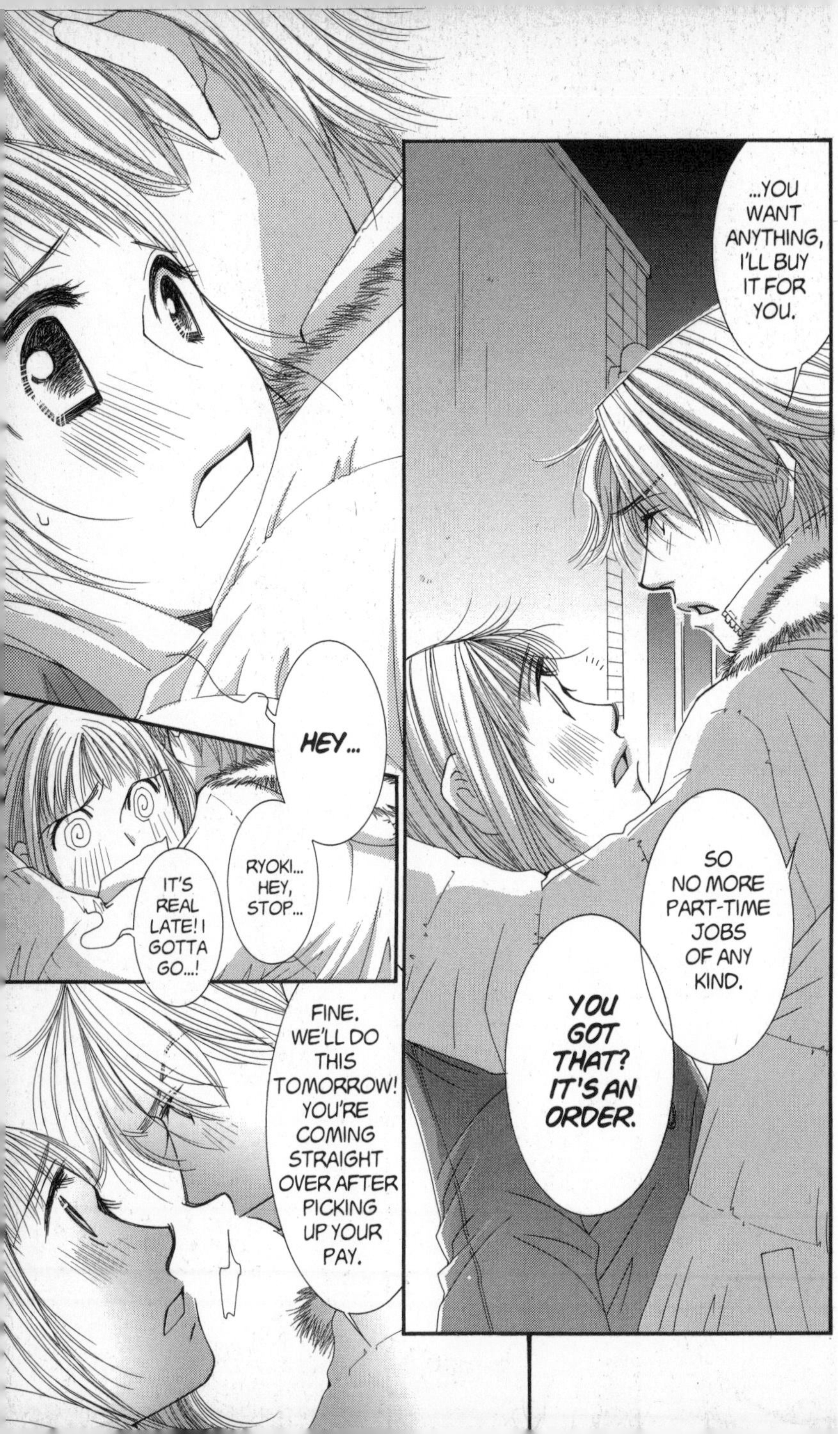
...YOU WANT ANYTHING, I'LL BUY IT FOR YOU.
SO NO MORE PART-TIME JOBS OF ANY KIND.
YOU GOT THAT? IT'S AN ORDER.
HEY...
RYOKI... HEY, STOP...
IT'S REAL LATE! I GOTTA GO...!
FINE. WE'LL DO THIS TOMORROW! YOU'RE COMING STRAIGHT OVER AFTER PICKING UP YOUR PAY.

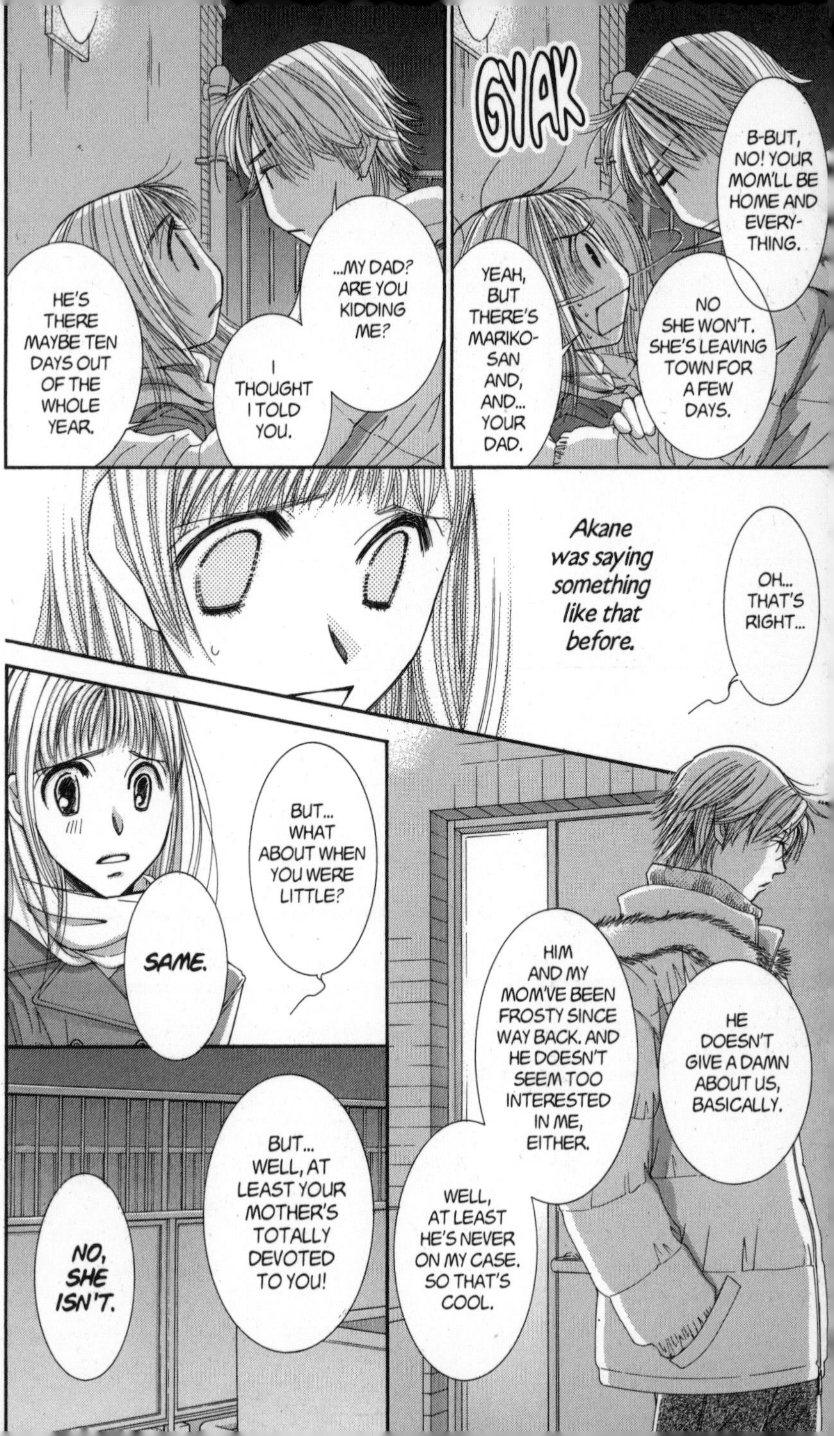

GYAK
B-BUT, NO! YOUR MOM'LL BE HOME AND EVERYTHING.
NO SHE WON'T. SHE'S LEAVING TOWN FOR A FEW DAYS.
YEAH, BUT THERE'S MARIKO-SAN AND, AND... YOUR DAD.
...MY DAD? ARE YOU KIDDING ME?
I THOUGHT I TOLD YOU.
HE'S THERE MAYBE TEN DAYS OUT OF THE WHOLE YEAR.
OH... THAT'S RIGHT...
Akane was saying something like that before.
HE DOESN'T GIVE A DAMN ABOUT US, BASICALLY.
HIM AND MY MOM'VE BEEN FROSTY SINCE WAY BACK. AND HE DOESN'T SEEM TOO INTERESTED IN ME, EITHER.
WELL, AT LEAST HE'S NEVER ON MY CASE. SO THAT'S COOL.
BUT... WHAT ABOUT WHEN YOU WERE LITTLE?
SAME.
BUT... WELL, AT LEAST YOUR MOTHER'S TOTALLY DEVOTED TO YOU!
NO, SHE ISN'T.

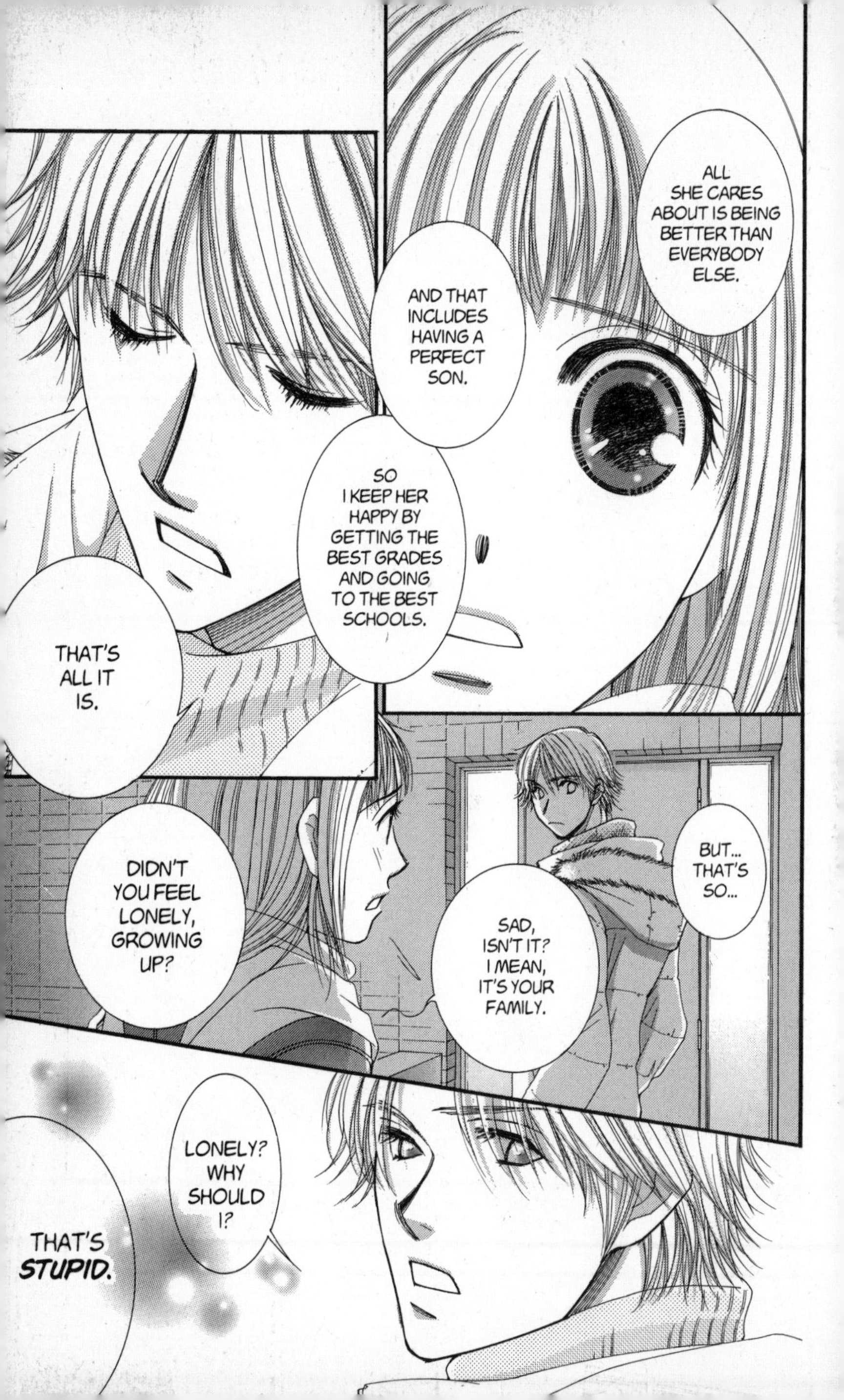
ALL SHE CARES ABOUT IS BEING BETTER THAN EVERYBODY ELSE.
AND THAT INCLUDES HAVING A PERFECT SON.
SO I KEEP HER HAPPY BY GETTING THE BEST GRADES AND GOING TO THE BEST SCHOOLS.
THAT'S ALL IT IS.
BUT... THAT'S SO...
SAD, ISN'T IT? I MEAN, IT'S YOUR FAMILY.
DIDN'T YOU FEEL LONELY, GROWING UP?
LONELY? WHY SHOULD I?
THAT'S **STUPID.**

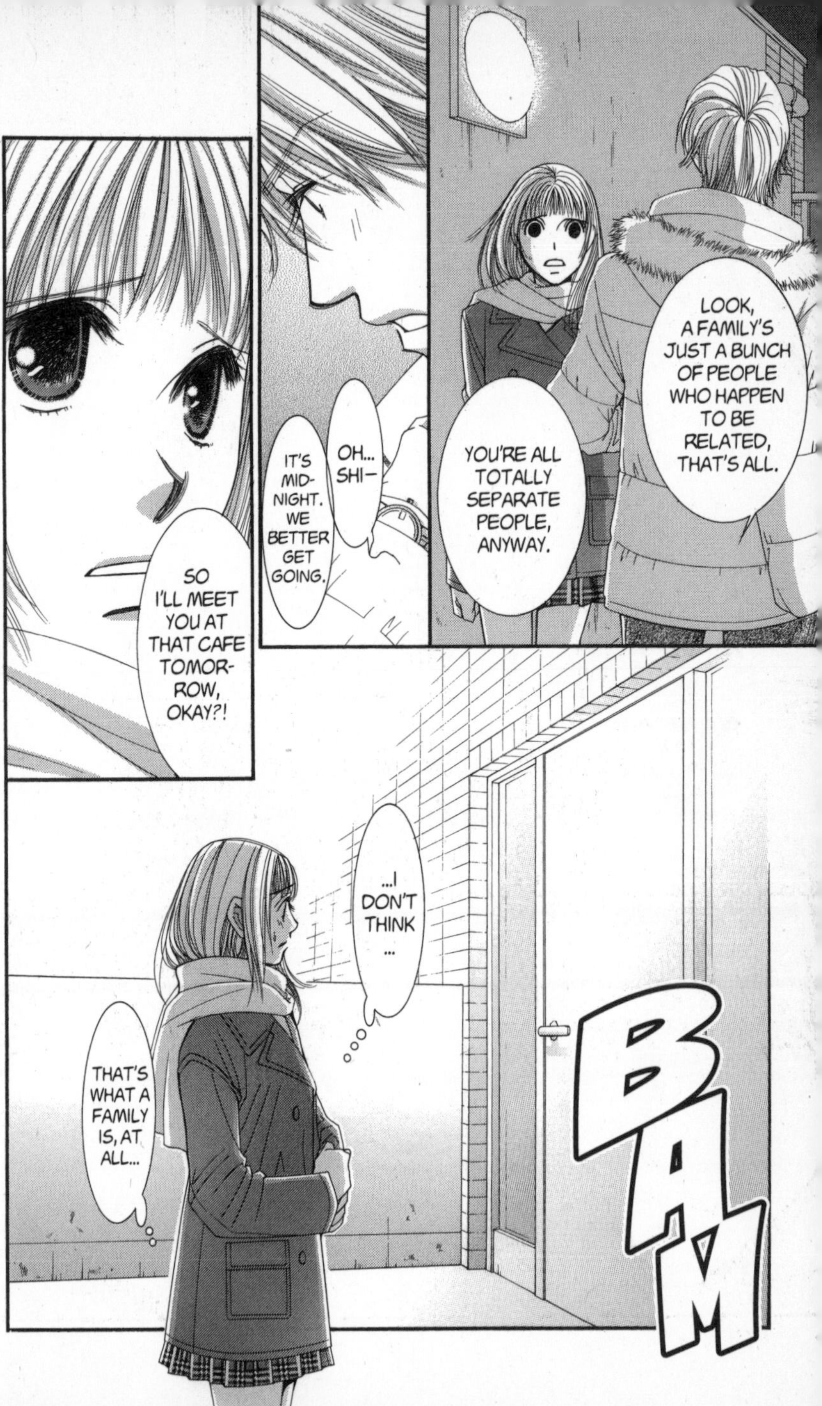
LOOK, A FAMILY'S JUST A BUNCH OF PEOPLE WHO HAPPEN TO BE RELATED, THAT'S ALL.
YOU'RE ALL TOTALLY SEPARATE PEOPLE, ANYWAY.
OH... SHI—
IT'S MID-NIGHT. WE BETTER GET GOING.
SO I'LL MEET YOU AT THAT CAFE TOMOR-ROW, OKAY?!
BAM
...I DON'T THINK ...
THAT'S WHAT A FAMILY IS, AT ALL...

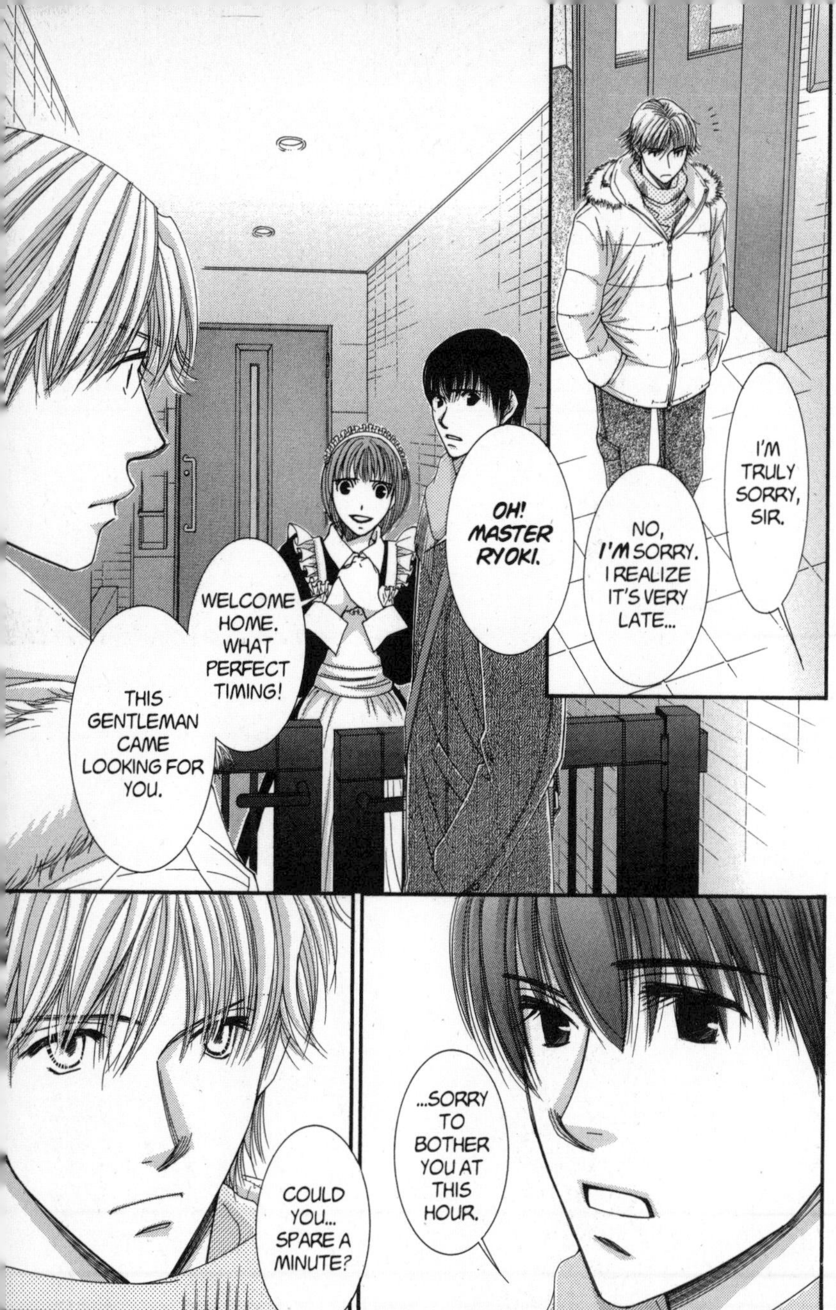
I'M TRULY SORRY, SIR.
NO, I'M SORRY. I REALIZE IT'S VERY LATE...
OH! MASTER RYOKI.
WELCOME HOME. WHAT PERFECT TIMING!
THIS GENTLEMAN CAME LOOKING FOR YOU.
...SORRY TO BOTHER YOU AT THIS HOUR.
COULD YOU... SPARE A MINUTE?

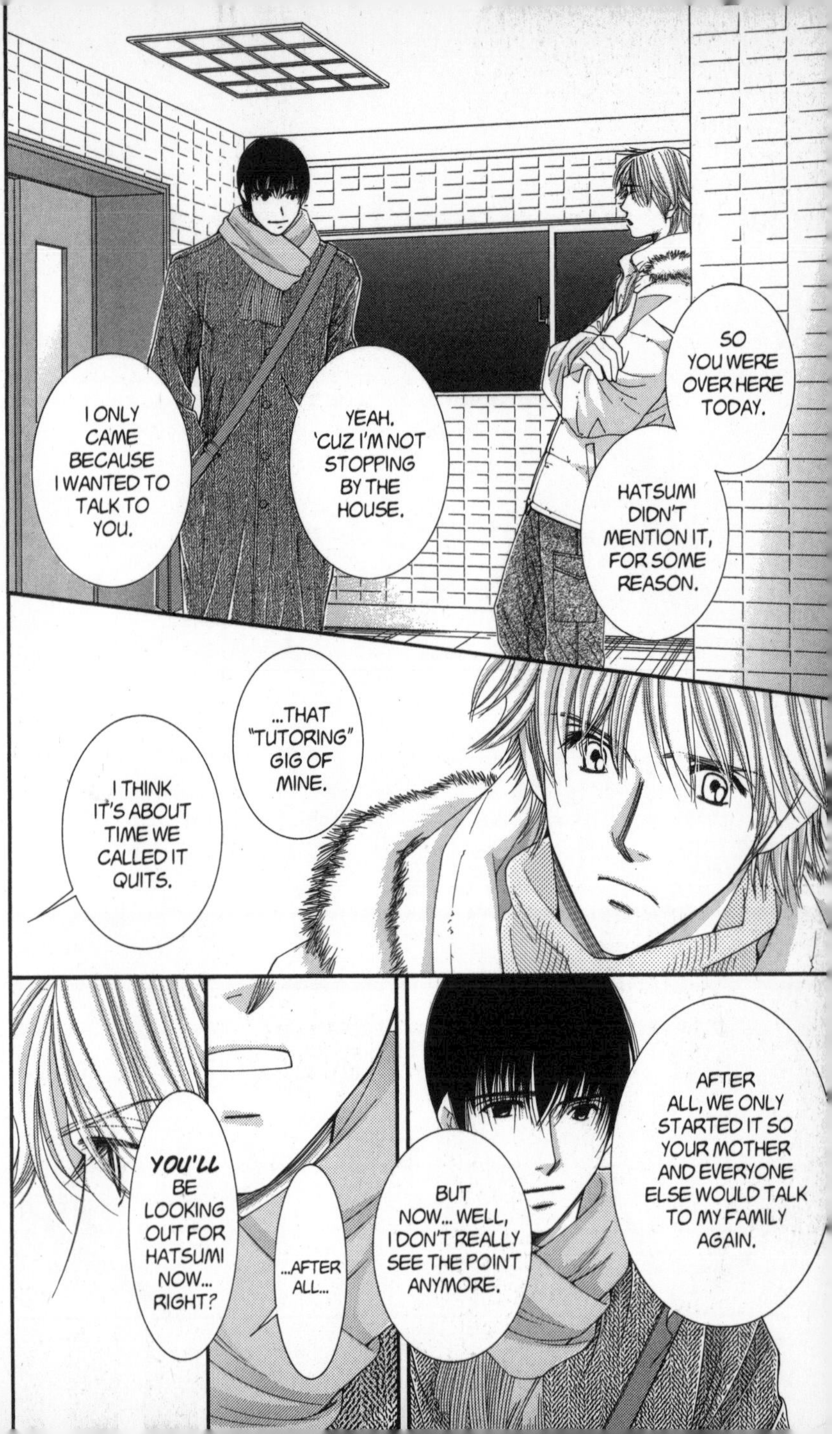
SO YOU WERE OVER HERE TODAY.
HATSUMI DIDN'T MENTION IT, FOR SOME REASON.
YEAH. 'CUZ I'M NOT STOPPING BY THE HOUSE.
I ONLY CAME BECAUSE I WANTED TO TALK TO YOU.
...THAT "TUTORING" GIG OF MINE.
I THINK IT'S ABOUT TIME WE CALLED IT QUITS.
AFTER ALL, WE ONLY STARTED IT SO YOUR MOTHER AND EVERYONE ELSE WOULD TALK TO MY FAMILY AGAIN.
BUT NOW... WELL, I DON'T REALLY SEE THE POINT ANYMORE.
...AFTER ALL...
YOU'LL BE LOOKING OUT FOR HATSUMI NOW... RIGHT?

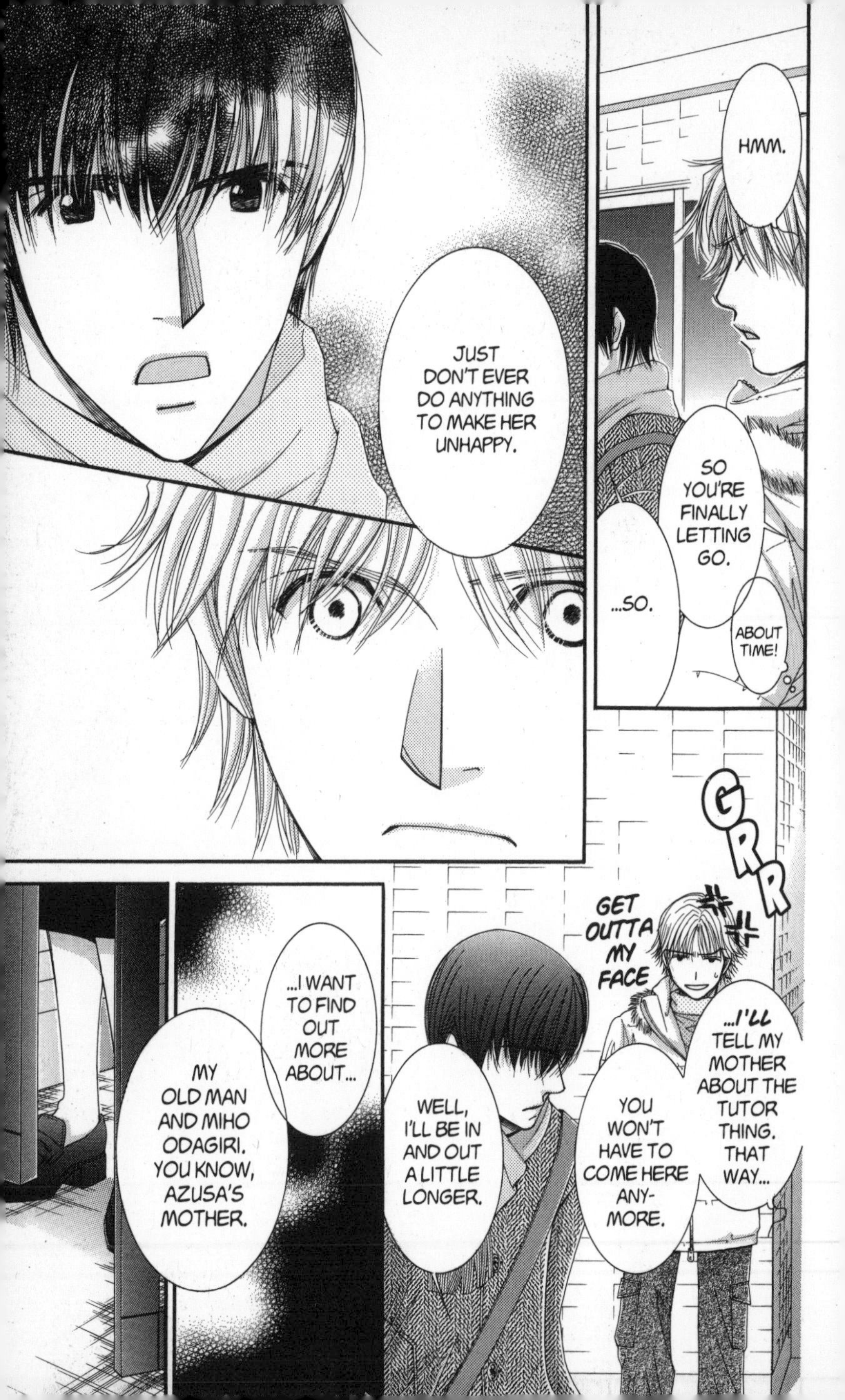
HMM.
SO YOU'RE FINALLY LETTING GO.
...SO.
ABOUT TIME!
JUST DON'T EVER DO ANYTHING TO MAKE HER UNHAPPY.
GRR
GET OUTTA MY FACE
...I'LL TELL MY MOTHER ABOUT THE TUTOR THING. THAT WAY...
YOU WON'T HAVE TO COME HERE ANY-MORE.
WELL, I'LL BE IN AND OUT A LITTLE LONGER.
...I WANT TO FIND OUT MORE ABOUT...
MY OLD MAN AND MIHO ODAGIRI. YOU KNOW, AZUSA'S MOTHER.

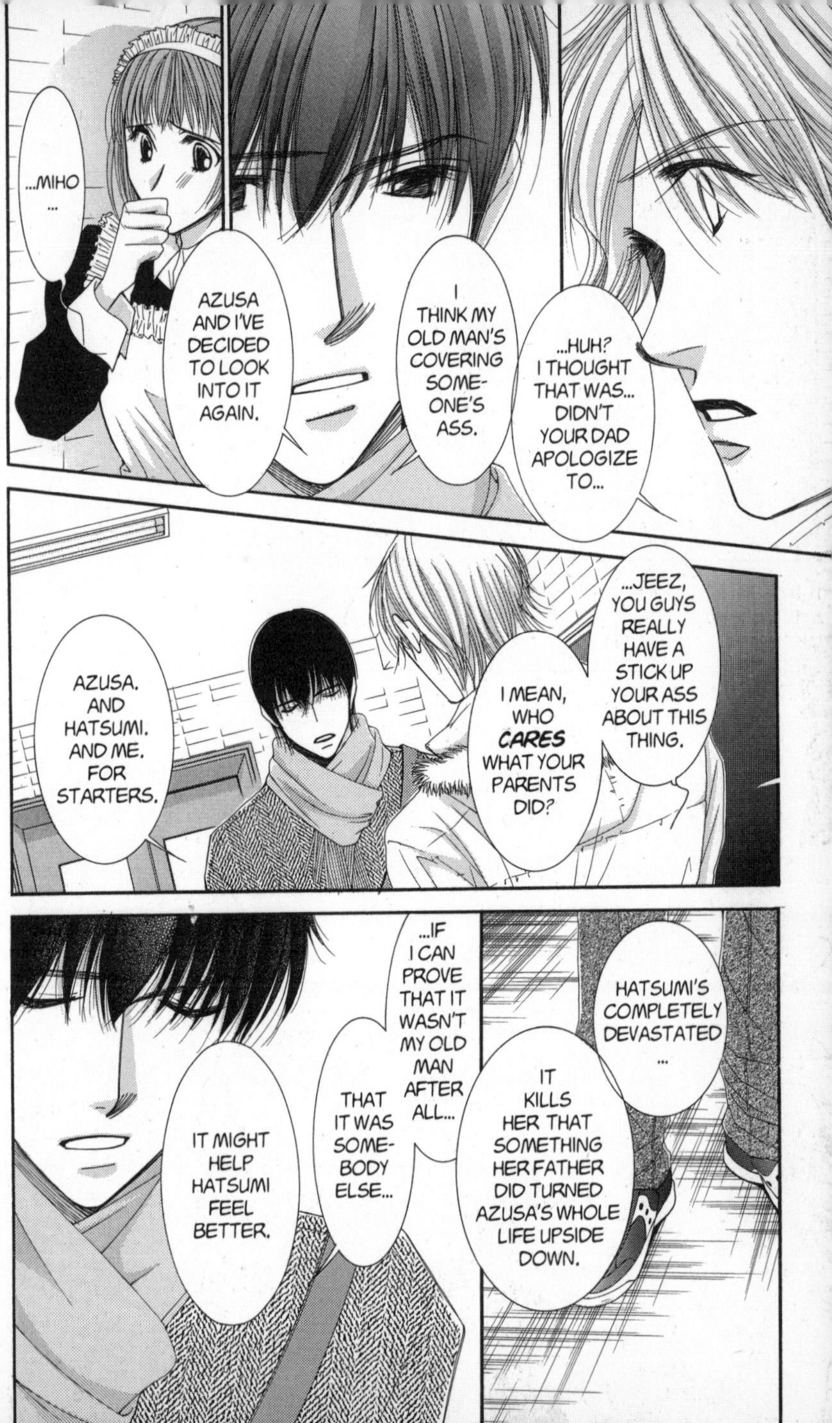
...HUH? I THOUGHT THAT WAS... DIDN'T YOUR DAD APOLOGIZE TO...
I THINK MY OLD MAN'S COVERING SOME-ONE'S ASS.
AZUSA AND I'VE DECIDED TO LOOK INTO IT AGAIN.
...MIHO ...
...JEEZ, YOU GUYS REALLY HAVE A STICK UP YOUR ASS ABOUT THIS THING.
I MEAN, WHO **CARES** WHAT YOUR PARENTS DID?
AZUSA. AND HATSUMI. AND ME. FOR STARTERS.
HATSUMI'S COMPLETELY DEVASTATED ...
IT KILLS HER THAT SOMETHING HER FATHER DID TURNED AZUSA'S WHOLE LIFE UPSIDE DOWN.
...IF I CAN PROVE THAT IT WASN'T MY OLD MAN AFTER ALL...
THAT IT WAS SOME-BODY ELSE...
IT MIGHT HELP HATSUMI FEEL BETTER.

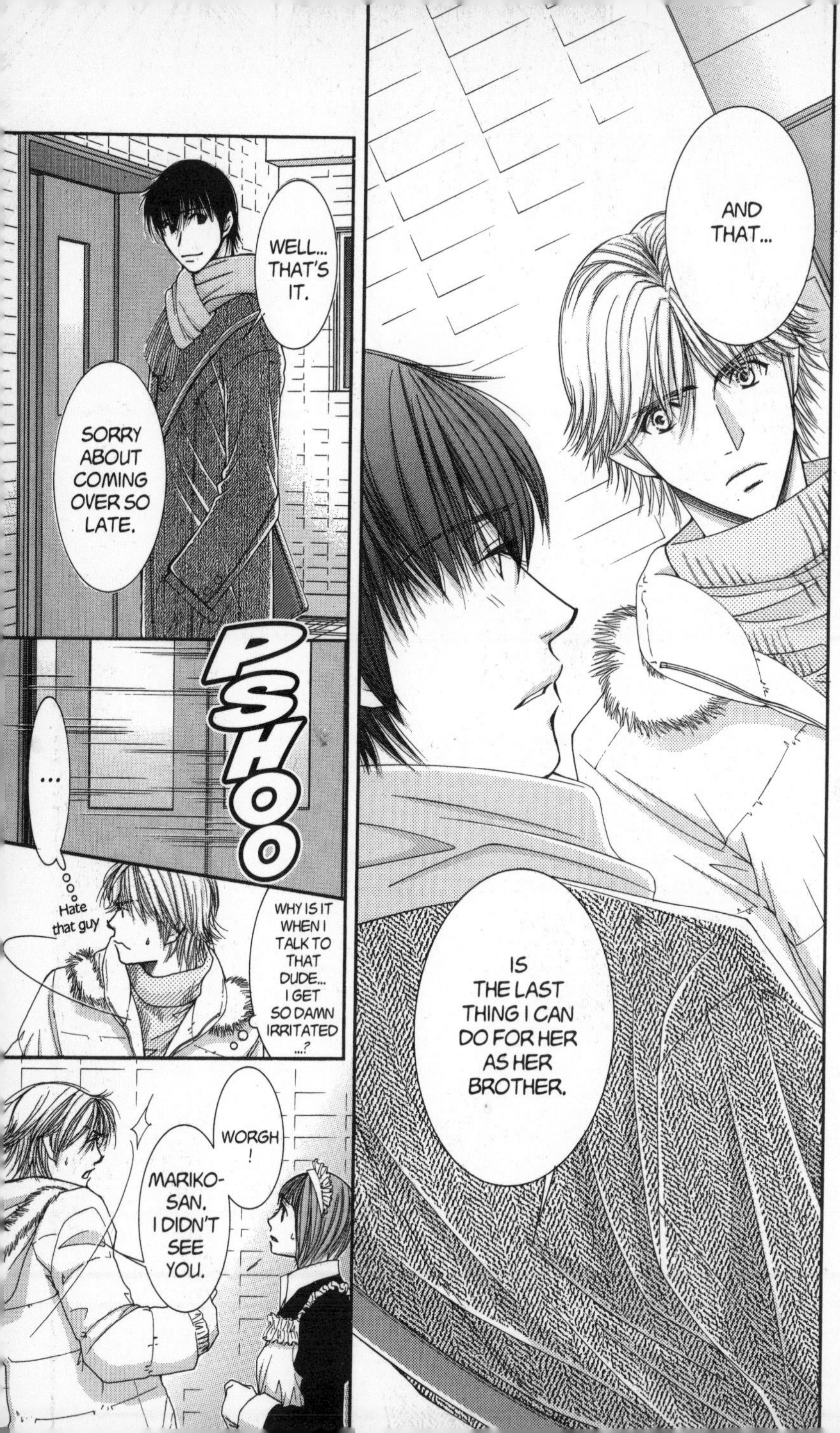
AND THAT...
IS THE LAST THING I CAN DO FOR HER AS HER BROTHER.
WELL... THAT'S IT.
SORRY ABOUT COMING OVER SO LATE.
PSHOO
...
WHY IS IT WHEN I TALK TO THAT DUDE... I GET SO DAMN IRRITATED...?
Hate that guy
WORGH!
MARIKO-SAN. I DIDN'T SEE YOU.

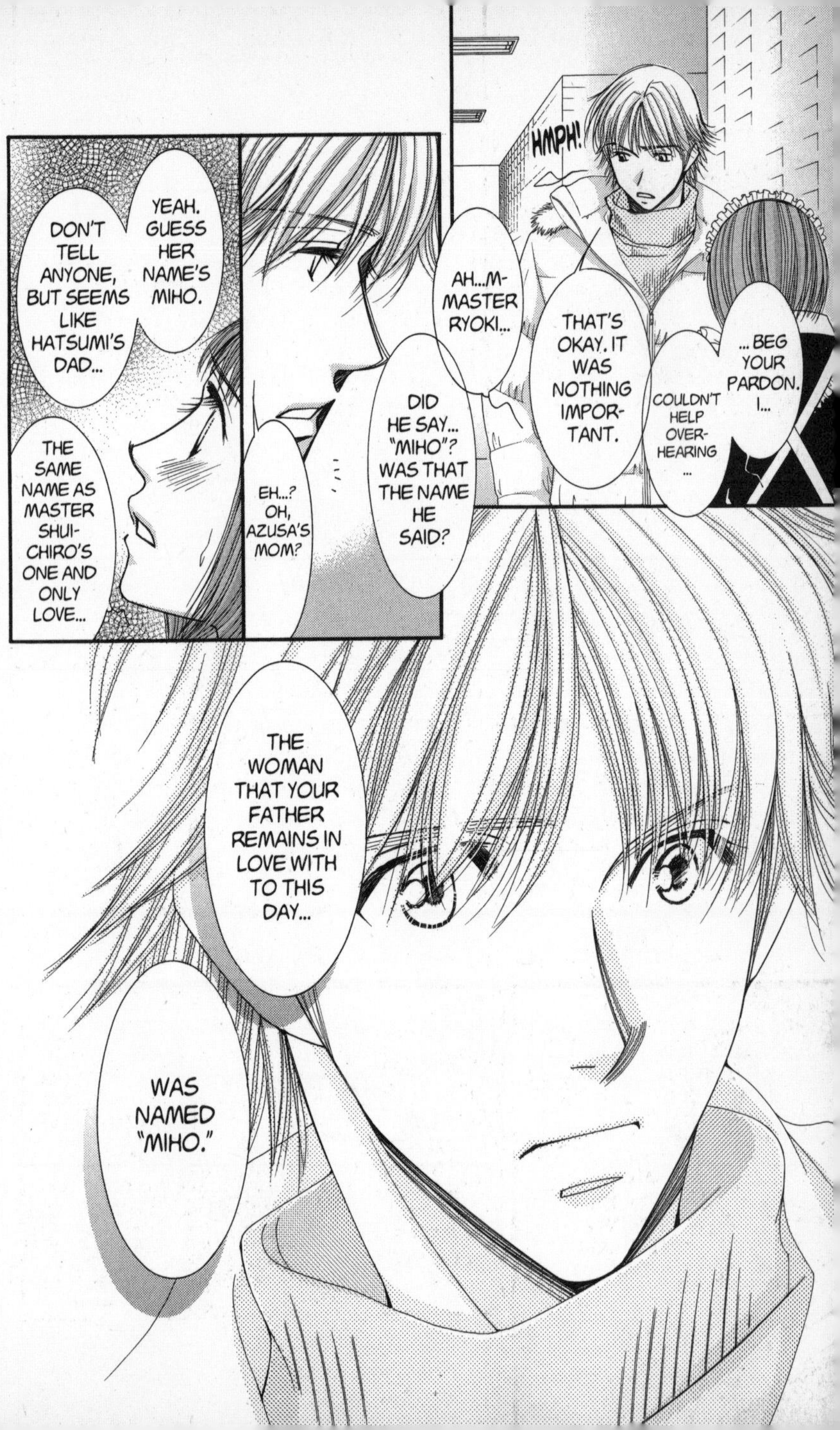
HMPH!
...BEG YOUR PARDON. I...
COULDN'T HELP OVER-HEARING...
THAT'S OKAY. IT WAS NOTHING IMPOR-TANT.
AH...M-MASTER RYOKI...
DID HE SAY... "MIHO"? WAS THAT THE NAME HE SAID?
EH...? OH, AZUSA'S MOM?
YEAH. GUESS HER NAME'S MIHO.
DON'T TELL ANYONE, BUT SEEMS LIKE HATSUMI'S DAD...
THE SAME NAME AS MASTER SHUI-CHIRO'S ONE AND ONLY LOVE...
THE WOMAN THAT YOUR FATHER REMAINS IN LOVE WITH TO THIS DAY...
WAS NAMED "MIHO."

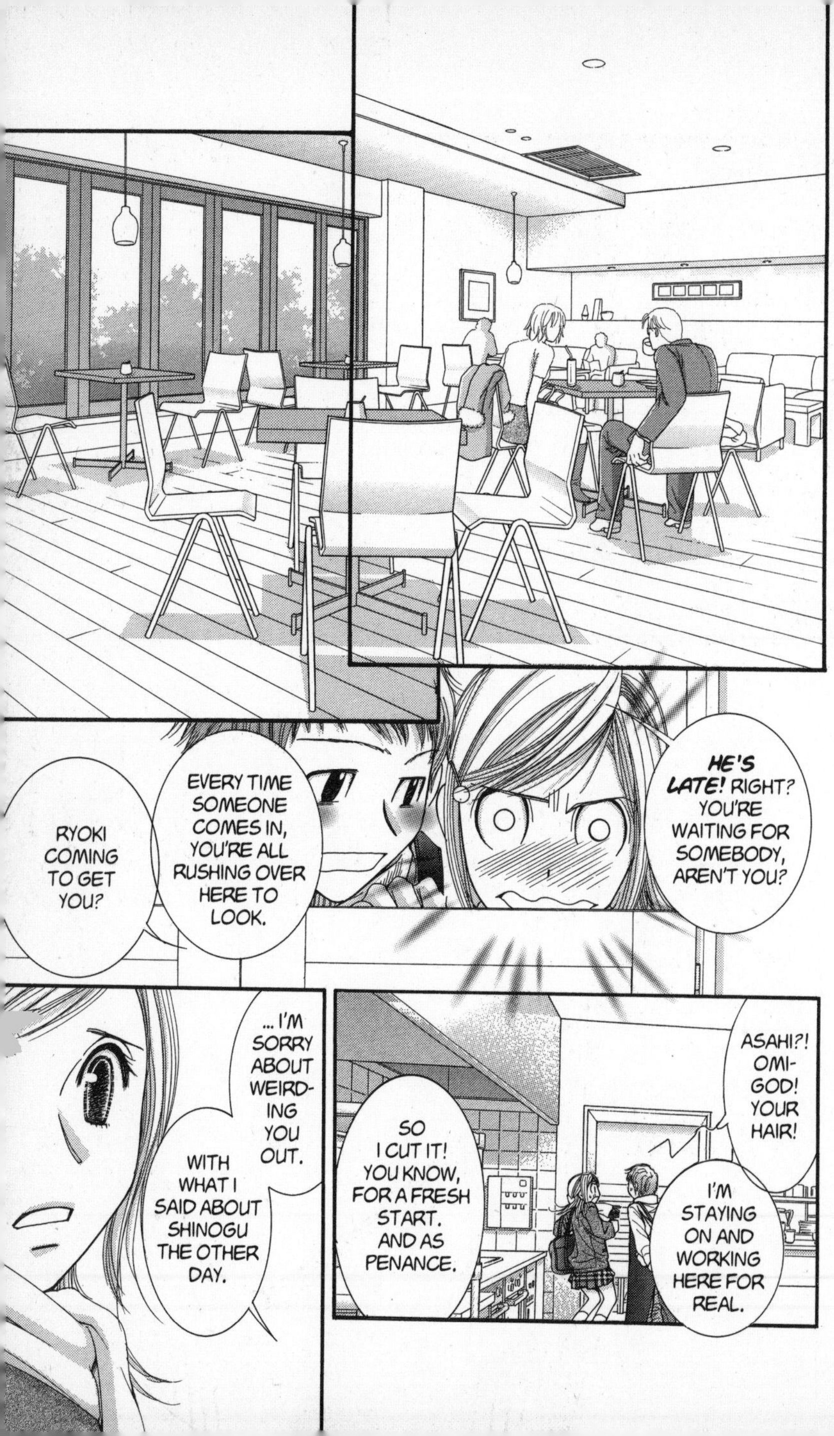
HE'S LATE! RIGHT? YOU'RE WAITING FOR SOMEBODY, AREN'T YOU?
EVERY TIME SOMEONE COMES IN, YOU'RE ALL RUSHING OVER HERE TO LOOK.
RYOKI COMING TO GET YOU?
ASAHI?! OMI-GOD! YOUR HAIR!
I'M STAYING ON AND WORKING HERE FOR REAL.
SO I CUT IT! YOU KNOW, FOR A FRESH START. AND AS PENANCE.
...I'M SORRY ABOUT WEIRD-ING YOU OUT.
WITH WHAT I SAID ABOUT SHINOGU THE OTHER DAY.

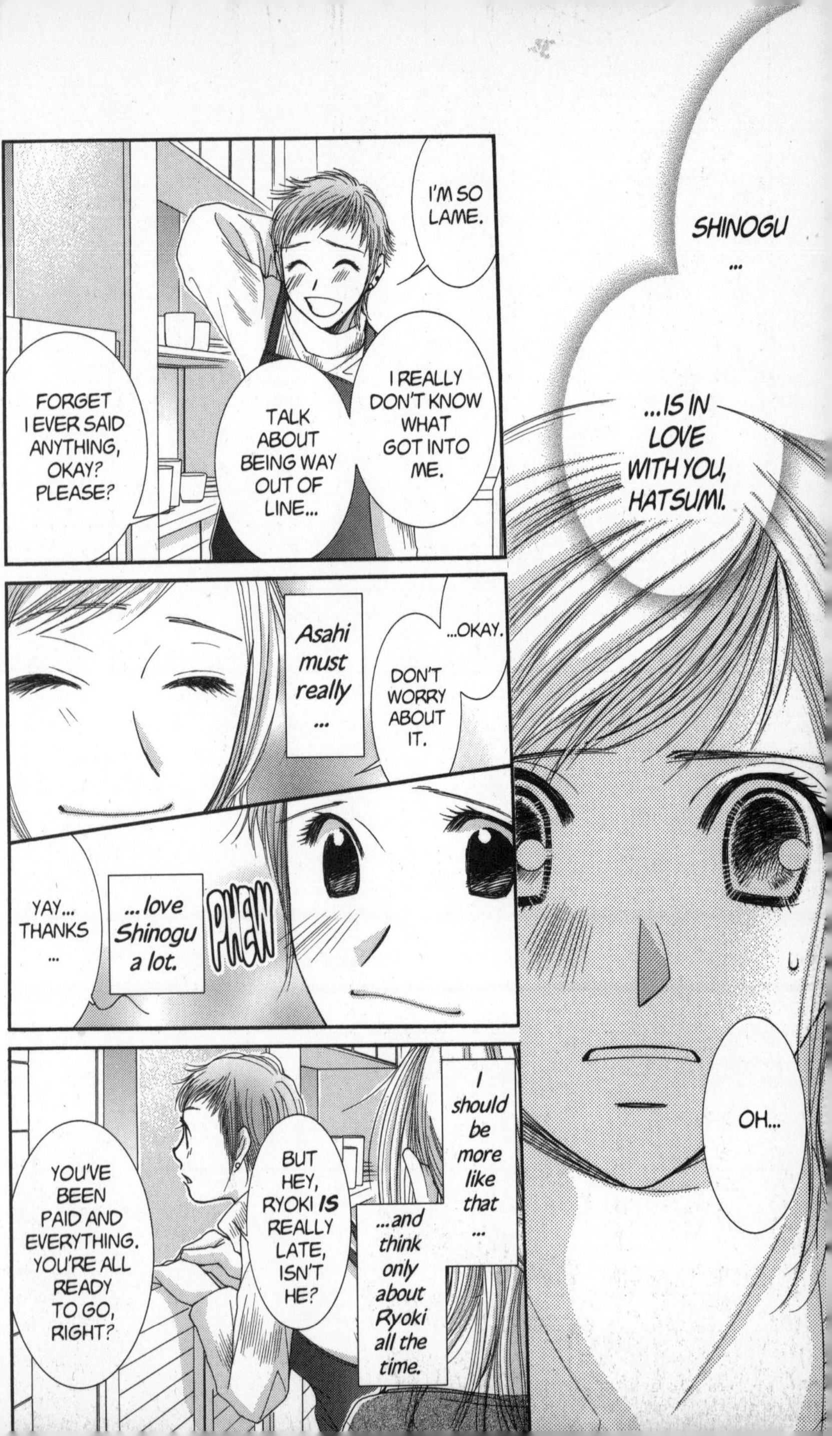
SHINOGU ...
...IS IN LOVE WITH YOU, HATSUMI.
OH...
I'M SO LAME.
I REALLY DON'T KNOW WHAT GOT INTO ME.
TALK ABOUT BEING WAY OUT OF LINE...
FORGET I EVER SAID ANYTHING, OKAY? PLEASE?
...OKAY.
DON'T WORRY ABOUT IT.
Asahi must really ...
PHEW
...love Shinogu a lot.
YAY... THANKS ...
I should be more like that ...
...and think only about Ryoki all the time.
BUT HEY, RYOKI IS REALLY LATE, ISN'T HE?
YOU'VE BEEN PAID AND EVERYTHING. YOU'RE ALL READY TO GO, RIGHT?

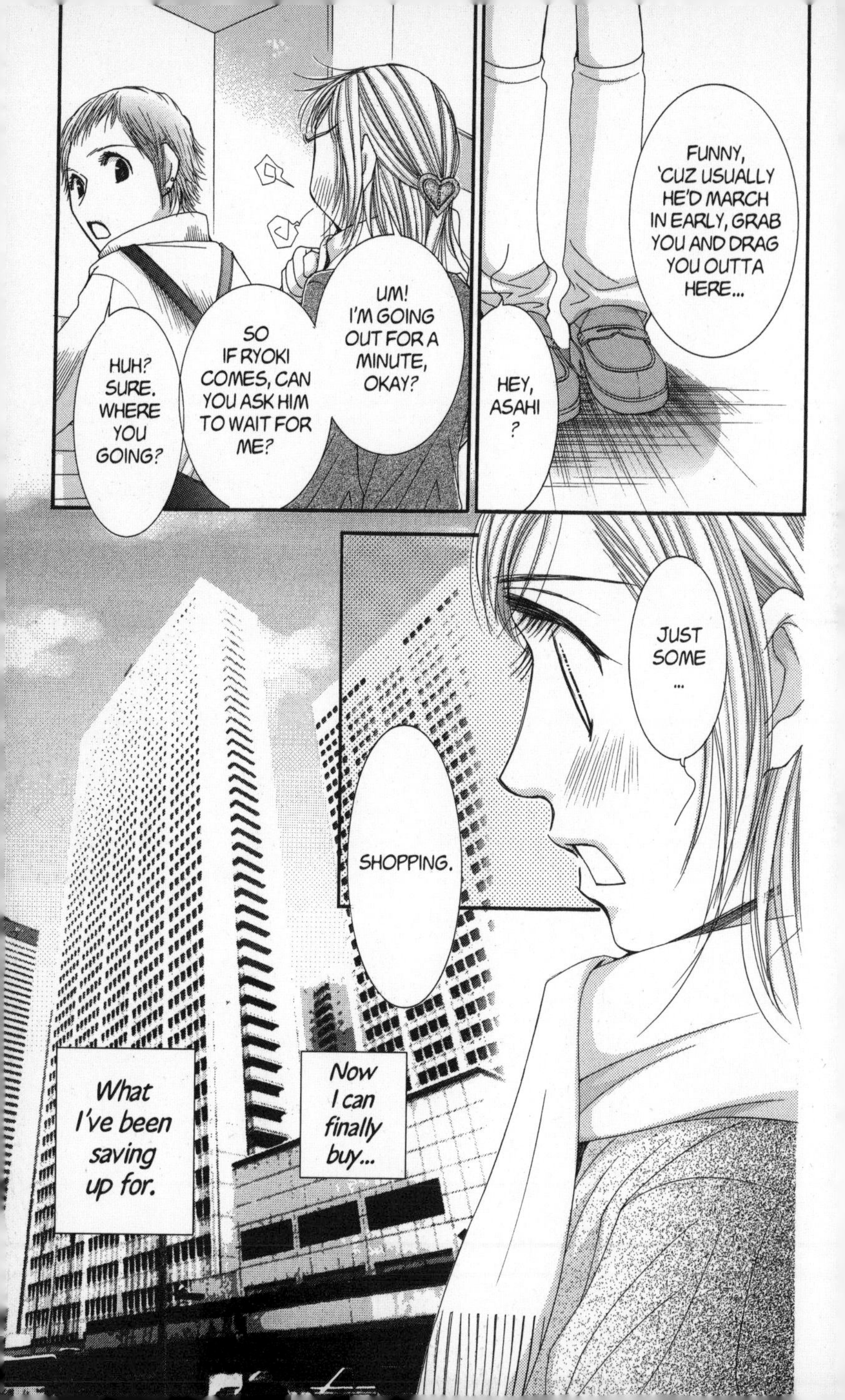
FUNNY, 'CUZ USUALLY HE'D MARCH IN EARLY, GRAB YOU AND DRAG YOU OUTTA HERE...
HEY, ASAHI?
UM! I'M GOING OUT FOR A MINUTE, OKAY?
SO IF RYOKI COMES, CAN YOU ASK HIM TO WAIT FOR ME?
HUH? SURE. WHERE YOU GOING?
JUST SOME...
SHOPPING.
Now I can finally buy...
What I've been saving up for.

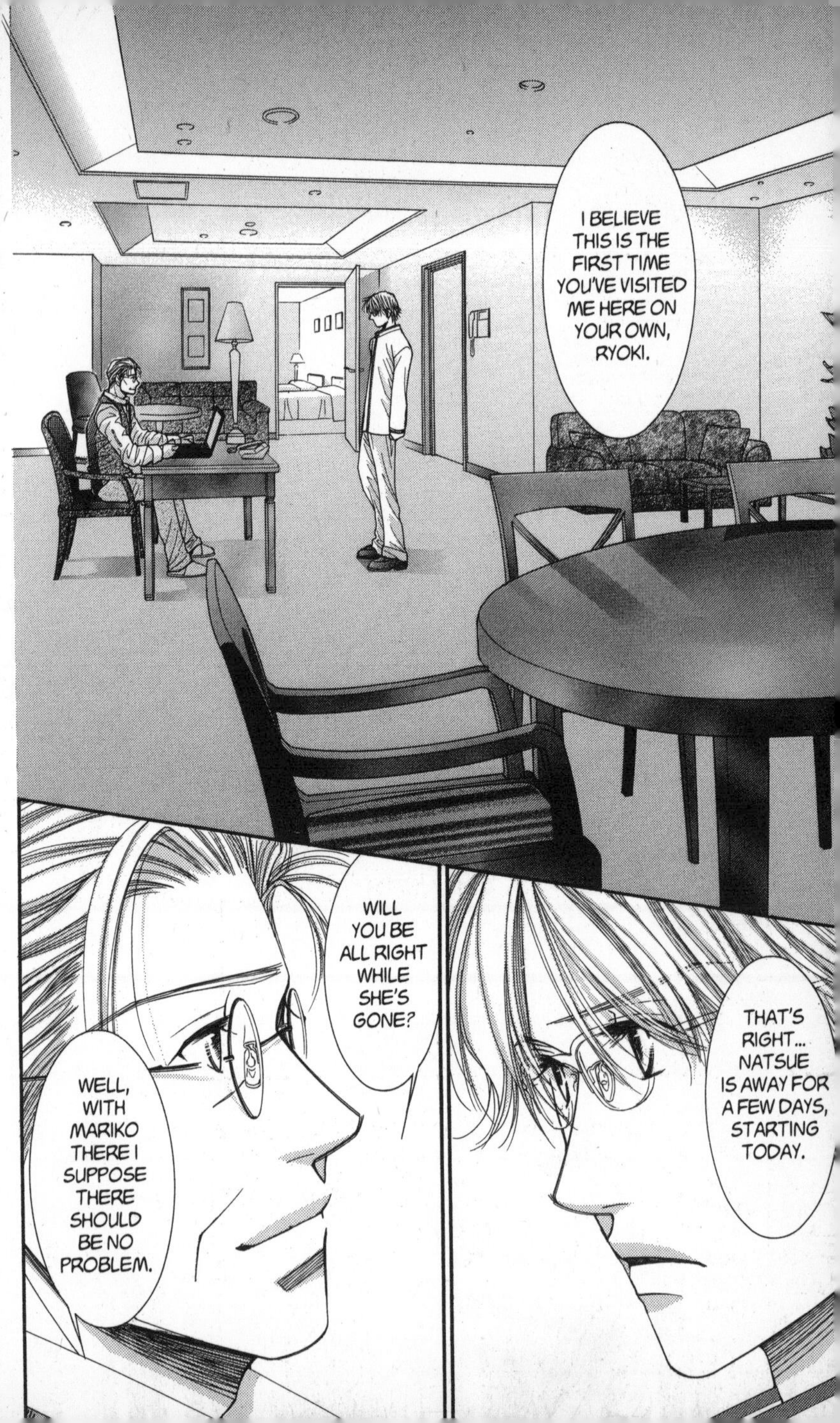
I BELIEVE THIS IS THE FIRST TIME YOU'VE VISITED ME HERE ON YOUR OWN, RYOKI.
THAT'S RIGHT... NATSUE IS AWAY FOR A FEW DAYS, STARTING TODAY.
WILL YOU BE ALL RIGHT WHILE SHE'S GONE?
WELL, WITH MARIKO THERE I SUPPOSE THERE SHOULD BE NO PROBLEM.

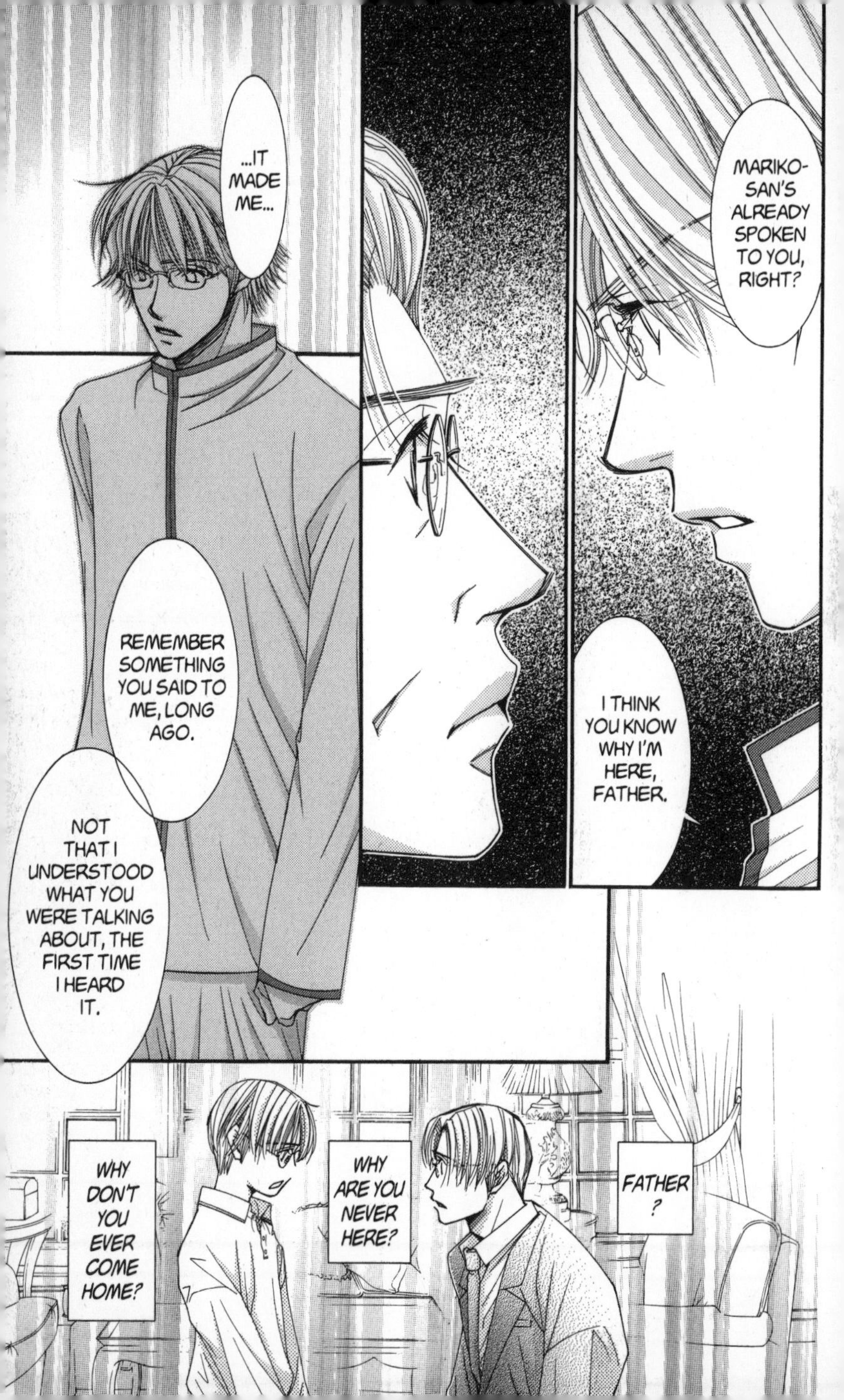
MARIKO-SAN'S ALREADY SPOKEN TO YOU, RIGHT?
I THINK YOU KNOW WHY I'M HERE, FATHER.
...IT MADE ME...
REMEMBER SOMETHING YOU SAID TO ME, LONG AGO.
NOT THAT I UNDERSTOOD WHAT YOU WERE TALKING ABOUT, THE FIRST TIME I HEARD IT.
FATHER?
WHY ARE YOU NEVER HERE?
WHY DON'T YOU EVER COME HOME?

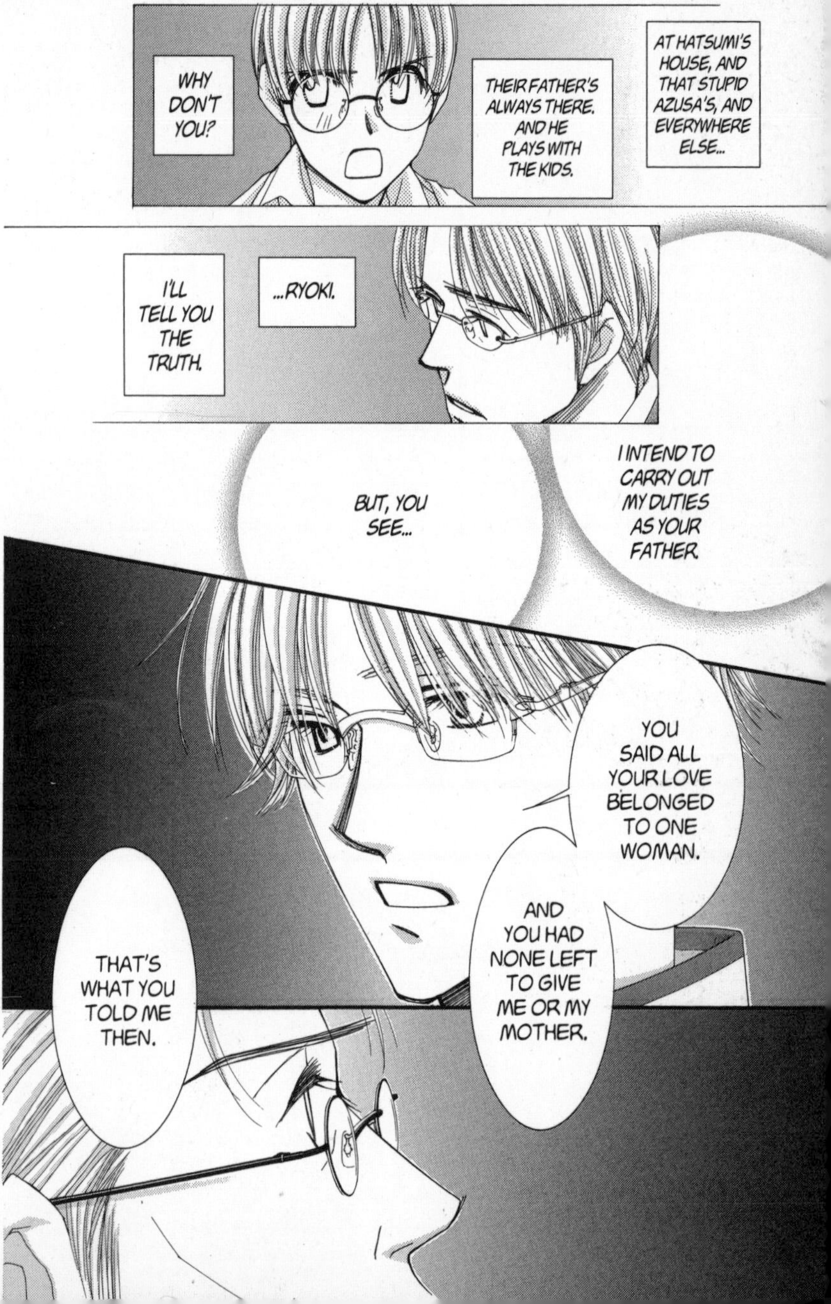
AT HATSUMI'S HOUSE, AND THAT STUPID AZUSA'S, AND EVERYWHERE ELSE...
THEIR FATHER'S ALWAYS THERE. AND HE PLAYS WITH THE KIDS.
WHY DON'T YOU?
...RYOKI.
I'LL TELL YOU THE TRUTH.
I INTEND TO CARRY OUT MY DUTIES AS YOUR FATHER.
BUT, YOU SEE...
YOU SAID ALL YOUR LOVE BELONGED TO ONE WOMAN.
AND YOU HAD NONE LEFT TO GIVE ME OR MY MOTHER.
THAT'S WHAT YOU TOLD ME THEN.

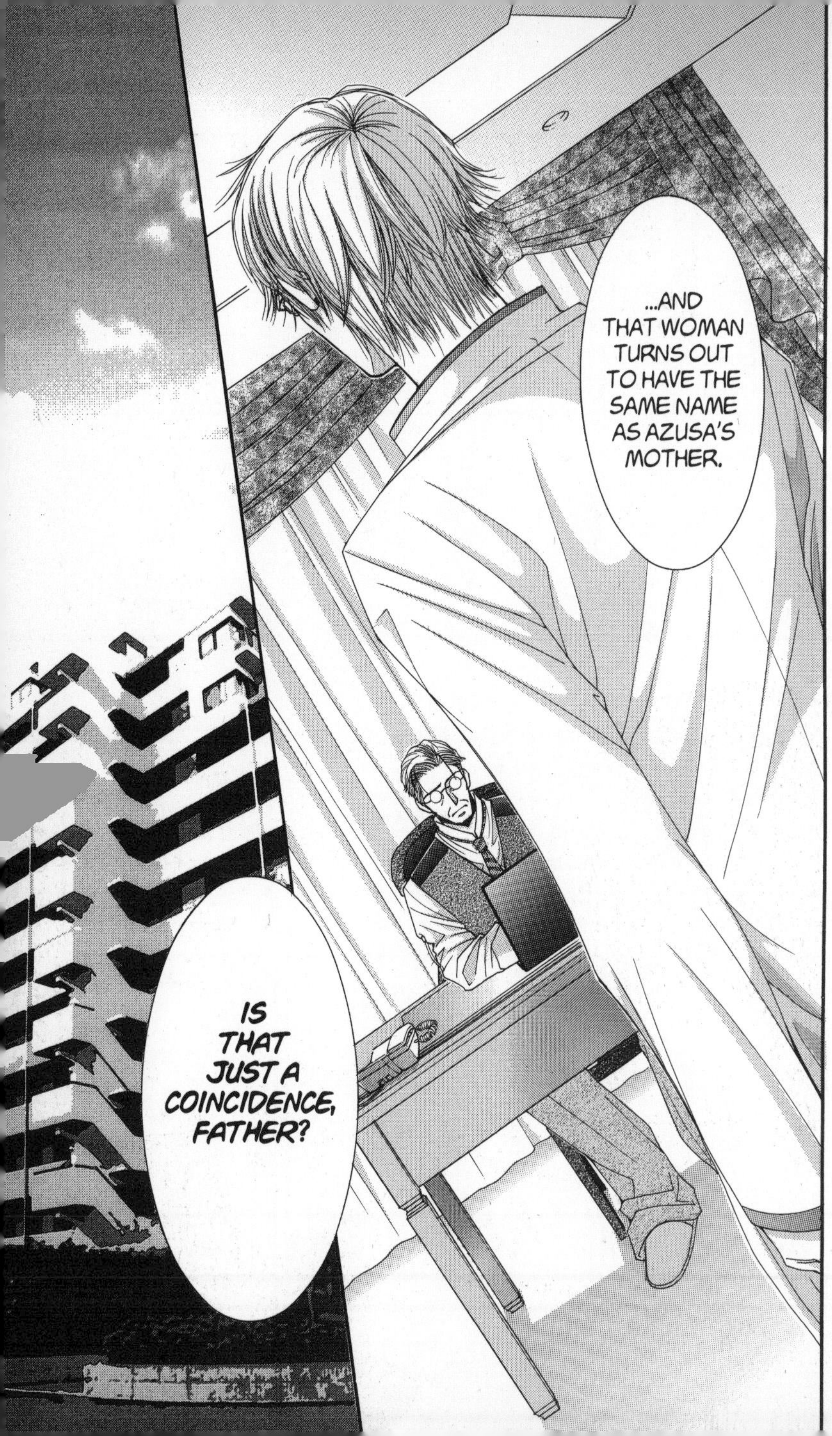
...AND THAT WOMAN TURNS OUT TO HAVE THE SAME NAME AS AZUSA'S MOTHER.
IS THAT JUST A COINCIDENCE, FATHER?

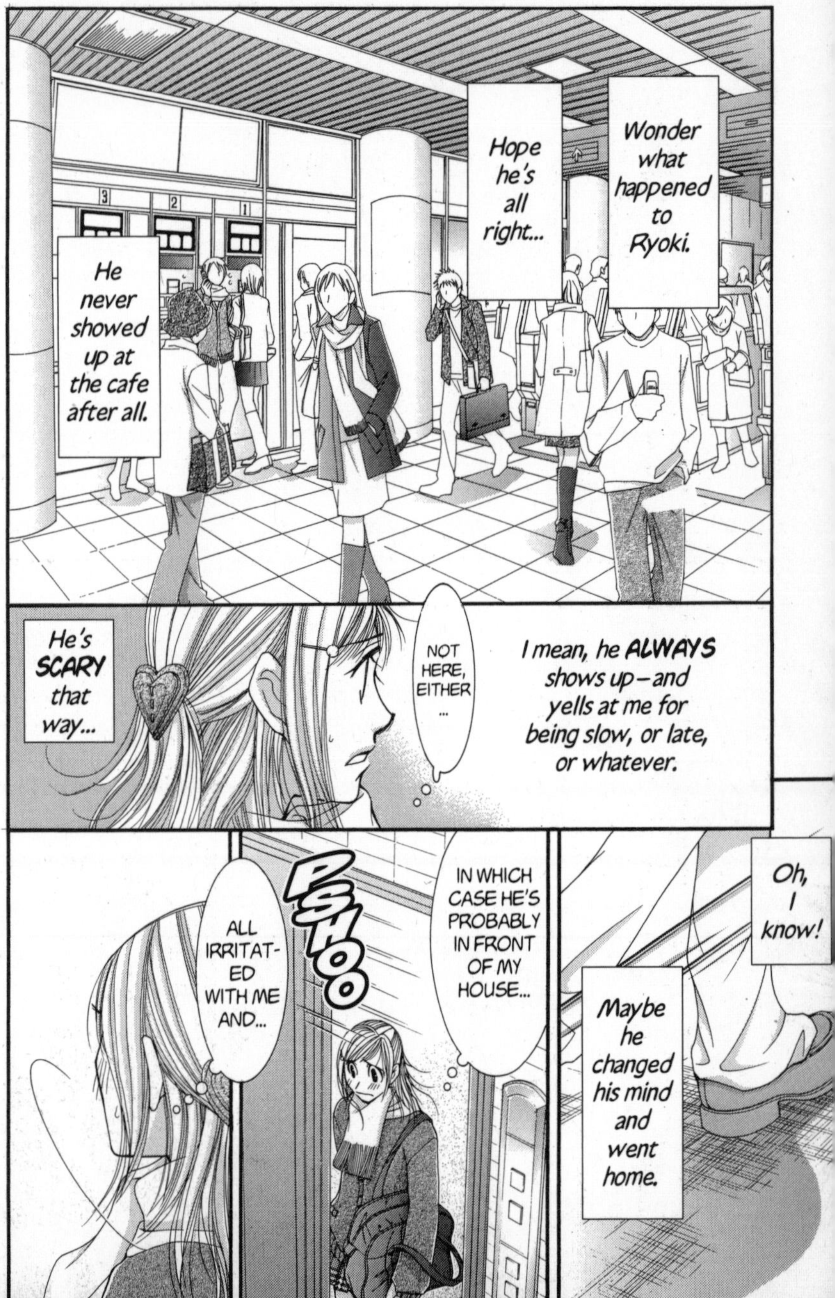
Wonder what happened to Ryoki.
Hope he's all right...
He never showed up at the cafe after all.
I mean, he **ALWAYS** shows up—and yells at me for being slow, or late, or whatever.
NOT HERE, EITHER...
He's **SCARY** that way...
Oh, I know!
Maybe he changed his mind and went home.
IN WHICH CASE HE'S PROBABLY IN FRONT OF MY HOUSE...
PSHOO
ALL IRRITAT-ED WITH ME AND...

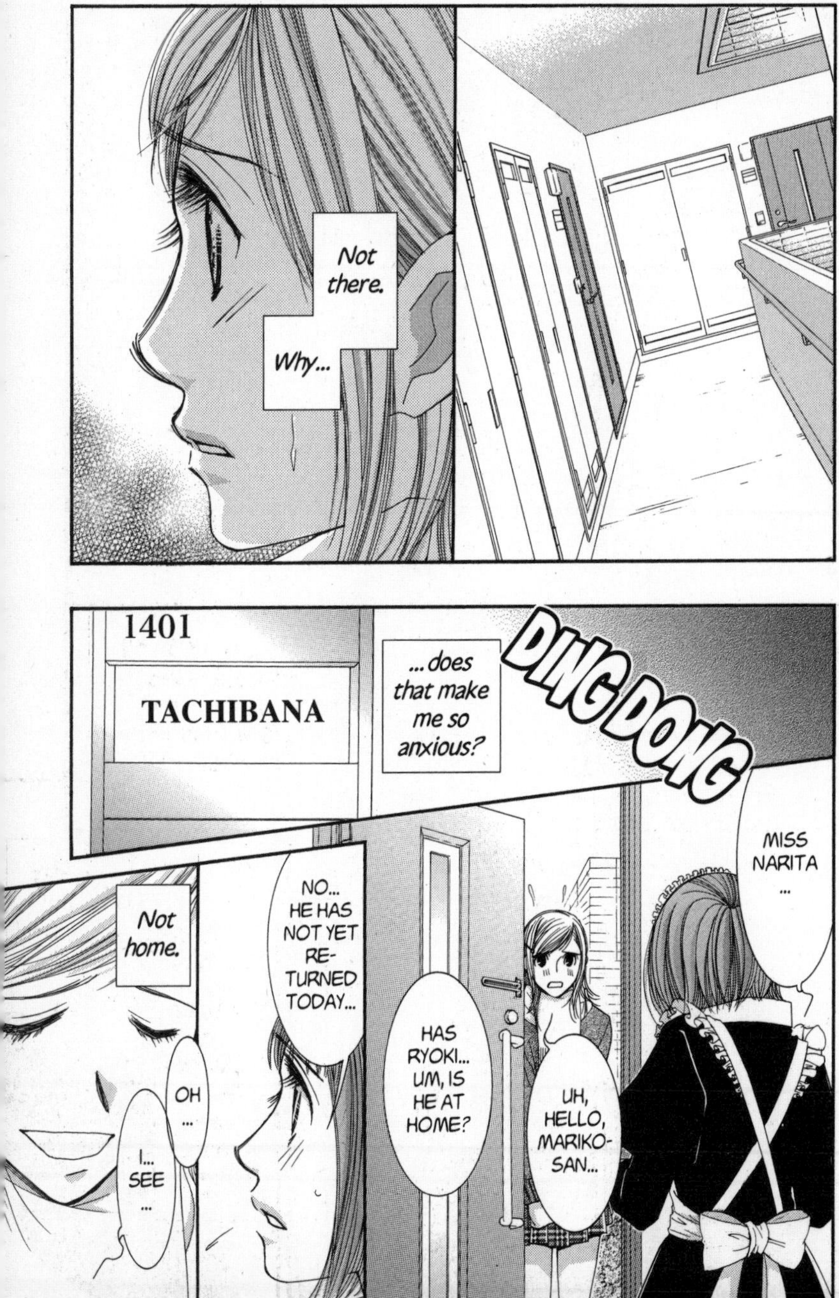
Not there.
Why...
1401
TACHIBANA
...does that make me so anxious?
DING DONG
MISS NARITA...
UH, HELLO, MARIKO-SAN...
HAS RYOKI... UM, IS HE AT HOME?
NO... HE HAS NOT YET RE-TURNED TODAY...
Not home.
OH...
I... SEE...

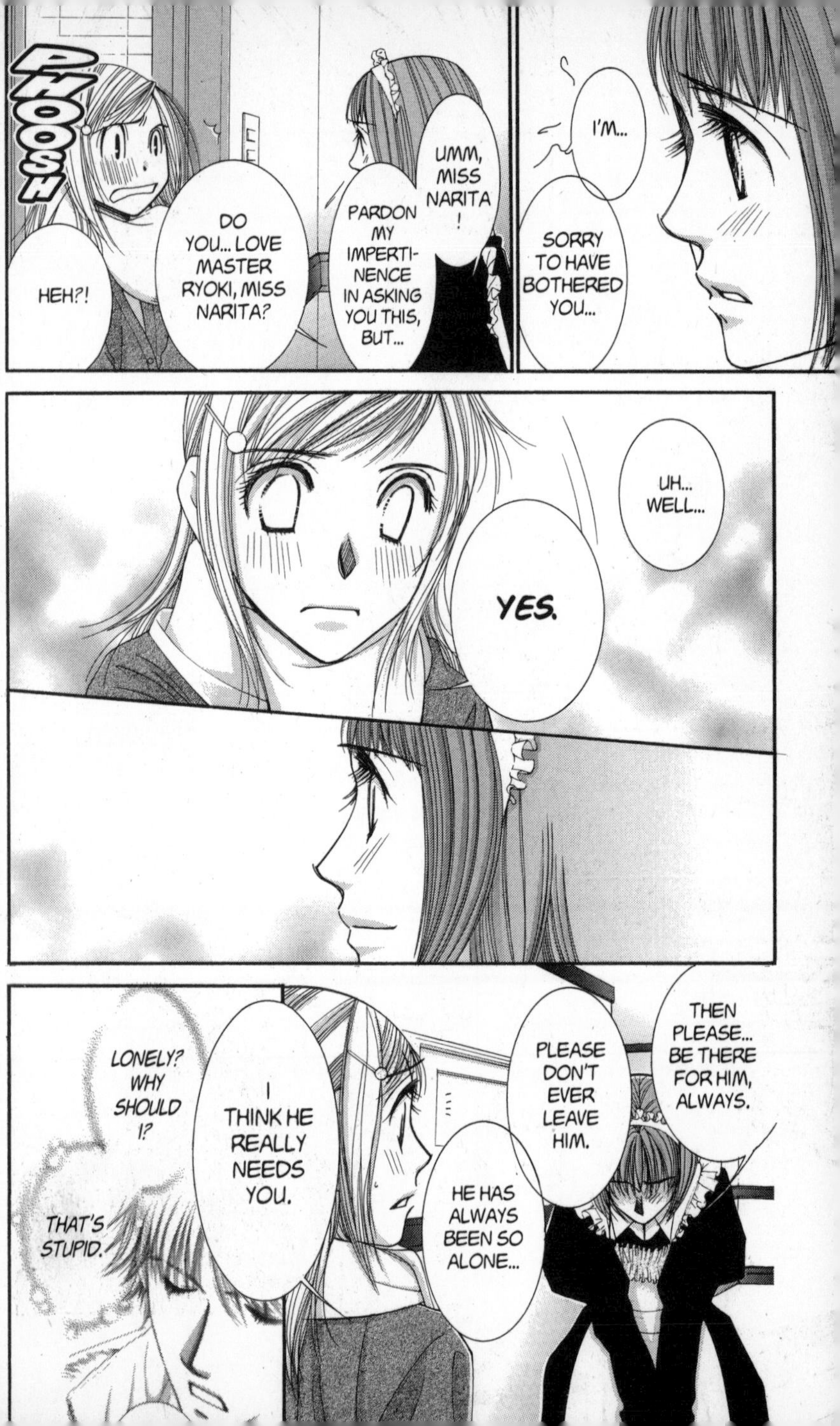
I'M...
SORRY TO HAVE BOTHERED YOU...
UMM, MISS NARITA!
PARDON MY IMPERTINENCE IN ASKING YOU THIS, BUT...
DO YOU... LOVE MASTER RYOKI, MISS NARITA?
PHOOSH
HEH?!
UH... WELL...
YES.
THEN PLEASE... BE THERE FOR HIM, ALWAYS.
PLEASE DON'T EVER LEAVE HIM.
HE HAS ALWAYS BEEN SO ALONE...
I THINK HE REALLY NEEDS YOU.
LONELY? WHY SHOULD I?
THAT'S STUPID.

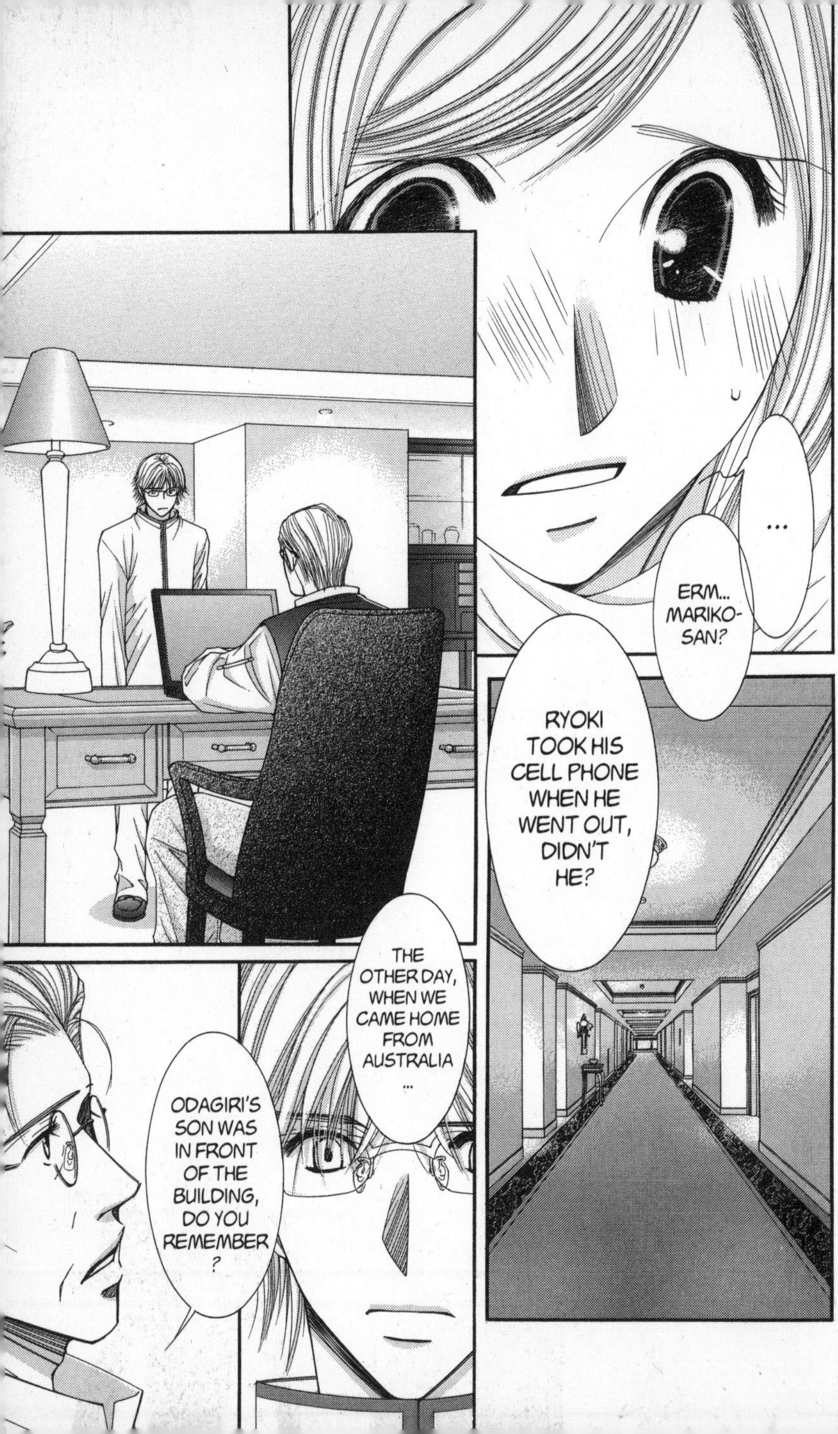
...
ERM... MARIKO-SAN?
RYOKI TOOK HIS CELL PHONE WHEN HE WENT OUT, DIDN'T HE?
THE OTHER DAY, WHEN WE CAME HOME FROM AUSTRALIA ...
ODAGIRI'S SON WAS IN FRONT OF THE BUILDING, DO YOU REMEMBER ?

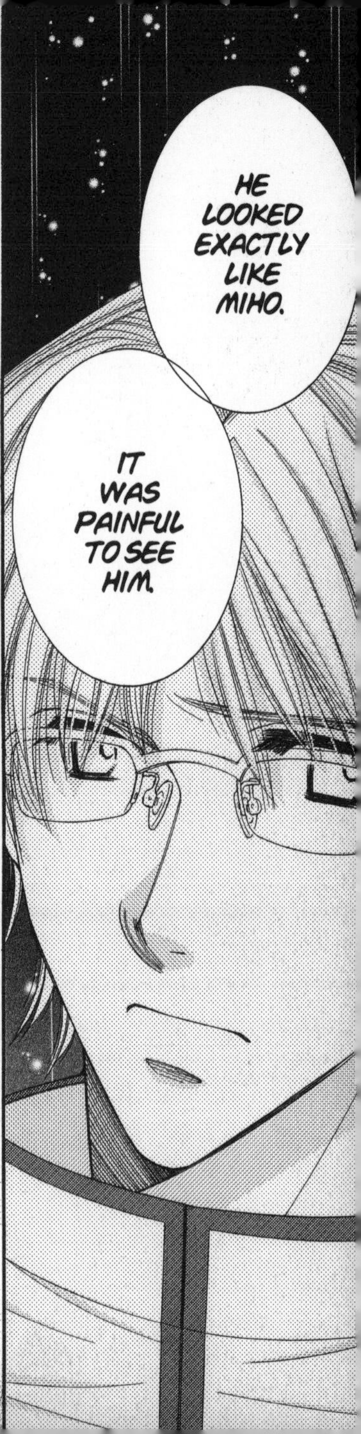
HE LOOKED EXACTLY LIKE MIHO.
IT WAS PAINFUL TO SEE HIM.

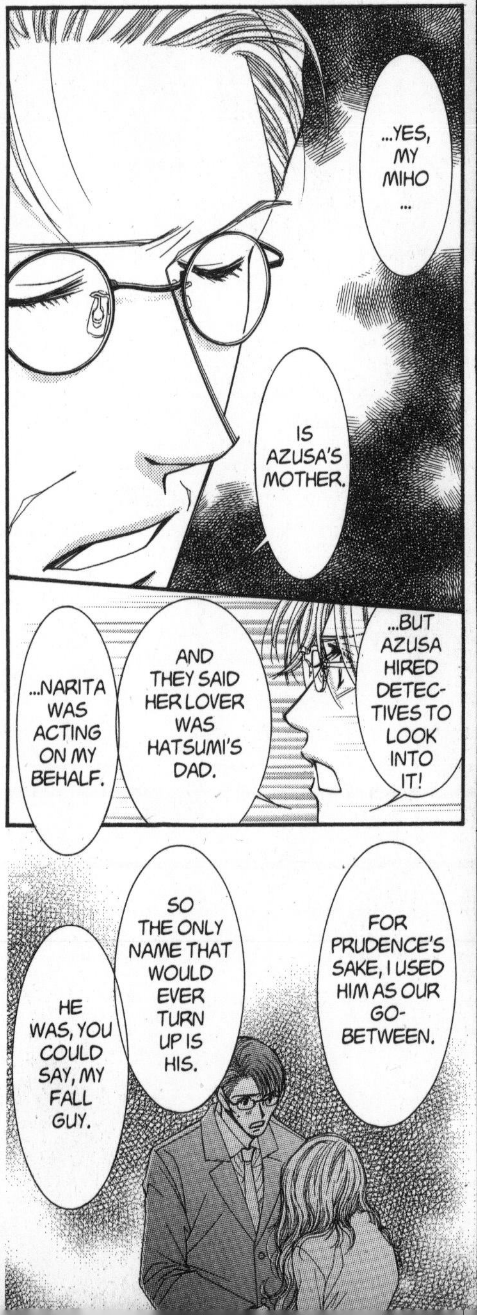
...YES, MY MIHO ...
IS AZUSA'S MOTHER.
...BUT AZUSA HIRED DETEC-TIVES TO LOOK INTO IT!
AND THEY SAID HER LOVER WAS HATSUMI'S DAD.
...NARITA WAS ACTING ON MY BEHALF.
FOR PRUDENCE'S SAKE, I USED HIM AS OUR GO-BETWEEN.
SO THE ONLY NAME THAT WOULD EVER TURN UP IS HIS.
HE WAS, YOU COULD SAY, MY FALL GUY.

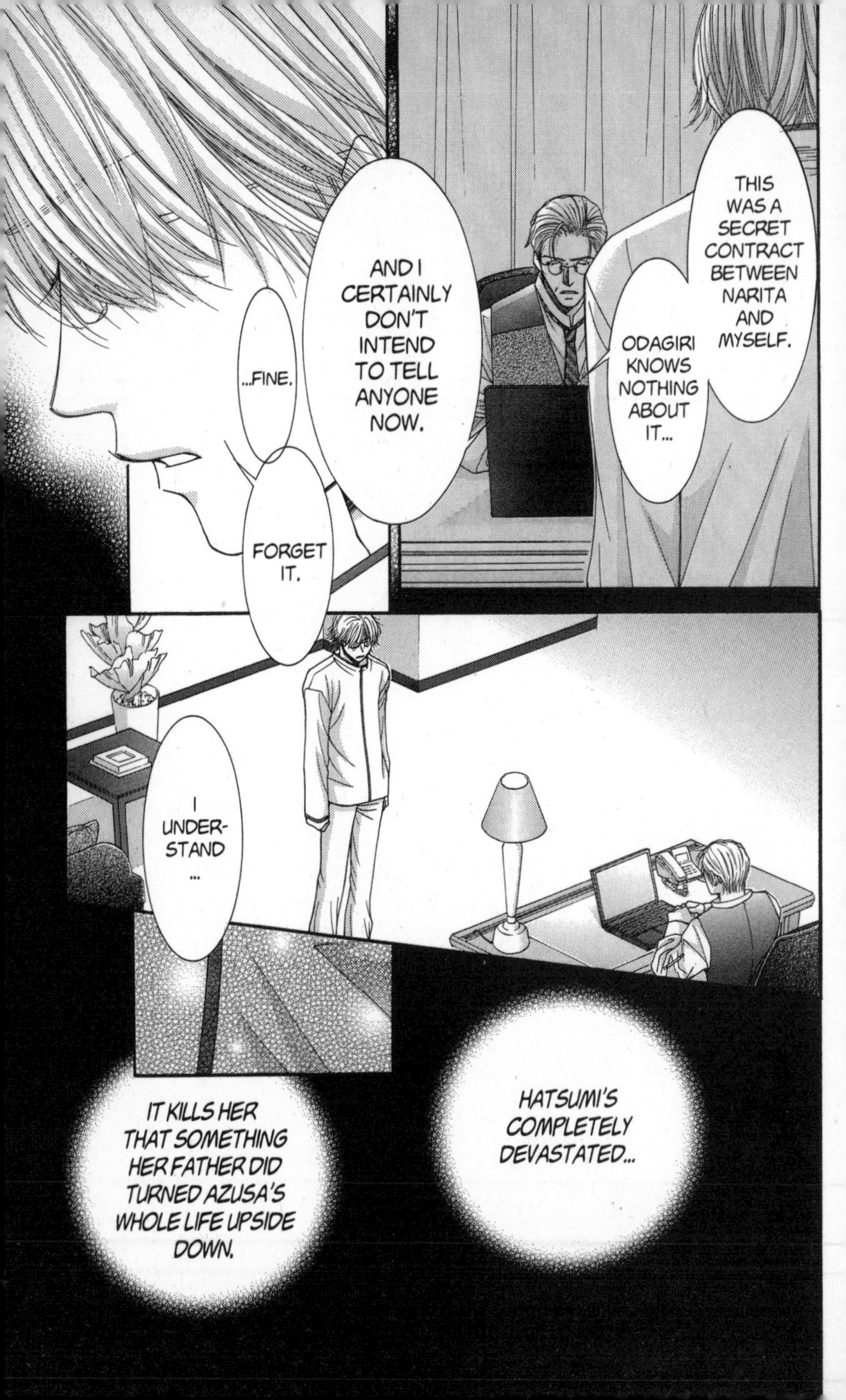
THIS WAS A SECRET CONTRACT BETWEEN NARITA AND MYSELF.
ODAGIRI KNOWS NOTHING ABOUT IT...
AND I CERTAINLY DON'T INTEND TO TELL ANYONE NOW.
...FINE.
FORGET IT.
I UNDER-STAND...
HATSUMI'S COMPLETELY DEVASTATED...
IT KILLS HER THAT SOMETHING HER FATHER DID TURNED AZUSA'S WHOLE LIFE UPSIDE DOWN.

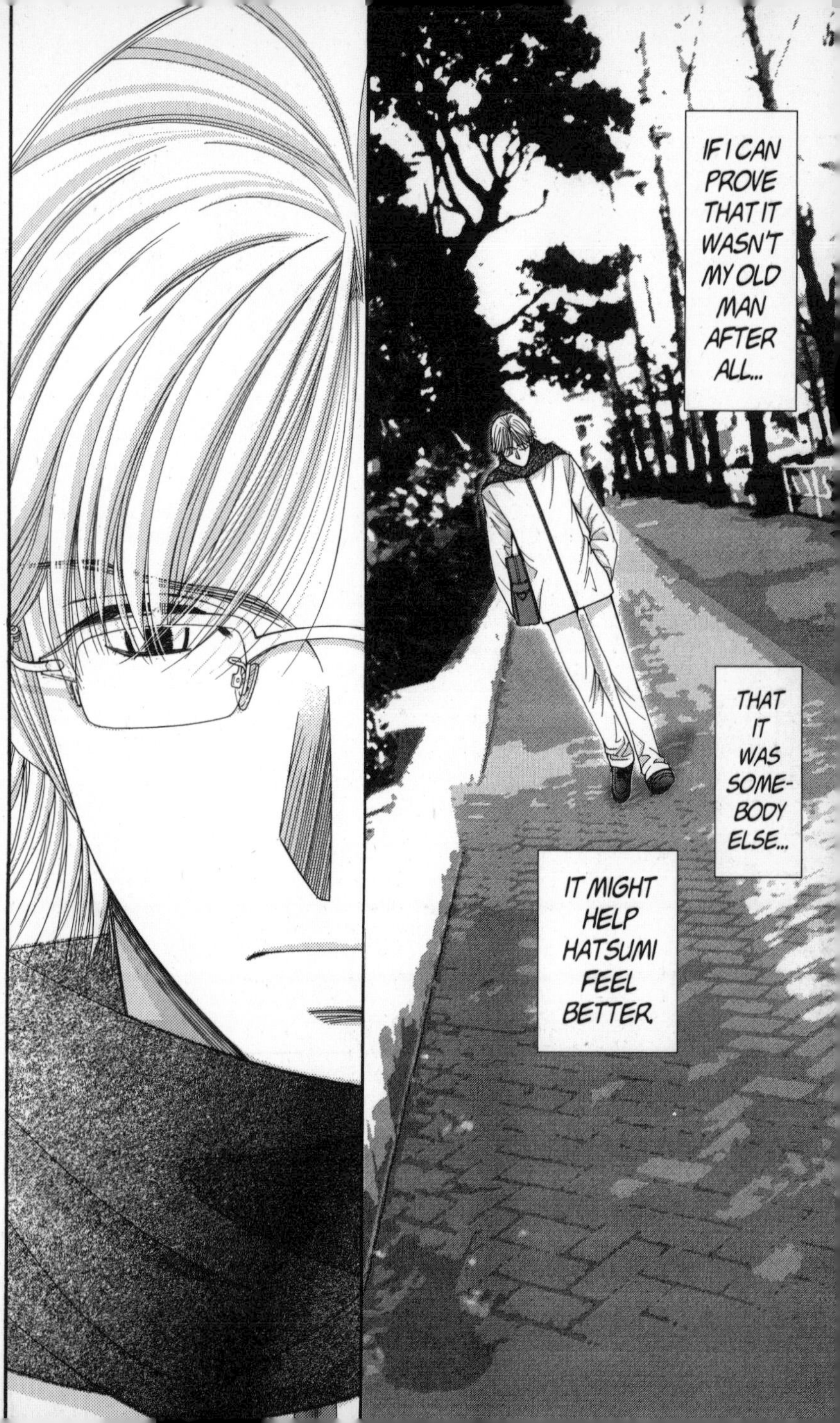
IF I CAN PROVE THAT IT WASN'T MY OLD MAN AFTER ALL...
THAT IT WAS SOME-BODY ELSE...
IT MIGHT HELP HATSUMI FEEL BETTER.

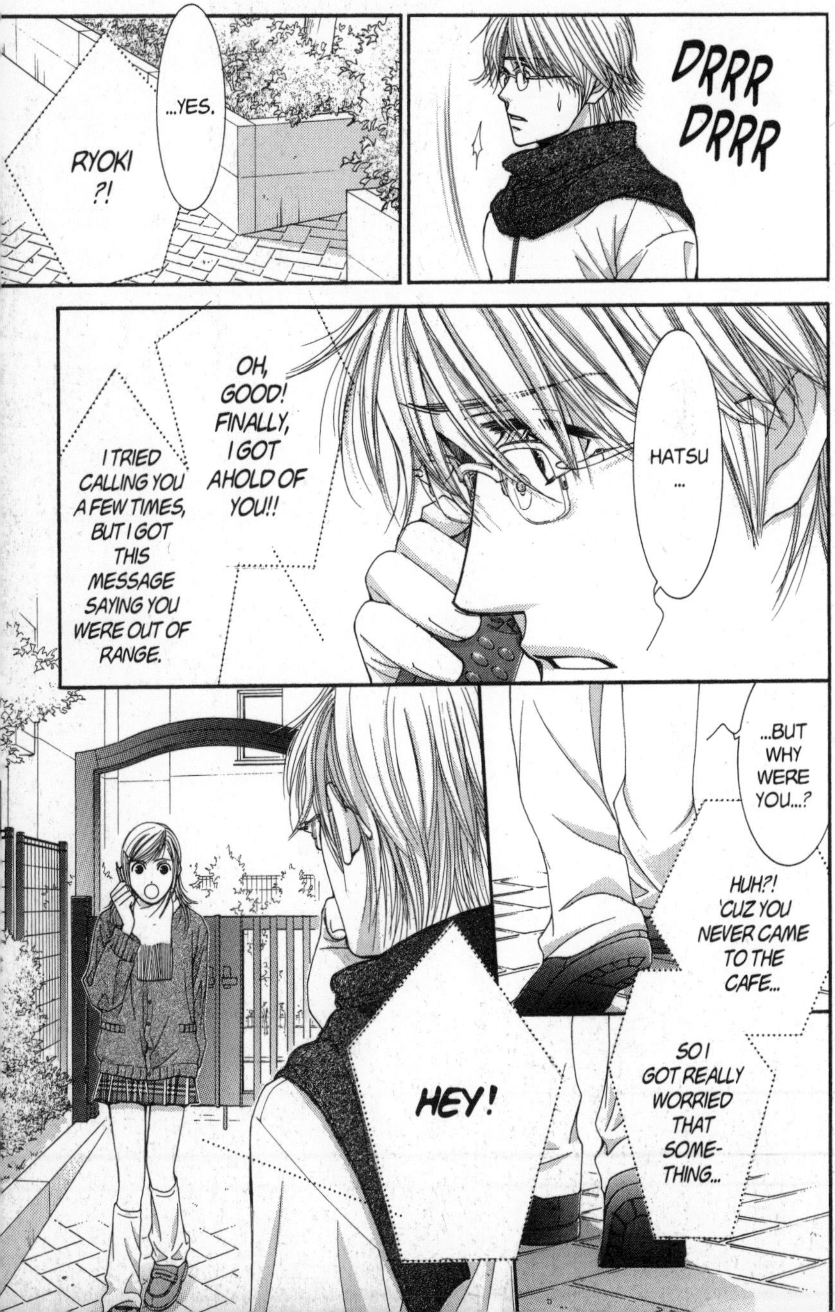
DRRR DRRR
...YES.
RYOKI ?!
HATSU ...
OH, GOOD! FINALLY, I GOT AHOLD OF YOU!!
I TRIED CALLING YOU A FEW TIMES, BUT I GOT THIS MESSAGE SAYING YOU WERE OUT OF RANGE.
...BUT WHY WERE YOU...?
HUH?! 'CUZ YOU NEVER CAME TO THE CAFE...
SO I GOT REALLY WORRIED THAT SOME-THING...
HEY!

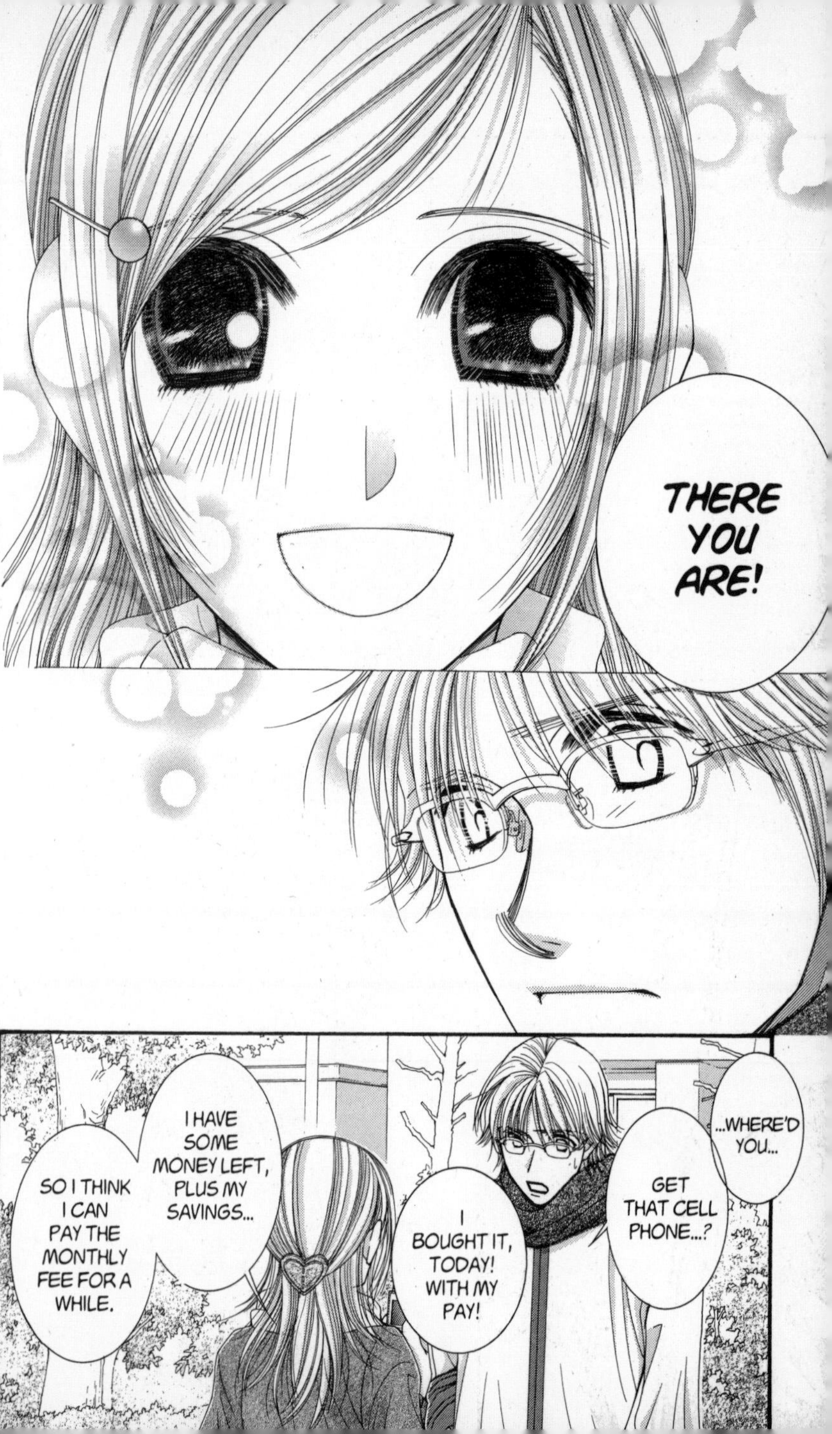
THERE YOU ARE!
...WHERE'D YOU...
GET THAT CELL PHONE...?
I BOUGHT IT, TODAY! WITH MY PAY!
I HAVE SOME MONEY LEFT, PLUS MY SAVINGS...
SO I THINK I CAN PAY THE MONTHLY FEE FOR A WHILE.

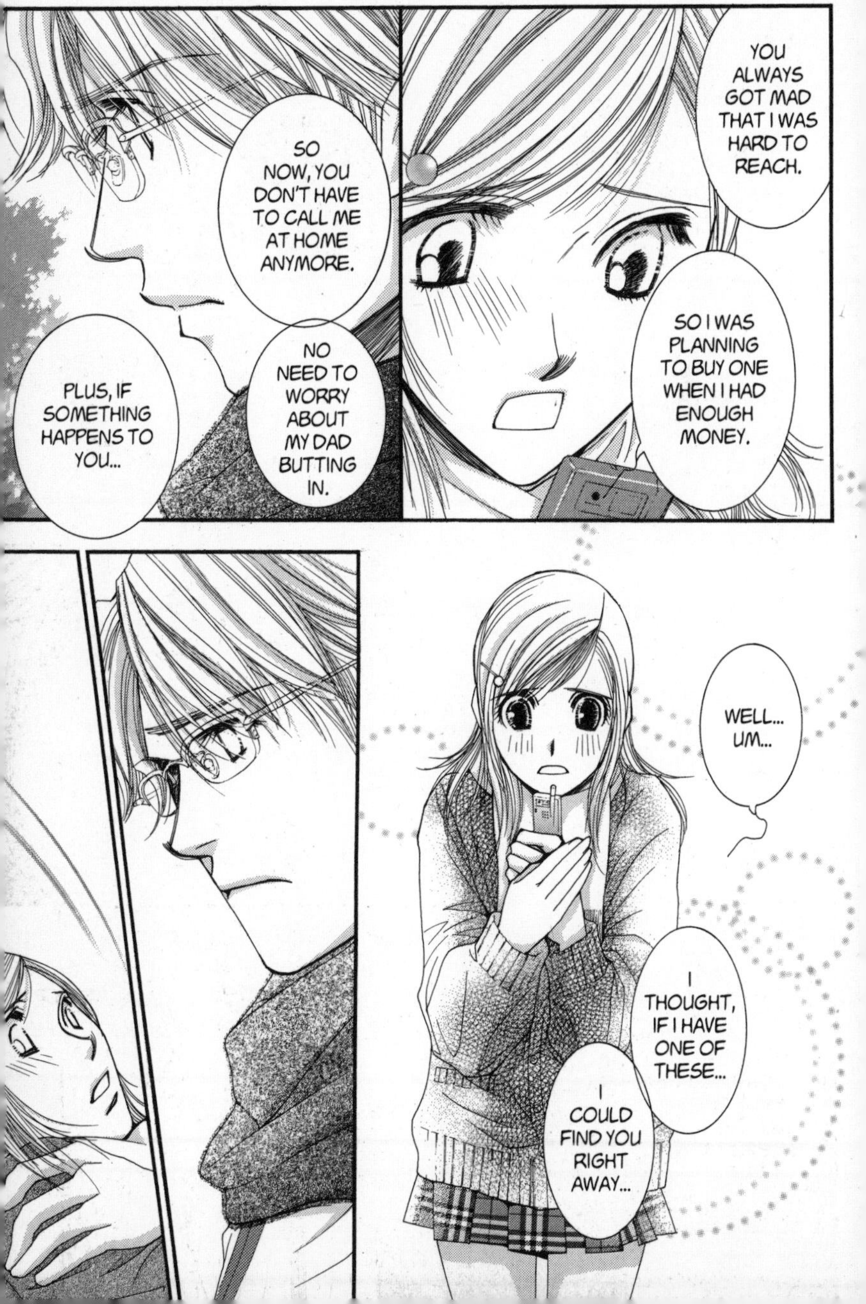
YOU ALWAYS GOT MAD THAT I WAS HARD TO REACH.
SO I WAS PLANNING TO BUY ONE WHEN I HAD ENOUGH MONEY.
SO NOW, YOU DON'T HAVE TO CALL ME AT HOME ANYMORE.
NO NEED TO WORRY ABOUT MY DAD BUTTING IN.
PLUS, IF SOMETHING HAPPENS TO YOU...
WELL... UM...
I THOUGHT, IF I HAVE ONE OF THESE...
I COULD FIND YOU RIGHT AWAY...

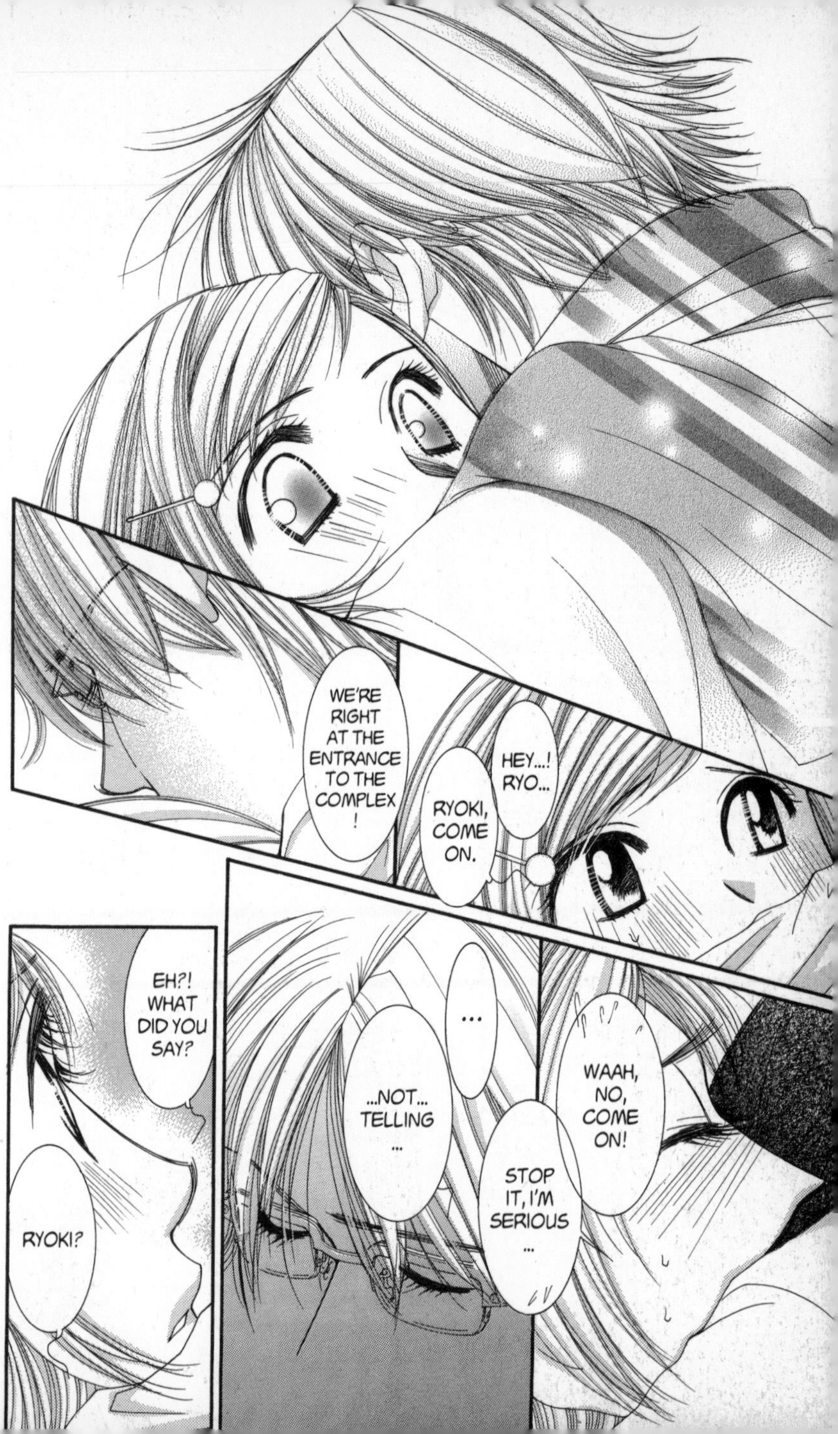
HEY...! RYO...
RYOKI, COME ON.
WE'RE RIGHT AT THE ENTRANCE TO THE COMPLEX!
WAAH, NO, COME ON!
STOP IT, I'M SERIOUS...
...
...NOT... TELLING...
EH?! WHAT DID YOU SAY?
RYOKI?

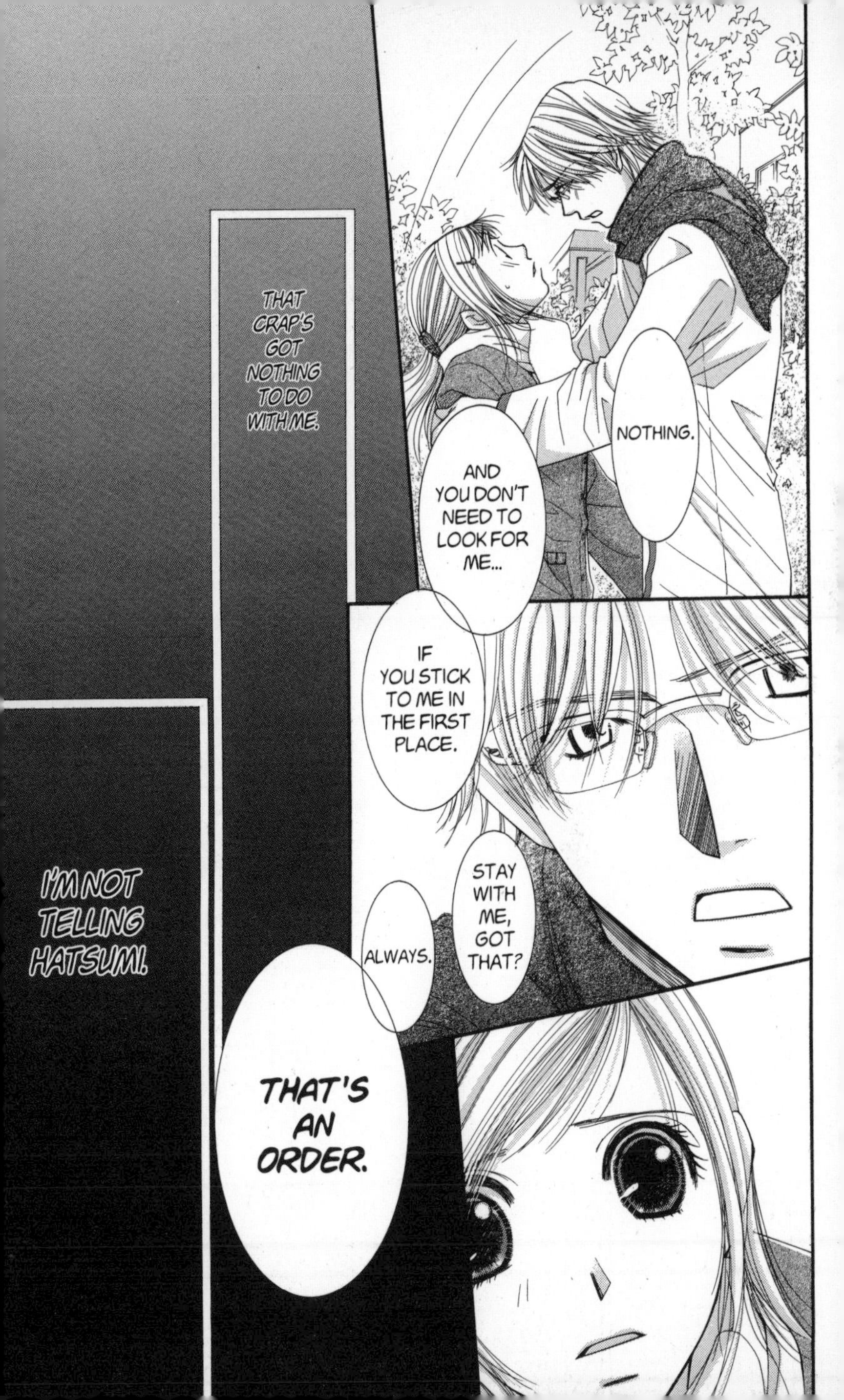
NOTHING.
AND YOU DON'T NEED TO LOOK FOR ME...
IF YOU STICK TO ME IN THE FIRST PLACE.
STAY WITH ME, GOT THAT?
ALWAYS.
THAT'S AN ORDER.
THAT CRAP'S GOT NOTHING TO DO WITH ME.
I'M NOT TELLING HATSUMI.

SPEAK NO EVIL.

Chapter 39

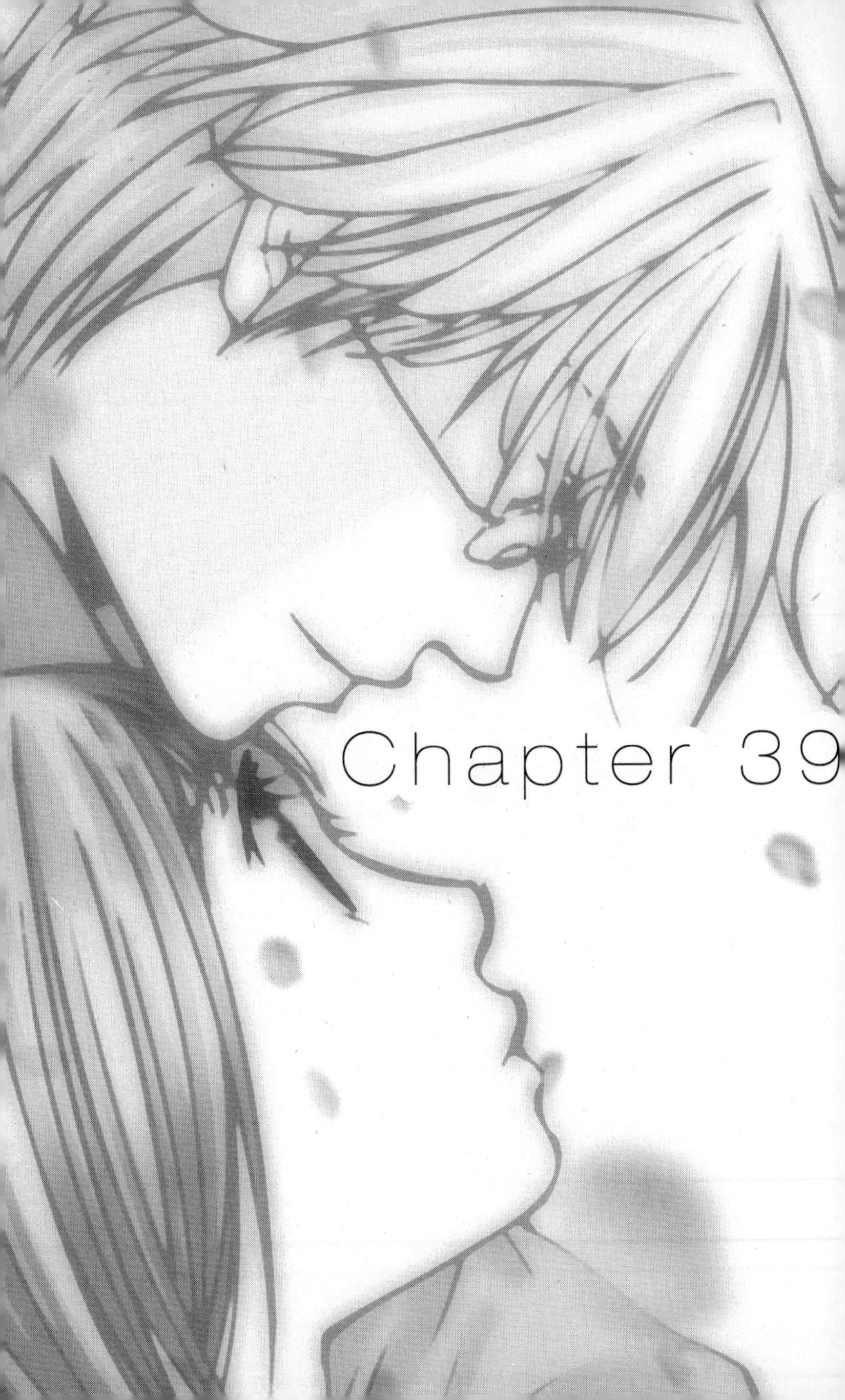

hot gimmick

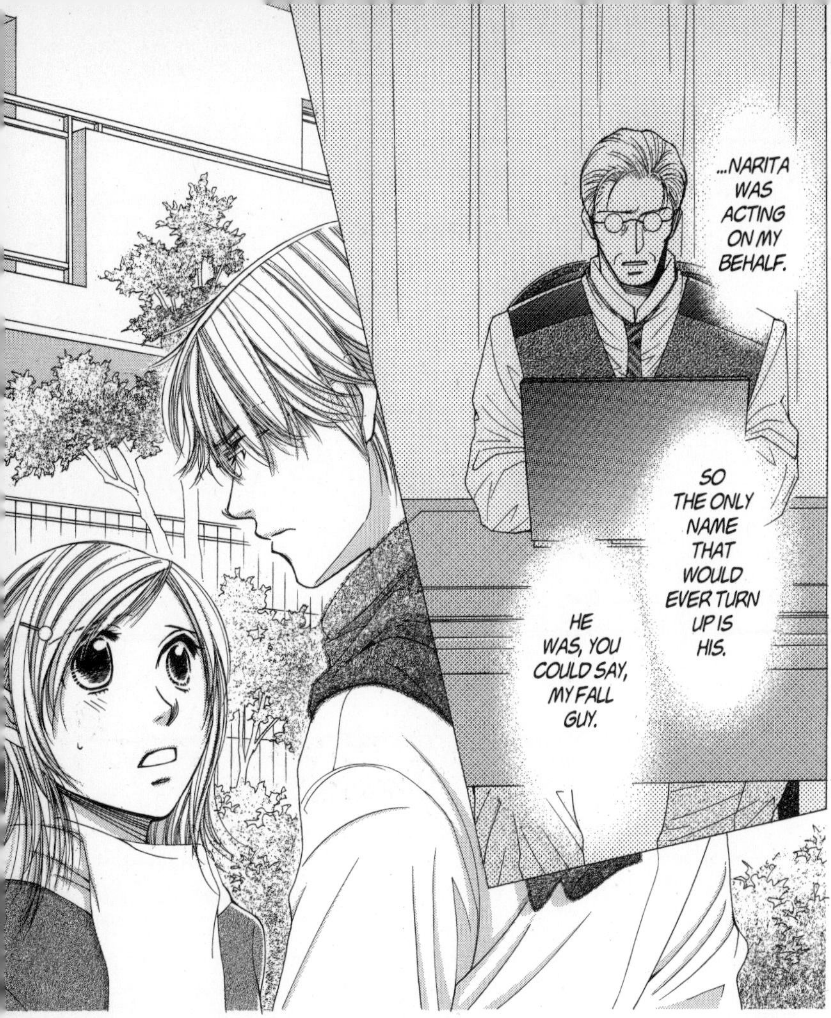
...NARITA WAS ACTING ON MY BEHALF.
SO THE ONLY NAME THAT WOULD EVER TURN UP IS HIS.
HE WAS, YOU COULD SAY, MY FALL GUY.

hot gimmick

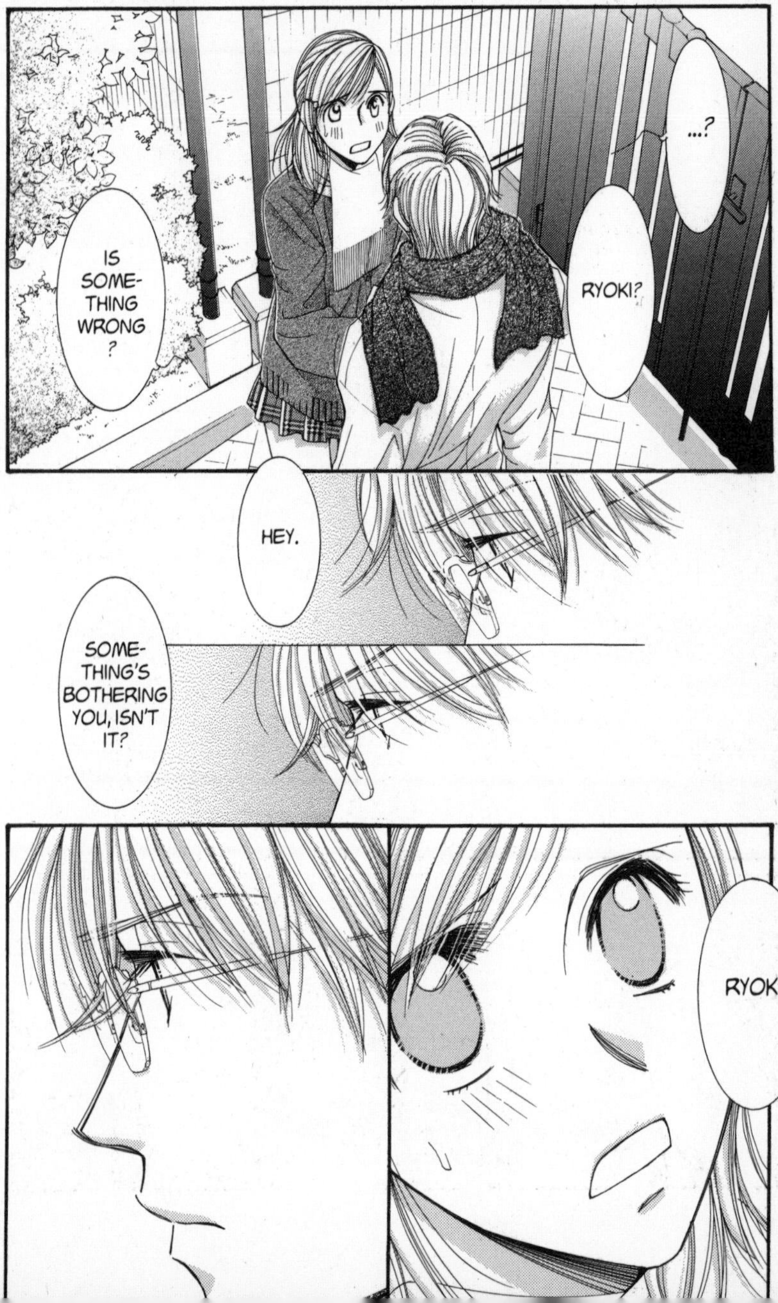
...?
RYOKI?
IS SOME-THING WRONG?
HEY.
SOME-THING'S BOTHERING YOU, ISN'T IT?
RYOKI.

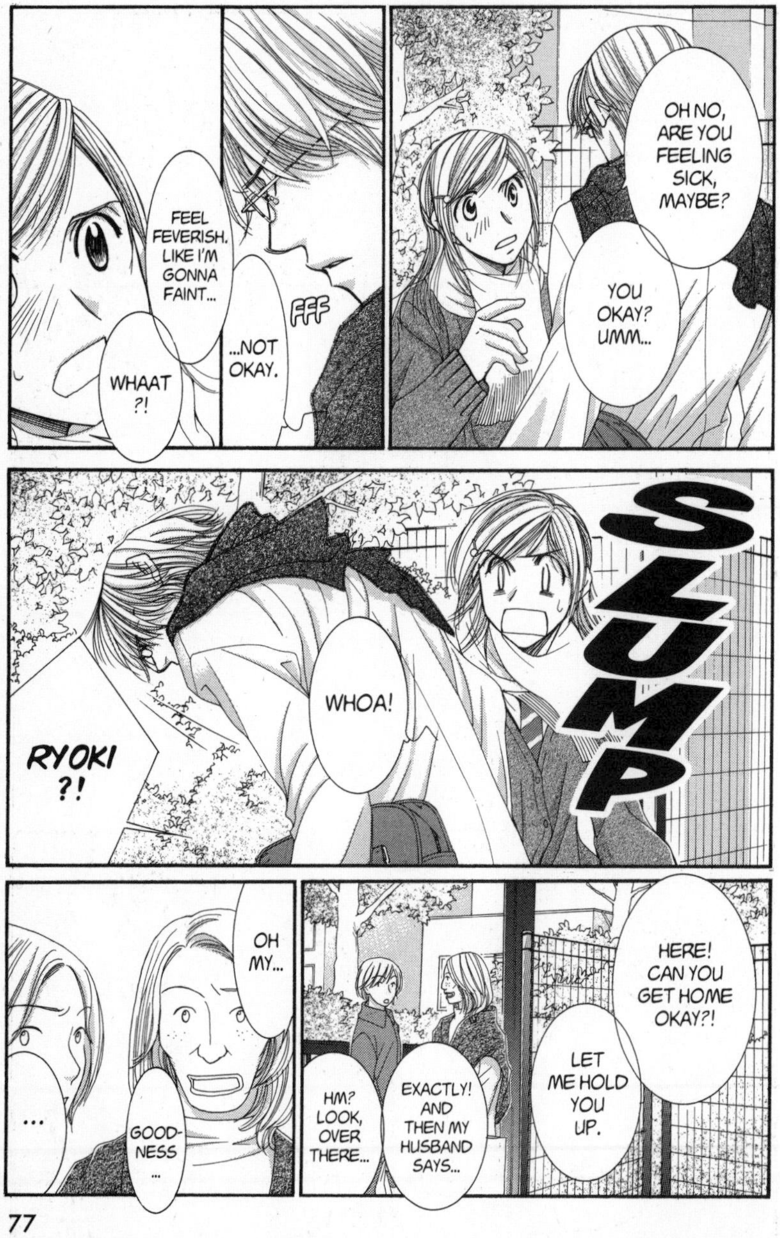
OH NO, ARE YOU FEELING SICK, MAYBE?
YOU OKAY? UMM...
...NOT OKAY.
FFF
FEEL FEVERISH. LIKE I'M GONNA FAINT...
WHAAT?!
SLUMP
WHOA!
RYOKI?!
HERE! CAN YOU GET HOME OKAY?!
LET ME HOLD YOU UP.
EXACTLY! AND THEN MY HUSBAND SAYS...
HM? LOOK, OVER THERE...
OH MY...
GOOD-NESS...
...

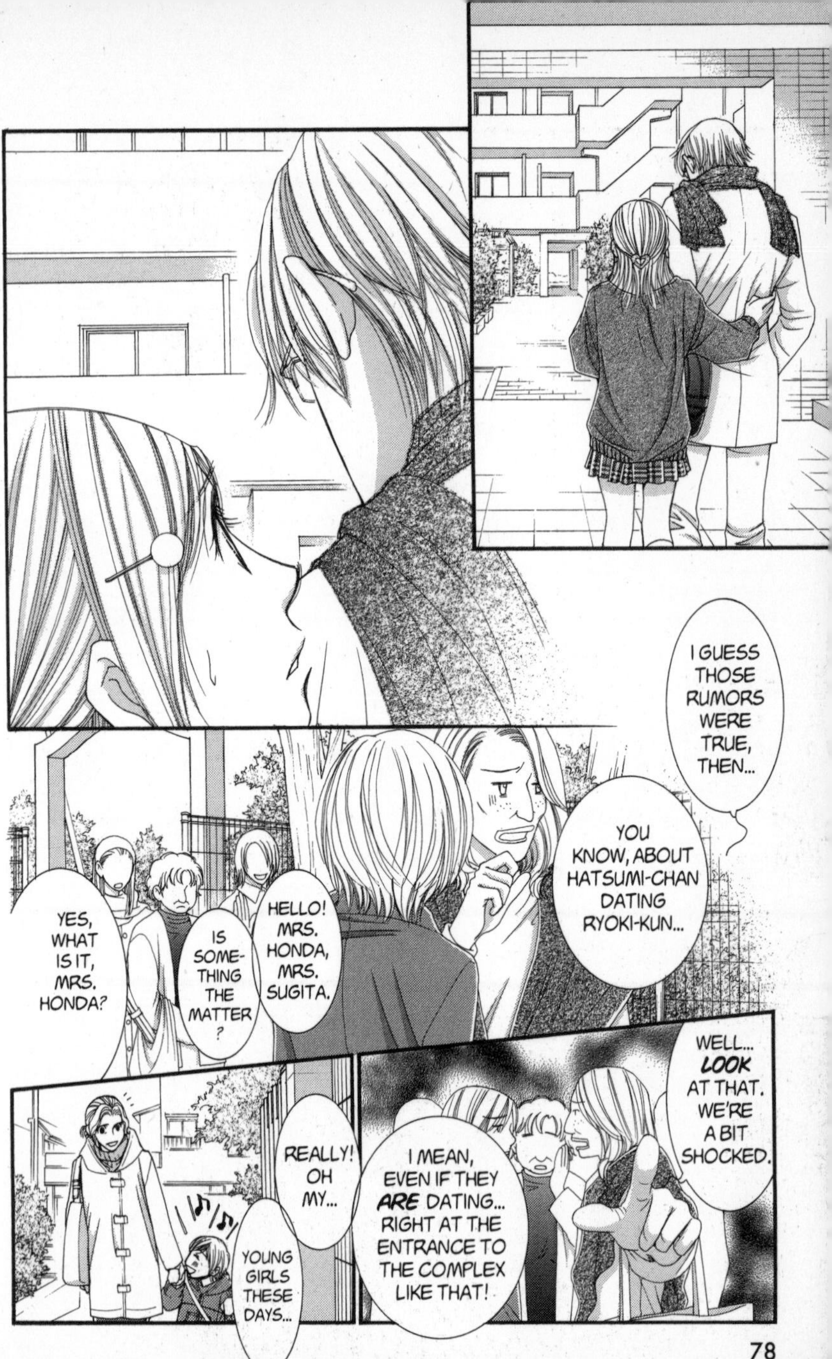
I GUESS THOSE RUMORS WERE TRUE, THEN...
YOU KNOW, ABOUT HATSUMI-CHAN DATING RYOKI-KUN...
HELLO! MRS. HONDA, MRS. SUGITA.
IS SOME-THING THE MATTER?
YES, WHAT IS IT, MRS. HONDA?
WELL... **LOOK** AT THAT. WE'RE A BIT SHOCKED.
I MEAN, EVEN IF THEY **ARE** DATING... RIGHT AT THE ENTRANCE TO THE COMPLEX LIKE THAT!
REALLY! OH MY...
YOUNG GIRLS THESE DAYS...

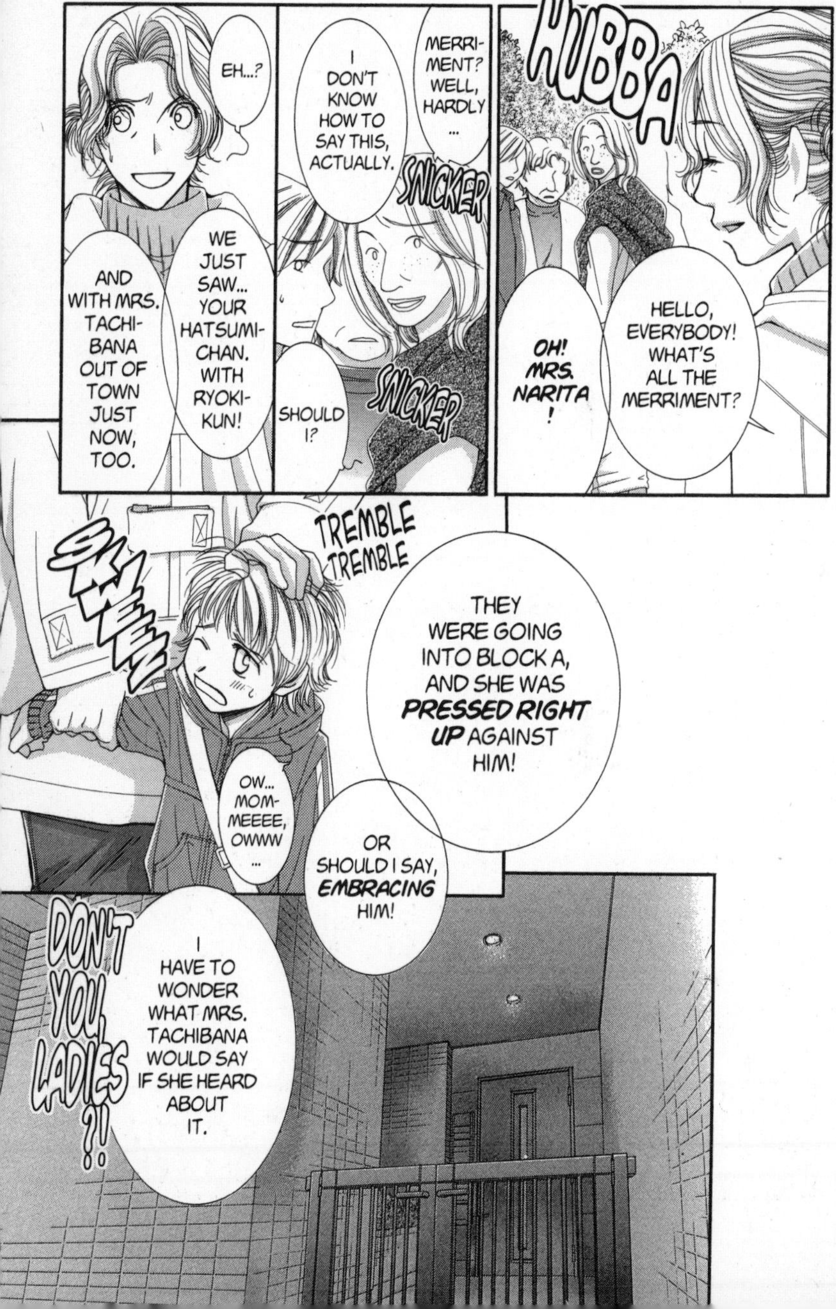
HUBBA
HELLO, EVERYBODY! WHAT'S ALL THE MERRIMENT?
OH! MRS. NARITA!
MERRIMENT? WELL, HARDLY...
I DON'T KNOW HOW TO SAY THIS, ACTUALLY.
SNICKER
SNICKER
SHOULD I?
EH...?
WE JUST SAW... YOUR HATSUMI-CHAN. WITH RYOKI-KUN!
AND WITH MRS. TACHIBANA OUT OF TOWN JUST NOW, TOO.
TREMBLE TREMBLE
THEY WERE GOING INTO BLOCK A, AND SHE WAS **PRESSED RIGHT UP** AGAINST HIM!
SKWEEZ
OW... MOM-MEEEE, OWWW...
OR SHOULD I SAY, **EMBRACING** HIM!
DON'T YOU, LADIES?!
I HAVE TO WONDER WHAT MRS. TACHIBANA WOULD SAY IF SHE HEARD ABOUT IT.

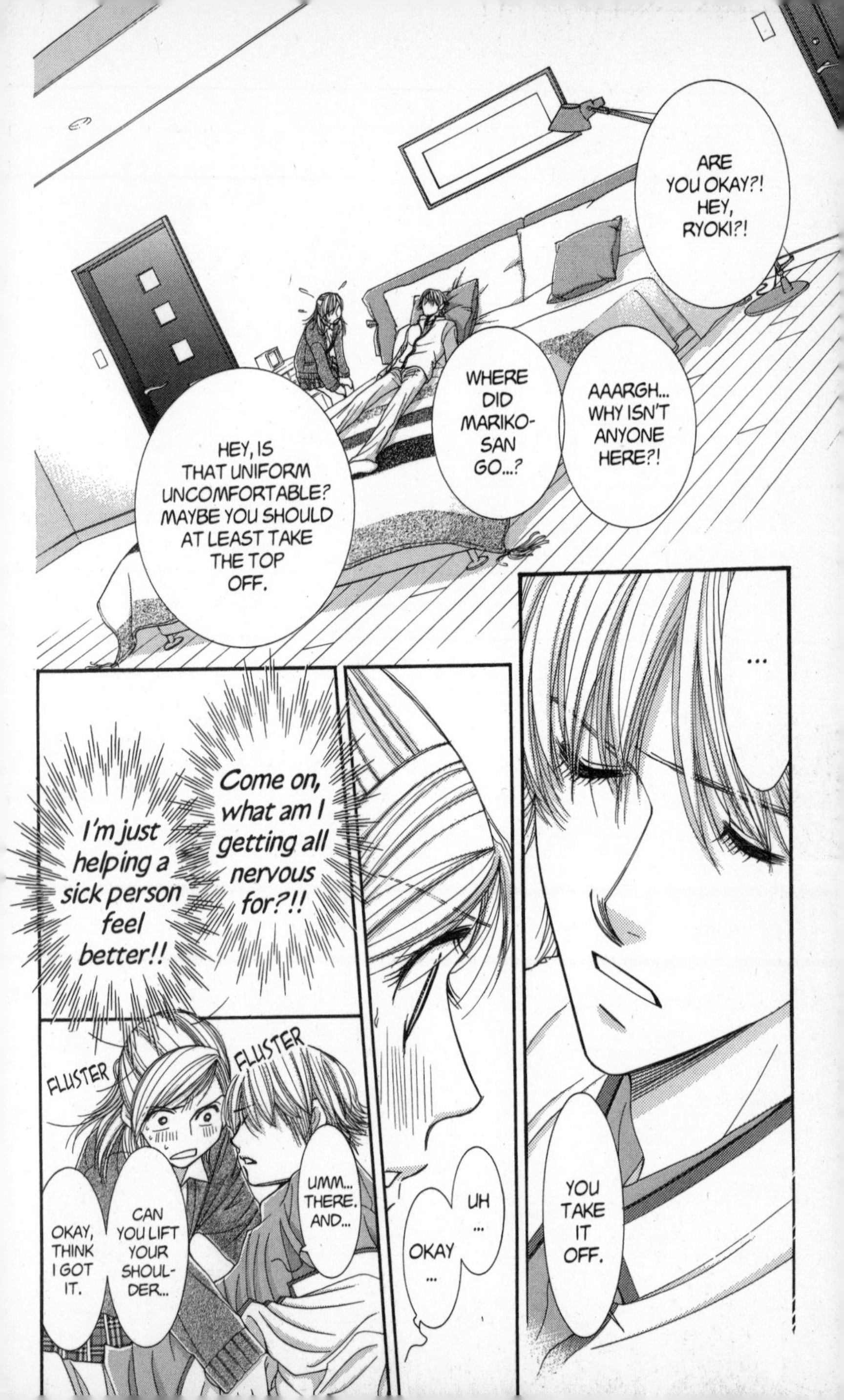
ARE YOU OKAY?! HEY, RYOKI?!
AAARGH... WHY ISN'T ANYONE HERE?!
WHERE DID MARIKO-SAN GO...?
HEY, IS THAT UNIFORM UNCOMFORTABLE? MAYBE YOU SHOULD AT LEAST TAKE THE TOP OFF.
...
YOU TAKE IT OFF.
UH ... OKAY ...
Come on, what am I getting all nervous for?!!
I'm just helping a sick person feel better!!
FLUSTER
FLUSTER
UMM... THERE. AND...
CAN YOU LIFT YOUR SHOULDER...
OKAY, THINK I GOT IT.

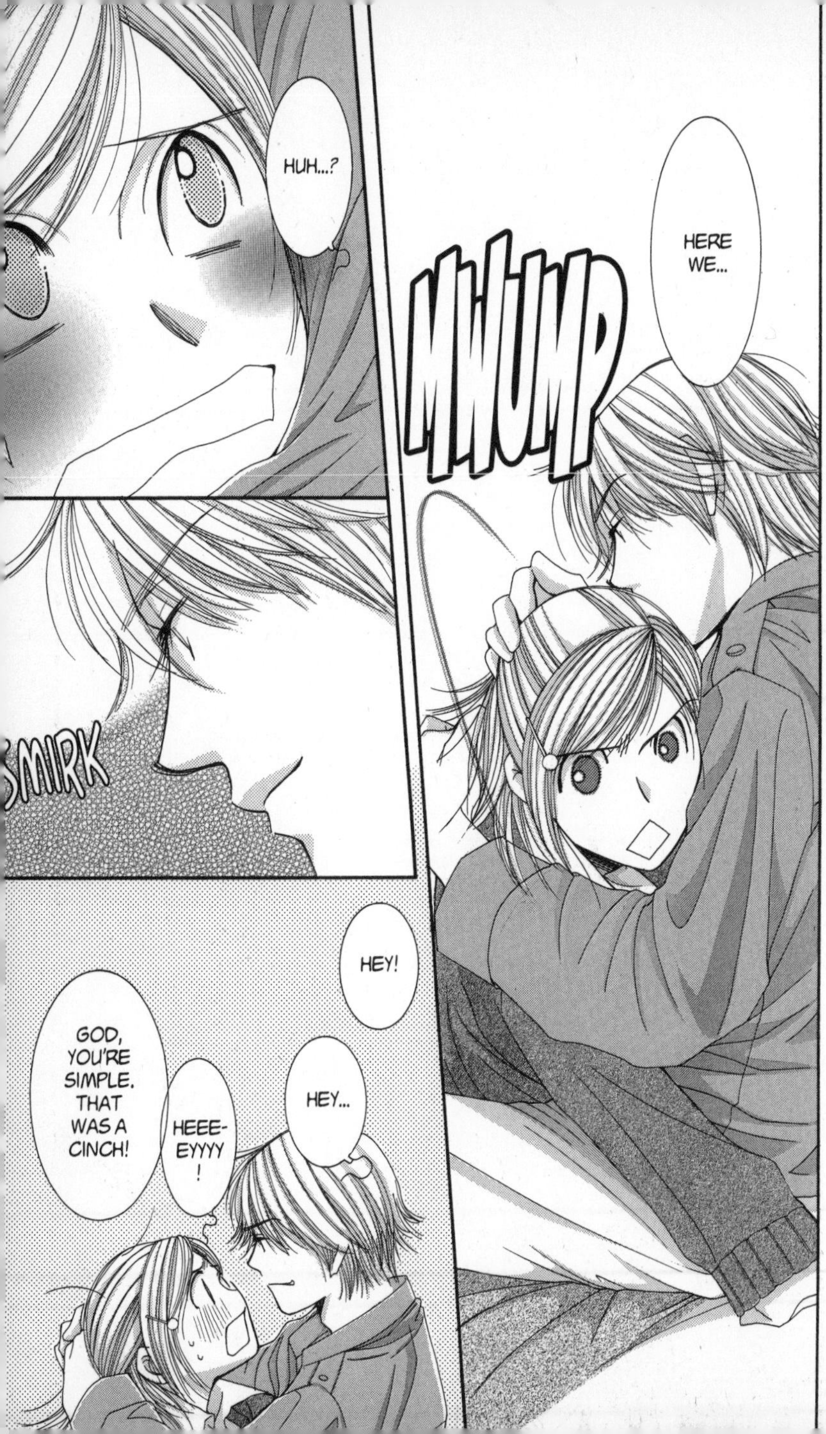
HERE WE...
MWUMP
HUH...?
SMIRK
HEY!
HEY...
GOD, YOU'RE SIMPLE. THAT WAS A CINCH!
HEEE-EYYYY!

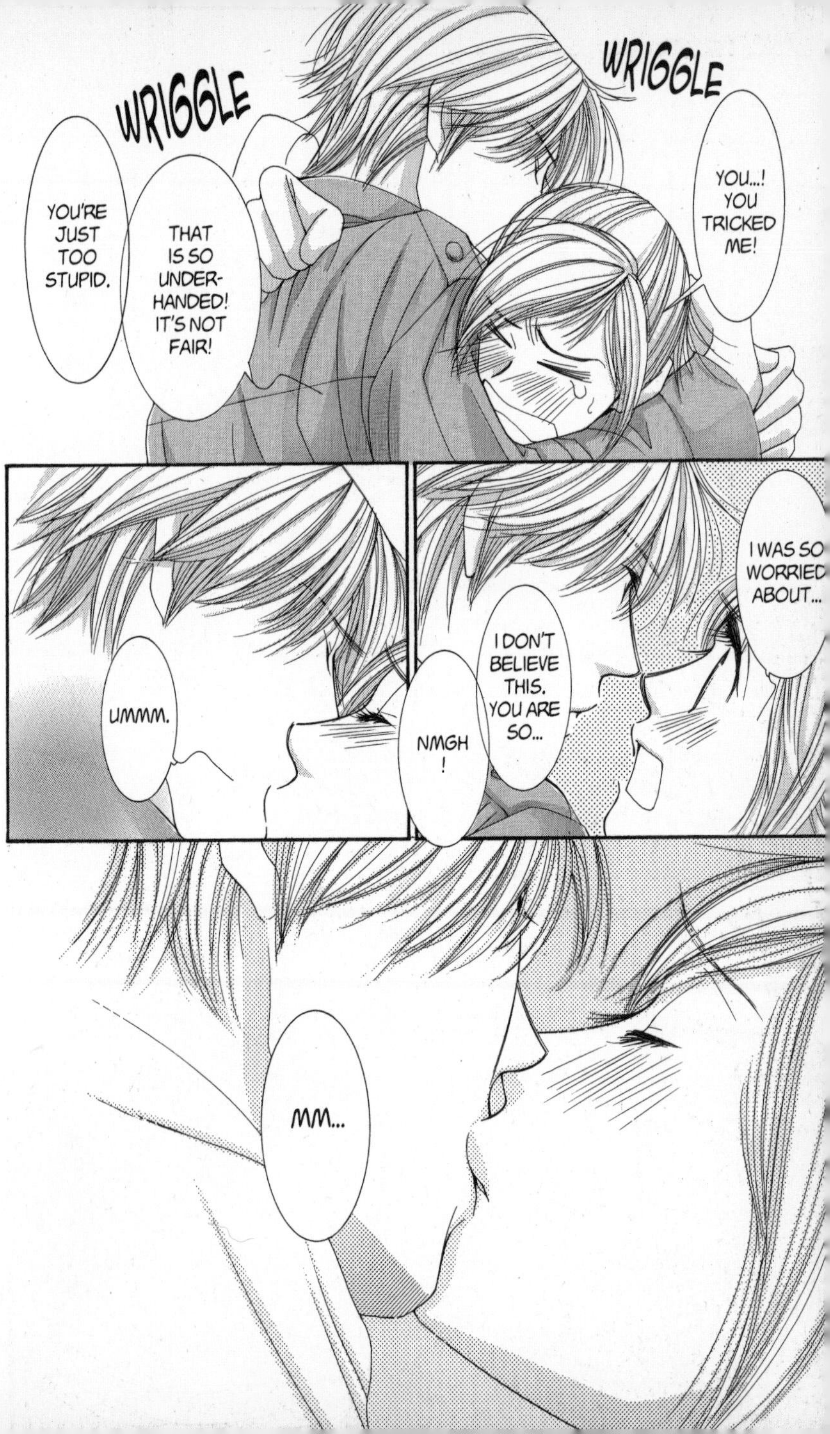
WRIGGLE
YOU...! YOU TRICKED ME!
WRIGGLE
THAT IS SO UNDER-HANDED! IT'S NOT FAIR!
YOU'RE JUST TOO STUPID.
I WAS SO WORRIED ABOUT...
I DON'T BELIEVE THIS. YOU ARE SO...
NMGH !
UMMM.
MM...

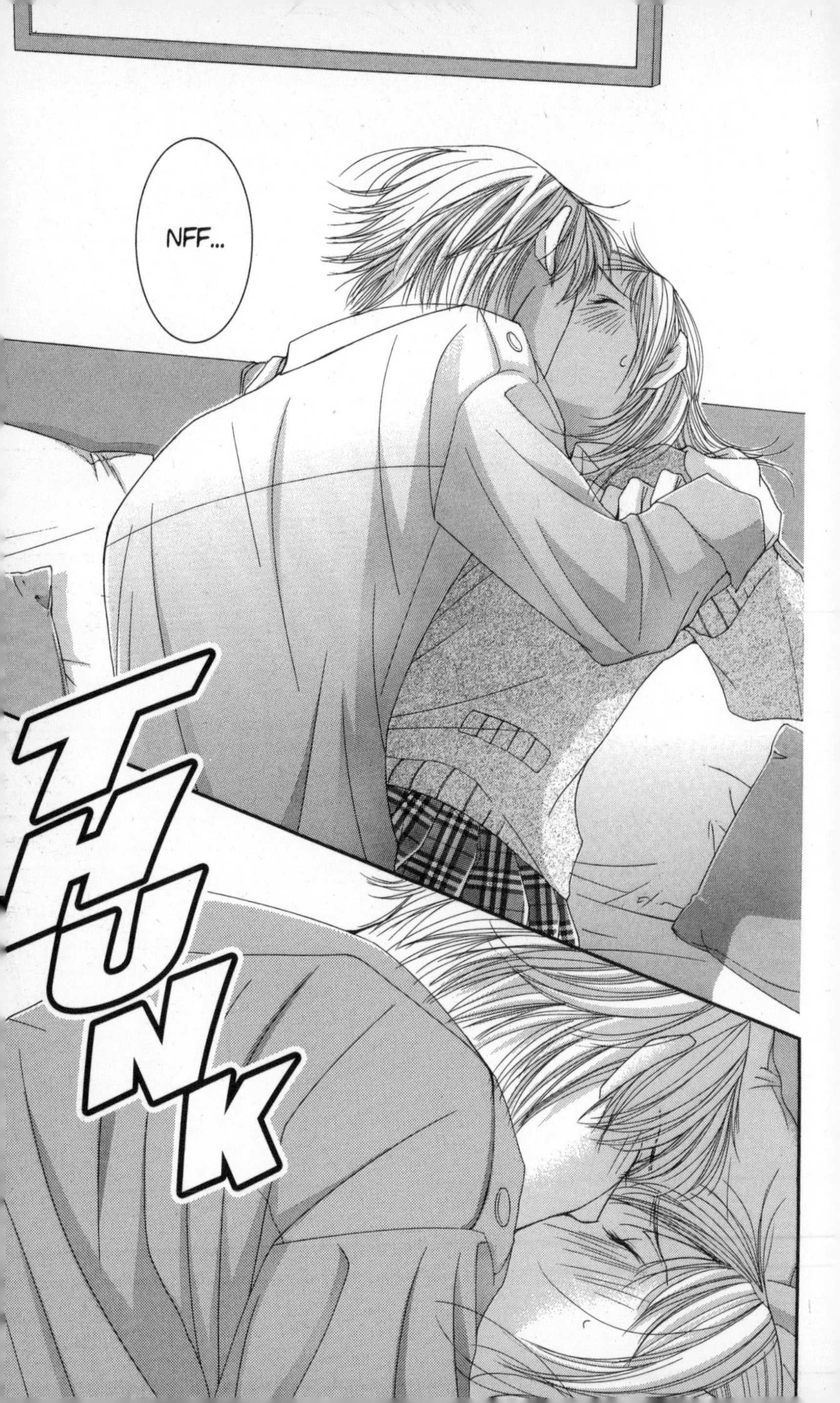
NFF...
THUNK

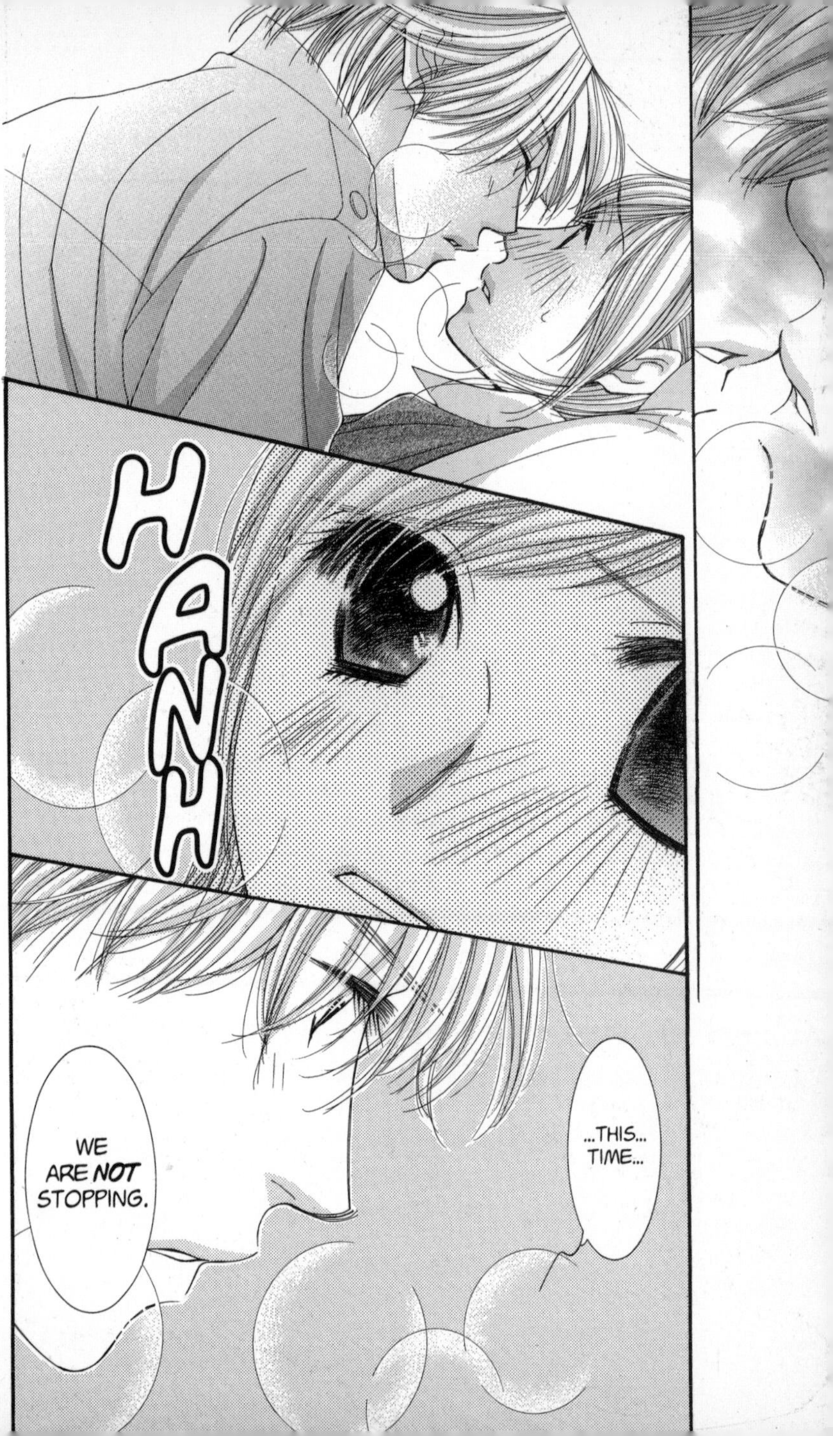
HANHH
...THIS... TIME...
WE ARE **NOT** STOPPING.

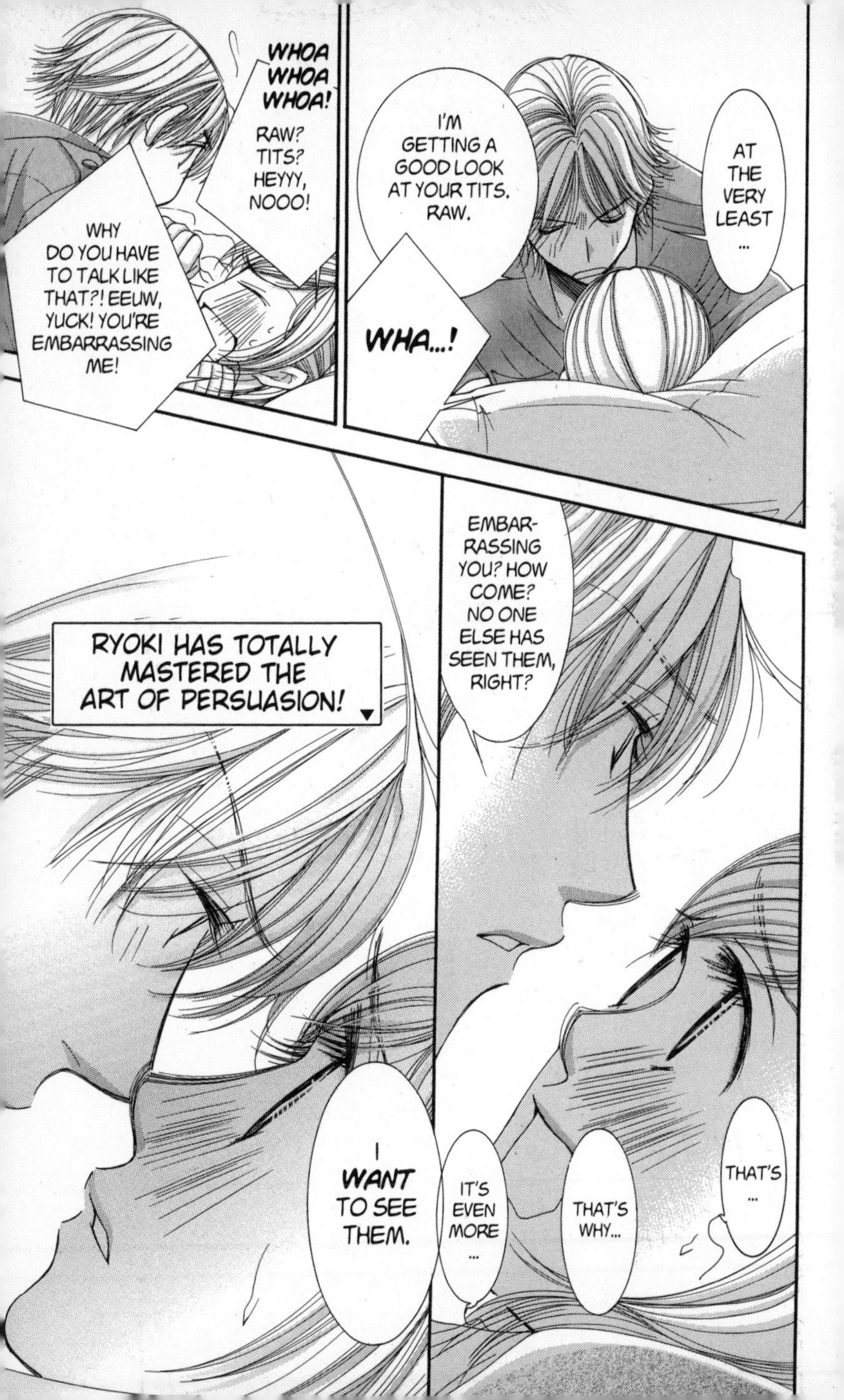
AT THE VERY LEAST ...
I'M GETTING A GOOD LOOK AT YOUR TITS. RAW.
WHA...!
WHOA WHOA WHOA!
RAW? TITS? HEYYY, NOOO!
WHY DO YOU HAVE TO TALK LIKE THAT?! EEUW, YUCK! YOU'RE EMBARRASSING ME!
EMBAR-RASSING YOU? HOW COME? NO ONE ELSE HAS SEEN THEM, RIGHT?
THAT'S ...
THAT'S WHY...
IT'S EVEN MORE ...
I WANT TO SEE THEM.
RYOKI HAS TOTALLY MASTERED THE ART OF PERSUASION!

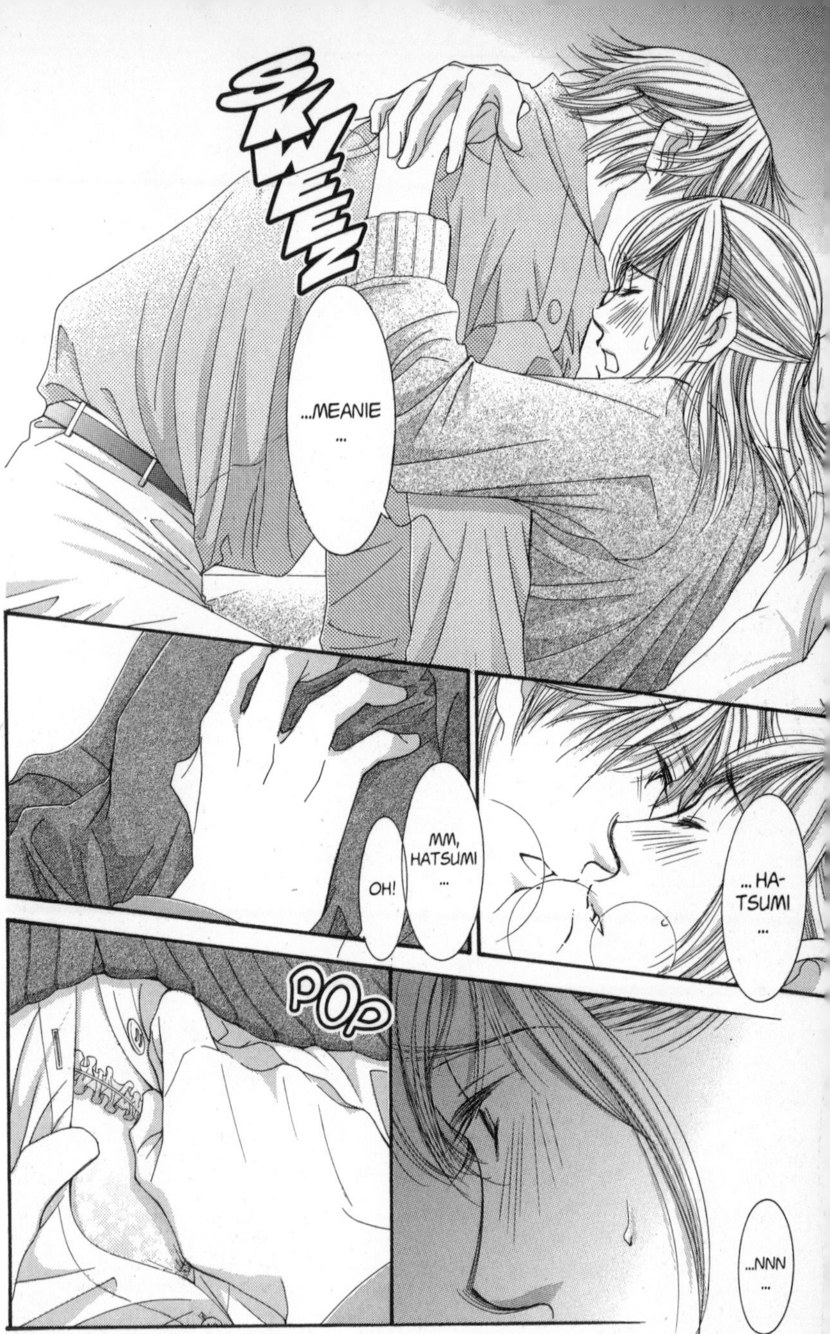
SKWEEZ
...MEANIE ...
... HA-TSUMI ...
MM, HATSUMI ...
OH!
...NNN ...
POP

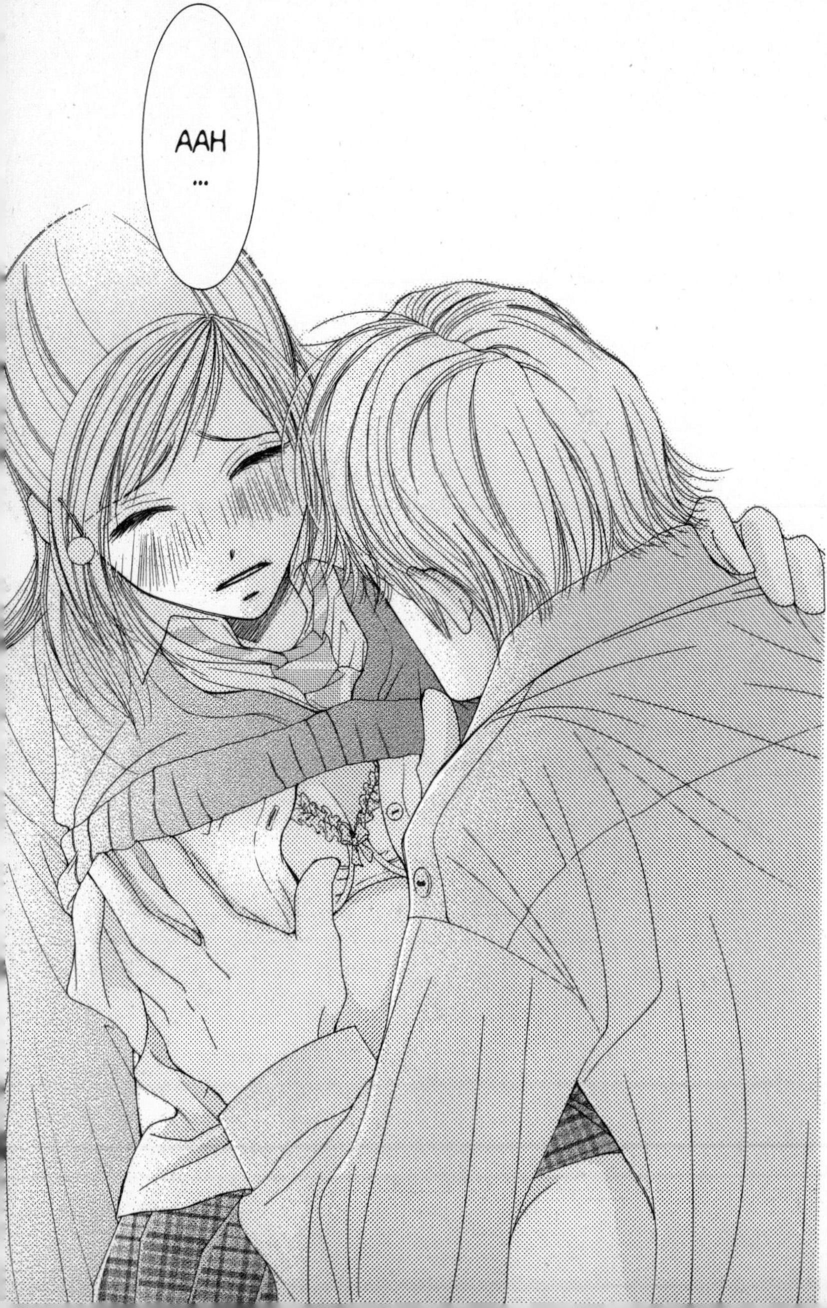
AAH ...

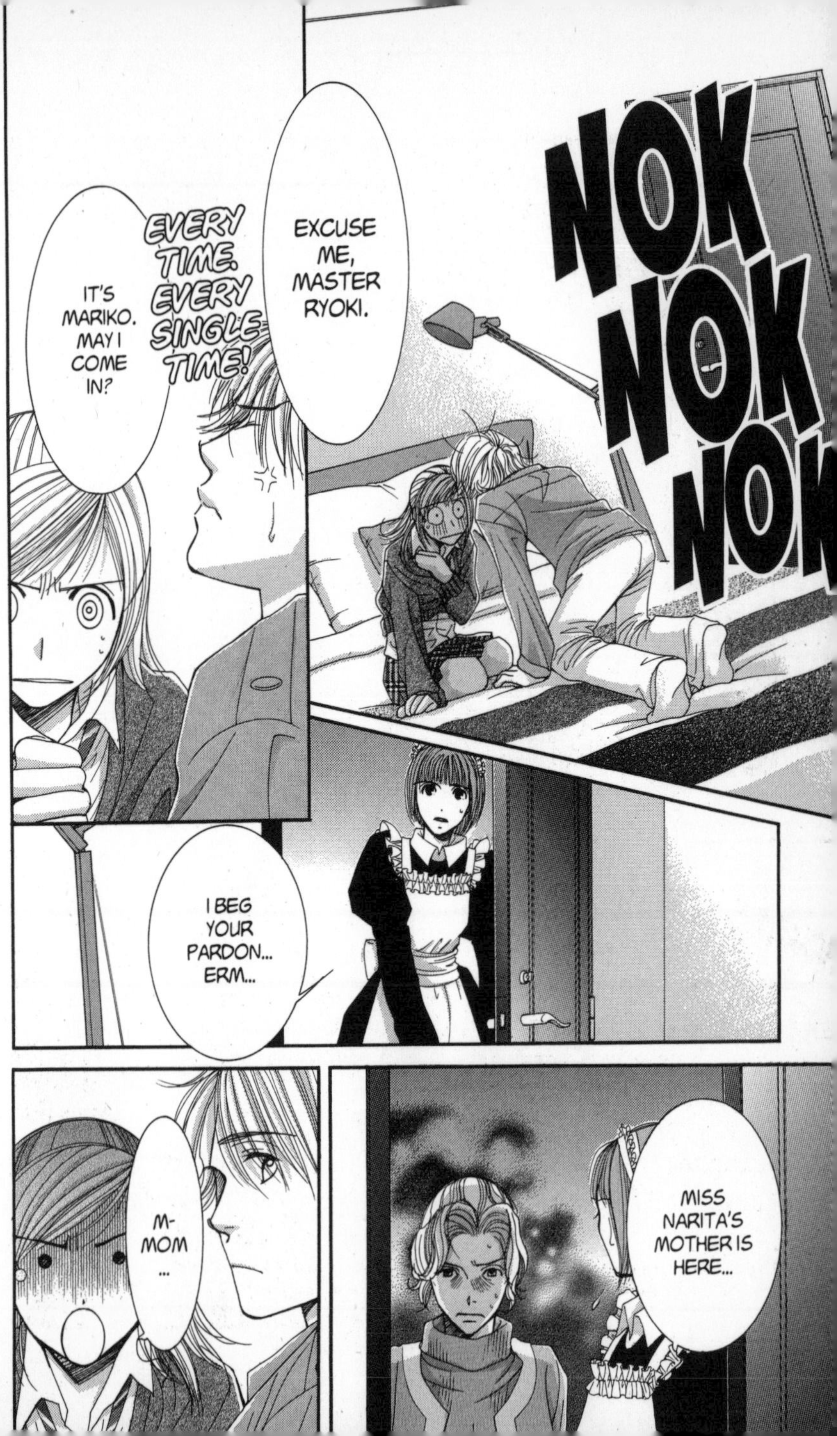
NOK NOK NOK
EXCUSE ME, MASTER RYOKI.
IT'S MARIKO. MAY I COME IN?
EVERY TIME. EVERY SINGLE TIME!
I BEG YOUR PARDON... ERM...
MISS NARITA'S MOTHER IS HERE...
M-MOM ...

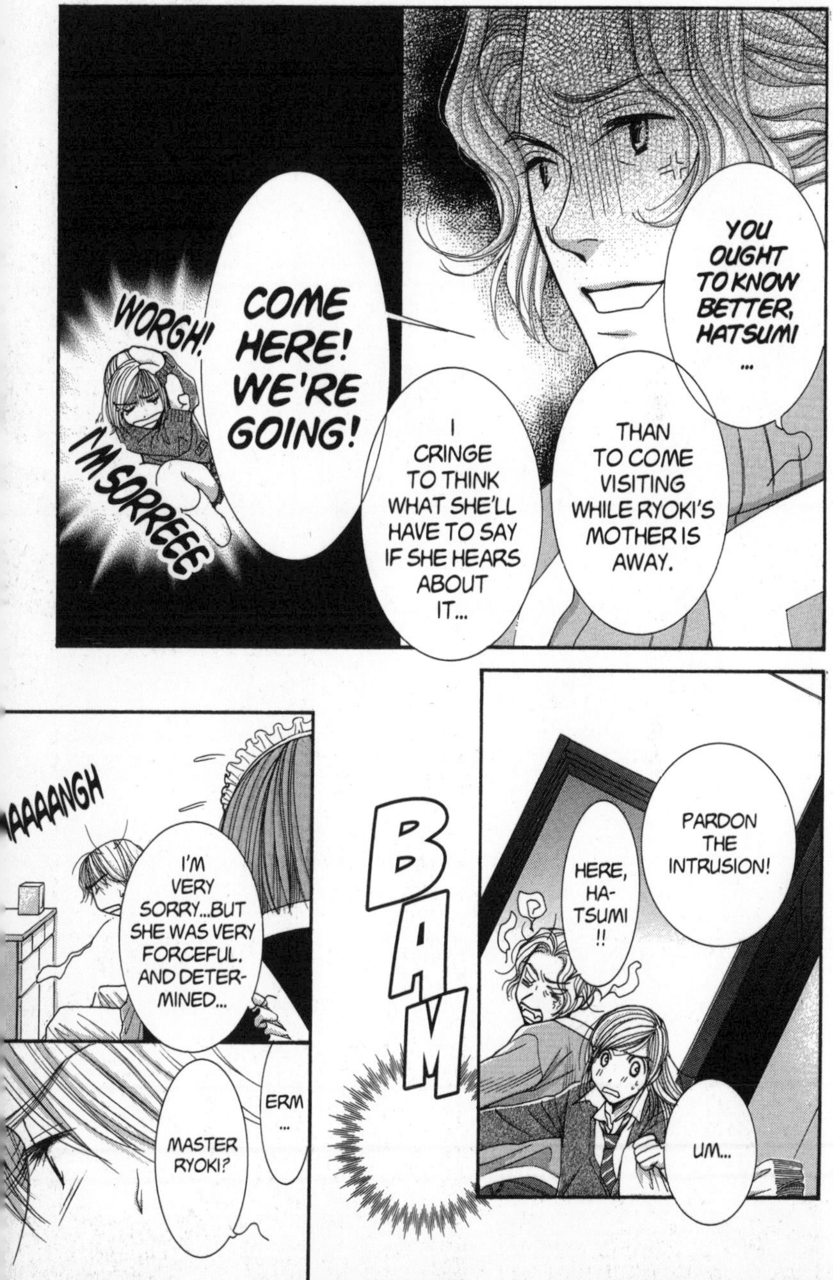
YOU OUGHT TO KNOW BETTER, HATSUMI ...
THAN TO COME VISITING WHILE RYOKI'S MOTHER IS AWAY.
I CRINGE TO THINK WHAT SHE'LL HAVE TO SAY IF SHE HEARS ABOUT IT...
COME HERE! WE'RE GOING!
WORGH!
I'M SORREEE
PARDON THE INTRUSION!
HERE, HA-TSUMI !!
UM...
BAM
AAAAANGH
I'M VERY SORRY...BUT SHE WAS VERY FORCEFUL. AND DETER-MINED...
ERM ...
MASTER RYOKI?

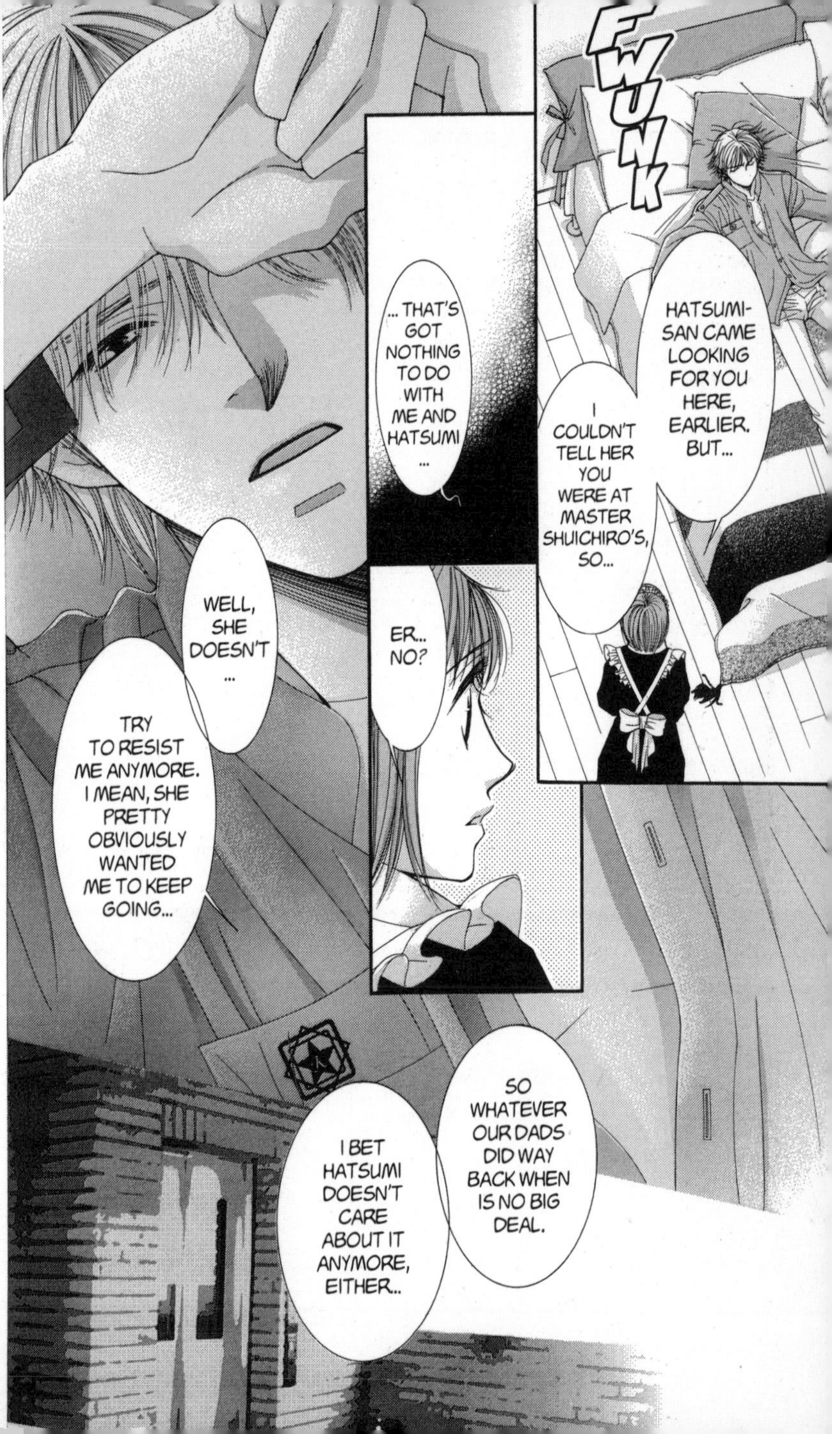
FWUNK
HATSUMI-SAN CAME LOOKING FOR YOU HERE, EARLIER. BUT...
I COULDN'T TELL HER YOU WERE AT MASTER SHUICHIRO'S, SO...
...THAT'S GOT NOTHING TO DO WITH ME AND HATSUMI...
ER.. NO?
WELL, SHE DOESN'T...
TRY TO RESIST ME ANYMORE. I MEAN, SHE PRETTY OBVIOUSLY WANTED ME TO KEEP GOING...
SO WHATEVER OUR DADS DID WAY BACK WHEN IS NO BIG DEAL.
I BET HATSUMI DOESN'T CARE ABOUT IT ANYMORE, EITHER..

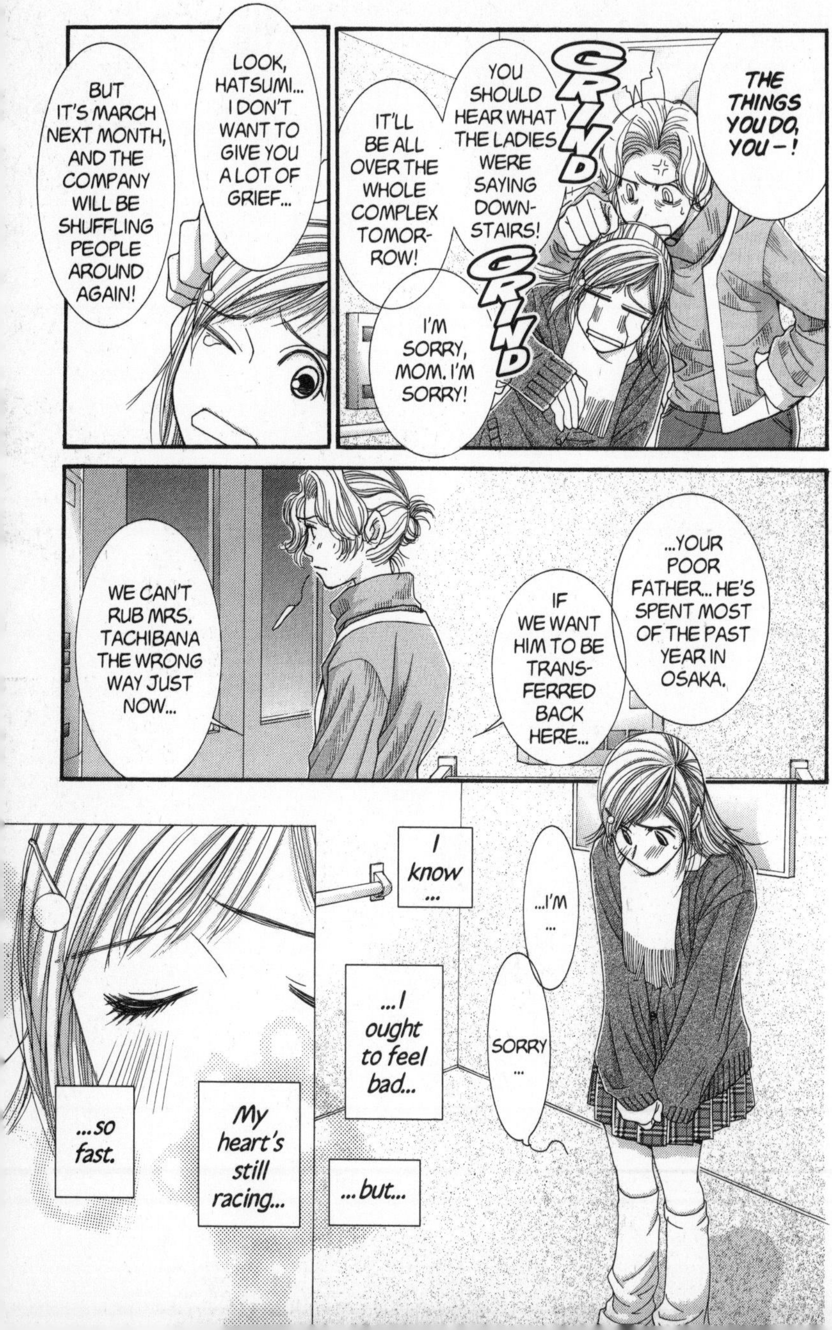
THE THINGS YOU DO, YOU—!
GRIND
YOU SHOULD HEAR WHAT THE LADIES WERE SAYING DOWN-STAIRS!
IT'LL BE ALL OVER THE WHOLE COMPLEX TOMOR-ROW!
GRIND
I'M SORRY, MOM. I'M SORRY!
LOOK, HATSUMI... I DON'T WANT TO GIVE YOU A LOT OF GRIEF...
BUT IT'S MARCH NEXT MONTH, AND THE COMPANY WILL BE SHUFFLING PEOPLE AROUND AGAIN!
...YOUR POOR FATHER... HE'S SPENT MOST OF THE PAST YEAR IN OSAKA.
IF WE WANT HIM TO BE TRANS-FERRED BACK HERE...
WE CAN'T RUB MRS. TACHIBANA THE WRONG WAY JUST NOW...
...I'M ...
I know ...
SORRY ...
...I ought to feel bad...
...but...
My heart's still racing...
...so fast.

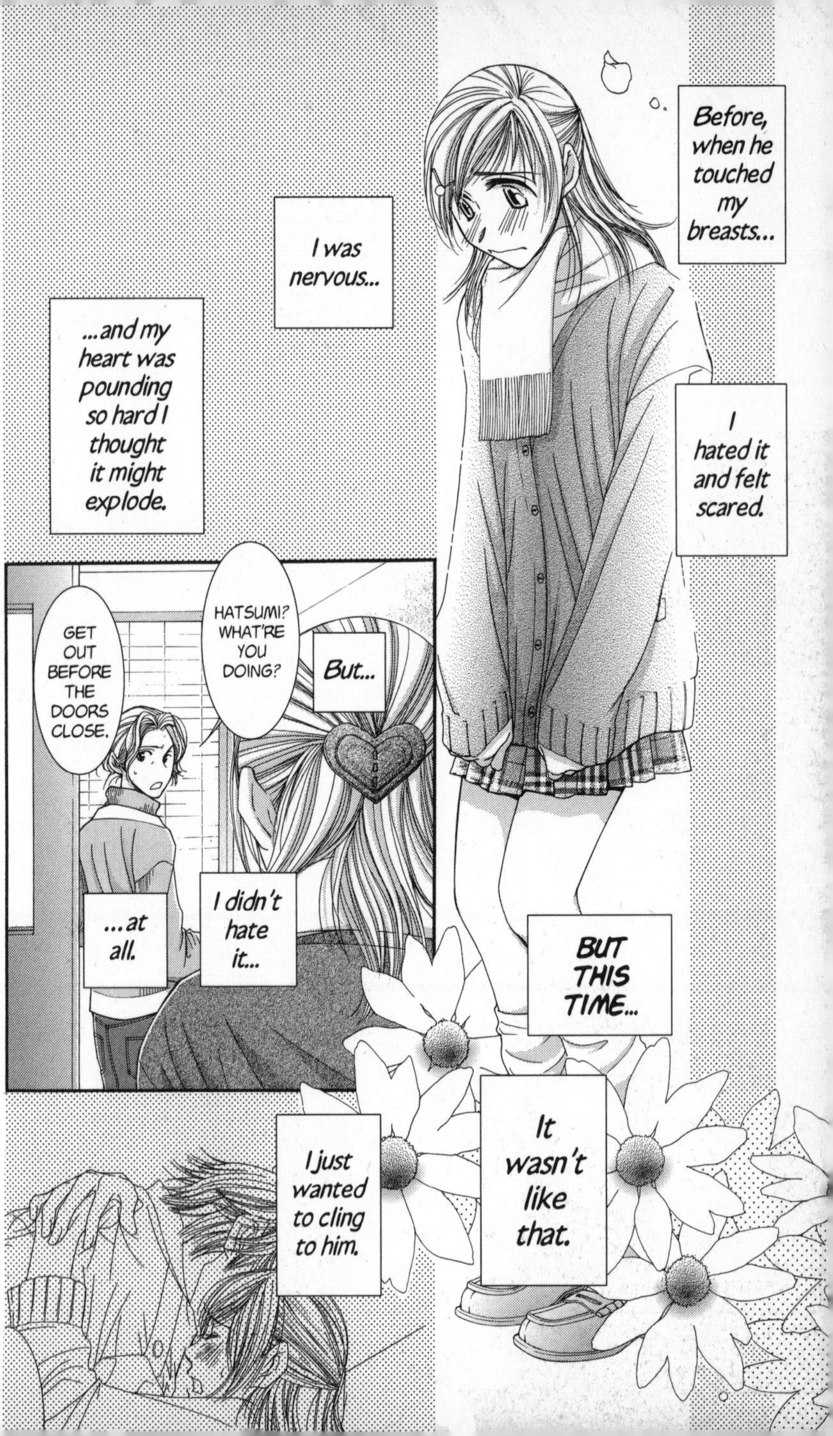
Before, when he touched my breasts...
I hated it and felt scared.
BUT THIS TIME...
It wasn't like that.
I was nervous...
...and my heart was pounding so hard I thought it might explode.
But...
HATSUMI? WHAT'RE YOU DOING?
GET OUT BEFORE THE DOORS CLOSE.
I didn't hate it...
...at all.
I just wanted to cling to him.

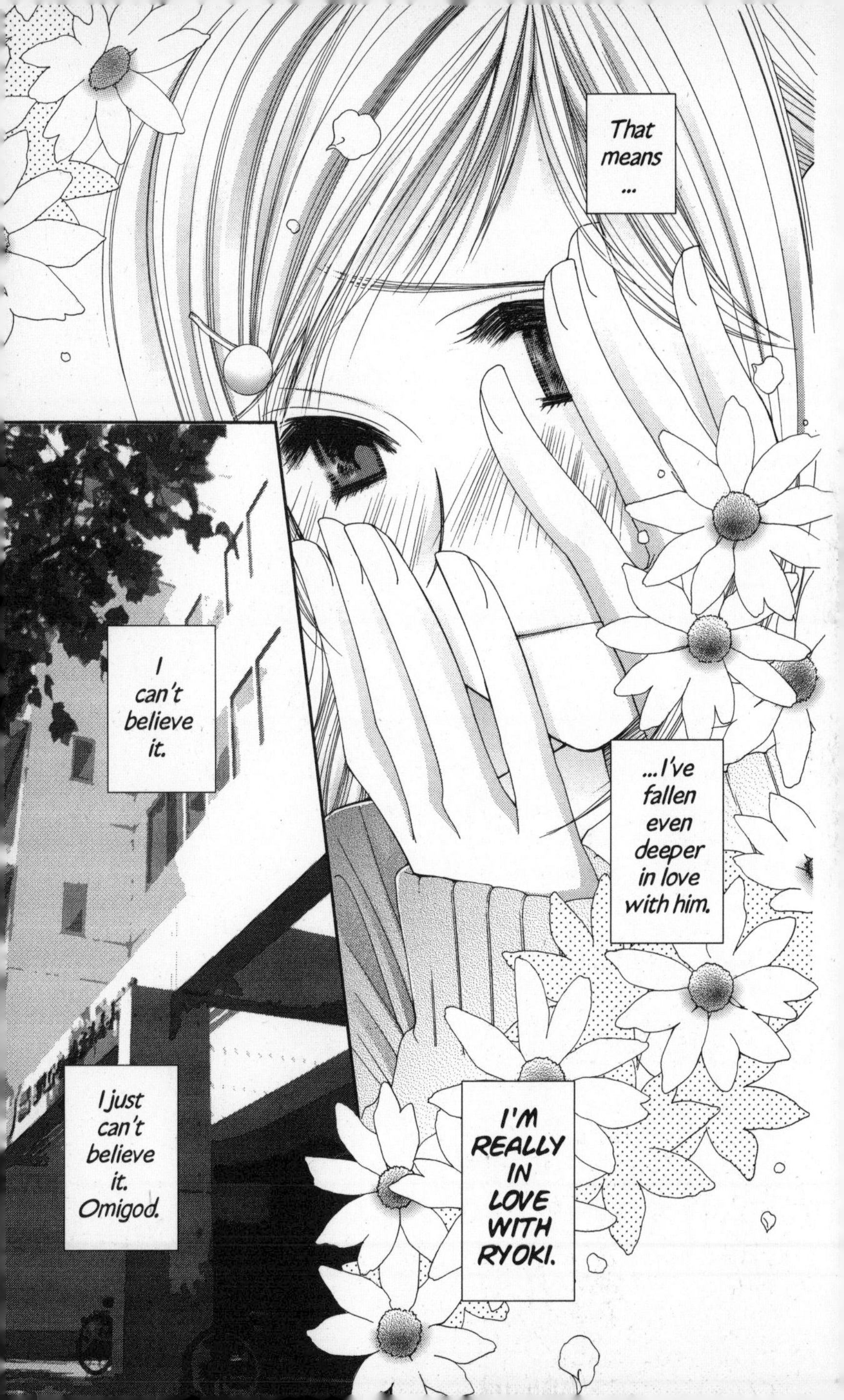
That means ...
...I've fallen even deeper in love with him.
I can't believe it.
I just can't believe it. Omigod.
I'M REALLY IN LOVE WITH RYOKI.

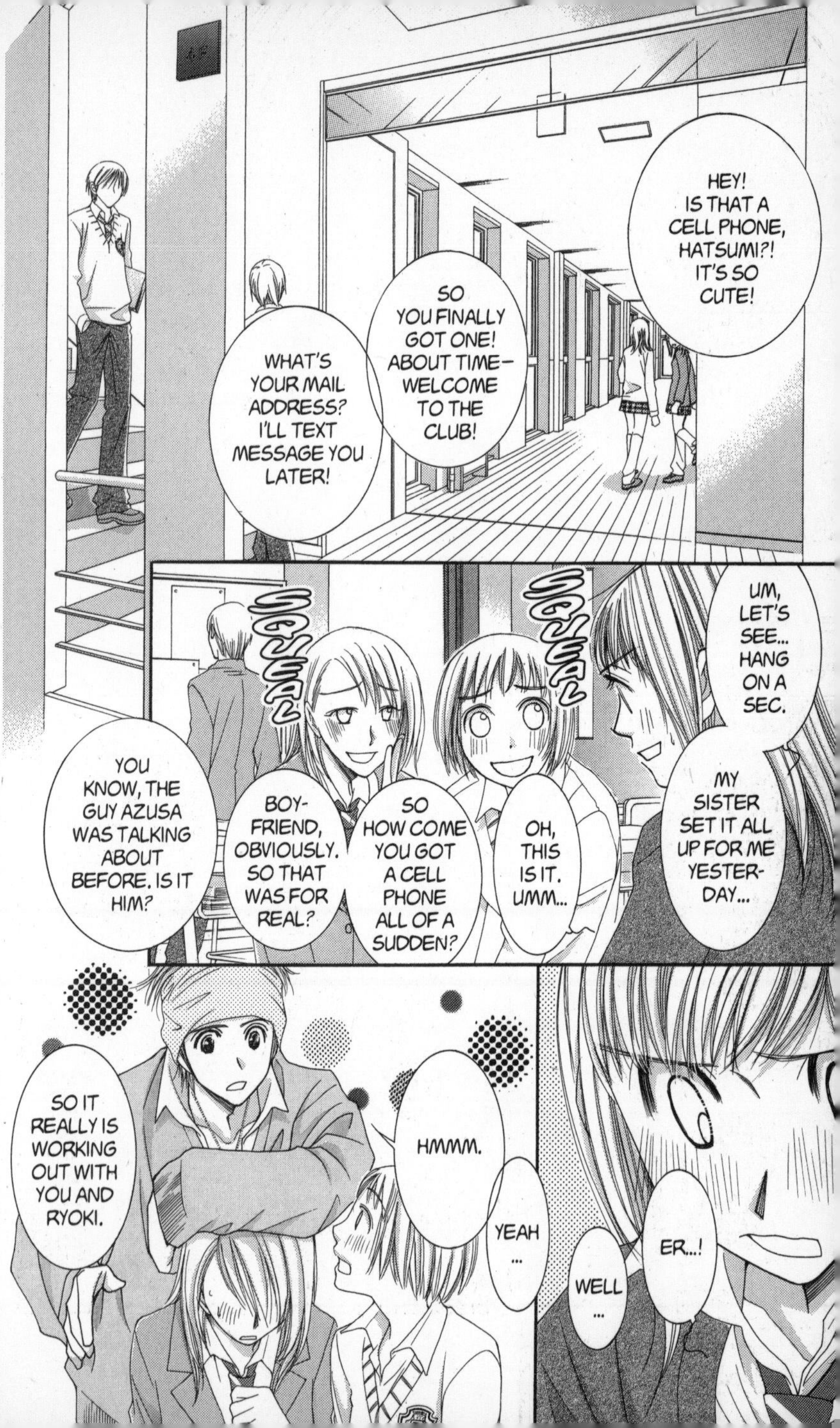
HEY! IS THAT A CELL PHONE, HATSUMI?! IT'S SO CUTE!
SO YOU FINALLY GOT ONE! ABOUT TIME— WELCOME TO THE CLUB!
WHAT'S YOUR MAIL ADDRESS? I'LL TEXT MESSAGE YOU LATER!
UM, LET'S SEE... HANG ON A SEC.
MY SISTER SET IT ALL UP FOR ME YESTER-DAY...
OH, THIS IS IT. UMM...
SO HOW COME YOU GOT A CELL PHONE ALL OF A SUDDEN?
BOY-FRIEND, OBVIOUSLY. SO THAT WAS FOR REAL?
YOU KNOW, THE GUY AZUSA WAS TALKING ABOUT BEFORE. IS IT HIM?
ER...!
WELL ...
HMMM.
YEAH ...
SO IT REALLY IS WORKING OUT WITH YOU AND RYOKI.

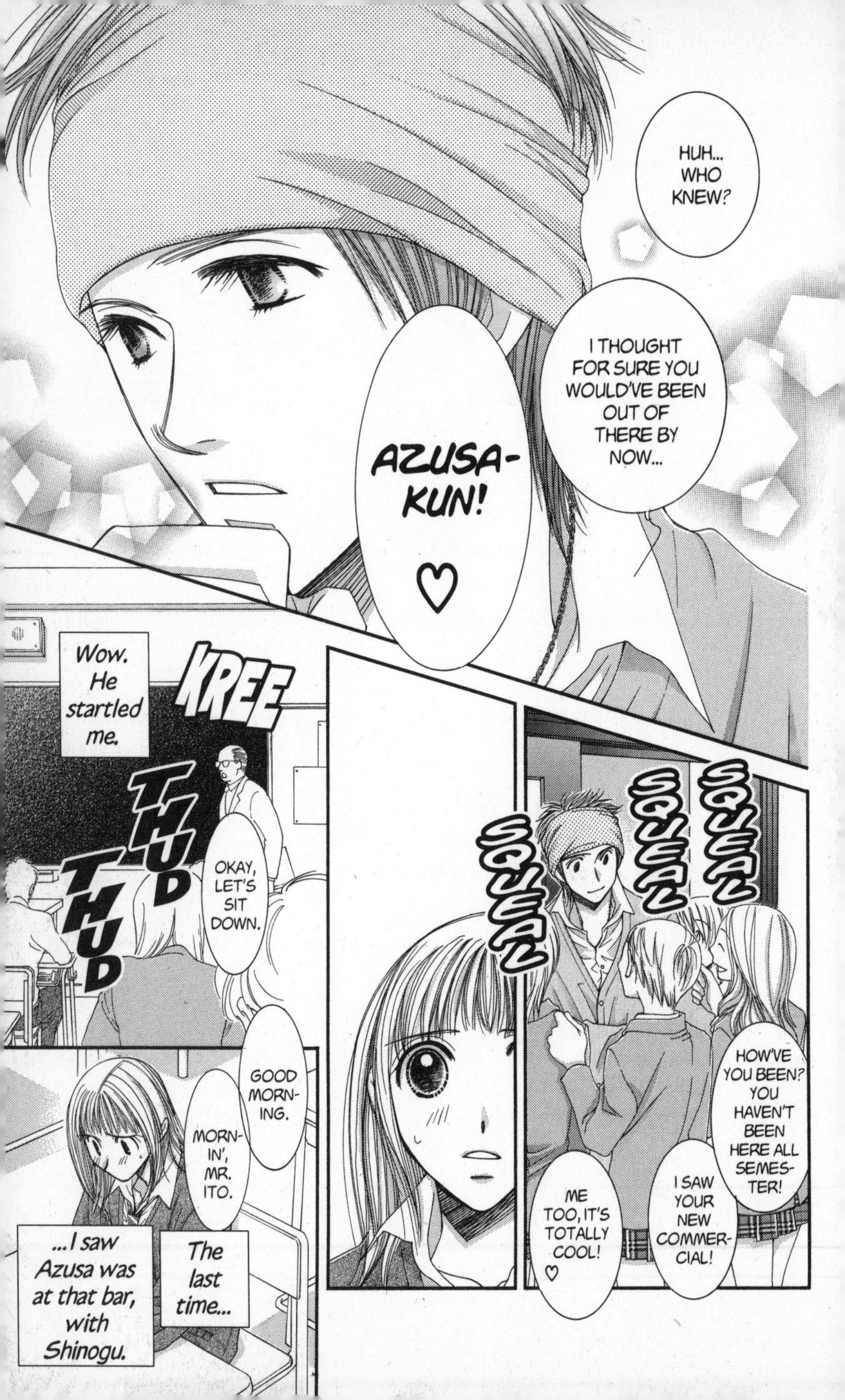
HUH... WHO KNEW?
I THOUGHT FOR SURE YOU WOULD'VE BEEN OUT OF THERE BY NOW...
AZUSA-KUN! ♡
SQUEAL
SQUEAL
SQUEAL
HOW'VE YOU BEEN? YOU HAVEN'T BEEN HERE ALL SEMESTER!
I SAW YOUR NEW COMMERCIAL!
ME TOO, IT'S TOTALLY COOL! ♡
KREE
Wow. He startled me.
THUD
THUD
OKAY, LET'S SIT DOWN.
GOOD MORNING.
MORNIN', MR. ITO.
The last time...
...I saw Azusa was at that bar, with Shinogu.

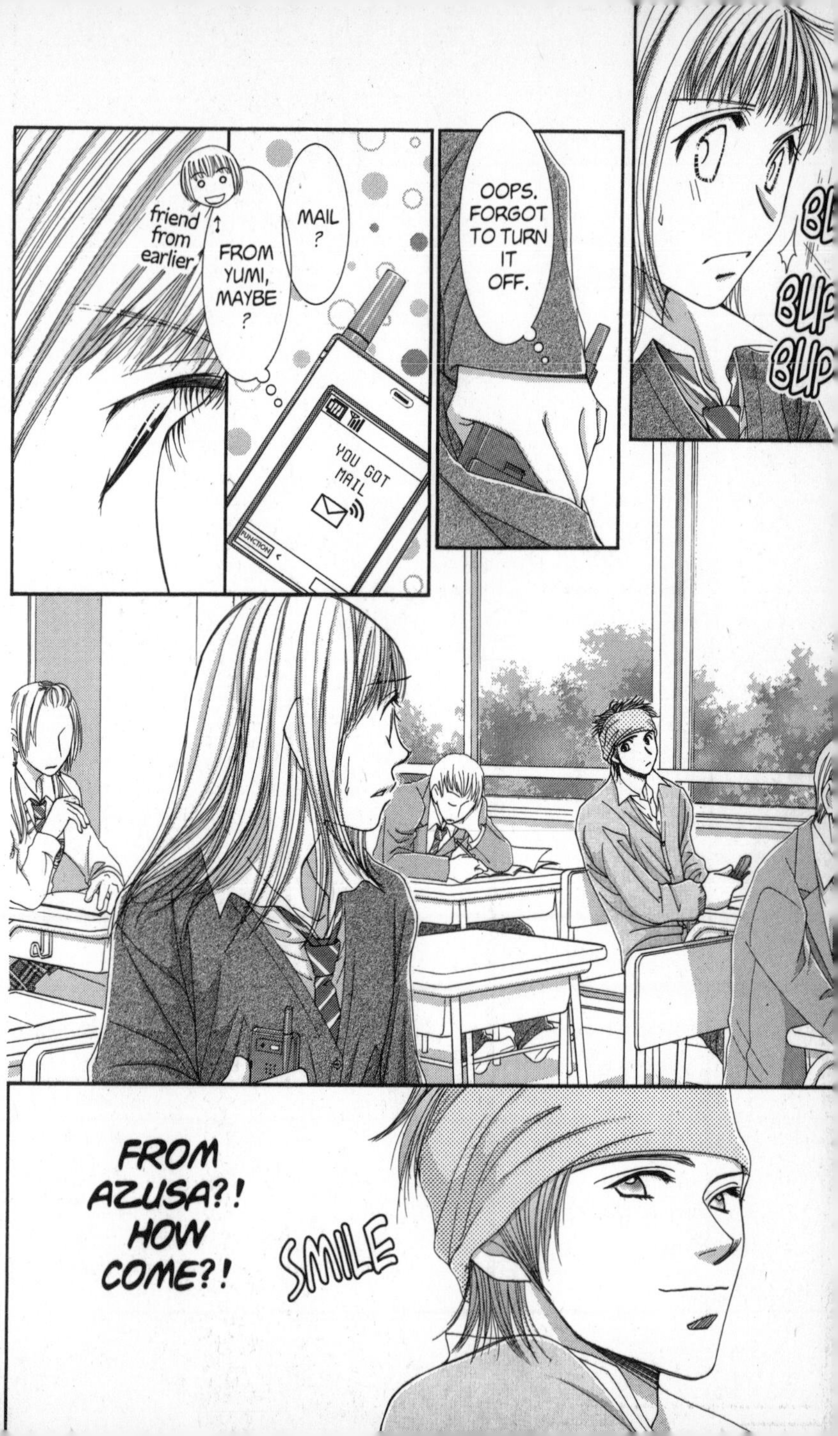
BLIP BLIP BLIP
OOPS. FORGOT TO TURN IT OFF.
MAIL ?
FROM YUMI, MAYBE ?
friend from earlier
YOU GOT MAIL
FUNCTION
FROM AZUSA?! HOW COME?!
SMILE

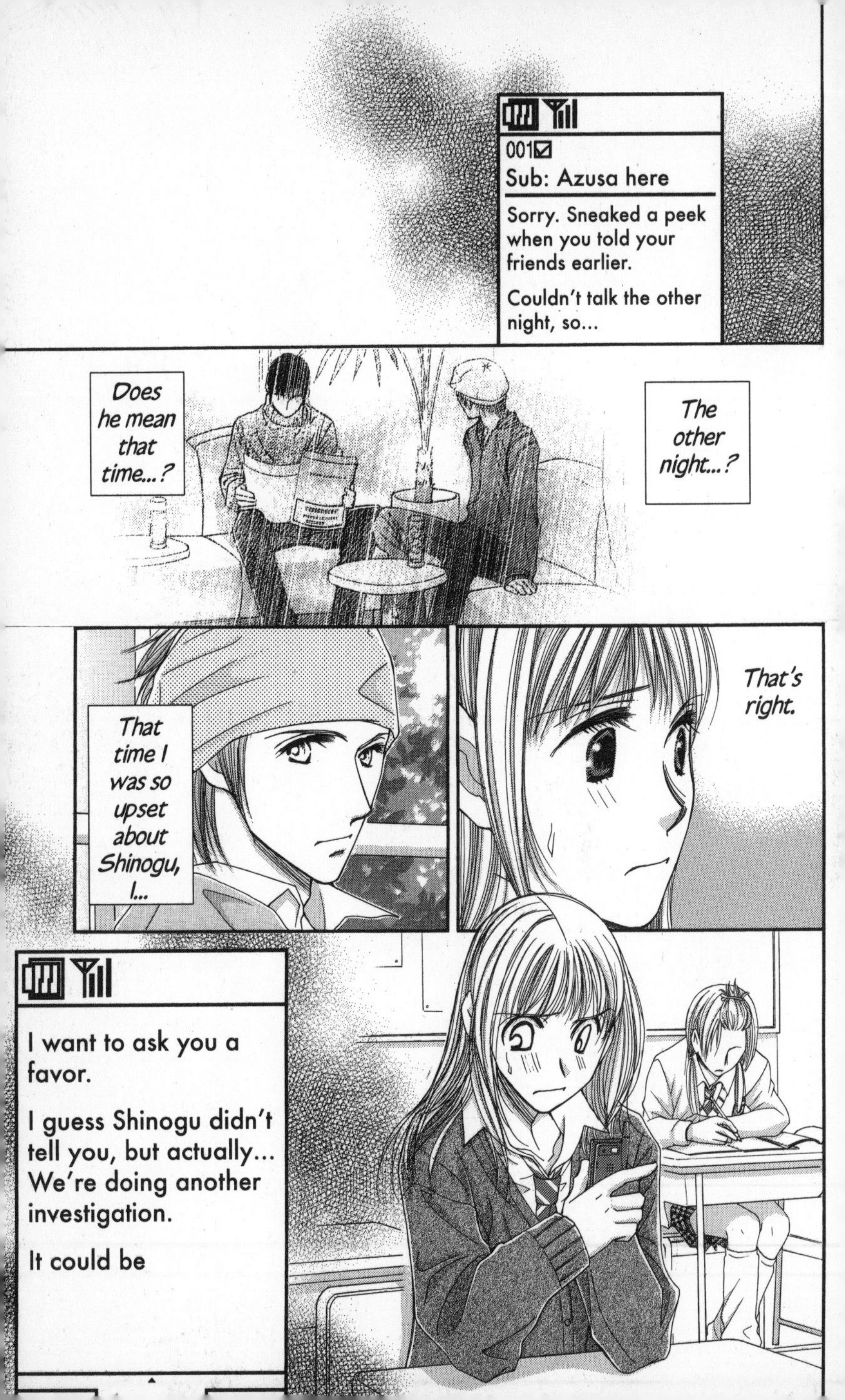
001
Sub: Azusa here
Sorry. Sneaked a peek when you told your friends earlier.
Couldn't talk the other night, so...
The other night...?
Does he mean that time...?
That's right.
That time I was so upset about Shinogu, I...
I want to ask you a favor.
I guess Shinogu didn't tell you, but actually... We're doing another investigation.
It could be

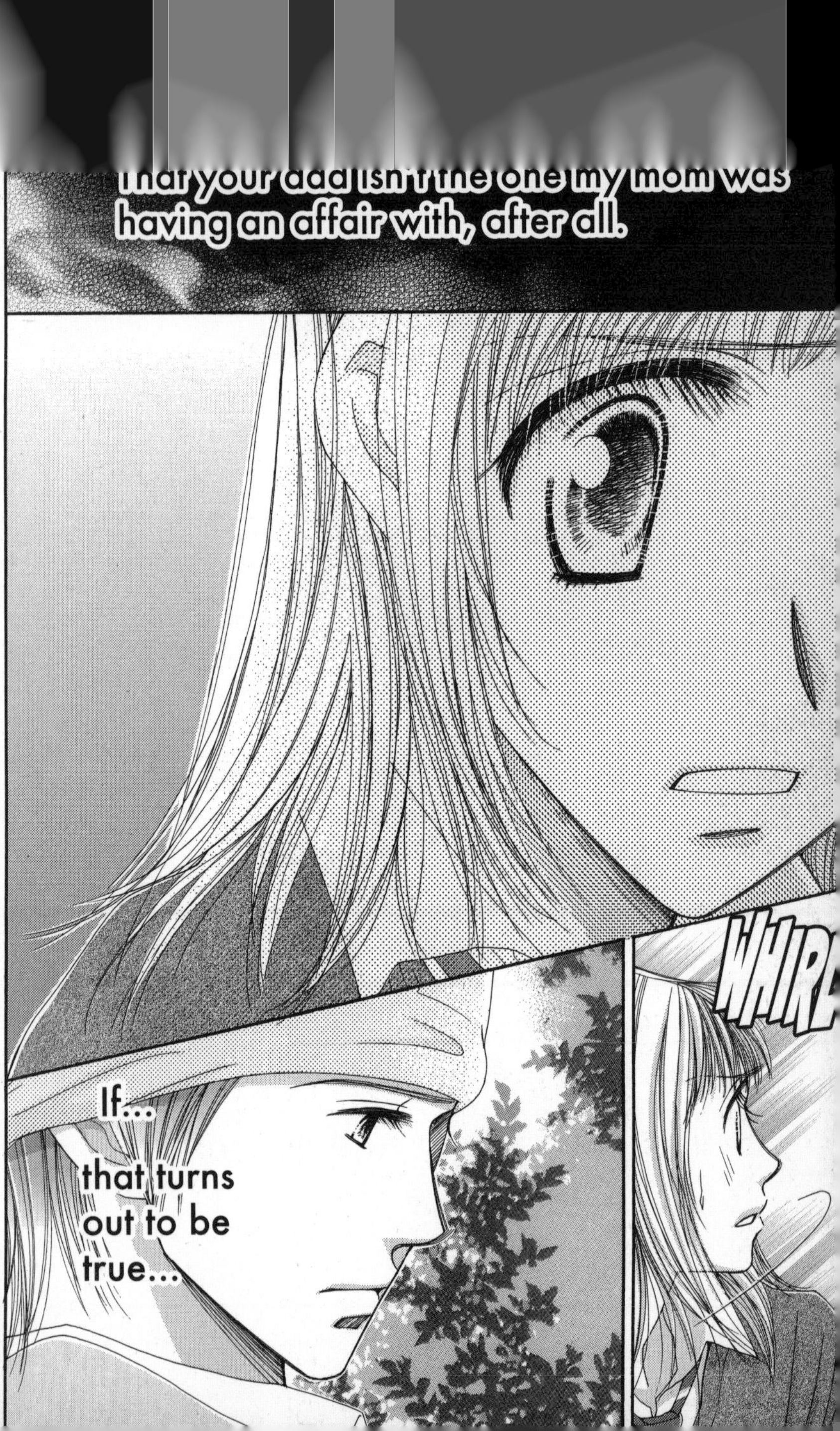
That your dad isn't the one my mom was having an affair with, after all.
WHIRL
If...
that turns out to be true...

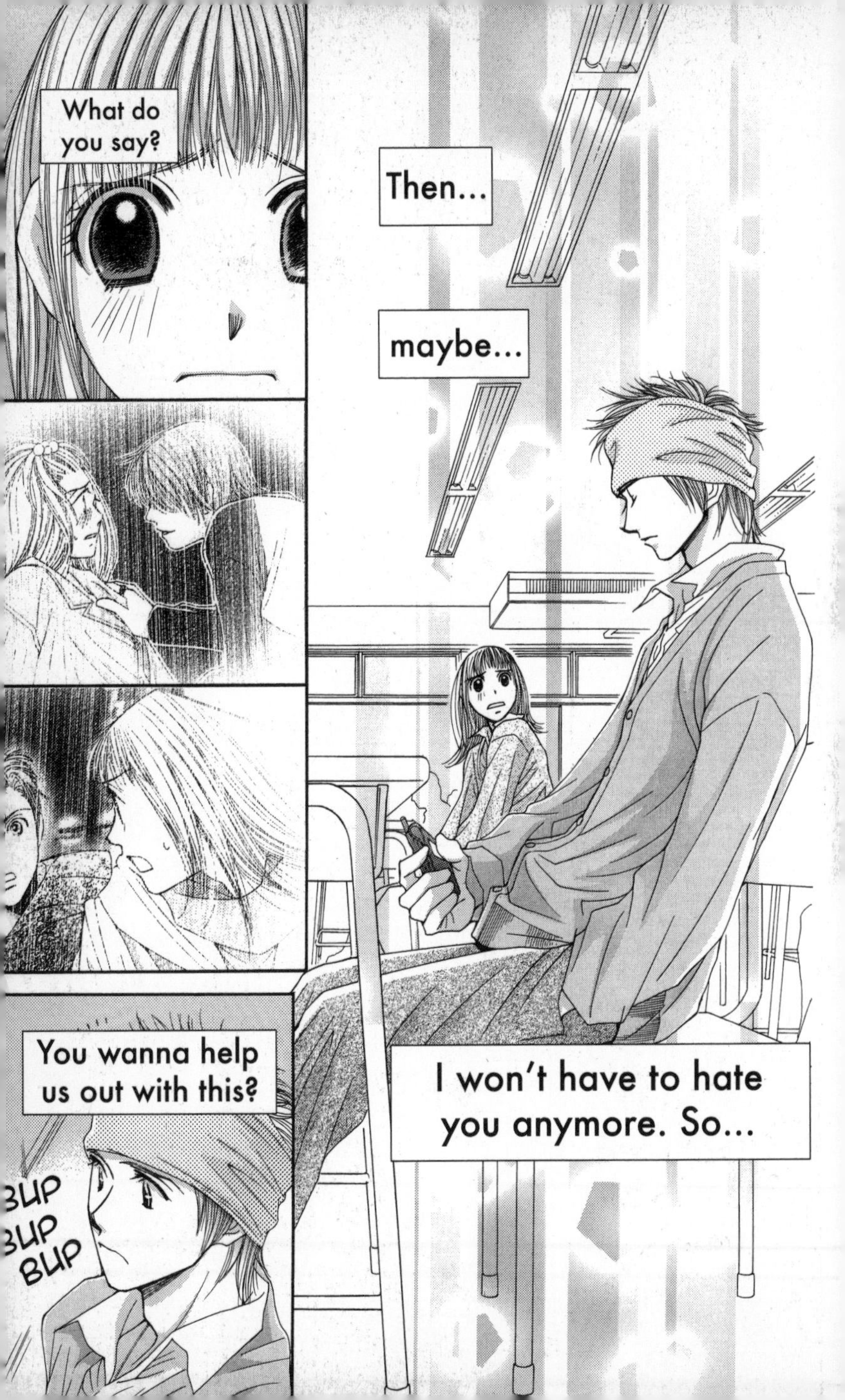
Then...
maybe...
I won't have to hate you anymore. So...
What do you say?
You wanna help us out with this?
BUP BUP BUP

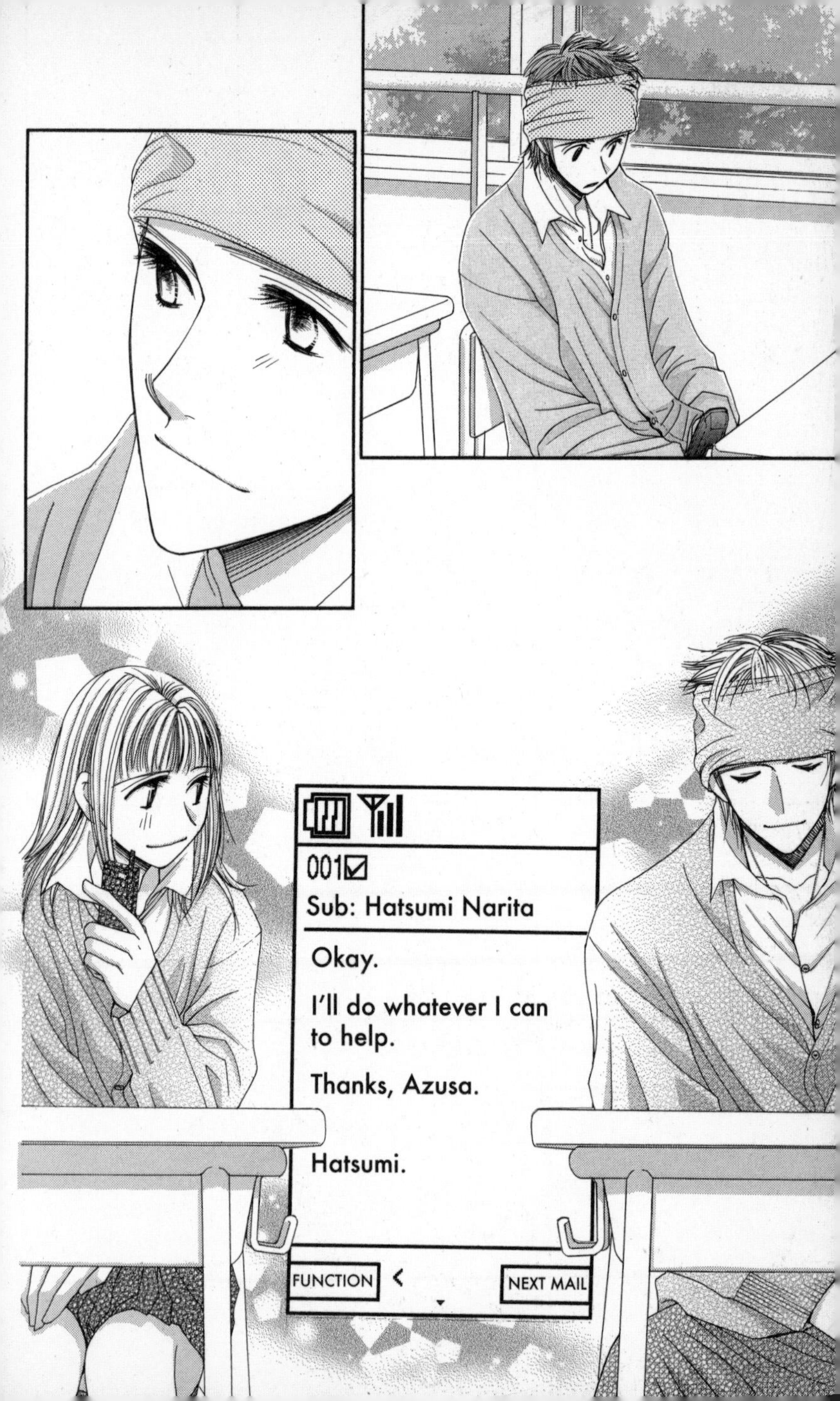
001
Sub: Hatsumi Narita
Okay.
I'll do whatever I can to help.
Thanks, Azusa.
Hatsumi.
FUNCTION
NEXT MAIL

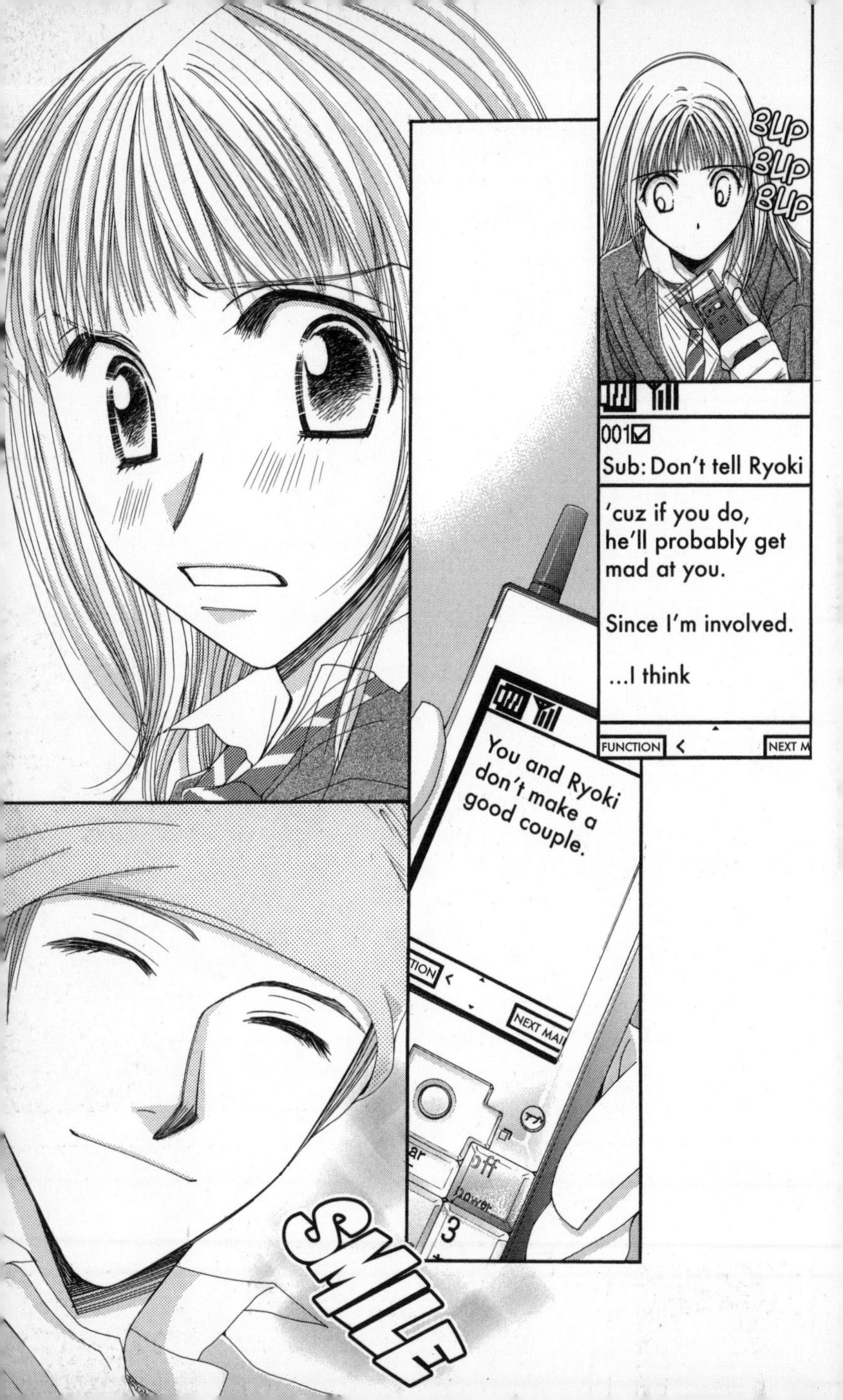

BLIP BLIP BLIP
001
Sub: Don't tell Ryoki
'cuz if you do, he'll probably get mad at you.
Since I'm involved.
...I think
FUNCTION
You and Ryoki don't make a good couple.
SMILE

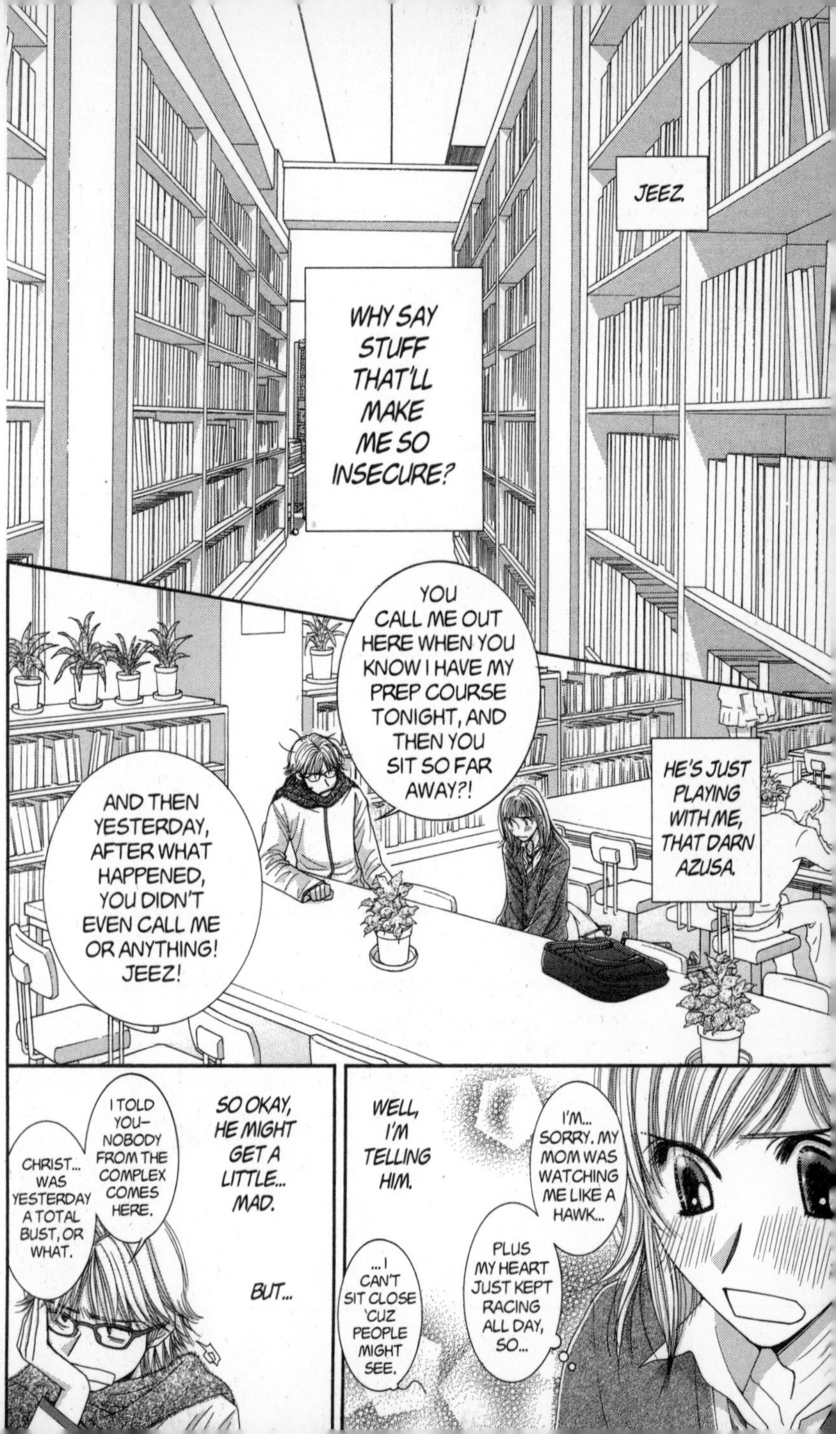

JEEZ.
WHY SAY STUFF THAT'LL MAKE ME SO INSECURE?
HE'S JUST PLAYING WITH ME, THAT DARN AZUSA.
YOU CALL ME OUT HERE WHEN YOU KNOW I HAVE MY PREP COURSE TONIGHT, AND THEN YOU SIT SO FAR AWAY?!
AND THEN YESTERDAY, AFTER WHAT HAPPENED, YOU DIDN'T EVEN CALL ME OR ANYTHING! JEEZ!
I'M... SORRY. MY MOM WAS WATCHING ME LIKE A HAWK...
WELL, I'M TELLING HIM.
PLUS MY HEART JUST KEPT RACING ALL DAY, SO...
...I CAN'T SIT CLOSE 'CUZ PEOPLE MIGHT SEE.
SO OKAY, HE MIGHT GET A LITTLE... MAD.
I TOLD YOU— NOBODY FROM THE COMPLEX COMES HERE.
CHRIST... WAS YESTERDAY A TOTAL BUST, OR WHAT.
BUT...

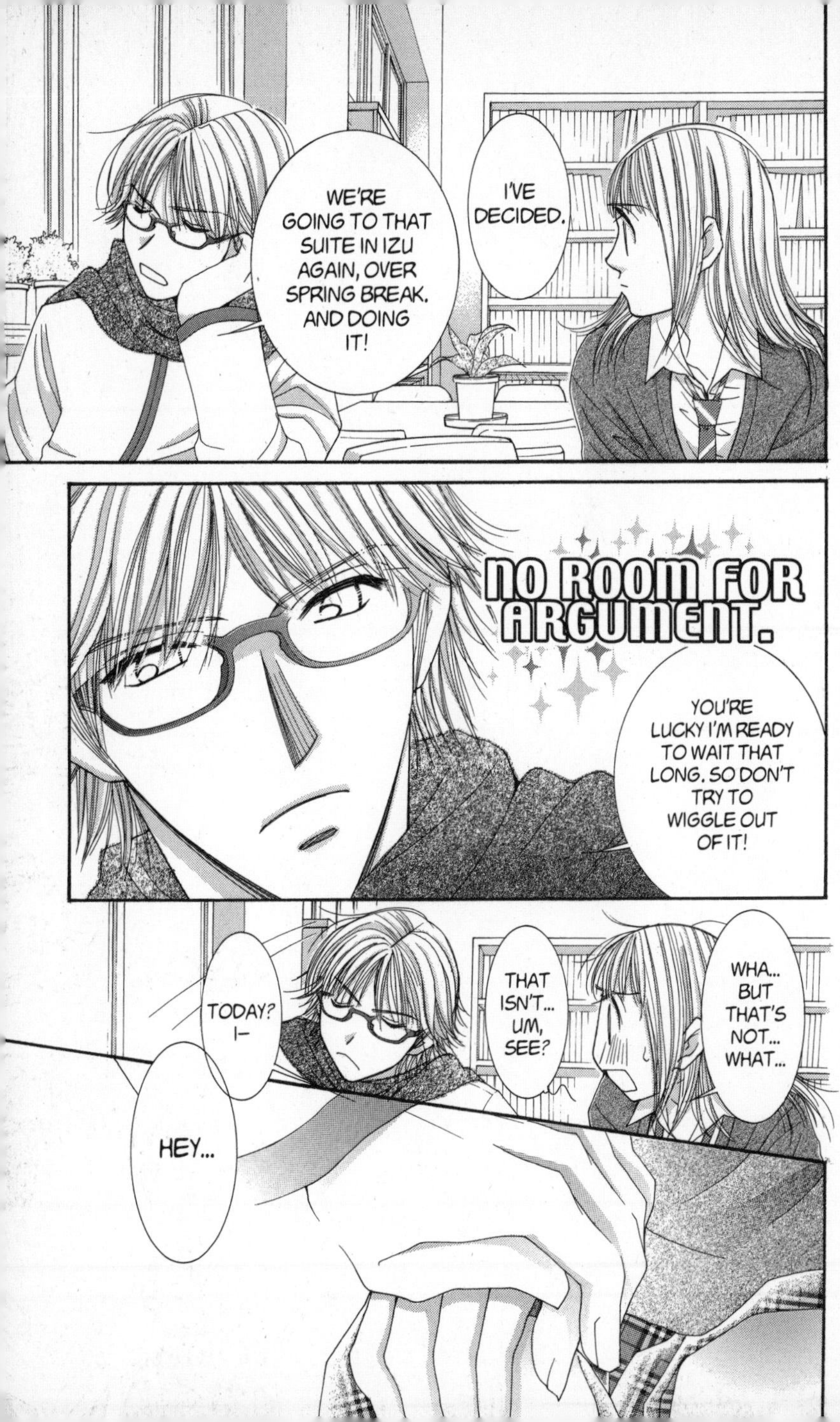
I'VE DECIDED.
WE'RE GOING TO THAT SUITE IN IZU AGAIN, OVER SPRING BREAK. AND DOING IT!
NO ROOM FOR ARGUMENT.
YOU'RE LUCKY I'M READY TO WAIT THAT LONG. SO DON'T TRY TO WIGGLE OUT OF IT!
WHA... BUT THAT'S NOT... WHAT...
THAT ISN'T... UM, SEE?
TODAY? I–
HEY...

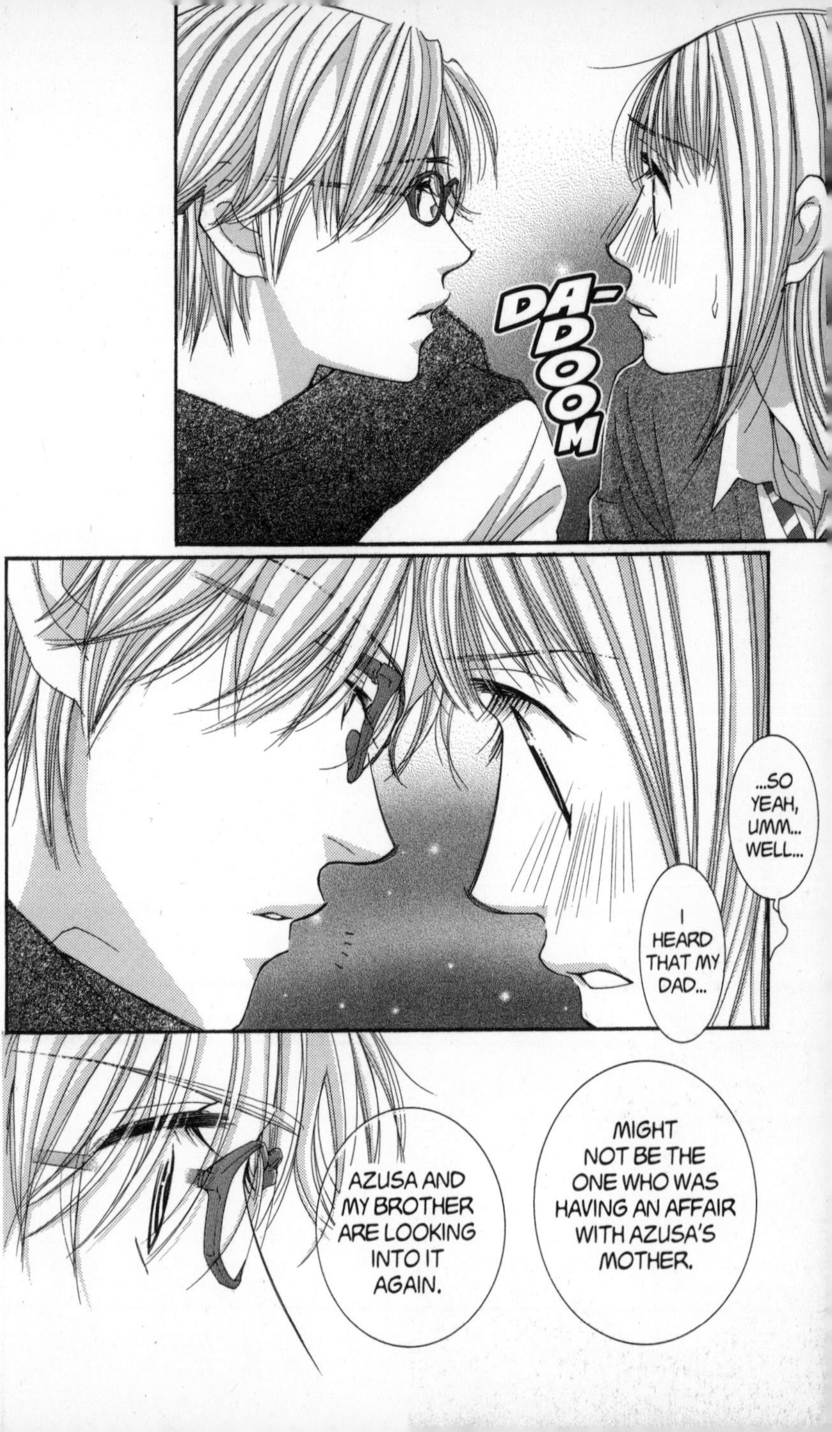
DA-DOOM
...SO YEAH, UMM... WELL...
I HEARD THAT MY DAD...
MIGHT NOT BE THE ONE WHO WAS HAVING AN AFFAIR WITH AZUSA'S MOTHER.
AZUSA AND MY BROTHER ARE LOOKING INTO IT AGAIN.

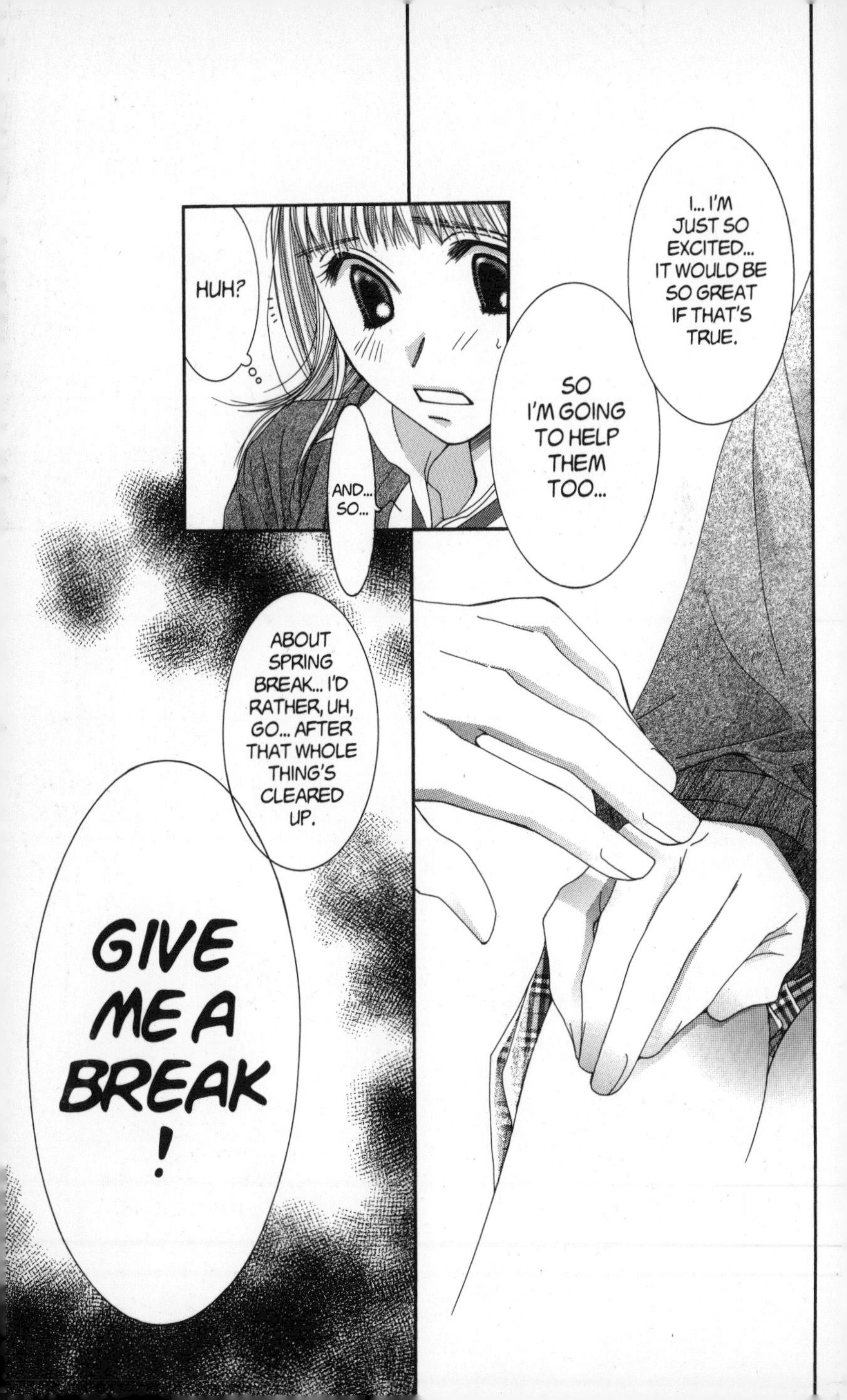
I... I'M JUST SO EXCITED... IT WOULD BE SO GREAT IF THAT'S TRUE.
SO I'M GOING TO HELP THEM TOO...
HUH?
AND... SO...
ABOUT SPRING BREAK... I'D RATHER, UH, GO... AFTER THAT WHOLE THING'S CLEARED UP.
GIVE ME A BREAK!

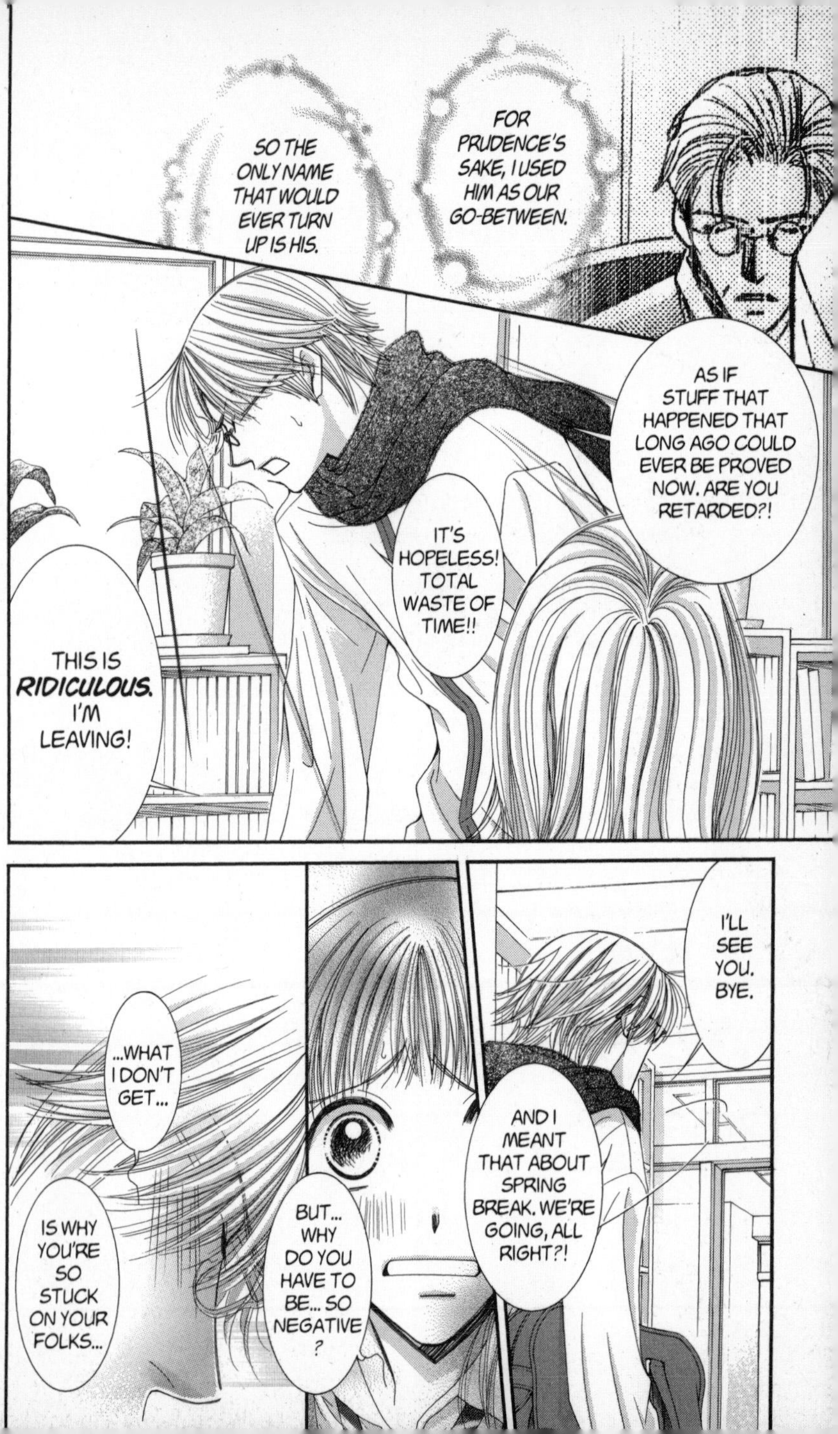
FOR PRUDENCE'S SAKE, I USED HIM AS OUR GO-BETWEEN.
SO THE ONLY NAME THAT WOULD EVER TURN UP IS HIS.
AS IF STUFF THAT HAPPENED THAT LONG AGO COULD EVER BE PROVED NOW. ARE YOU RETARDED?!
IT'S HOPELESS! TOTAL WASTE OF TIME!!
THIS IS **RIDICULOUS.** I'M LEAVING!
I'LL SEE YOU. BYE.
AND I MEANT THAT ABOUT SPRING BREAK. WE'RE GOING, ALL RIGHT?!
BUT... WHY DO YOU HAVE TO BE... SO NEGATIVE?
...WHAT I DON'T GET...
IS WHY YOU'RE SO STUCK ON YOUR FOLKS...

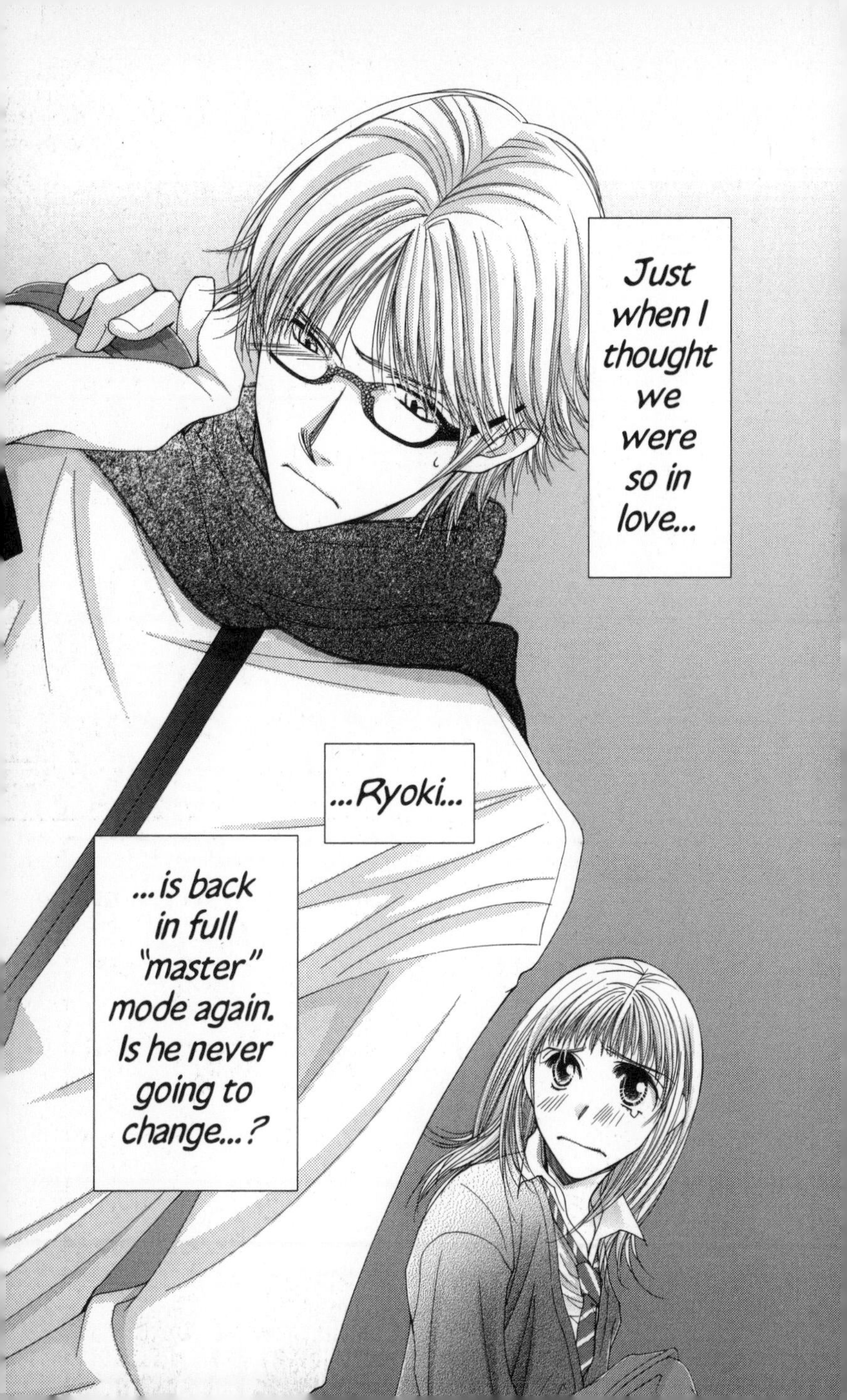
Just when I thought we were so in love...
...Ryoki...
...is back in full "master" mode again. Is he never going to change...?

SPEAK NO EVIL
PART 2.

Chapter 40

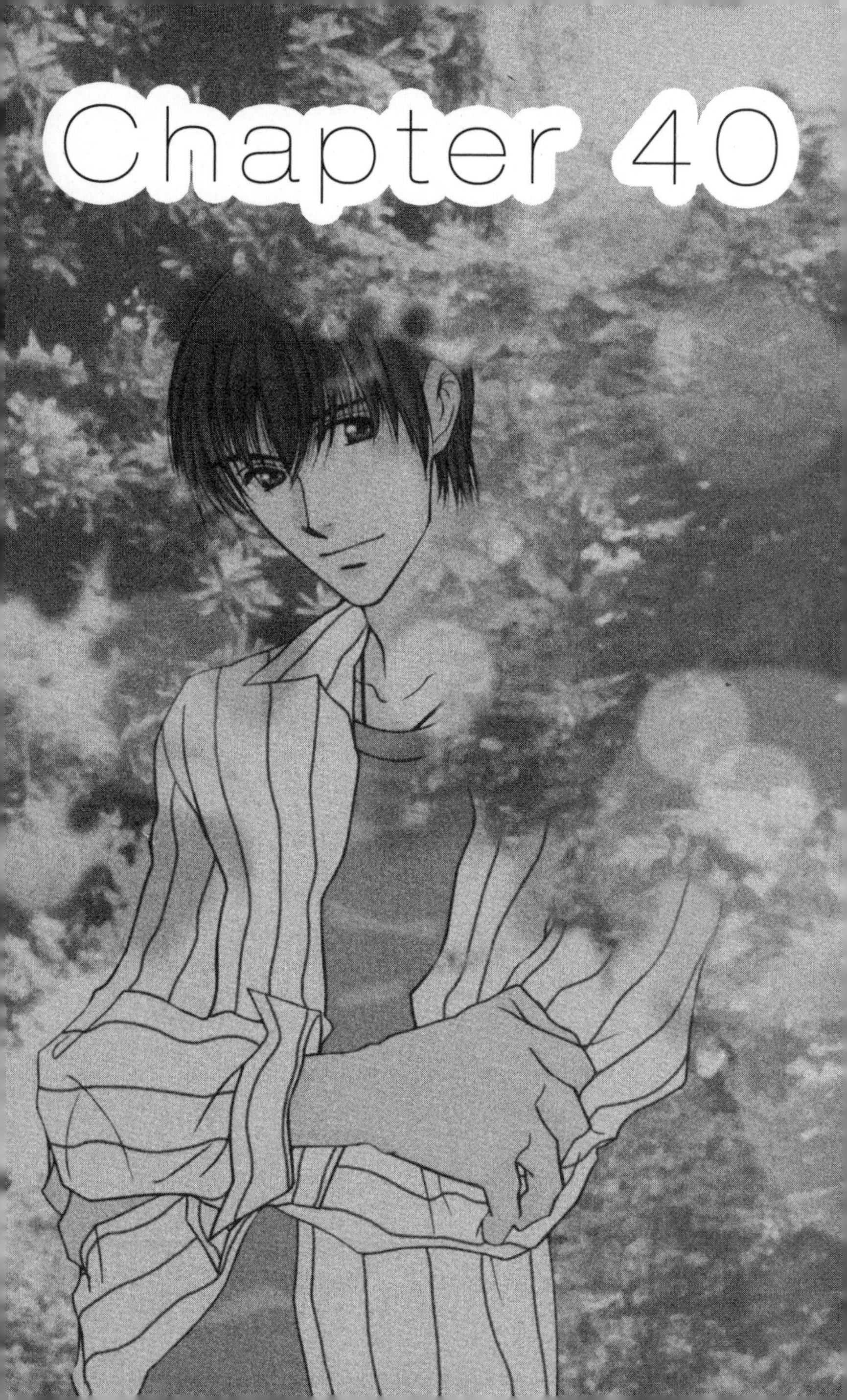

hot gimmick

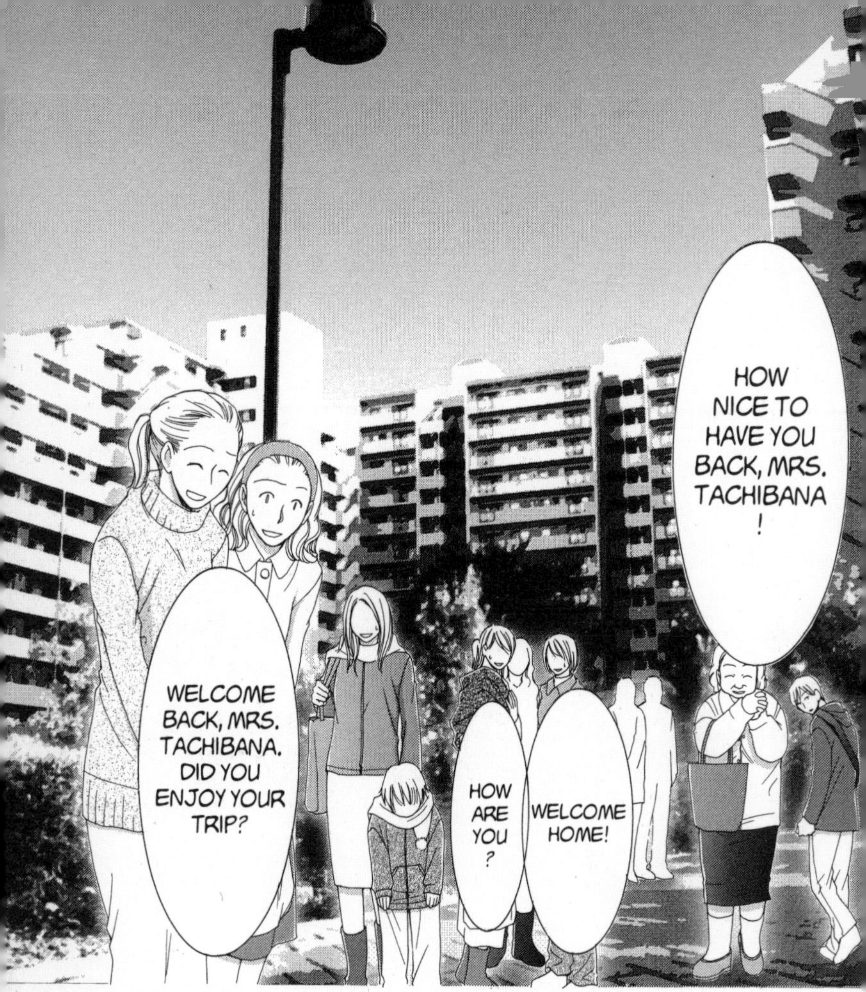
HOW NICE TO HAVE YOU BACK, MRS. TACHIBANA!
WELCOME HOME!
HOW ARE YOU?
WELCOME BACK, MRS. TACHIBANA. DID YOU ENJOY YOUR TRIP?

hot gimmick

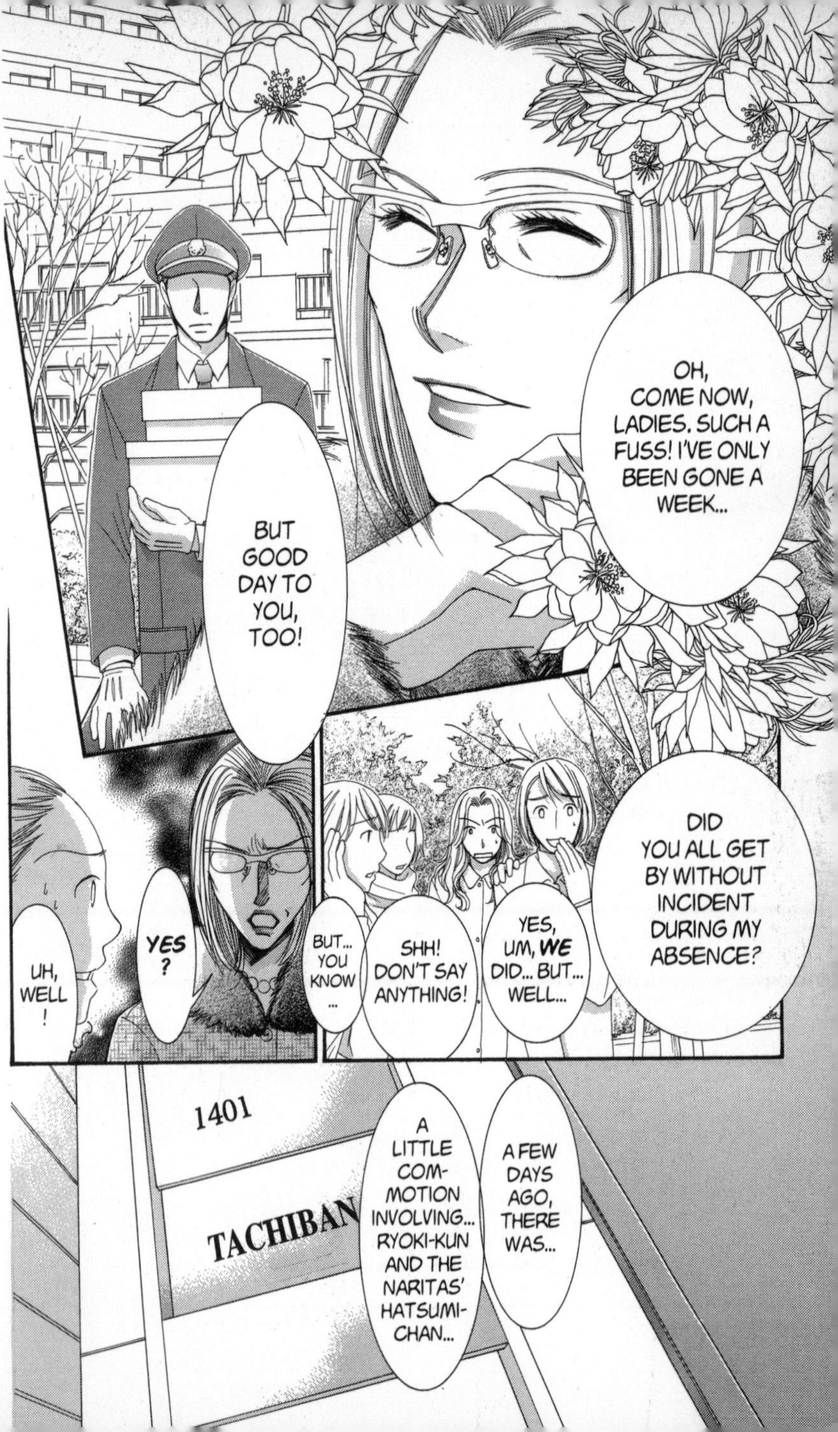
OH, COME NOW, LADIES. SUCH A FUSS! I'VE ONLY BEEN GONE A WEEK...
BUT GOOD DAY TO YOU, TOO!
DID YOU ALL GET BY WITHOUT INCIDENT DURING MY ABSENCE?
YES, UM, **WE** DID... BUT... WELL...
SHH! DON'T SAY ANYTHING!
BUT... YOU KNOW...
YES?
UH, WELL!
1401
TACHIBAN
A FEW DAYS AGO, THERE WAS...
A LITTLE COM-MOTION INVOLVING... RYOKI-KUN AND THE NARITAS' HATSUMI-CHAN...

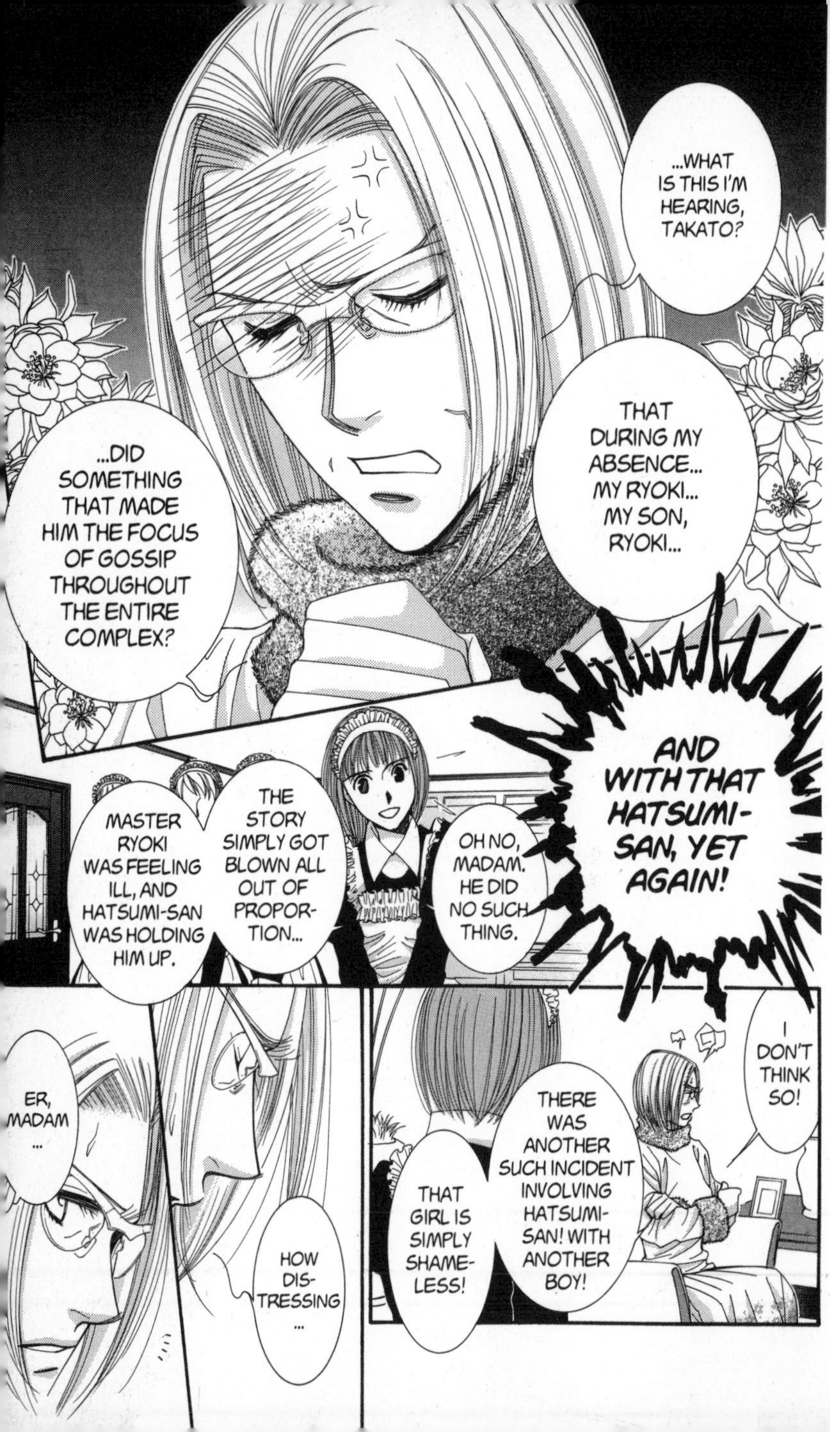
...WHAT IS THIS I'M HEARING, TAKATO?
THAT DURING MY ABSENCE... MY RYOKI... MY SON, RYOKI...
...DID SOMETHING THAT MADE HIM THE FOCUS OF GOSSIP THROUGHOUT THE ENTIRE COMPLEX?
AND WITH THAT HATSUMI-SAN, YET AGAIN!
OH NO, MADAM. HE DID NO SUCH THING.
THE STORY SIMPLY GOT BLOWN ALL OUT OF PROPORTION...
MASTER RYOKI WAS FEELING ILL, AND HATSUMI-SAN WAS HOLDING HIM UP.
I DON'T THINK SO!
THERE WAS ANOTHER SUCH INCIDENT INVOLVING HATSUMI-SAN! WITH ANOTHER BOY!
THAT GIRL IS SIMPLY SHAMELESS!
HOW DISTRESSING...
ER, MADAM...

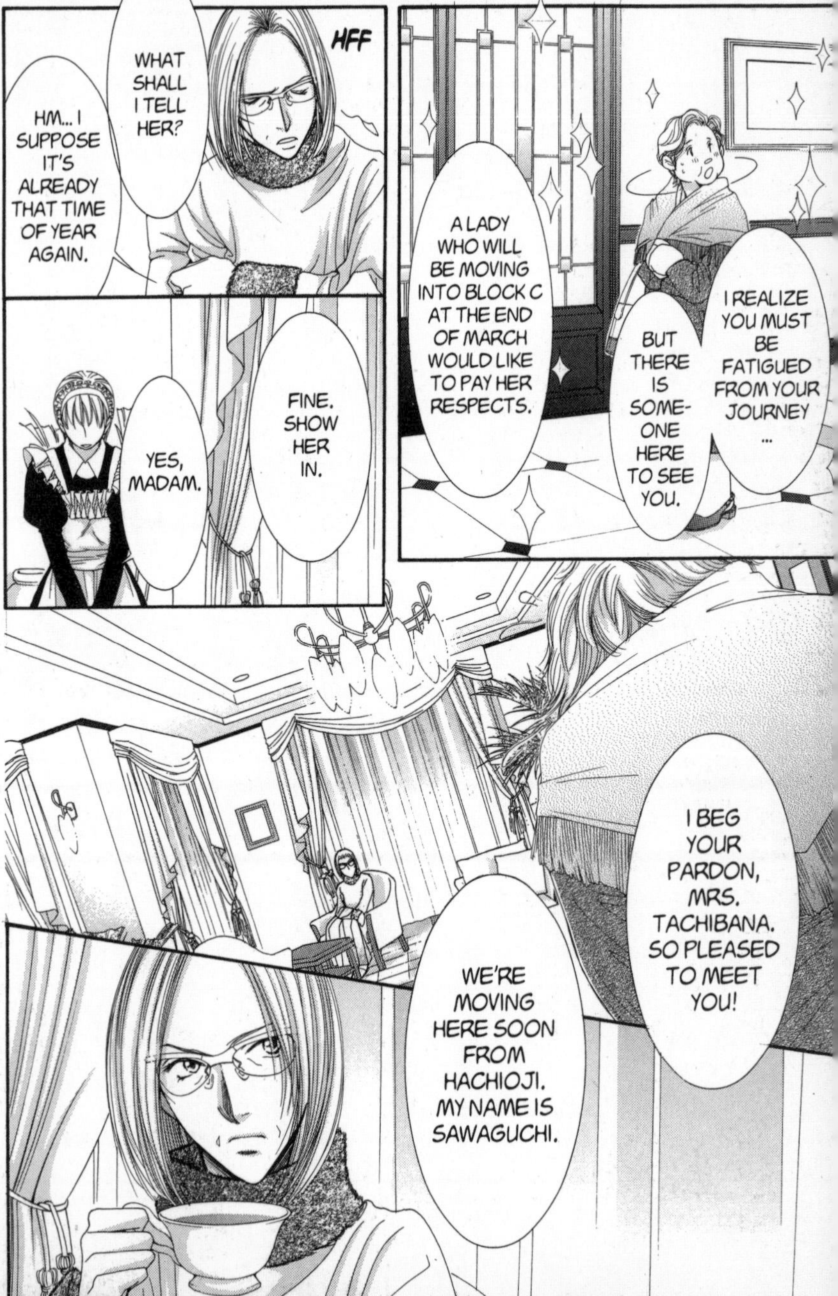
I REALIZE YOU MUST BE FATIGUED FROM YOUR JOURNEY ...
BUT THERE IS SOME-ONE HERE TO SEE YOU.
A LADY WHO WILL BE MOVING INTO BLOCK C AT THE END OF MARCH WOULD LIKE TO PAY HER RESPECTS.
HFF
WHAT SHALL I TELL HER?
HM... I SUPPOSE IT'S ALREADY THAT TIME OF YEAR AGAIN.
FINE. SHOW HER IN.
YES, MADAM.
I BEG YOUR PARDON, MRS. TACHIBANA. SO PLEASED TO MEET YOU!
WE'RE MOVING HERE SOON FROM HACHIOJI. MY NAME IS SAWAGUCHI.

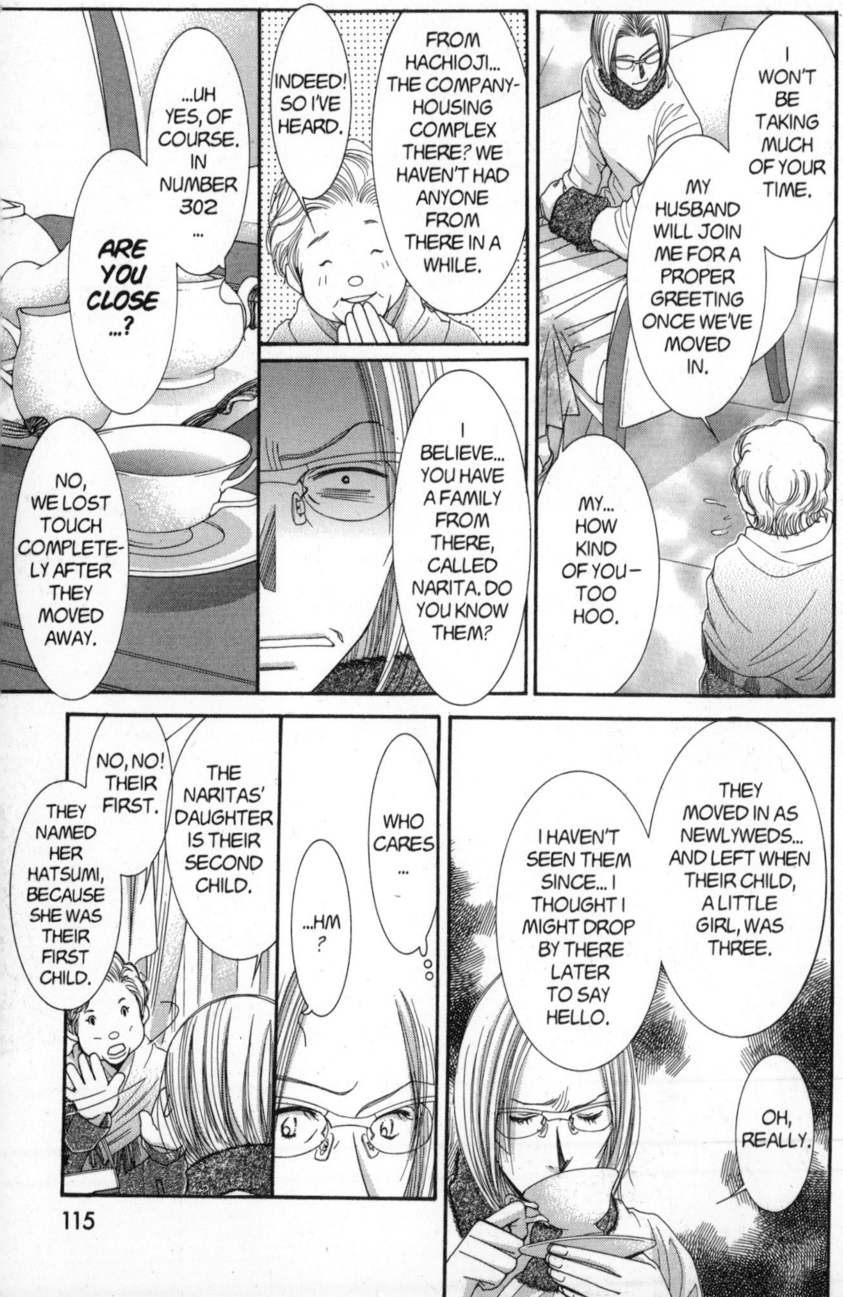

I WON'T BE TAKING MUCH OF YOUR TIME.
MY HUSBAND WILL JOIN ME FOR A PROPER GREETING ONCE WE'VE MOVED IN.
MY... HOW KIND OF YOU— TOO HOO.
FROM HACHIOJI... THE COMPANY-HOUSING COMPLEX THERE? WE HAVEN'T HAD ANYONE FROM THERE IN A WHILE.
INDEED! SO I'VE HEARD.
I BELIEVE... YOU HAVE A FAMILY FROM THERE, CALLED NARITA. DO YOU KNOW THEM?
...UH YES, OF COURSE. IN NUMBER 302 ...
ARE YOU CLOSE ...?
NO, WE LOST TOUCH COMPLETE-LY AFTER THEY MOVED AWAY.
THEY MOVED IN AS NEWLYWEDS... AND LEFT WHEN THEIR CHILD, A LITTLE GIRL, WAS THREE.
I HAVEN'T SEEN THEM SINCE... I THOUGHT I MIGHT DROP BY THERE LATER TO SAY HELLO.
OH, REALLY.
WHO CARES ...
...HM ?
THE NARITAS' DAUGHTER IS THEIR SECOND CHILD.
NO, NO! THEIR FIRST.
THEY NAMED HER HATSUMI, BECAUSE SHE WAS THEIR FIRST CHILD.

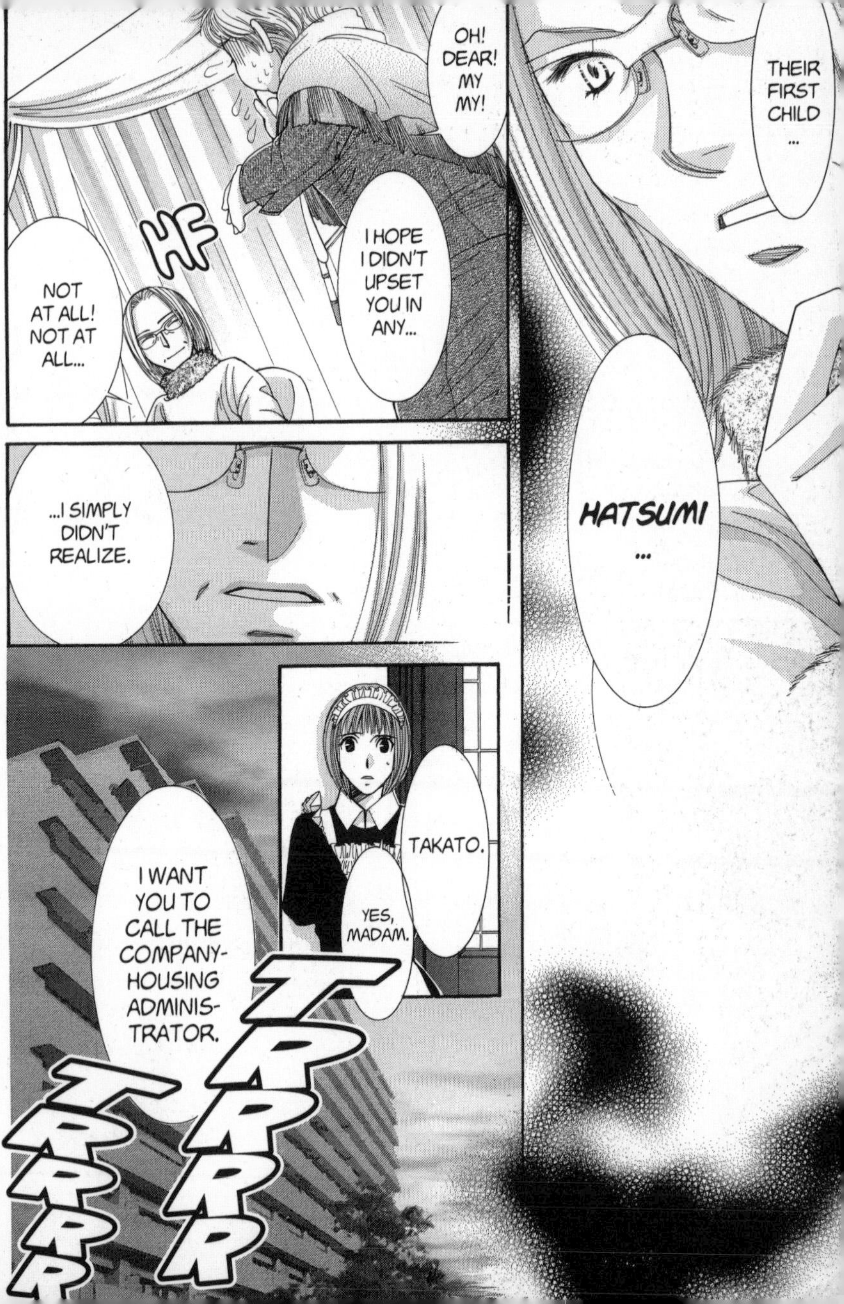
THEIR FIRST CHILD ...
HATSUMI ...
OH! DEAR! MY MY!
I HOPE I DIDN'T UPSET YOU IN ANY...
HF
NOT AT ALL! NOT AT ALL...
...I SIMPLY DIDN'T REALIZE.
TAKATO.
YES, MADAM.
I WANT YOU TO CALL THE COMPANY-HOUSING ADMINISTRATOR.
TRRRR
TRRRR

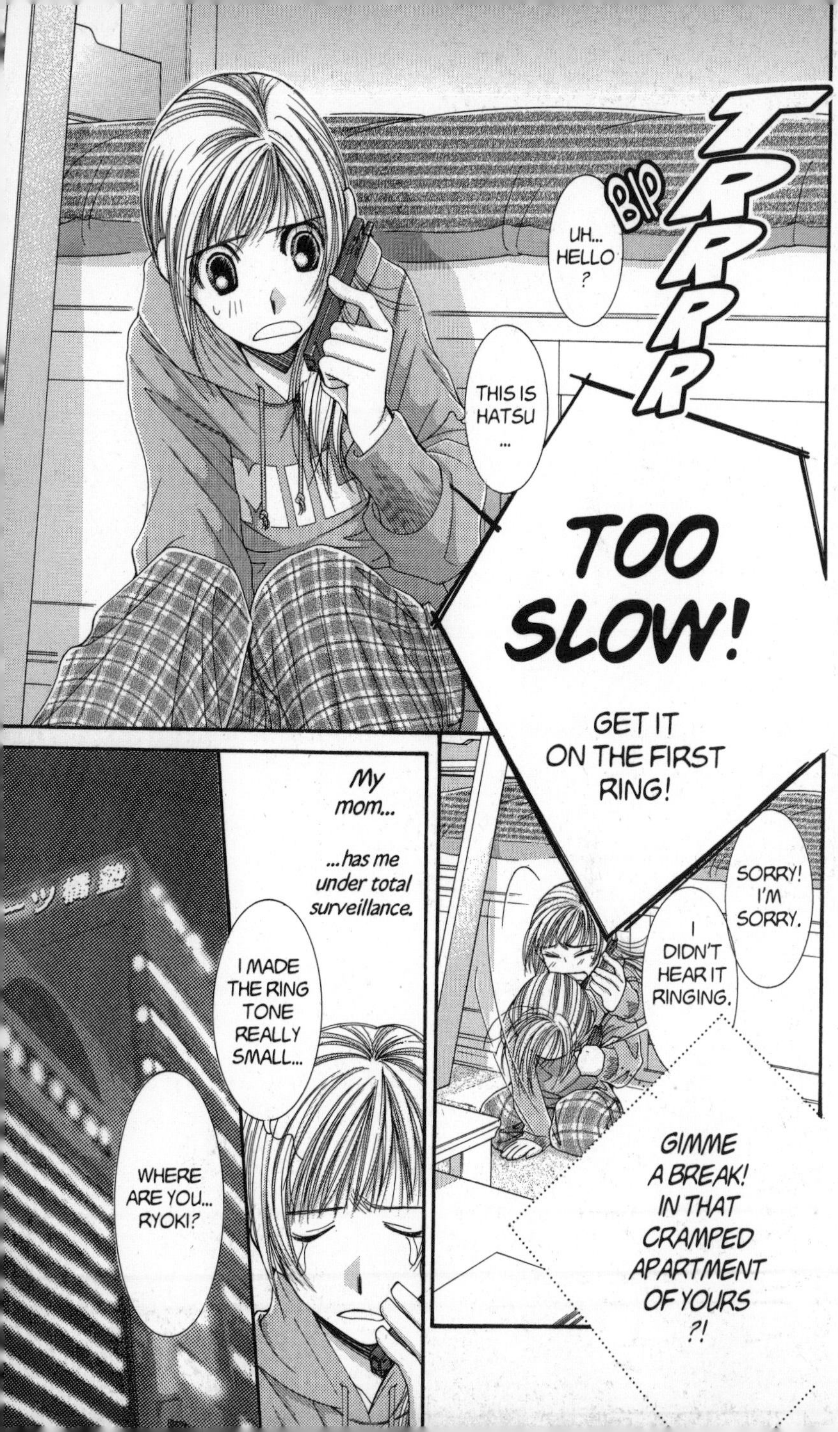
TRRRR
BLIP
UH... HELLO?
THIS IS HATSU...
TOO SLOW!
GET IT ON THE FIRST RING!
SORRY! I'M SORRY.
I DIDN'T HEAR IT RINGING.
GIMME A BREAK! IN THAT CRAMPED APARTMENT OF YOURS?!
My mom...
...has me under total surveillance.
I MADE THE RING TONE REALLY SMALL...
WHERE ARE YOU... RYOKI?

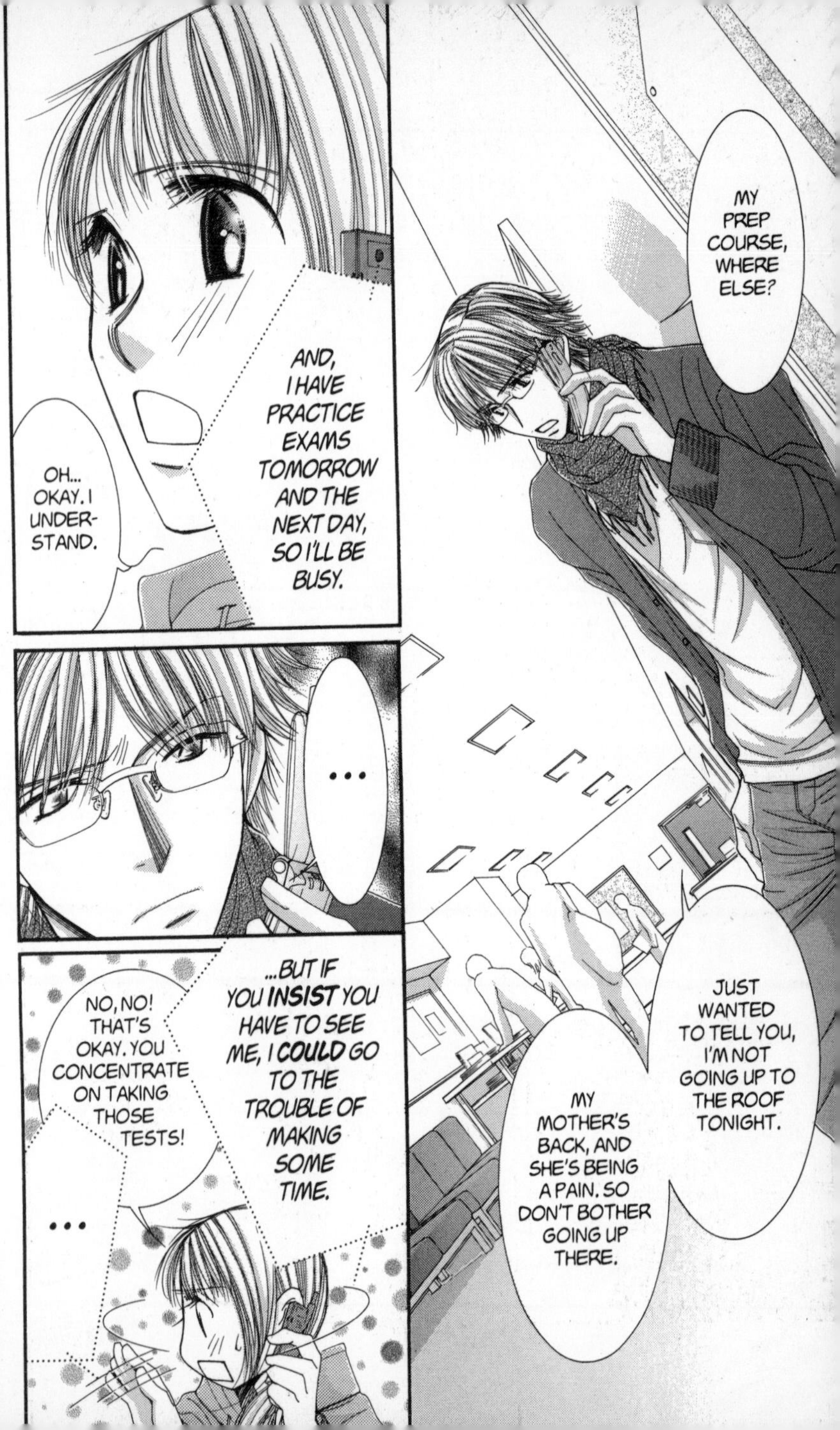
MY PREP COURSE, WHERE ELSE?
JUST WANTED TO TELL YOU, I'M NOT GOING UP TO THE ROOF TONIGHT.
MY MOTHER'S BACK, AND SHE'S BEING A PAIN. SO DON'T BOTHER GOING UP THERE.
AND, I HAVE PRACTICE EXAMS TOMORROW AND THE NEXT DAY, SO I'LL BE BUSY.
OH... OKAY. I UNDERSTAND.
...
...BUT IF YOU **INSIST** YOU HAVE TO SEE ME, I **COULD** GO TO THE TROUBLE OF MAKING SOME TIME.
NO, NO! THAT'S OKAY. YOU CONCENTRATE ON TAKING THOSE TESTS!
...

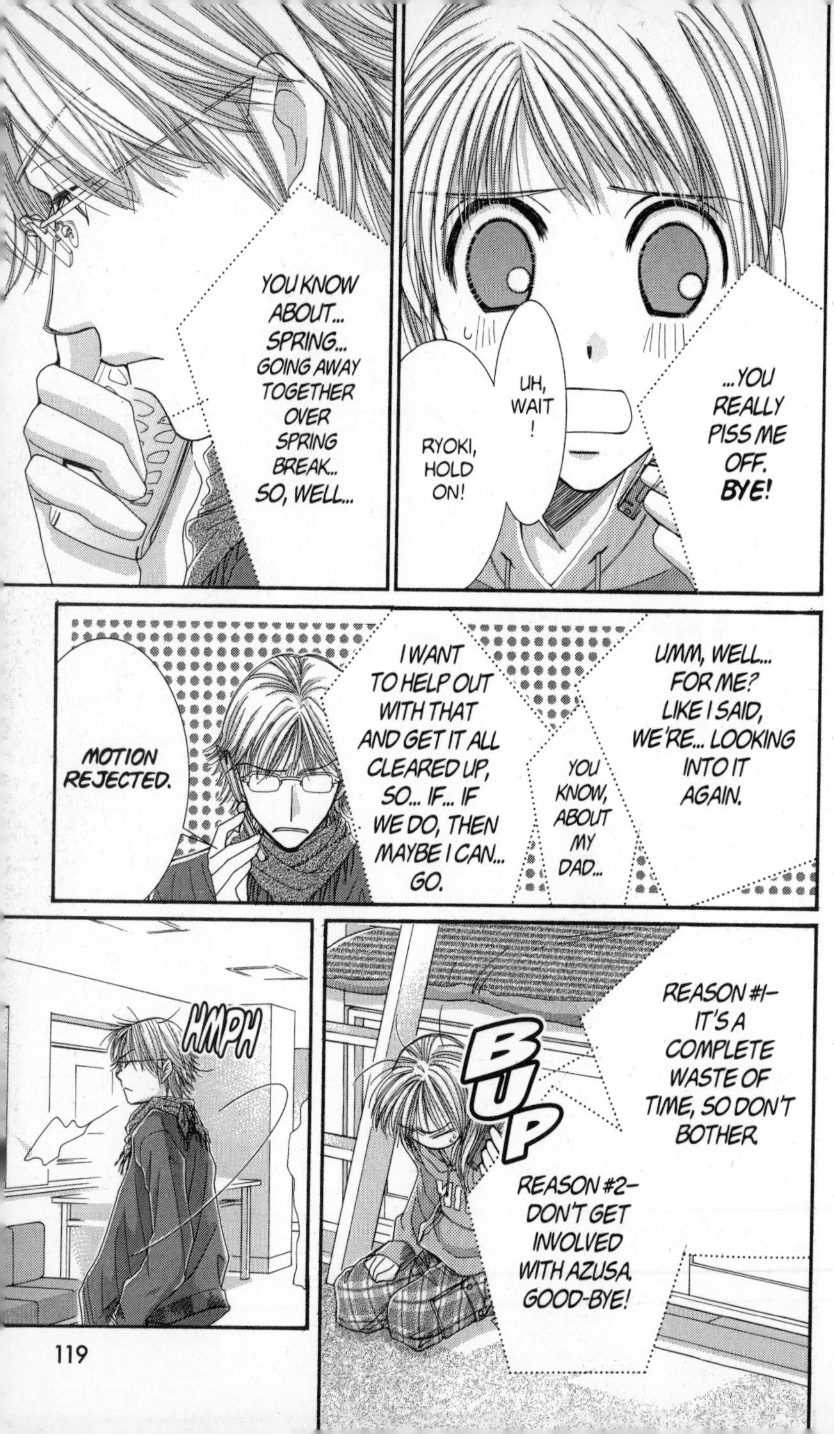
...YOU REALLY PISS ME OFF. BYE!
UH, WAIT!
RYOKI, HOLD ON!
YOU KNOW ABOUT... SPRING... GOING AWAY TOGETHER OVER SPRING BREAK... SO, WELL...
UMM, WELL... FOR ME? LIKE I SAID, WE'RE... LOOKING INTO IT AGAIN.
YOU KNOW, ABOUT MY DAD...
I WANT TO HELP OUT WITH THAT AND GET IT ALL CLEARED UP, SO... IF... IF WE DO, THEN MAYBE I CAN... GO.
MOTION REJECTED.
REASON #1— IT'S A COMPLETE WASTE OF TIME, SO DON'T BOTHER.
BUP
REASON #2— DON'T GET INVOLVED WITH AZUSA. GOOD-BYE!
HMPH

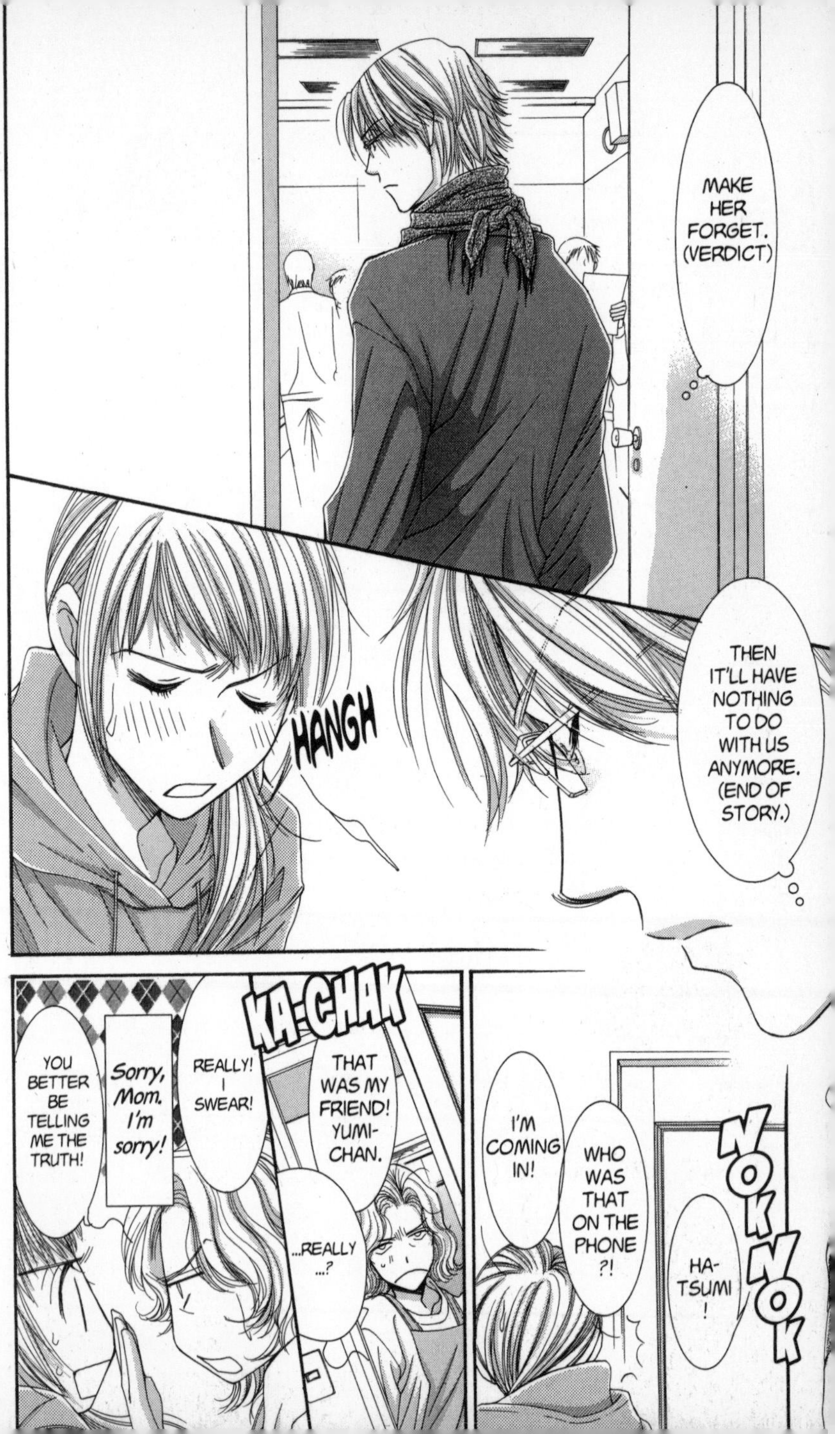
MAKE HER FORGET. (VERDICT)
THEN IT'LL HAVE NOTHING TO DO WITH US ANYMORE. (END OF STORY.)
HANGH
NOKNOK
HA-TSUMI!
WHO WAS THAT ON THE PHONE?!
I'M COMING IN!
KA-CHAK
THAT WAS MY FRIEND! YUMI-CHAN.
...REALLY...?
REALLY! I SWEAR!
Sorry, Mom. I'm sorry!
YOU BETTER BE TELLING ME THE TRUTH!

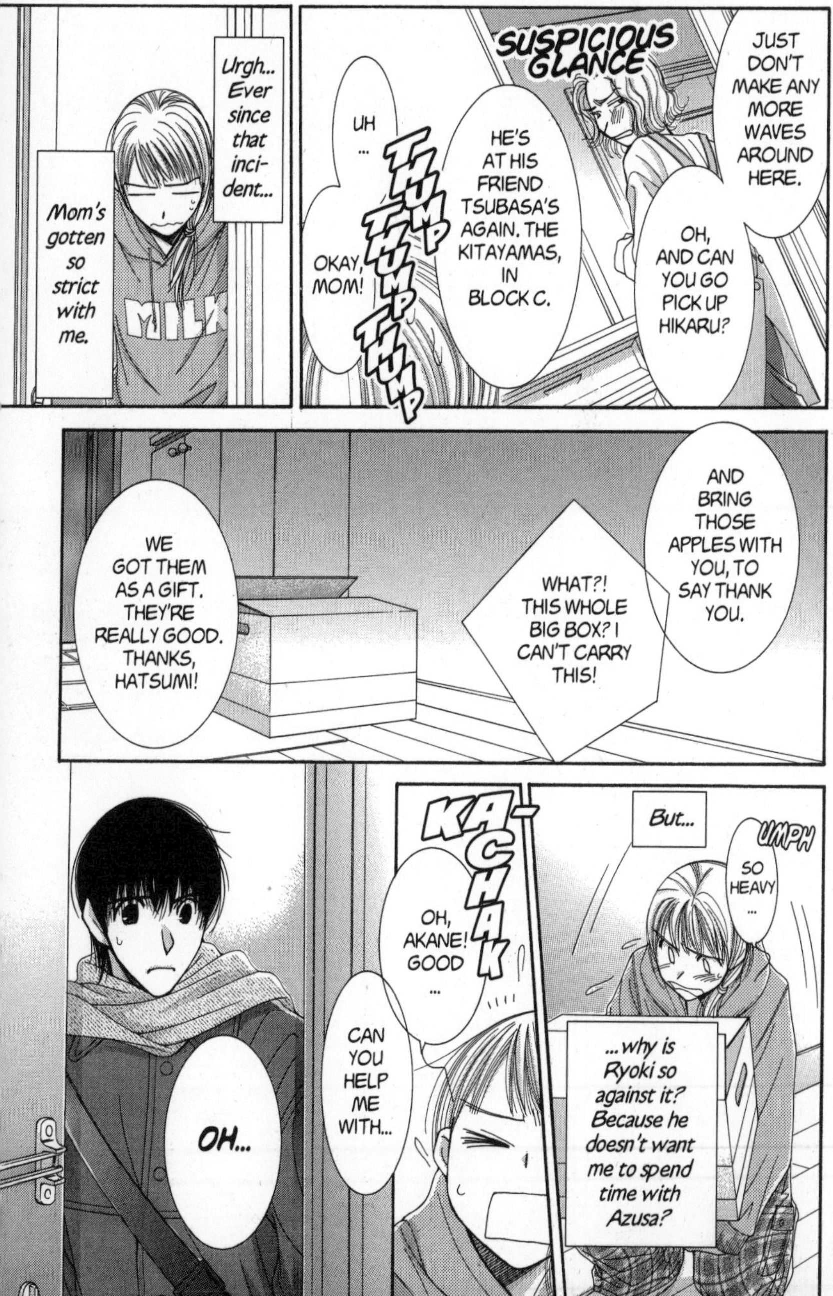
JUST DON'T MAKE ANY MORE WAVES AROUND HERE.
SUSPICIOUS GLANCE
OH, AND CAN YOU GO PICK UP HIKARU?
HE'S AT HIS FRIEND TSUBASA'S AGAIN. THE KITAYAMAS, IN BLOCK C.
UH ...
THUMP THUMP THUMP THUMP
OKAY, MOM!
Urgh... Ever since that incident...
Mom's gotten so strict with me.
AND BRING THOSE APPLES WITH YOU, TO SAY THANK YOU.
WHAT?! THIS WHOLE BIG BOX? I CAN'T CARRY THIS!
WE GOT THEM AS A GIFT. THEY'RE REALLY GOOD. THANKS, HATSUMI!
UMPH
SO HEAVY ...
But...
...why is Ryoki so against it? Because he doesn't want me to spend time with Azusa?
KA-CHAK
OH, AKANE! GOOD ...
CAN YOU HELP ME WITH...
OH...

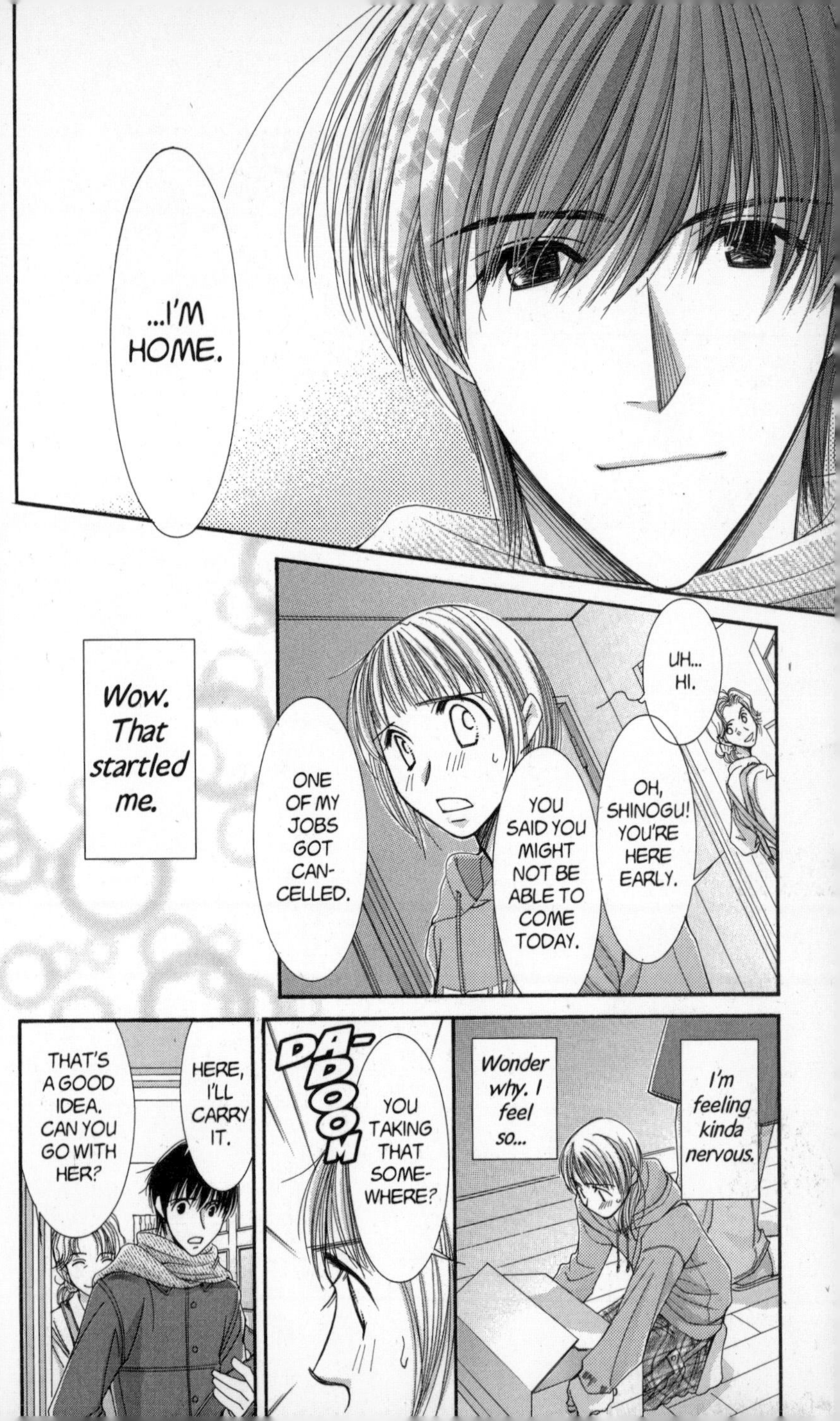
...I'M HOME.
UH... HI.
OH, SHINOGU! YOU'RE HERE EARLY.
YOU SAID YOU MIGHT NOT BE ABLE TO COME TODAY.
ONE OF MY JOBS GOT CAN-CELLED.
Wow. That startled me.
I'm feeling kinda nervous.
Wonder why. I feel so...
DA-DOOM
YOU TAKING THAT SOME-WHERE?
HERE, I'LL CARRY IT.
THAT'S A GOOD IDEA. CAN YOU GO WITH HER?

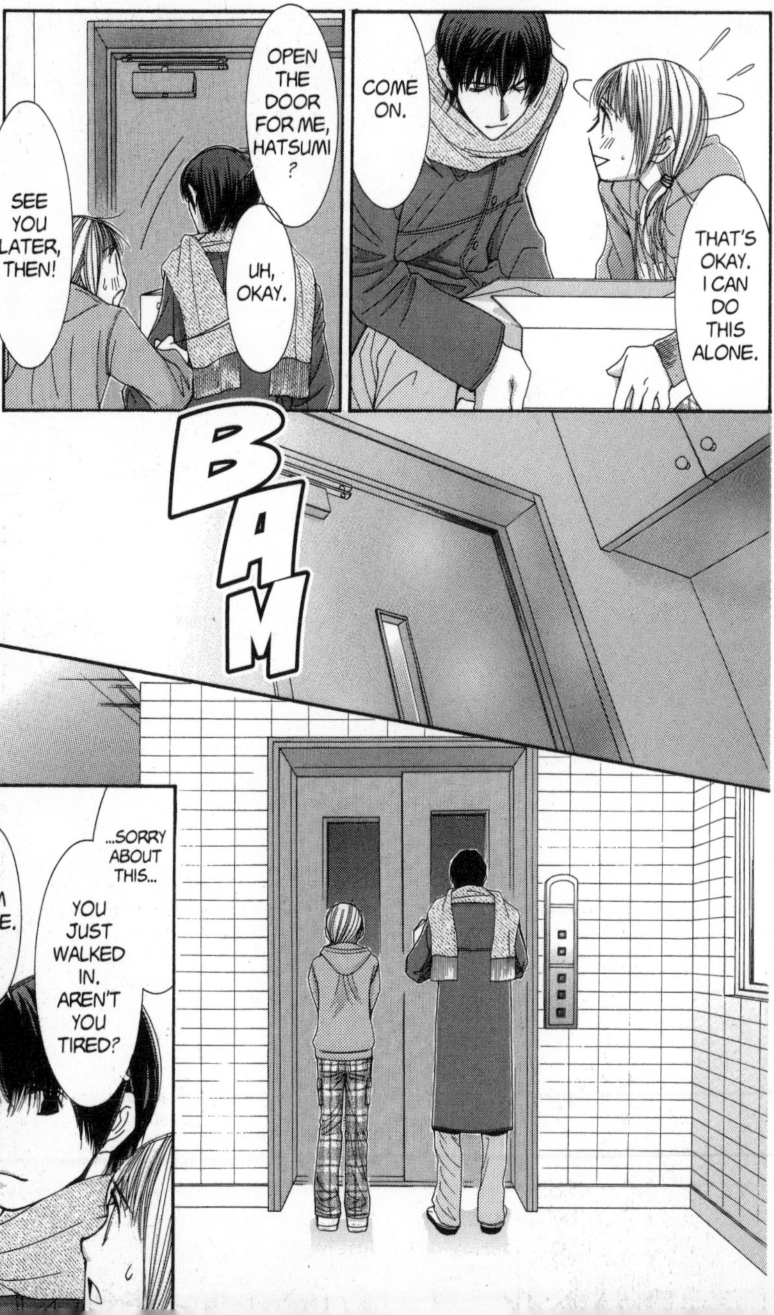
THAT'S OKAY. I CAN DO THIS ALONE.
COME ON.
OPEN THE DOOR FOR ME, HATSUMI?
UH, OKAY.
SEE YOU LATER, THEN!
BAM
...SORRY ABOUT THIS...
YOU JUST WALKED IN. AREN'T YOU TIRED?
I'M FINE.

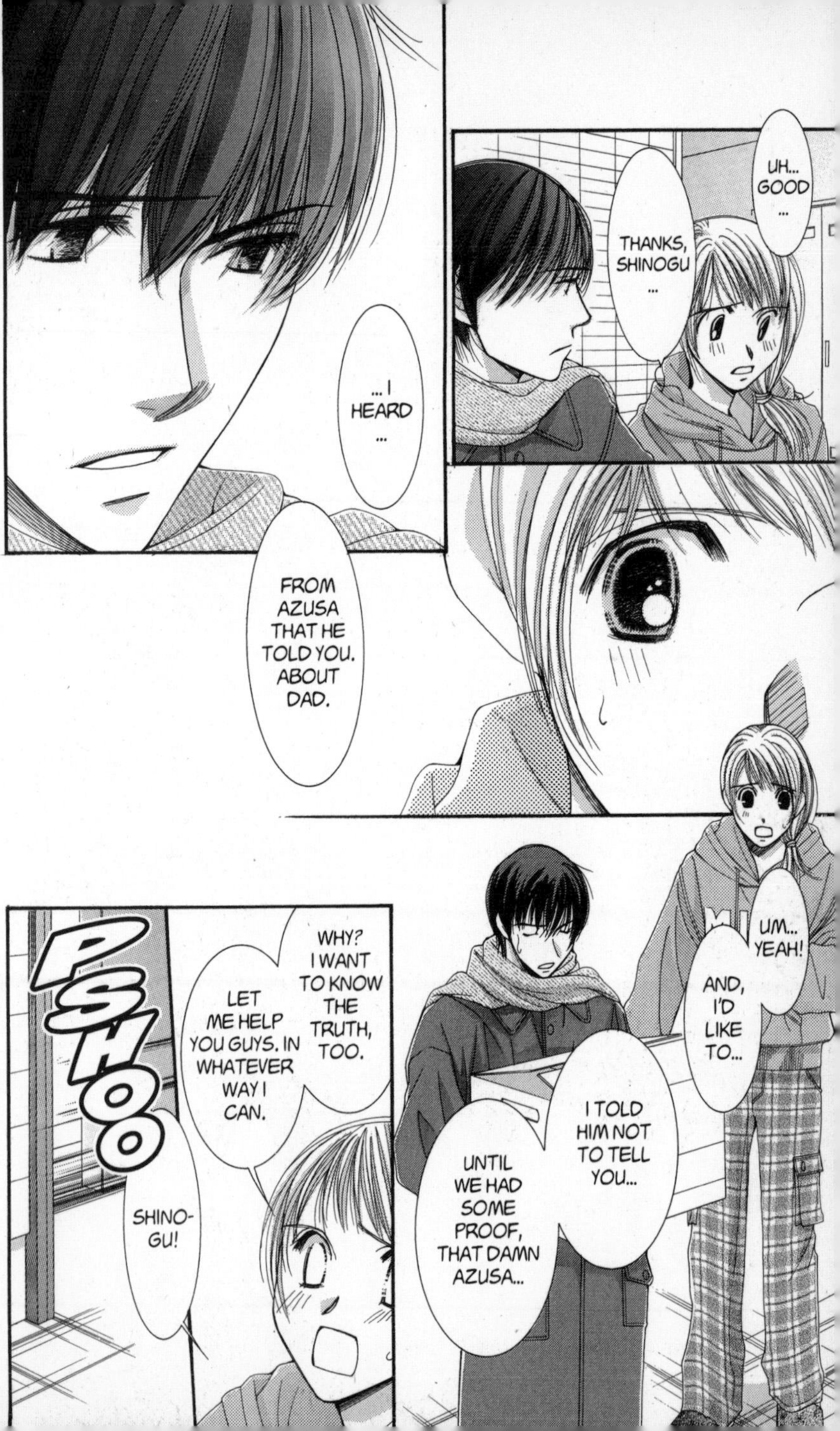
UH... GOOD...
THANKS, SHINOGU...
...I HEARD...
FROM AZUSA THAT HE TOLD YOU. ABOUT DAD.
UM... YEAH!
AND, I'D LIKE TO...
I TOLD HIM NOT TO TELL YOU...
UNTIL WE HAD SOME PROOF, THAT DAMN AZUSA...
PSHOO
WHY? I WANT TO KNOW THE TRUTH, TOO.
LET ME HELP YOU GUYS. IN WHATEVER WAY I CAN.
SHINO-GU!

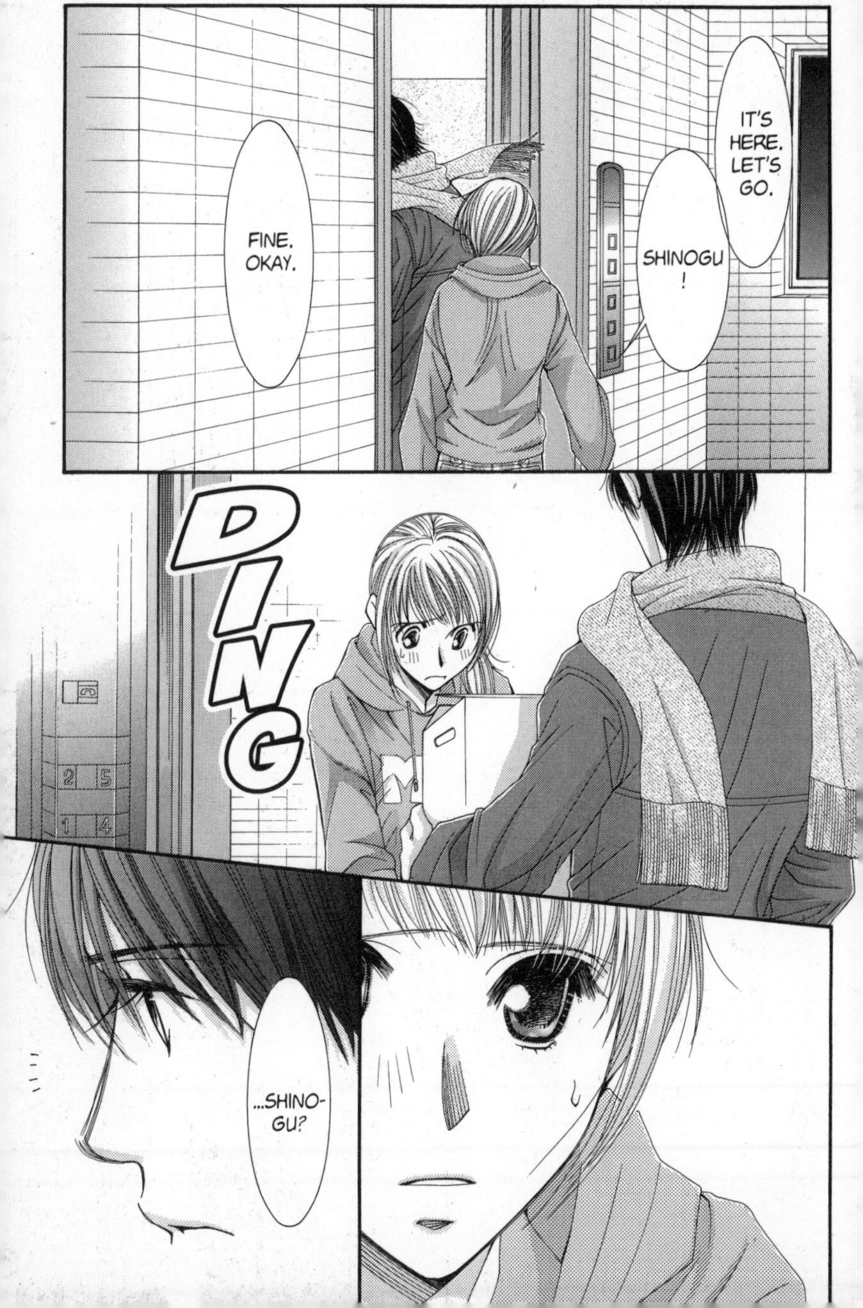

IT'S HERE. LET'S GO.
SHINOGU!
FINE. OKAY.
DING
...SHINO-GU?

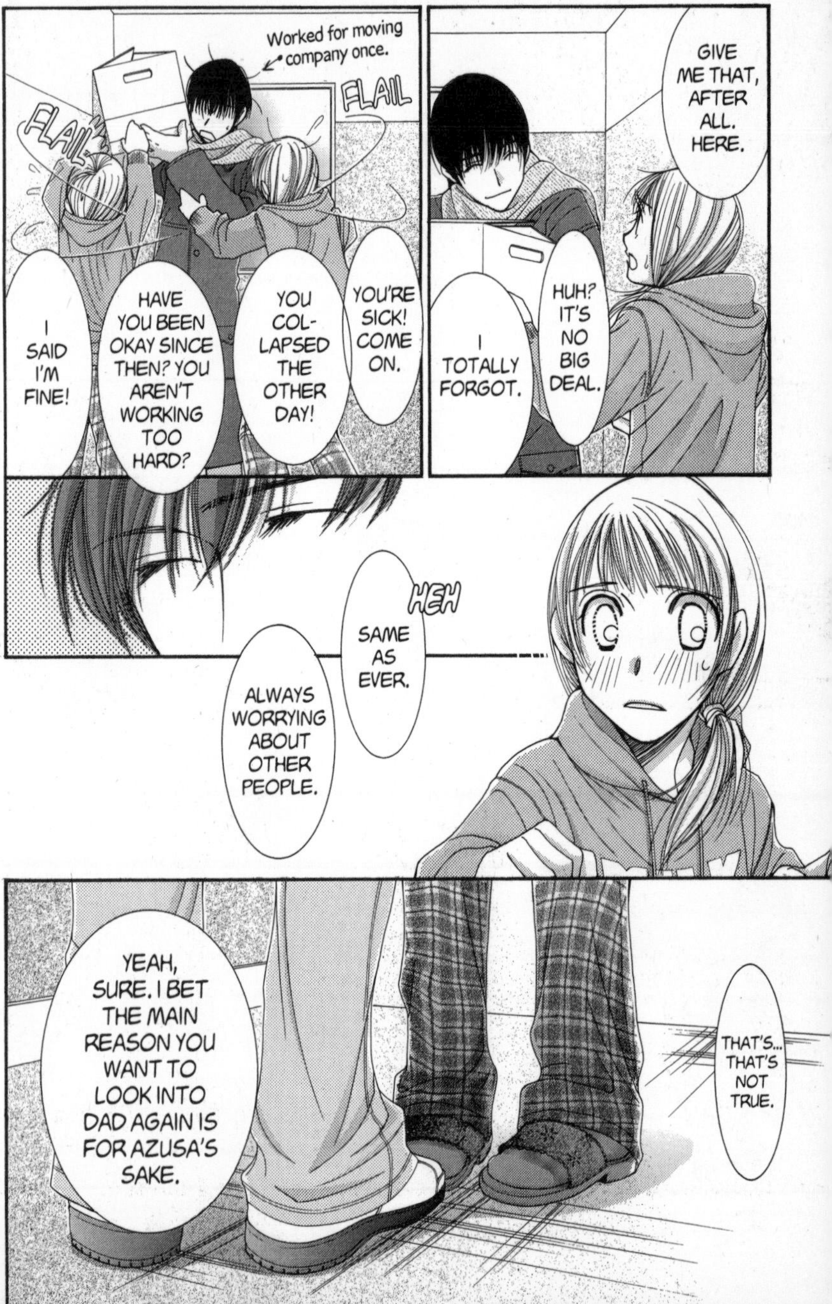
GIVE ME THAT, AFTER ALL. HERE.
HUH? IT'S NO BIG DEAL.
I TOTALLY FORGOT.
FLAIL
Worked for moving company once.
FLAIL
YOU'RE SICK! COME ON.
YOU COL-LAPSED THE OTHER DAY!
HAVE YOU BEEN OKAY SINCE THEN? YOU AREN'T WORKING TOO HARD?
I SAID I'M FINE!
HEH
SAME AS EVER.
ALWAYS WORRYING ABOUT OTHER PEOPLE.
THAT'S... THAT'S NOT TRUE.
YEAH, SURE. I BET THE MAIN REASON YOU WANT TO LOOK INTO DAD AGAIN IS FOR AZUSA'S SAKE.

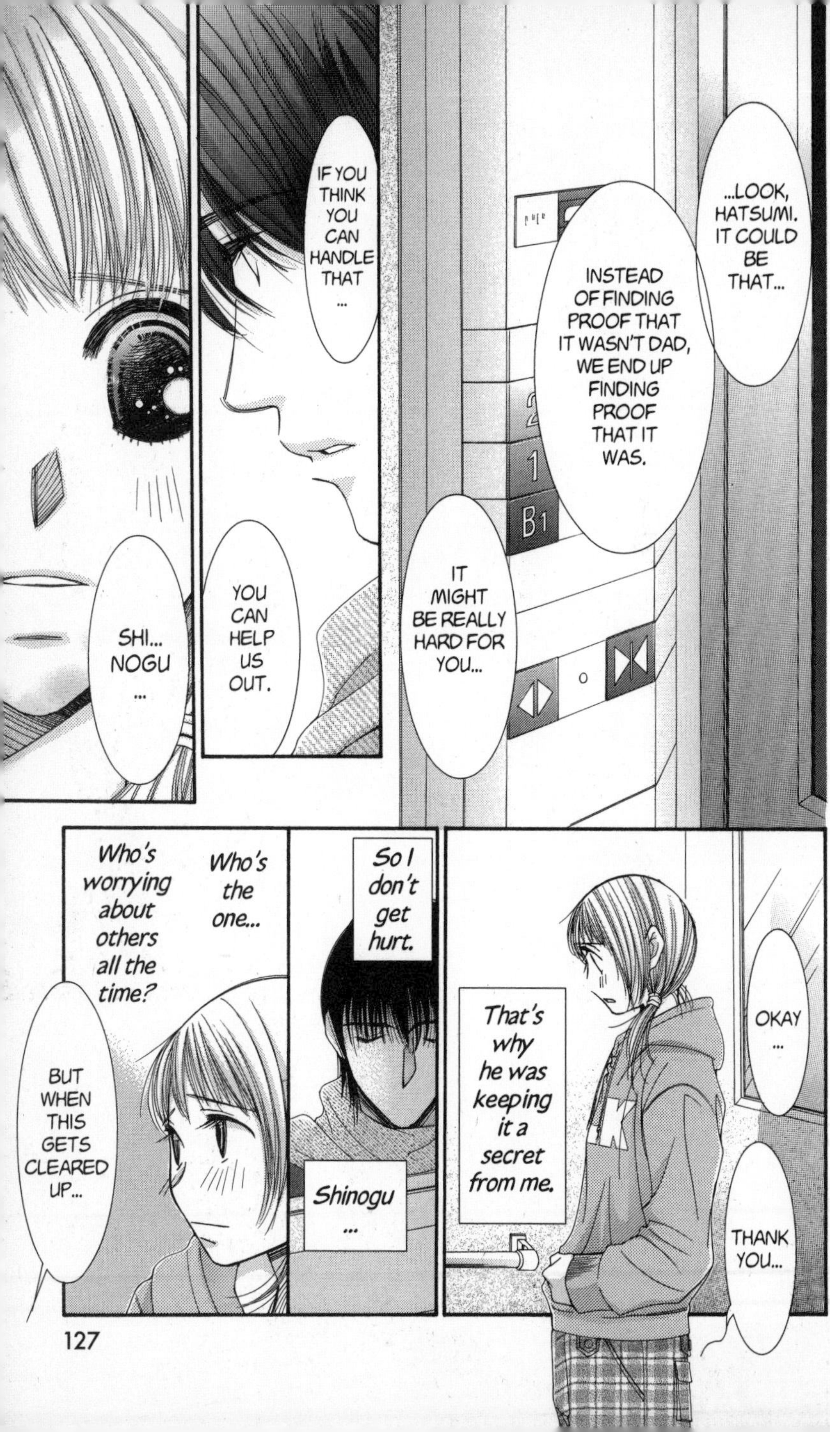
...LOOK, HATSUMI. IT COULD BE THAT...
INSTEAD OF FINDING PROOF THAT IT WASN'T DAD, WE END UP FINDING PROOF THAT IT WAS.
IT MIGHT BE REALLY HARD FOR YOU...
IF YOU THINK YOU CAN HANDLE THAT ...
YOU CAN HELP US OUT.
SHI... NOGU ...
OKAY ...
That's why he was keeping it a secret from me.
THANK YOU...
So I don't get hurt.
Shinogu ...
Who's the one...
Who's worrying about others all the time?
BUT WHEN THIS GETS CLEARED UP...

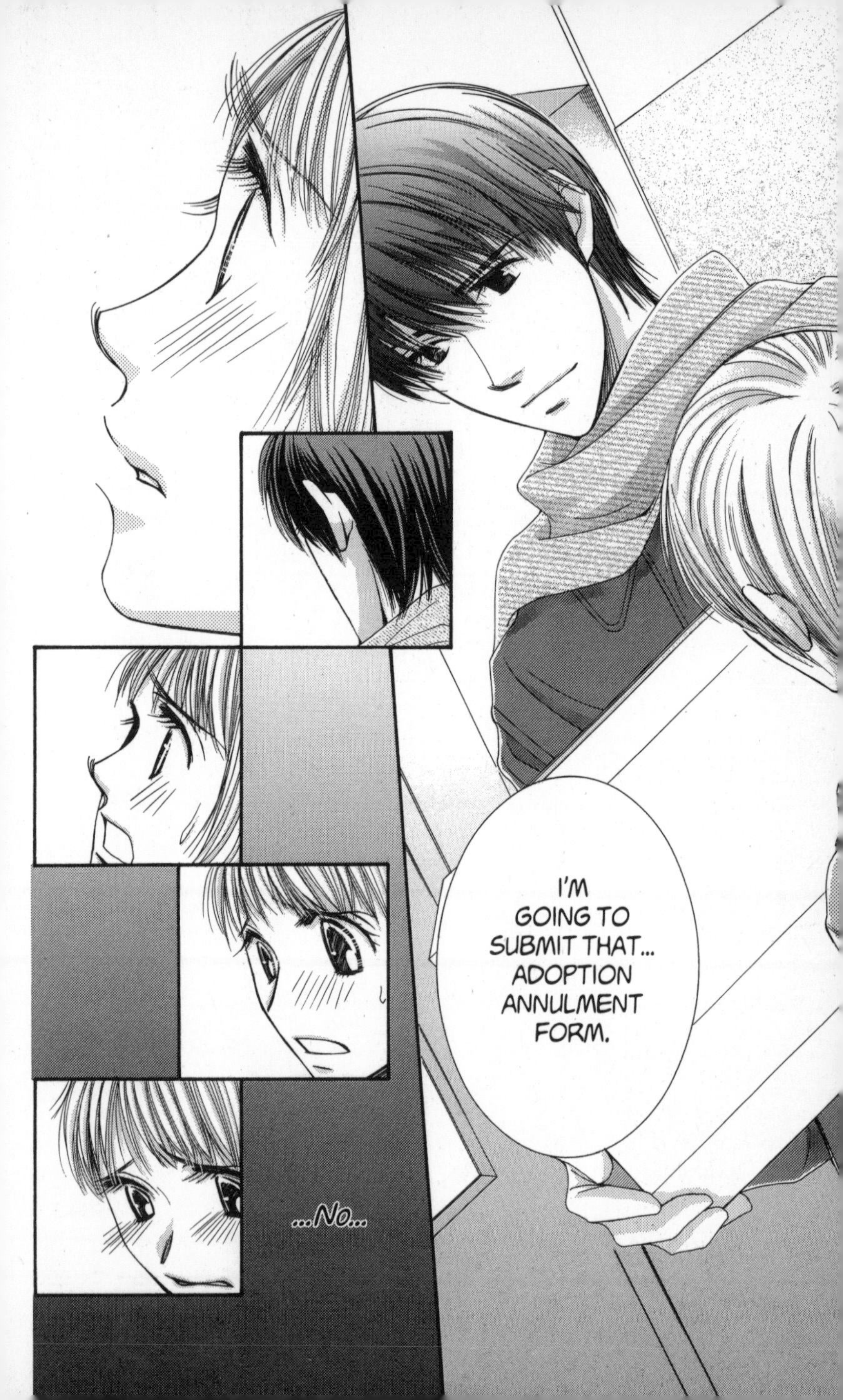
I'M GOING TO SUBMIT THAT... ADOPTION ANNULMENT FORM.
...No...

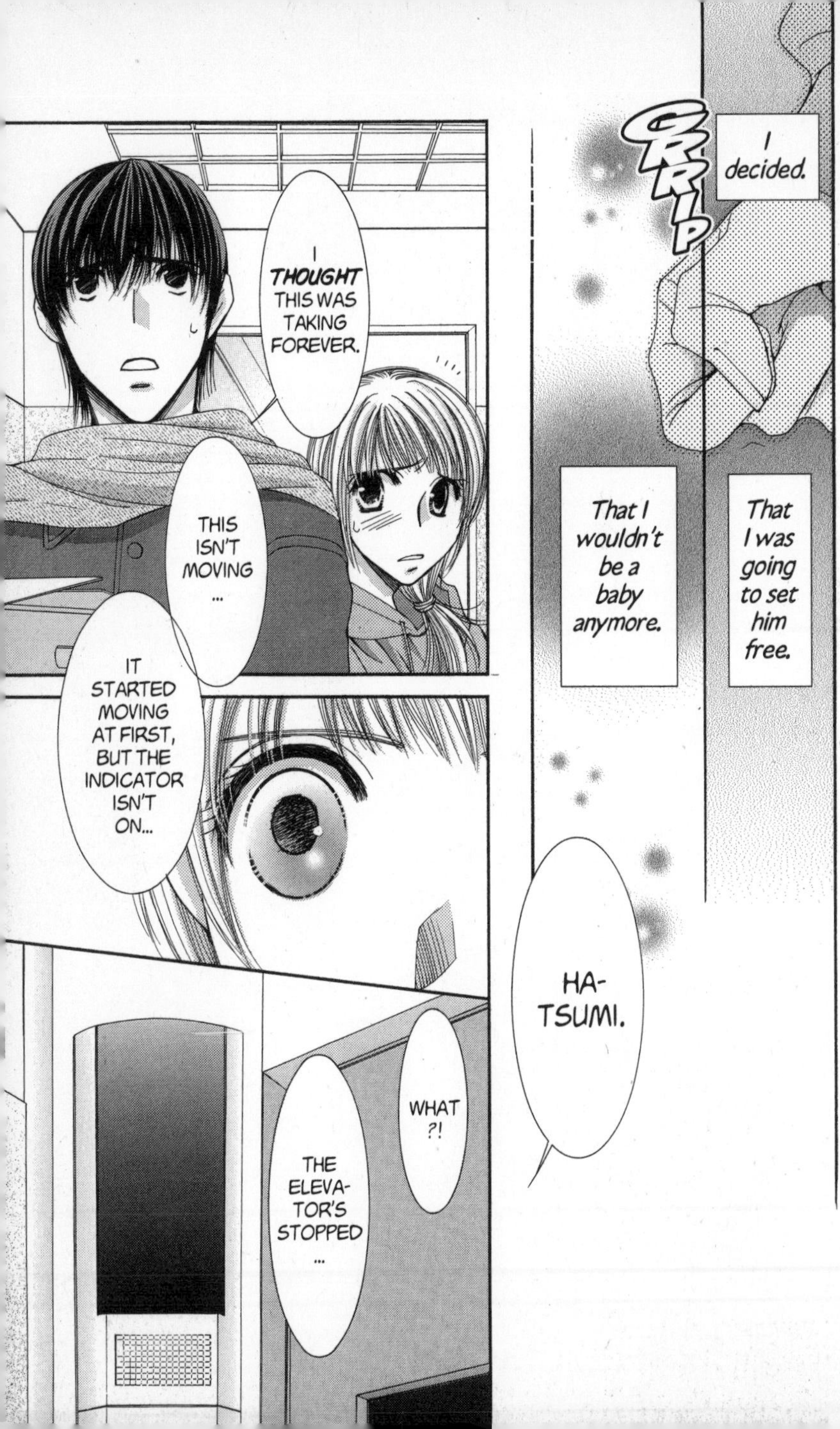
I decided.
GRIP
That I was going to set him free.
That I wouldn't be a baby anymore.
HA-TSUMI.
I *THOUGHT* THIS WAS TAKING FOREVER.
THIS ISN'T MOVING ...
IT STARTED MOVING AT FIRST, BUT THE INDICATOR ISN'T ON...
WHAT?!
THE ELEVA-TOR'S STOPPED ...

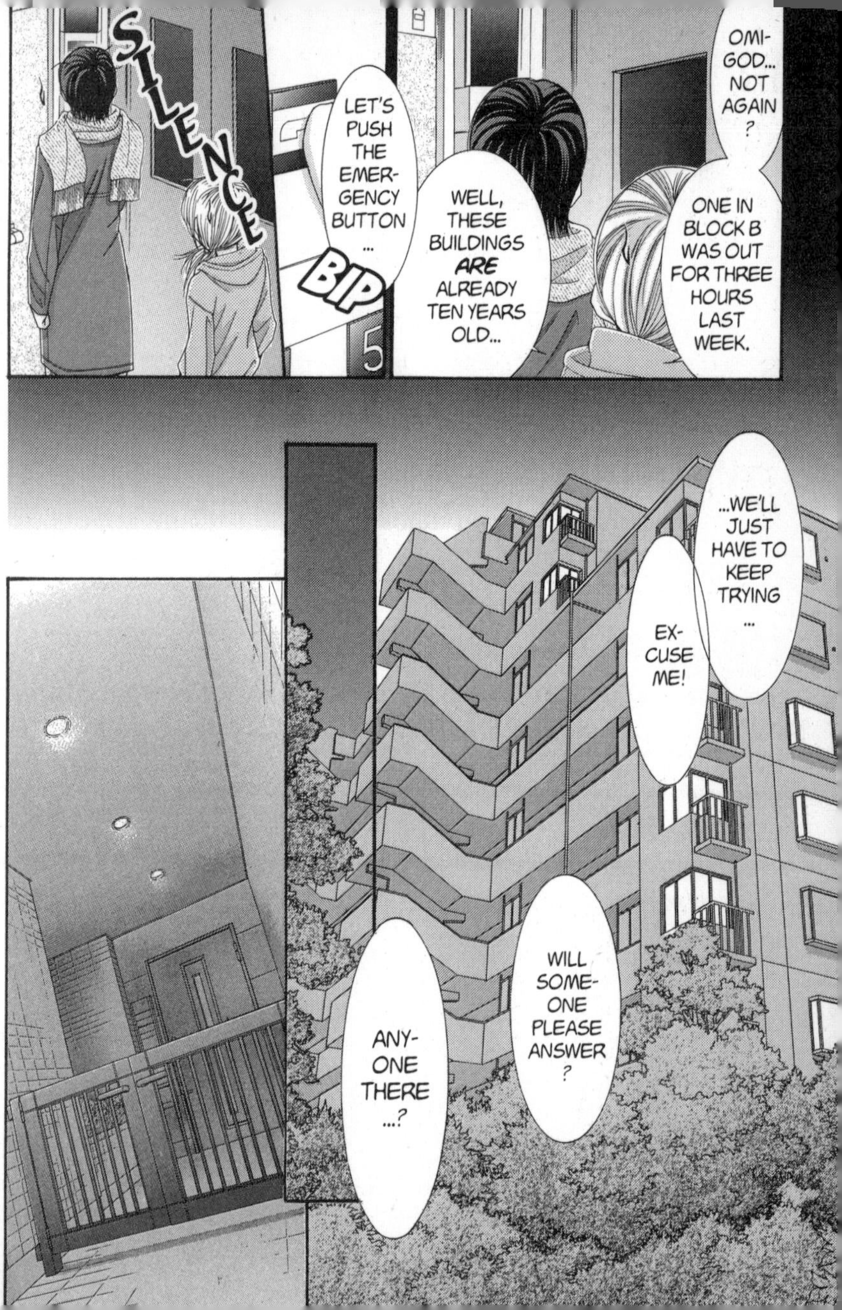
OMIGOD... NOT AGAIN?
ONE IN BLOCK B WAS OUT FOR THREE HOURS LAST WEEK.
WELL, THESE BUILDINGS ARE ALREADY TEN YEARS OLD...
LET'S PUSH THE EMERGENCY BUTTON...
BIP
SILENCE
...WE'LL JUST HAVE TO KEEP TRYING...
EXCUSE ME!
WILL SOMEONE PLEASE ANSWER?
ANYONE THERE...?

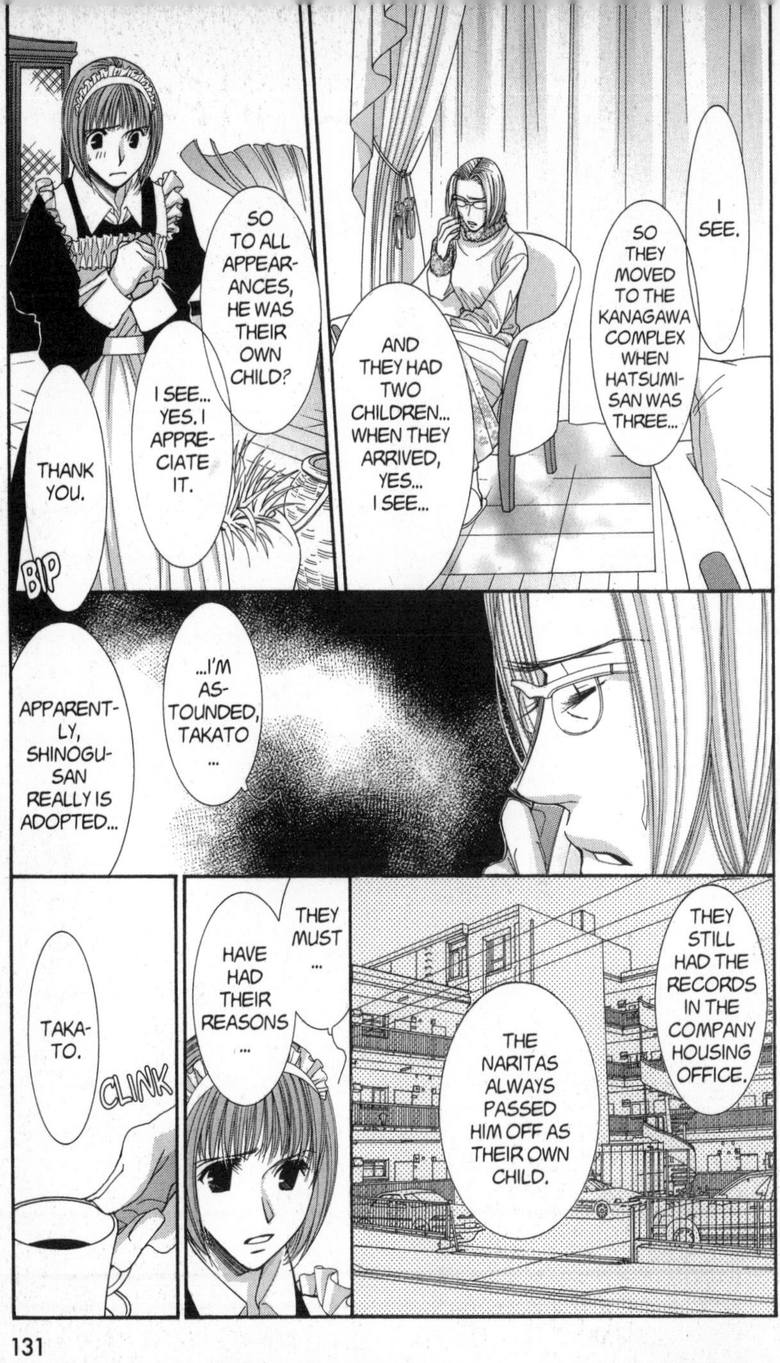
I SEE.
SO THEY MOVED TO THE KANAGAWA COMPLEX WHEN HATSUMI-SAN WAS THREE...
AND THEY HAD TWO CHILDREN... WHEN THEY ARRIVED, YES... I SEE...
SO TO ALL APPEARANCES, HE WAS THEIR OWN CHILD?
I SEE... YES. I APPRECIATE IT.
THANK YOU.
BIP
...I'M ASTOUNDED, TAKATO...
APPARENTLY, SHINOGU-SAN REALLY IS ADOPTED...
THEY STILL HAD THE RECORDS IN THE COMPANY HOUSING OFFICE.
THE NARITAS ALWAYS PASSED HIM OFF AS THEIR OWN CHILD.
THEY MUST...
HAVE HAD THEIR REASONS...
TAKA-TO.
CLINK

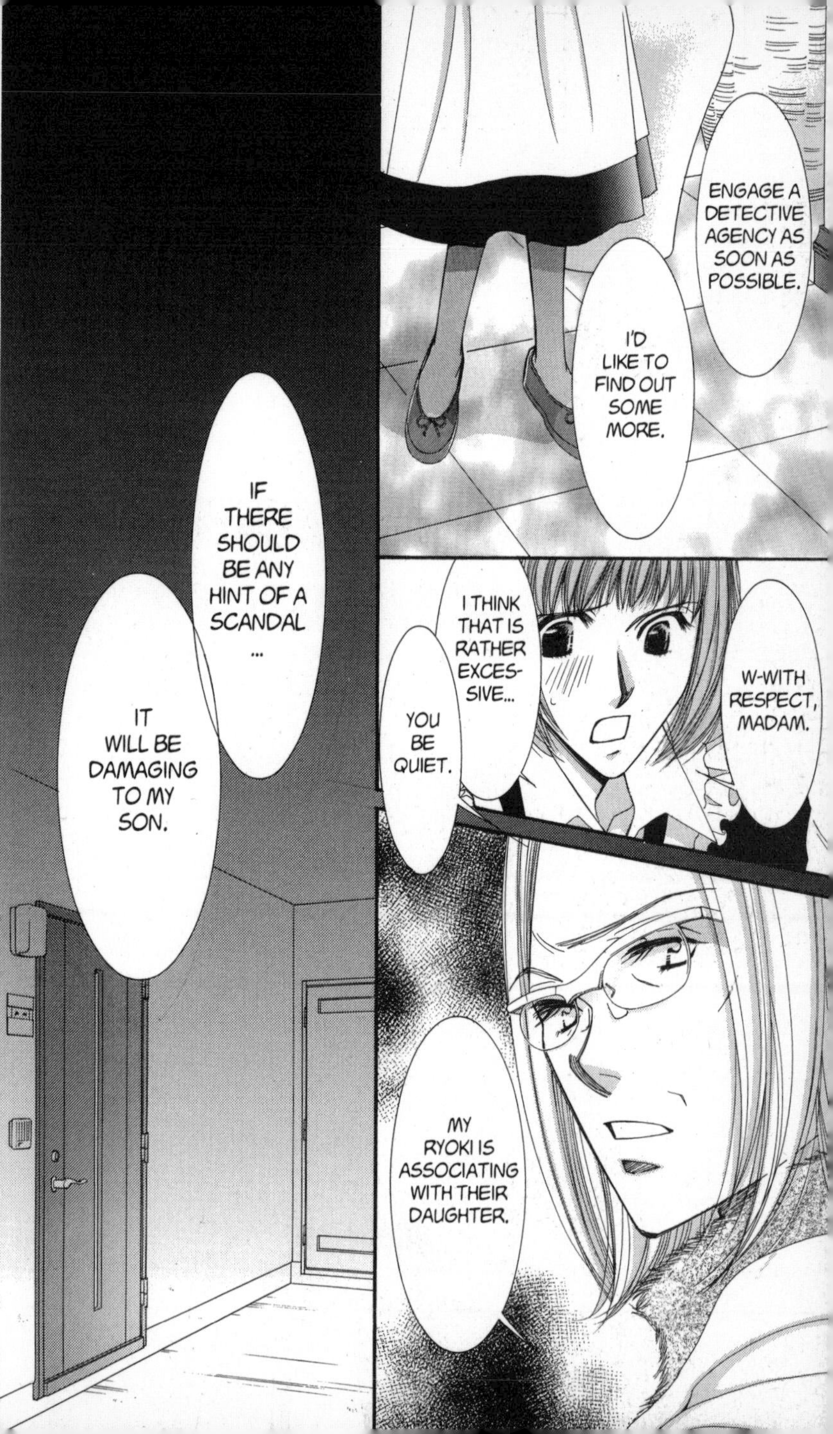
ENGAGE A DETECTIVE AGENCY AS SOON AS POSSIBLE.
I'D LIKE TO FIND OUT SOME MORE.
W-WITH RESPECT, MADAM.
I THINK THAT IS RATHER EXCES-SIVE...
YOU BE QUIET.
MY RYOKI IS ASSOCIATING WITH THEIR DAUGHTER.
IF THERE SHOULD BE ANY HINT OF A SCANDAL...
IT WILL BE DAMAGING TO MY SON.

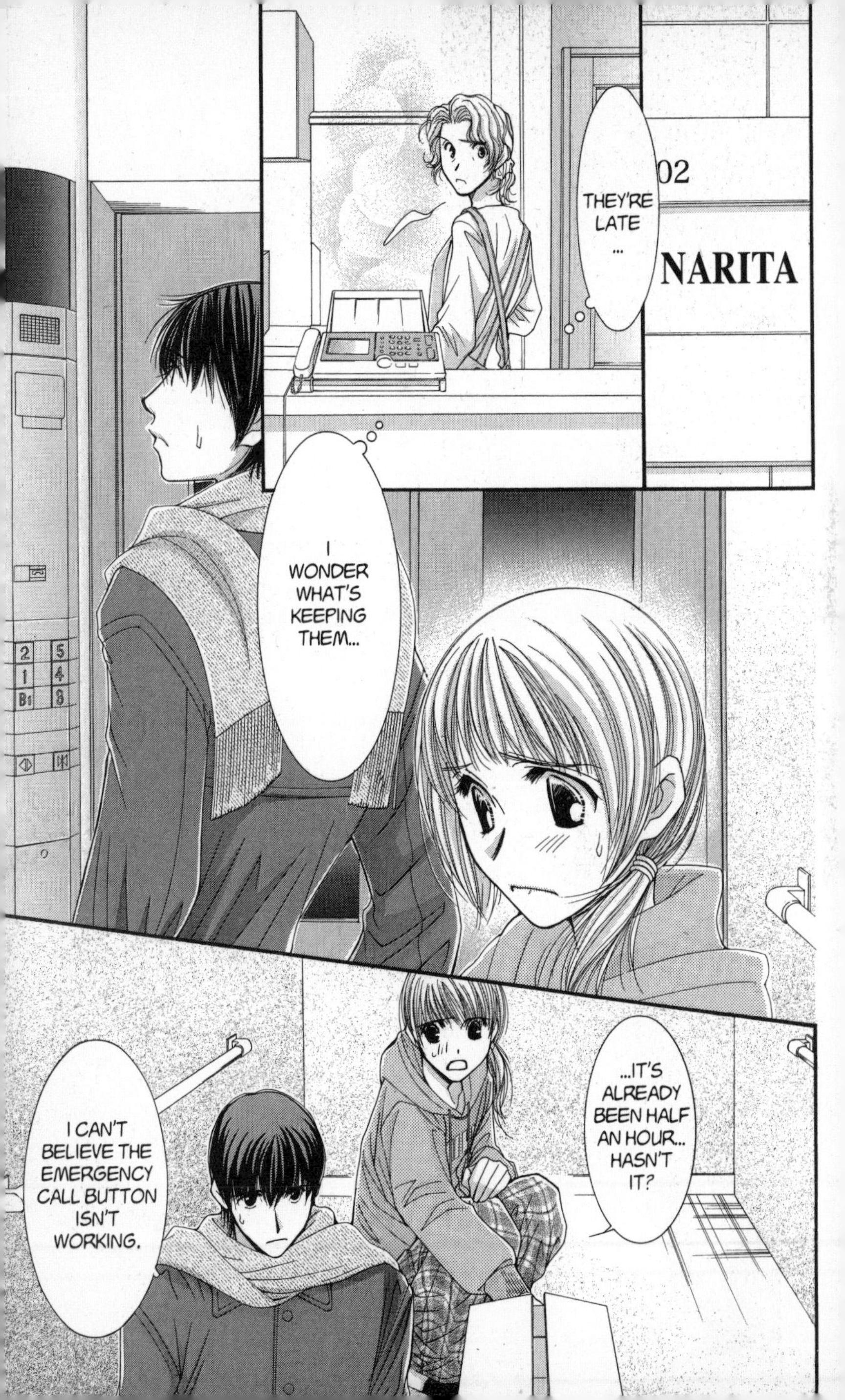
02
NARITA
THEY'RE LATE ...
I WONDER WHAT'S KEEPING THEM...
...IT'S ALREADY BEEN HALF AN HOUR... HASN'T IT?
I CAN'T BELIEVE THE EMERGENCY CALL BUTTON ISN'T WORKING.

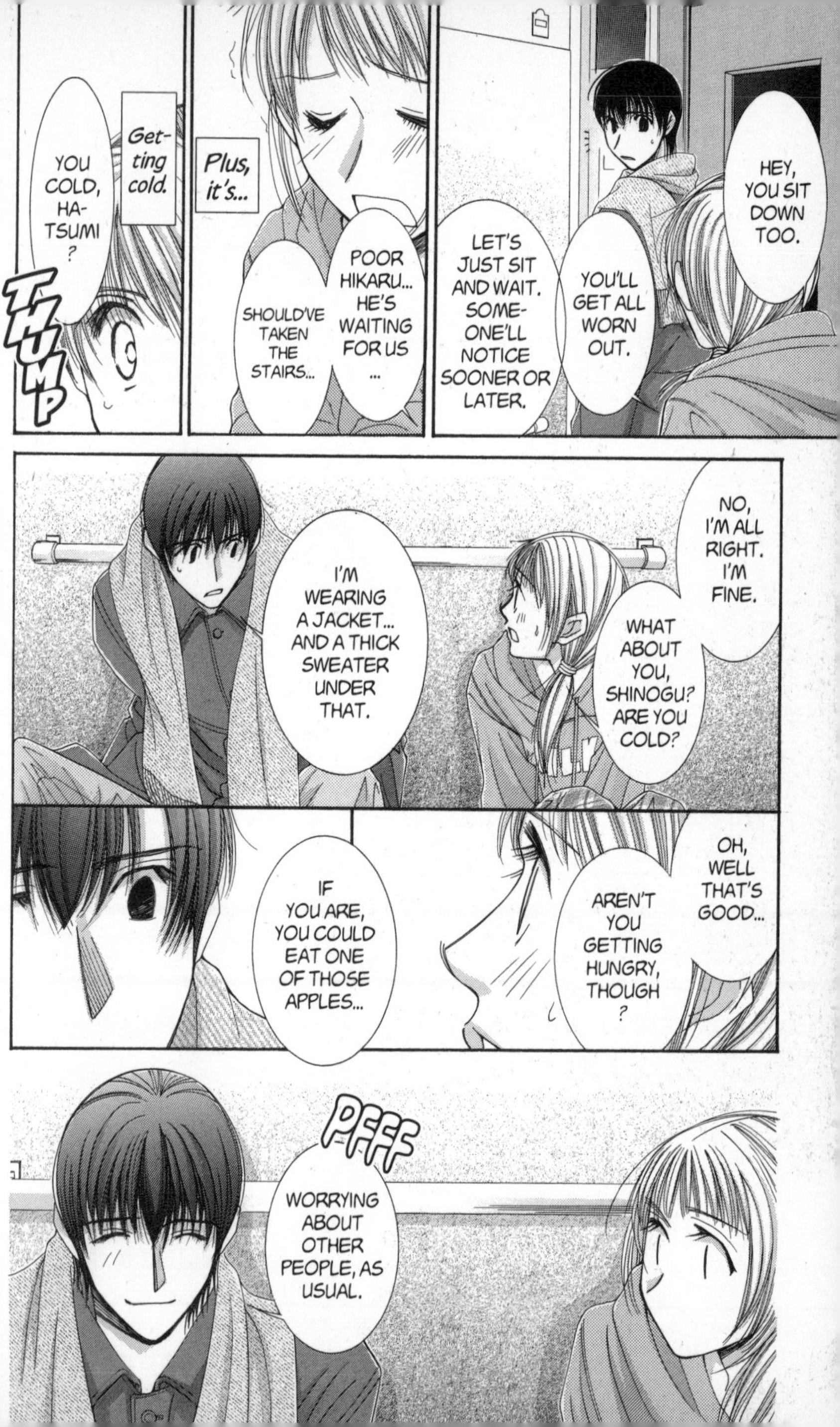
HEY, YOU SIT DOWN TOO.
YOU'LL GET ALL WORN OUT.
LET'S JUST SIT AND WAIT. SOME-ONE'LL NOTICE SOONER OR LATER.
POOR HIKARU... HE'S WAITING FOR US ...
SHOULD'VE TAKEN THE STAIRS...
Plus, it's...
Get-ting cold.
YOU COLD, HA-TSUMI ?
THUMP
NO, I'M ALL RIGHT. I'M FINE.
WHAT ABOUT YOU, SHINOGU? ARE YOU COLD?
I'M WEARING A JACKET... AND A THICK SWEATER UNDER THAT.
OH, WELL THAT'S GOOD...
AREN'T YOU GETTING HUNGRY, THOUGH ?
IF YOU ARE, YOU COULD EAT ONE OF THOSE APPLES...
PFFF
WORRYING ABOUT OTHER PEOPLE, AS USUAL.

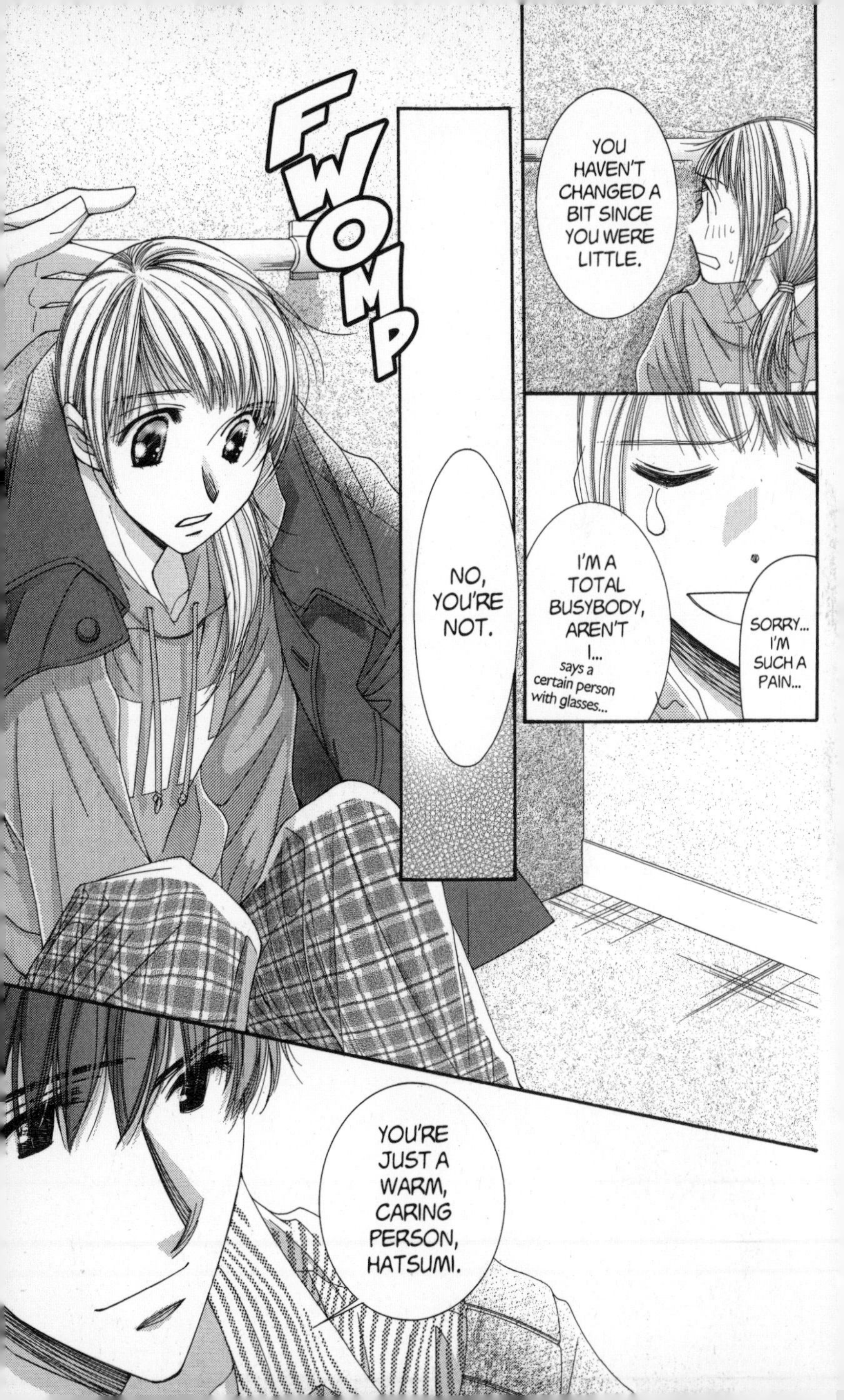
YOU HAVEN'T CHANGED A BIT SINCE YOU WERE LITTLE.
SORRY... I'M SUCH A PAIN...
I'M A TOTAL BUSYBODY, AREN'T I...
says a certain person with glasses...
FWOMP
NO, YOU'RE NOT.
YOU'RE JUST A WARM, CARING PERSON, HATSUMI.

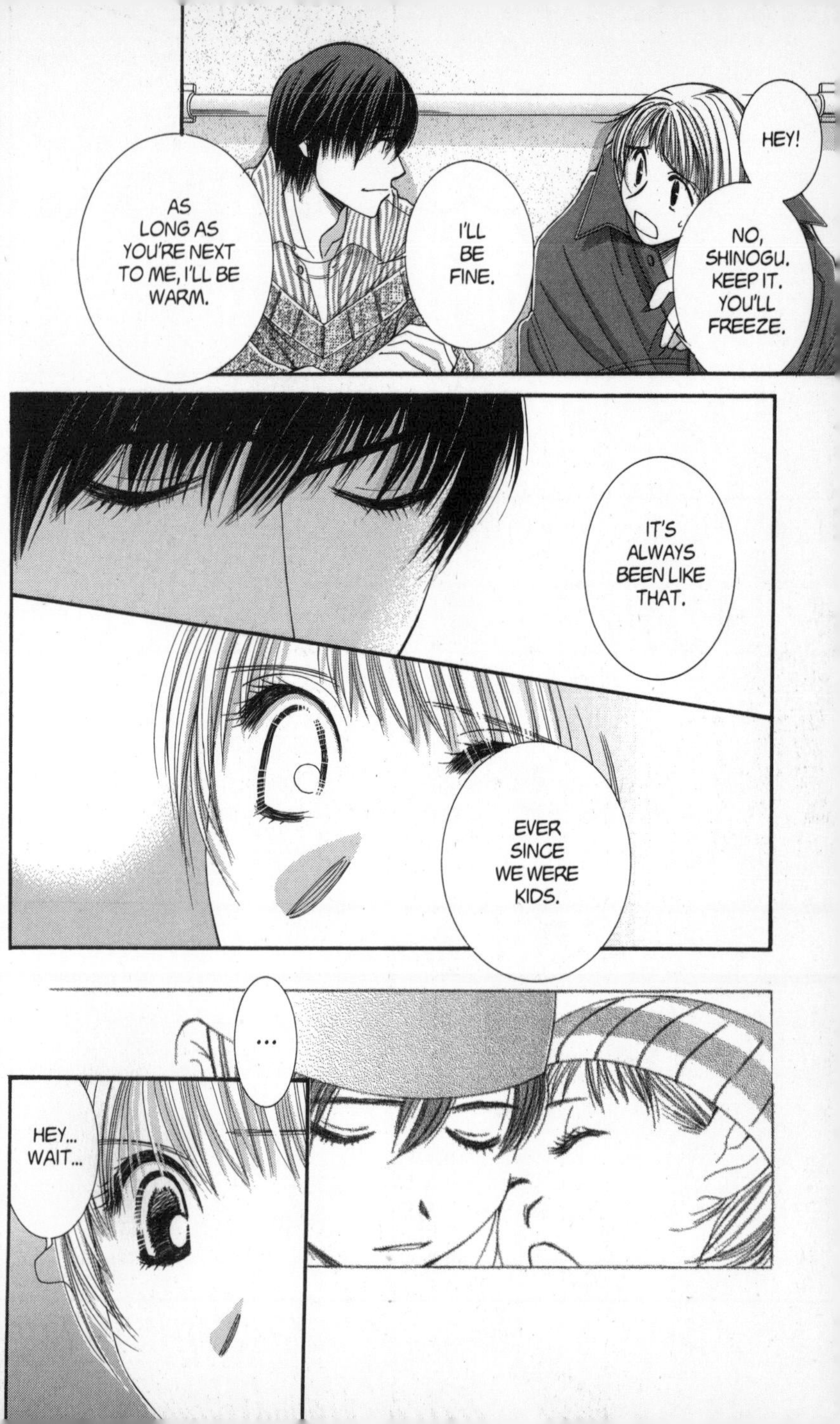
HEY!
NO, SHINOGU. KEEP IT. YOU'LL FREEZE.
I'LL BE FINE.
AS LONG AS YOU'RE NEXT TO ME, I'LL BE WARM.
IT'S ALWAYS BEEN LIKE THAT.
EVER SINCE WE WERE KIDS.
...
HEY... WAIT...

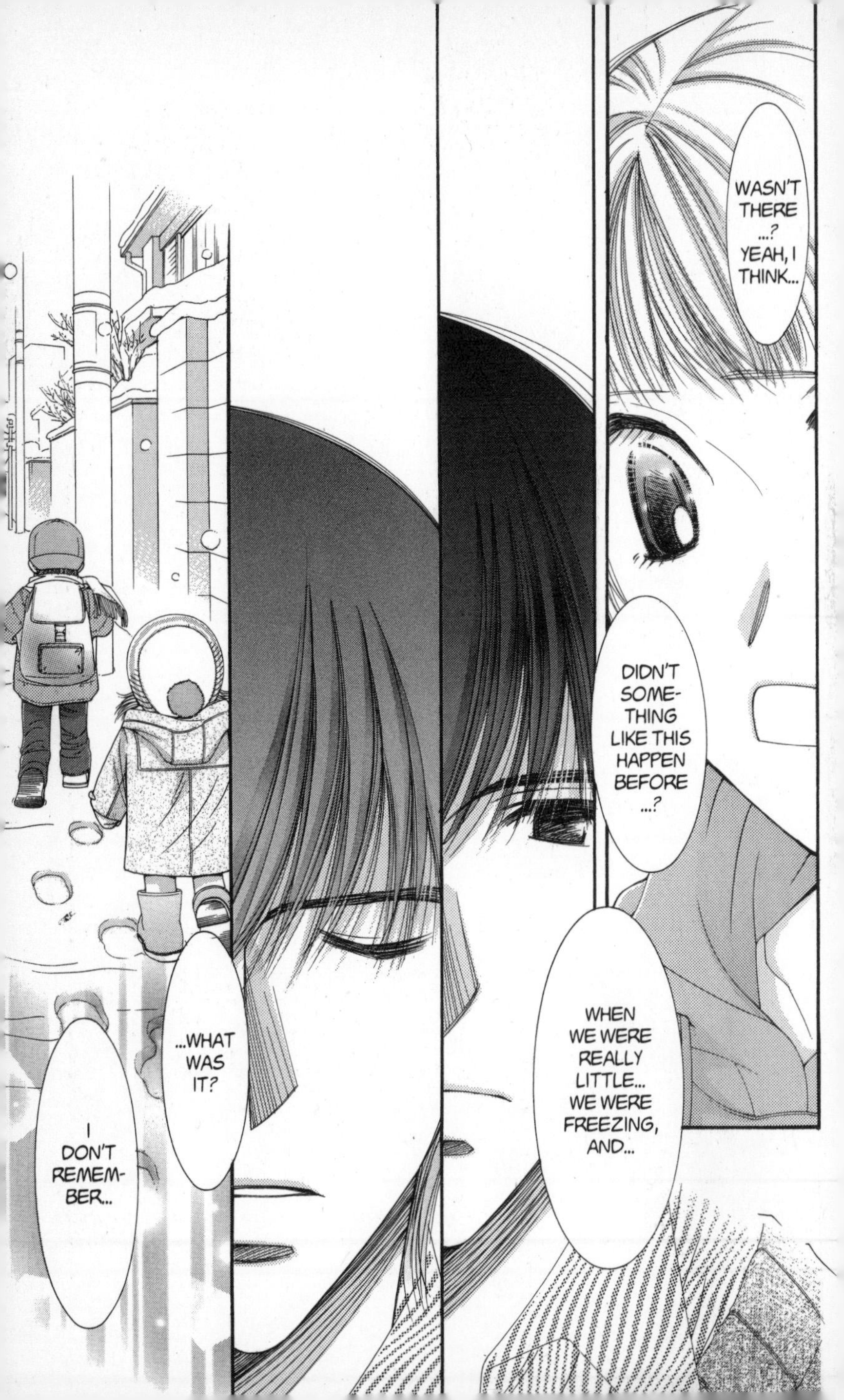
WASN'T THERE ...? YEAH, I THINK...
DIDN'T SOME-THING LIKE THIS HAPPEN BEFORE ...?
WHEN WE WERE REALLY LITTLE... WE WERE FREEZING, AND...
...WHAT WAS IT?
I DON'T REMEM-BER...

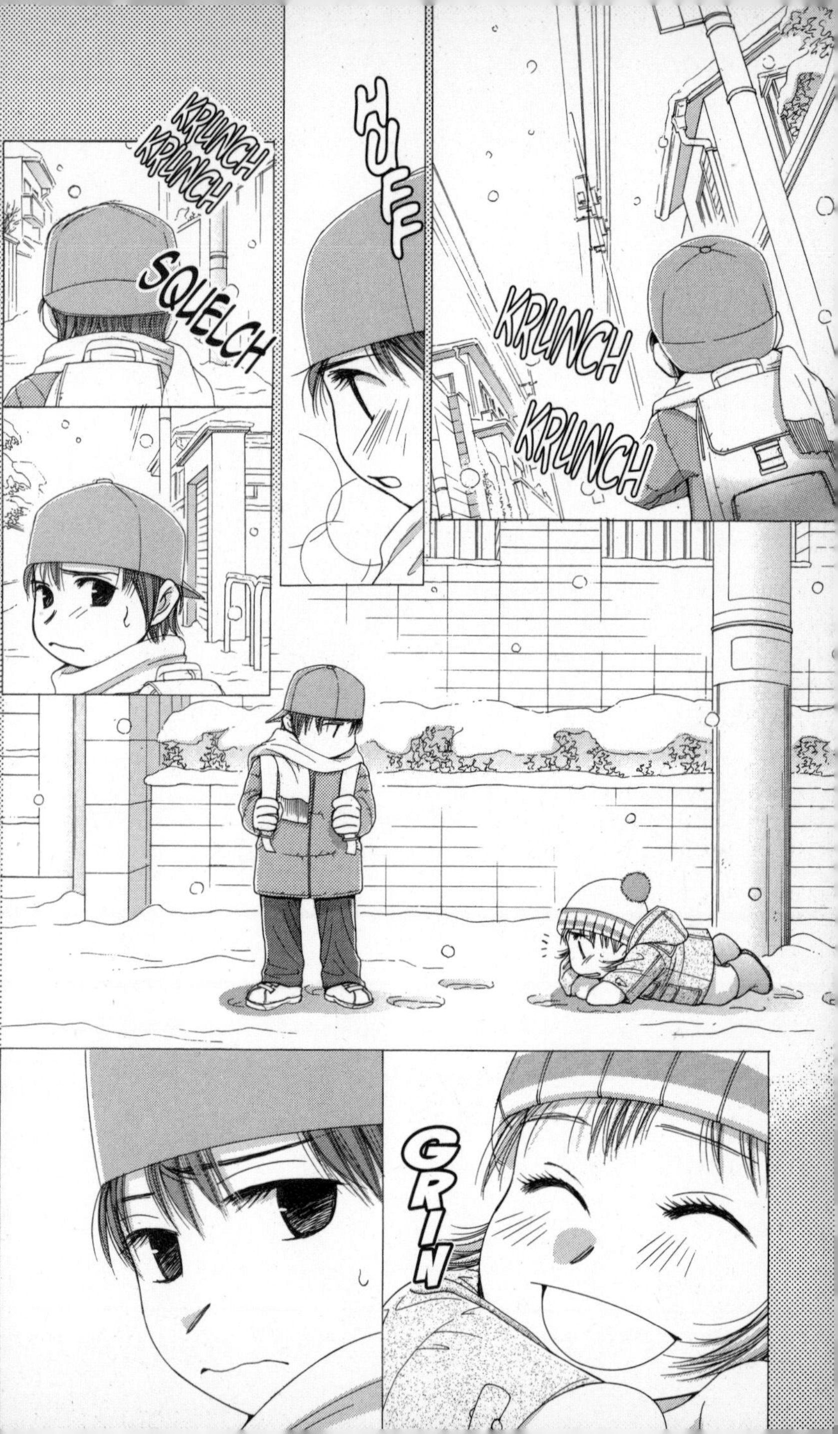
KRUNCH
KRUNCH
HUFF
KRUNCH
KRUNCH
SQUELCH
GRIN

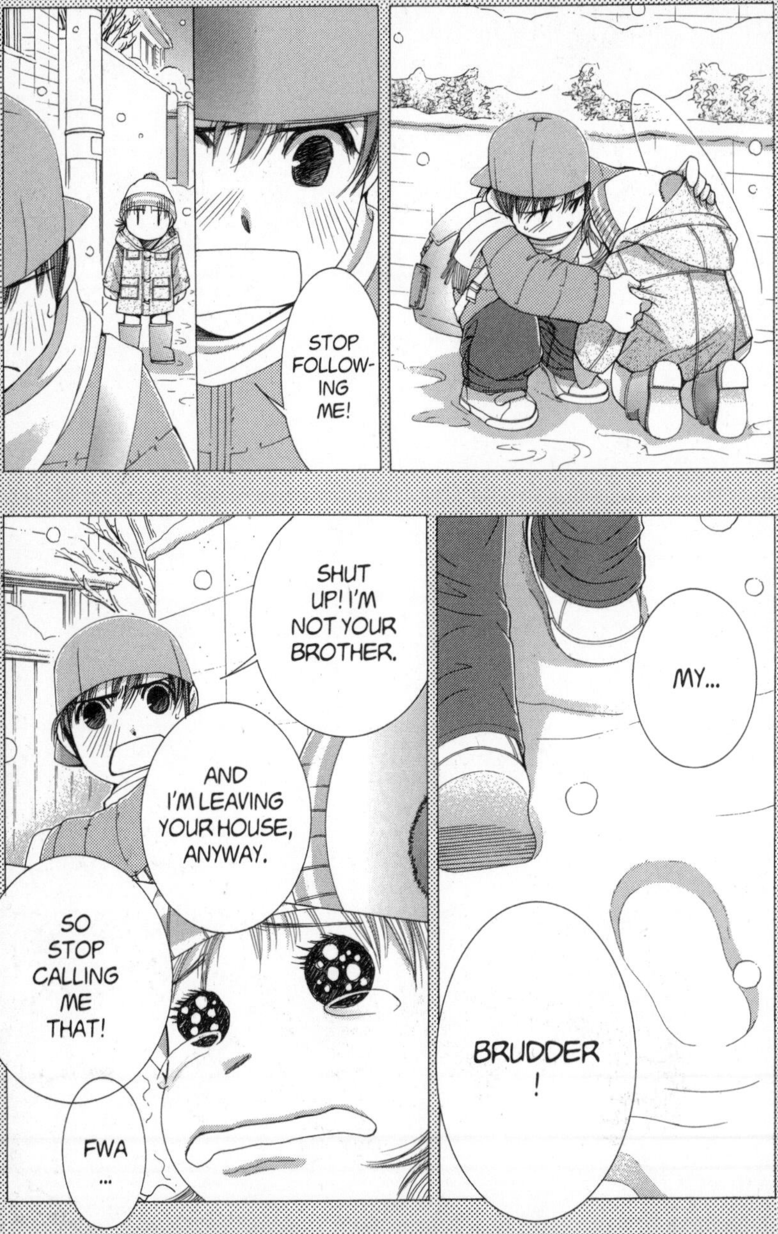
STOP FOLLOWING ME!
MY...
BRUDDER!
SHUT UP! I'M NOT YOUR BROTHER.
AND I'M LEAVING YOUR HOUSE, ANYWAY.
SO STOP CALLING ME THAT!
FWA...

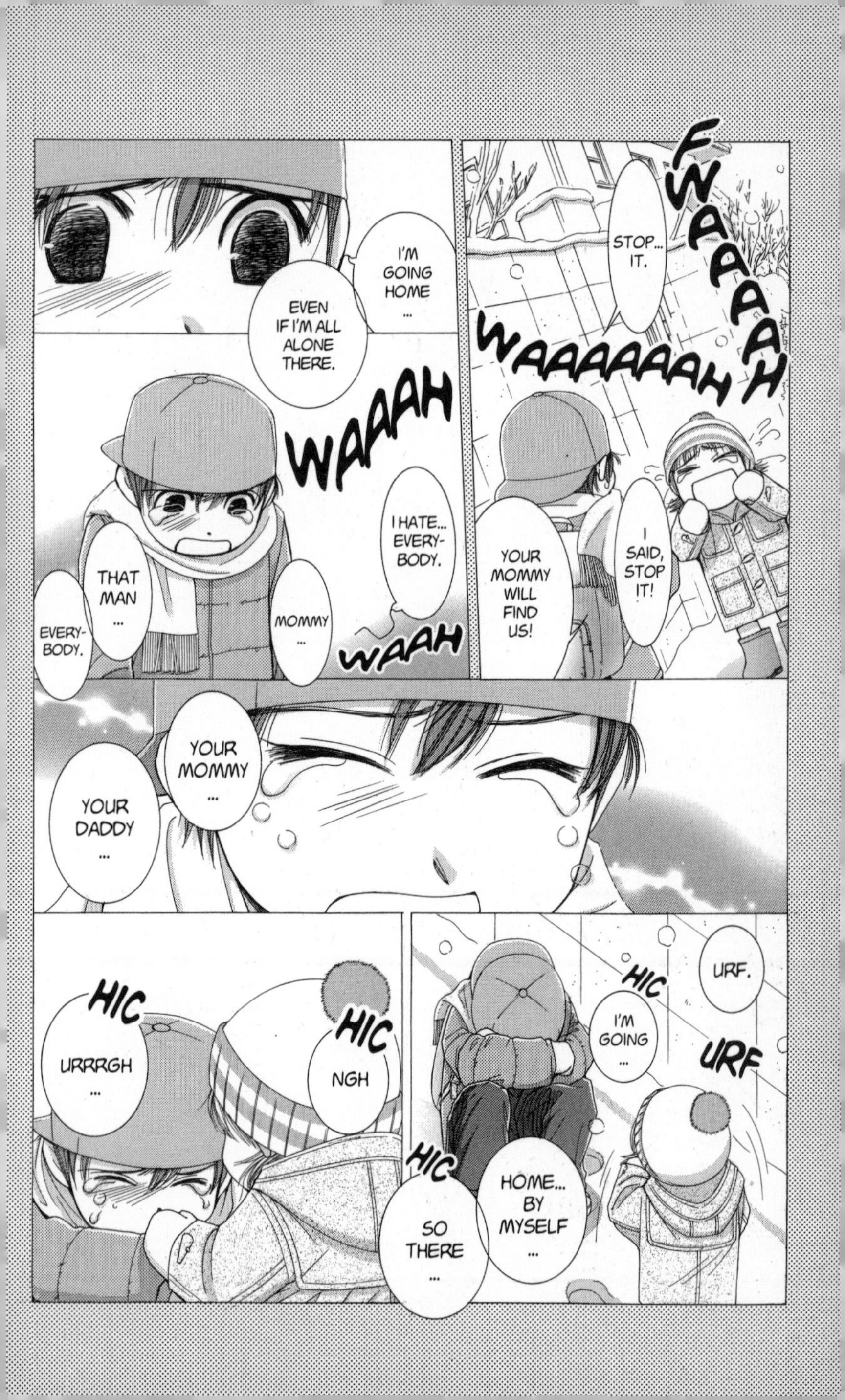
STOP... IT.
FWAAAAAH
WAAAAAAAH
I SAID, STOP IT!
YOUR MOMMY WILL FIND US!
I'M GOING HOME ...
EVEN IF I'M ALL ALONE THERE.
WAAAH
I HATE... EVERY-BODY.
MOMMY ...
THAT MAN ...
EVERY-BODY.
WAAH
YOUR MOMMY ...
YOUR DADDY ...
URF.
HIC
I'M GOING ...
URF
HOME... BY MYSELF ...
HIC
SO THERE ...
HIC
NGH
HIC
URRRGH ...

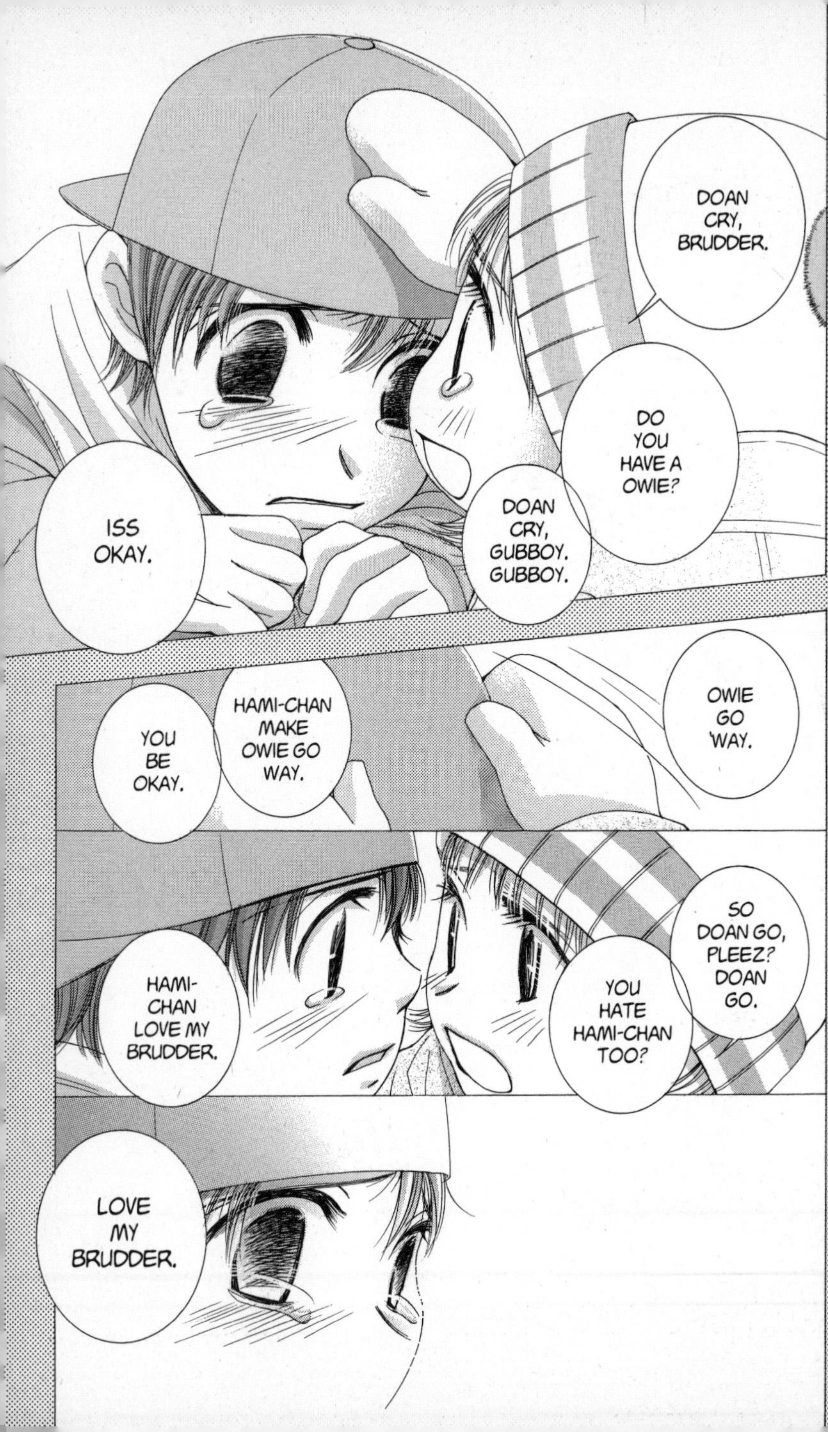
DOAN CRY, BRUDDER.
DO YOU HAVE A OWIE?
DOAN CRY, GUBBOY. GUBBOY.
ISS OKAY.
OWIE GO 'WAY.
HAMI-CHAN MAKE OWIE GO WAY.
YOU BE OKAY.
SO DOAN GO, PLEEZ? DOAN GO.
YOU HATE HAMI-CHAN TOO?
HAMI-CHAN LOVE MY BRUDDER.
LOVE MY BRUDDER.

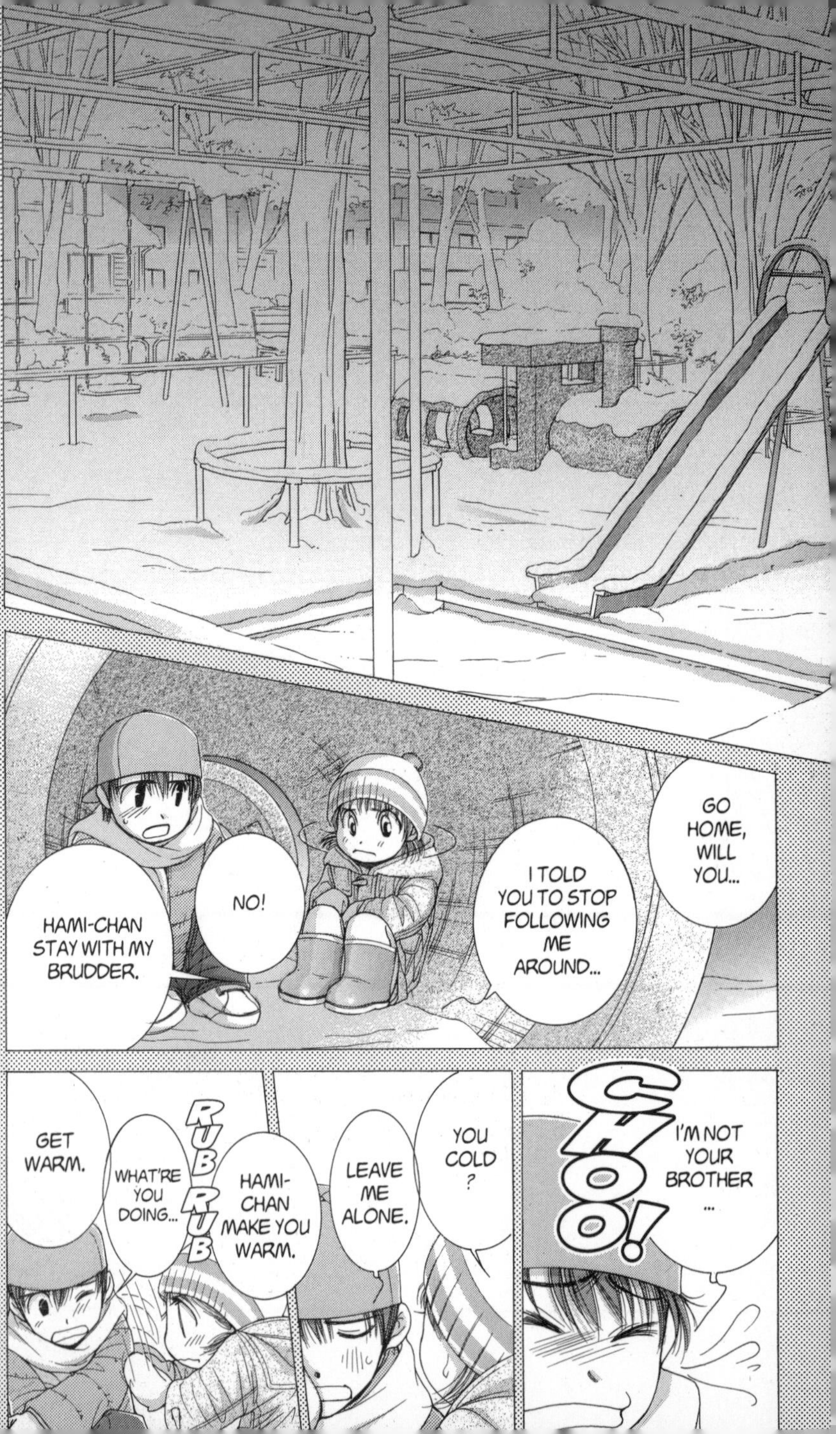
GO HOME, WILL YOU...
I TOLD YOU TO STOP FOLLOWING ME AROUND...
NO!
HAMI-CHAN STAY WITH MY BRUDDER.
CHOO!
I'M NOT YOUR BROTHER ...
YOU COLD ?
LEAVE ME ALONE.
HAMI-CHAN MAKE YOU WARM.
RUB RUB
WHAT'RE YOU DOING...
GET WARM.

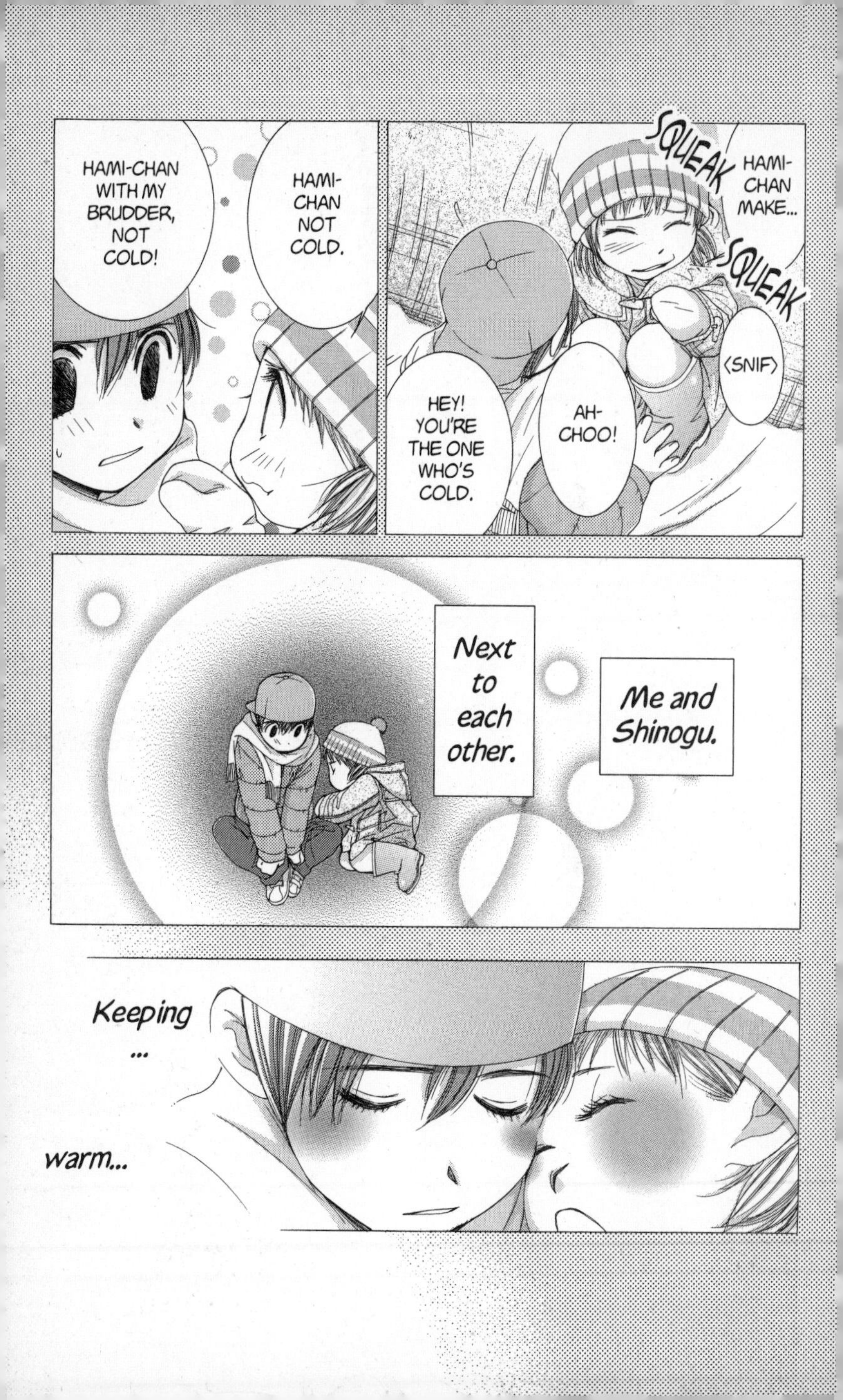
SQUEAK
HAMI-CHAN MAKE...
SQUEAK
<SNIF>
AH-CHOO!
HEY! YOU'RE THE ONE WHO'S COLD.
HAMI-CHAN NOT COLD.
HAMI-CHAN WITH MY BRUDDER, NOT COLD!
Me and Shinogu.
Next to each other.
Keeping ...
warm...

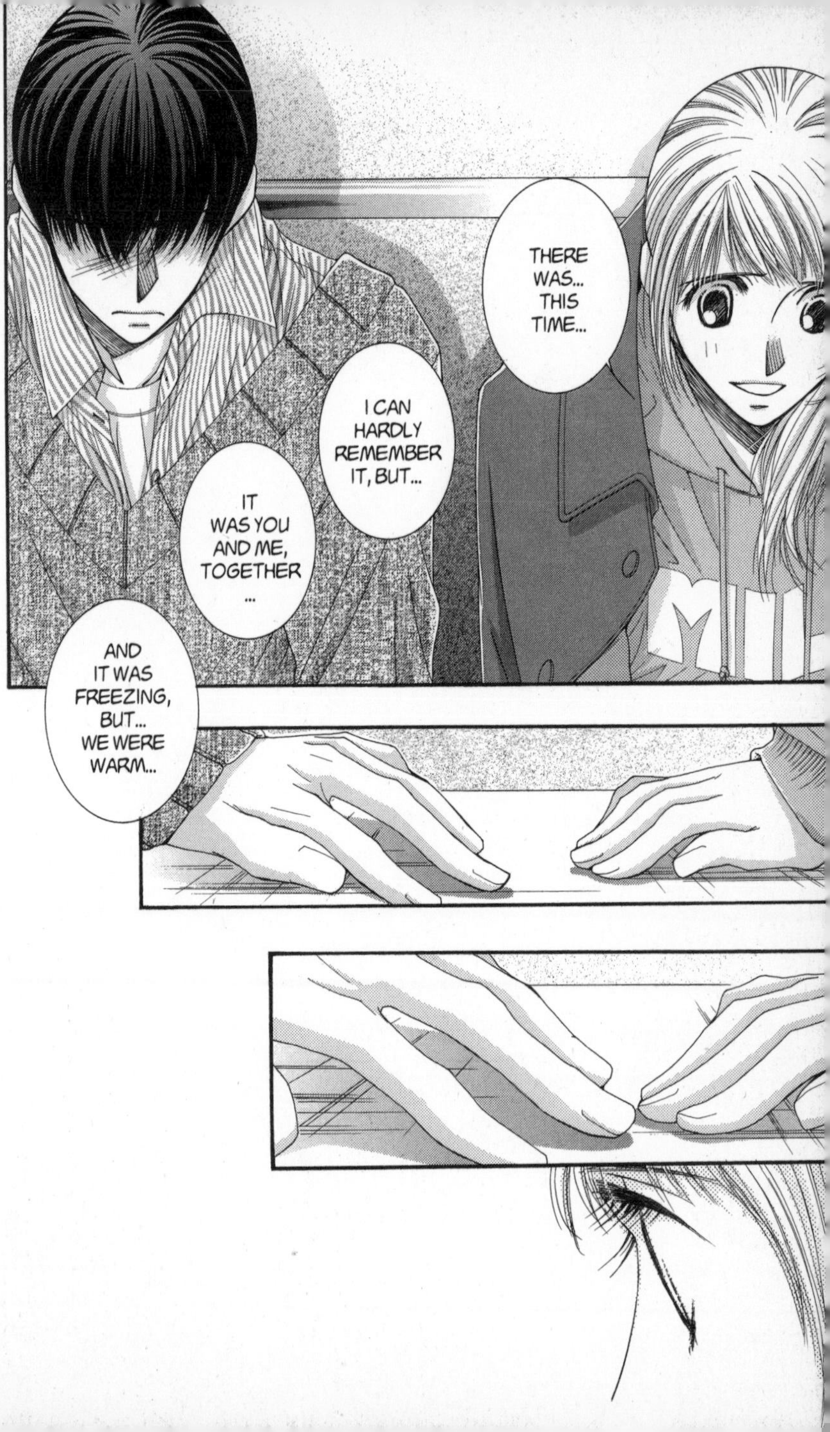
THERE WAS... THIS TIME...
I CAN HARDLY REMEMBER IT, BUT...
IT WAS YOU AND ME, TOGETHER ...
AND IT WAS FREEZING, BUT... WE WERE WARM...

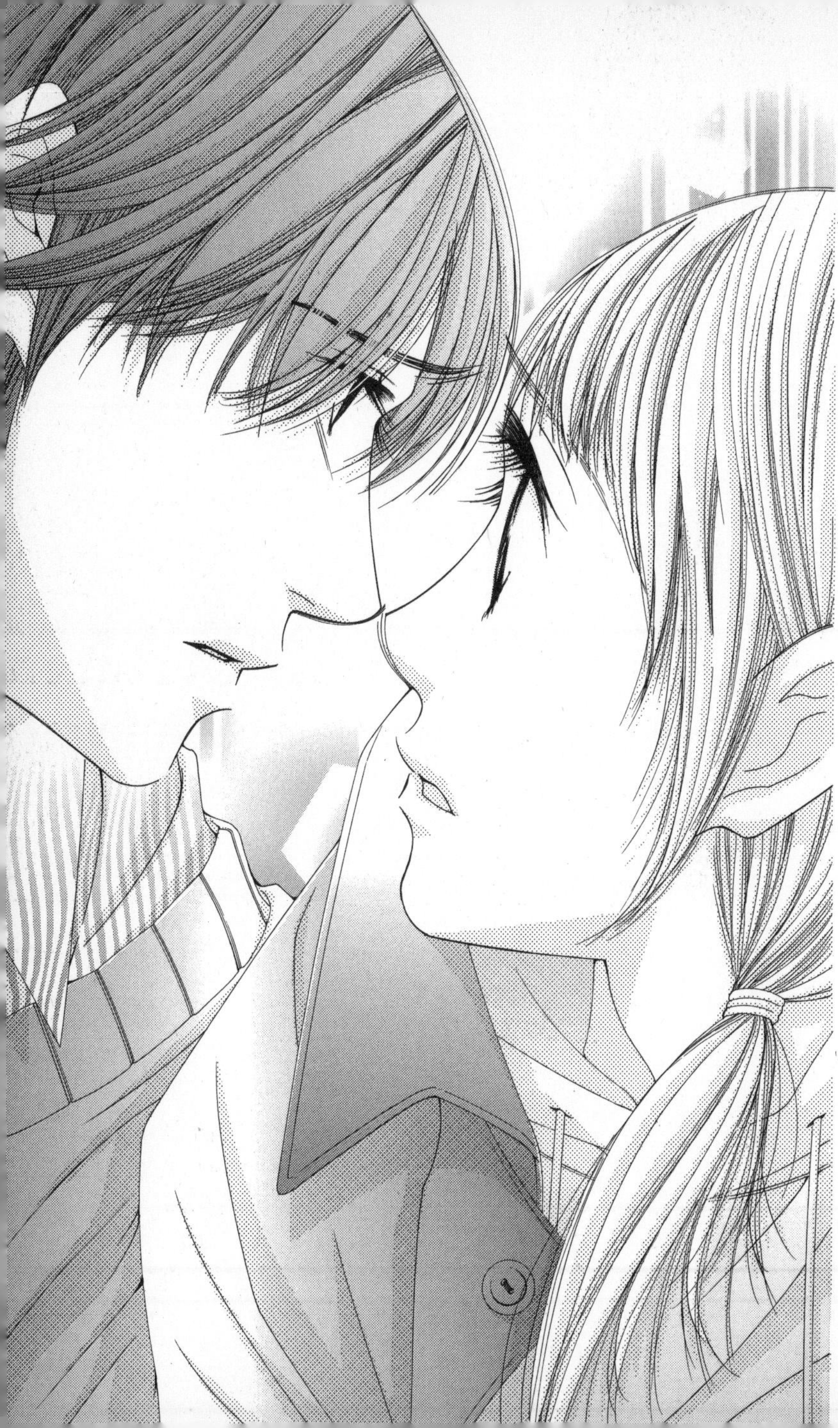

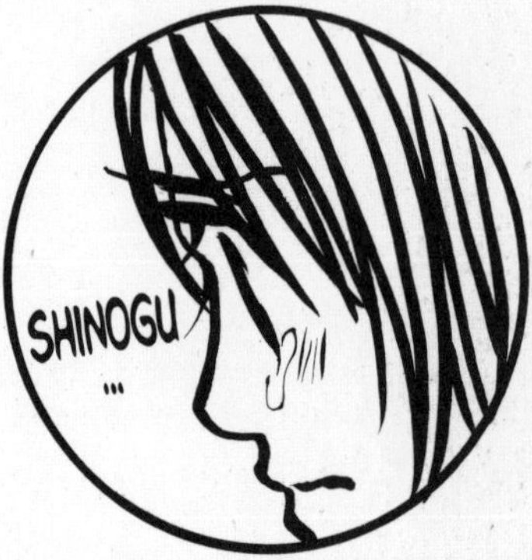
SHINOGU
...

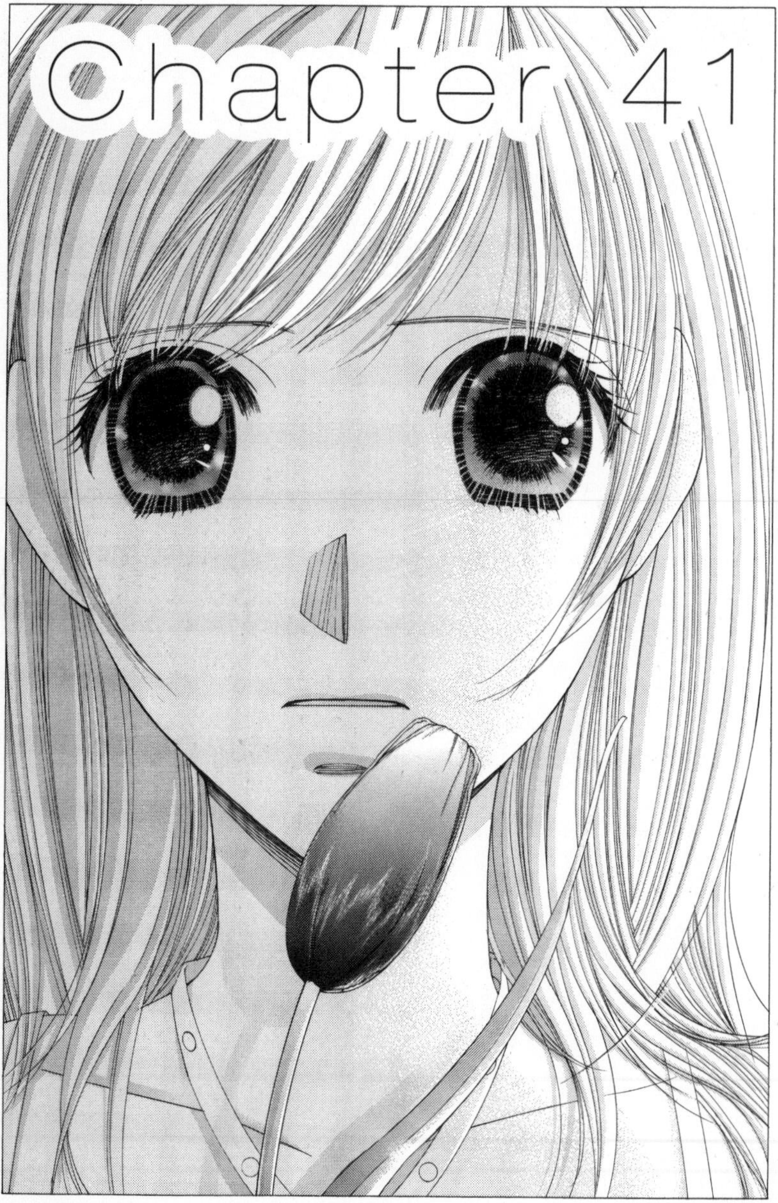
Chapter 41

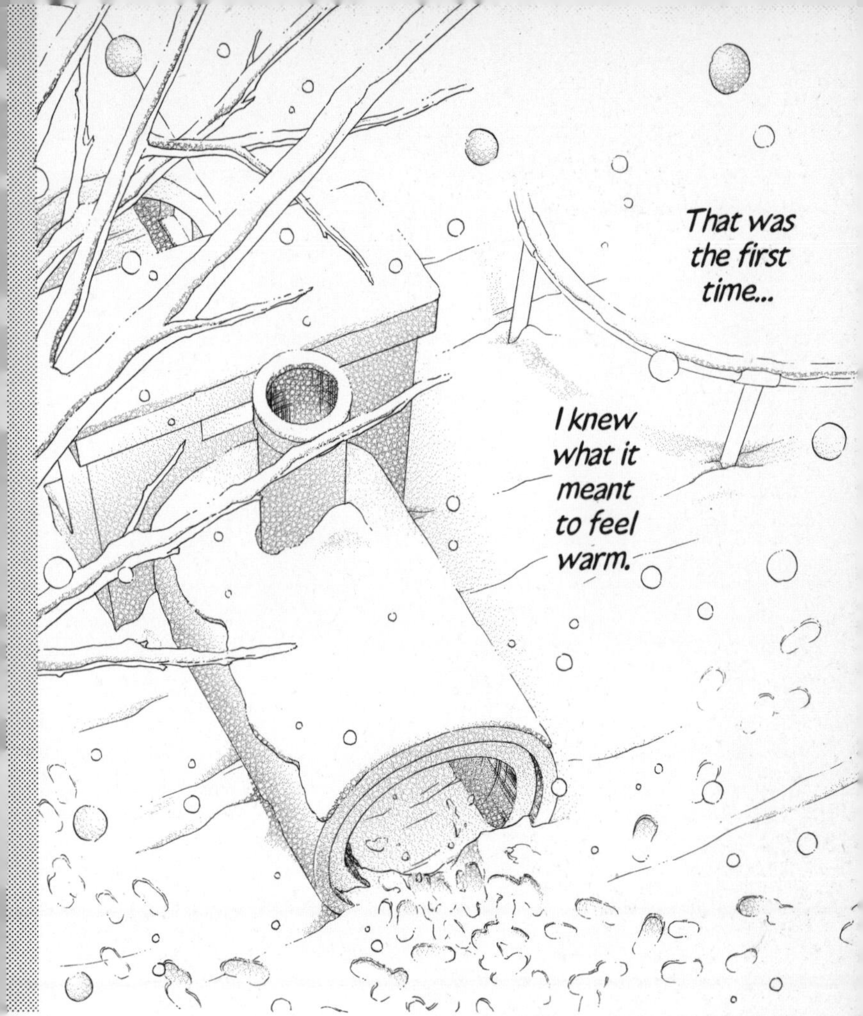
That was the first time...
I knew what it meant to feel warm.

hot gimmick

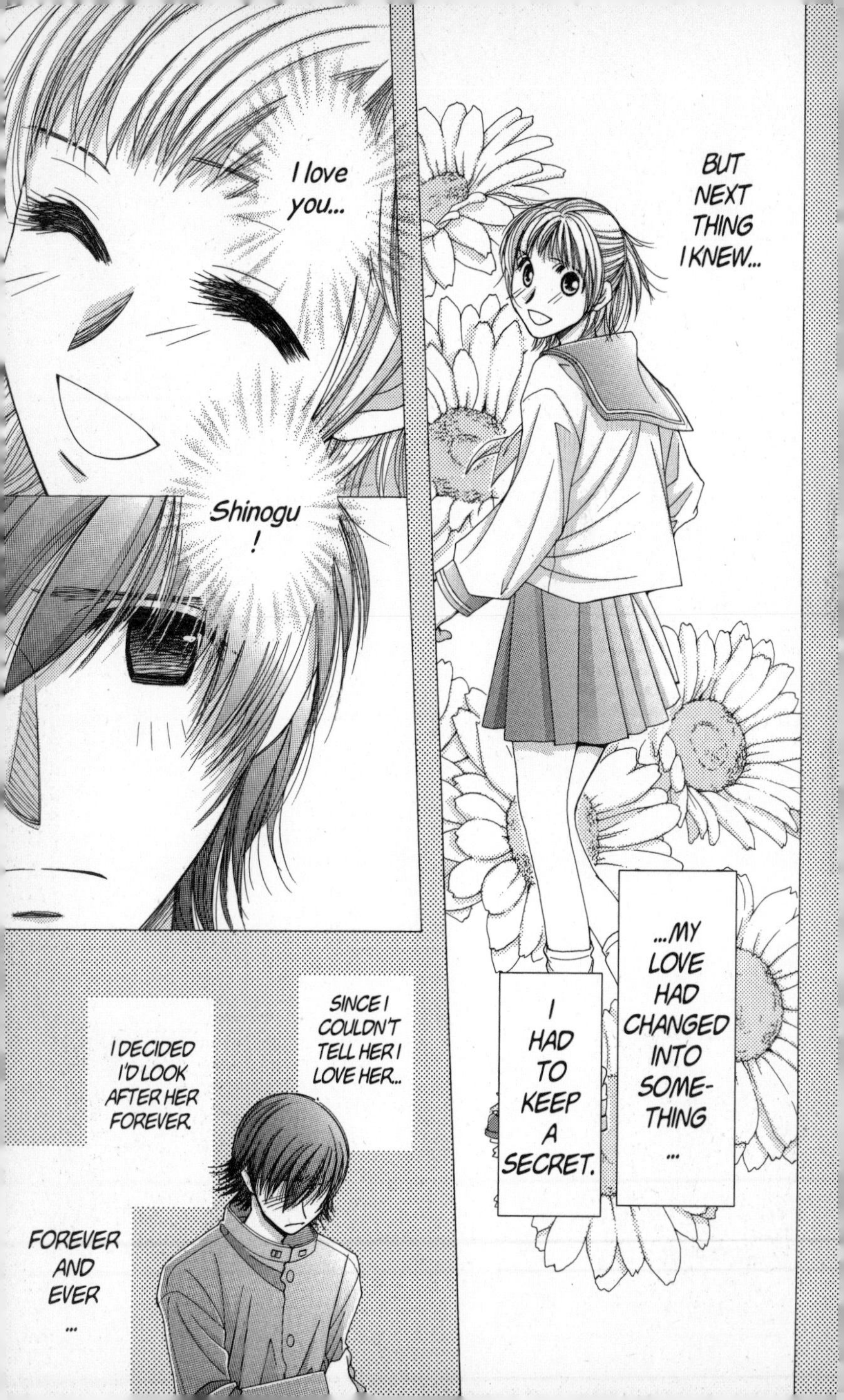
BUT NEXT THING I KNEW...
...MY LOVE HAD CHANGED INTO SOME-THING...
I HAD TO KEEP A SECRET.
I love you...
Shinogu!
SINCE I COULDN'T TELL HER I LOVE HER...
I DECIDED I'D LOOK AFTER HER FOREVER.
FOREVER AND EVER...

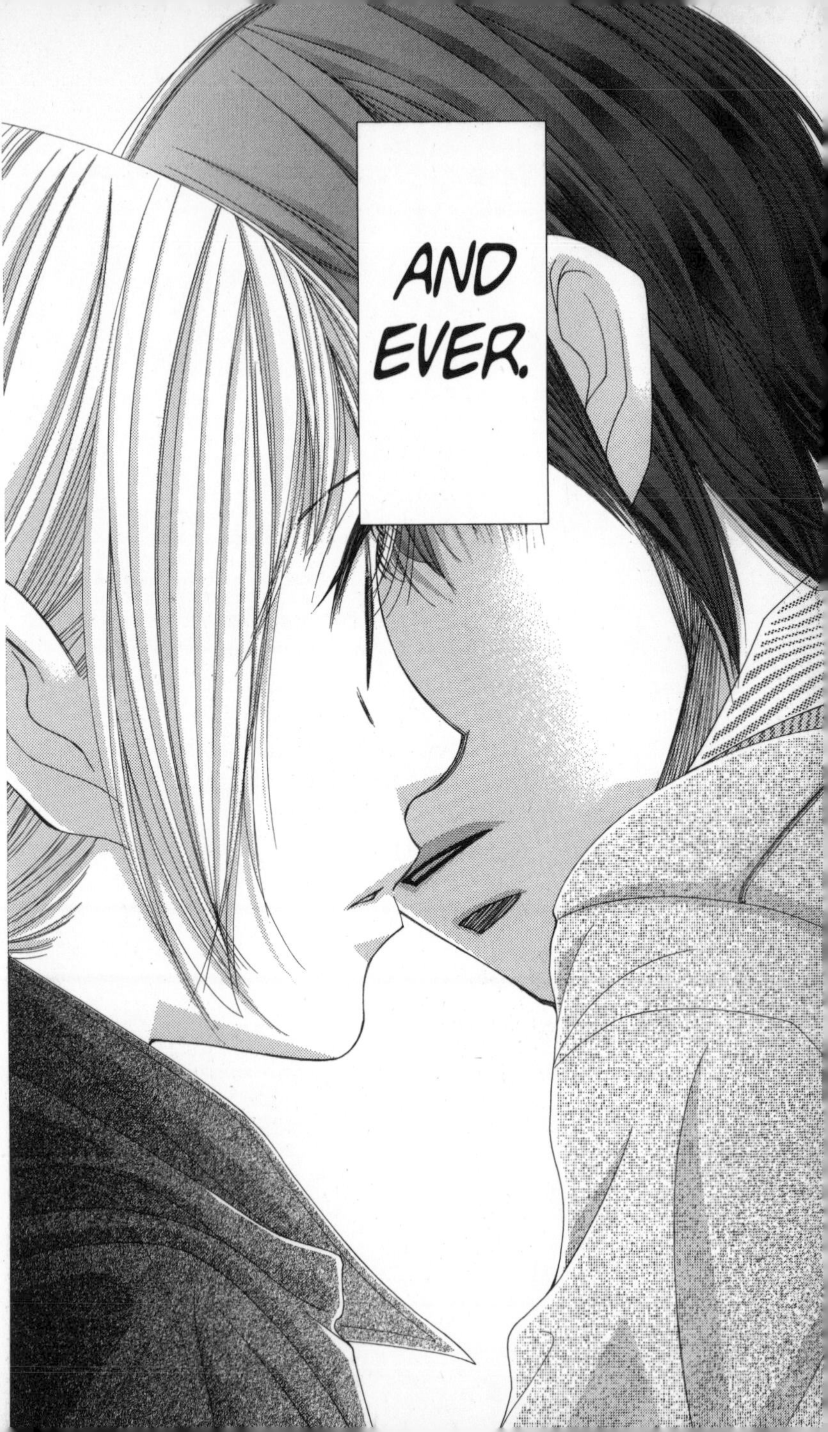
AND EVER.

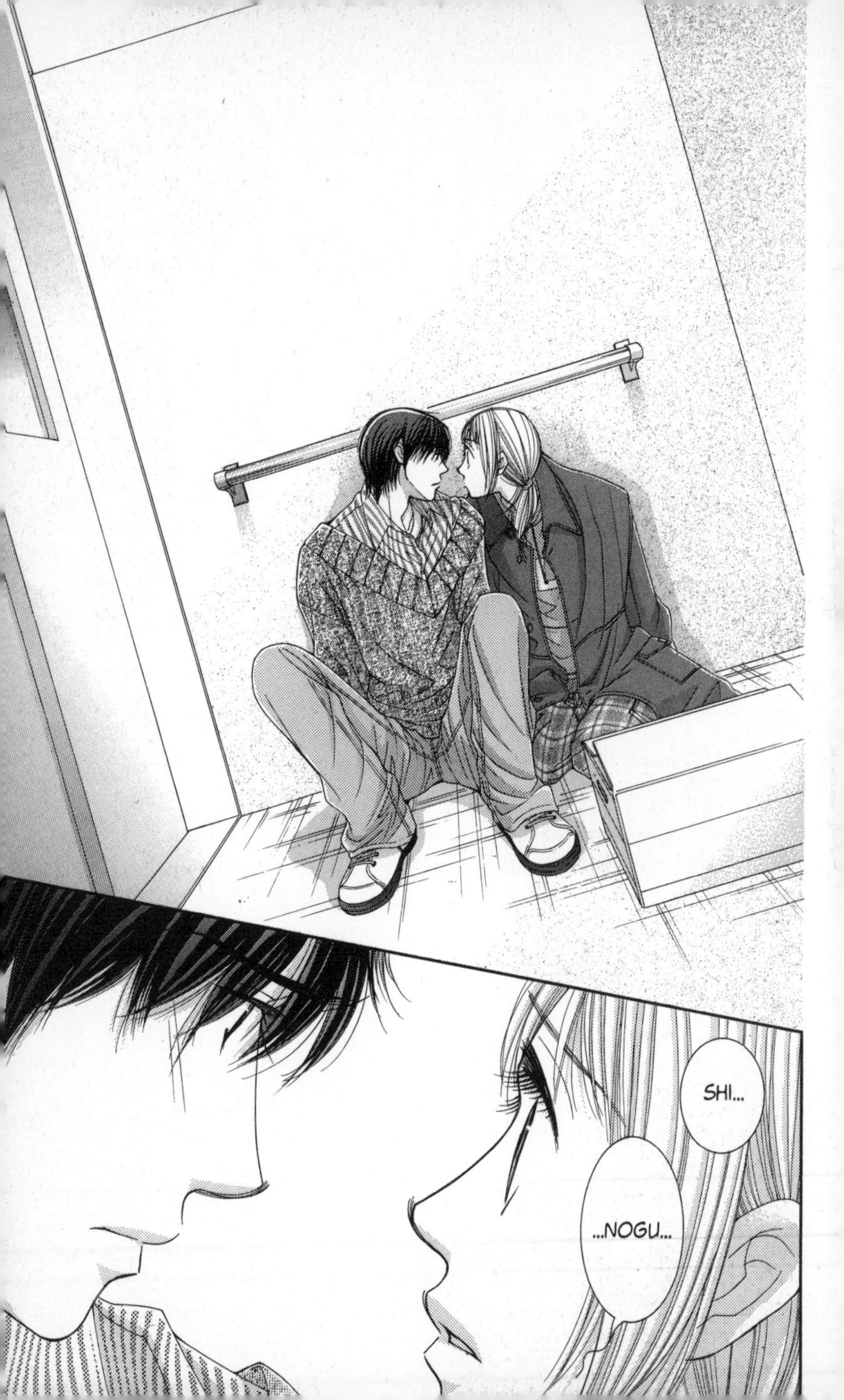
SHI...
...NOGU...

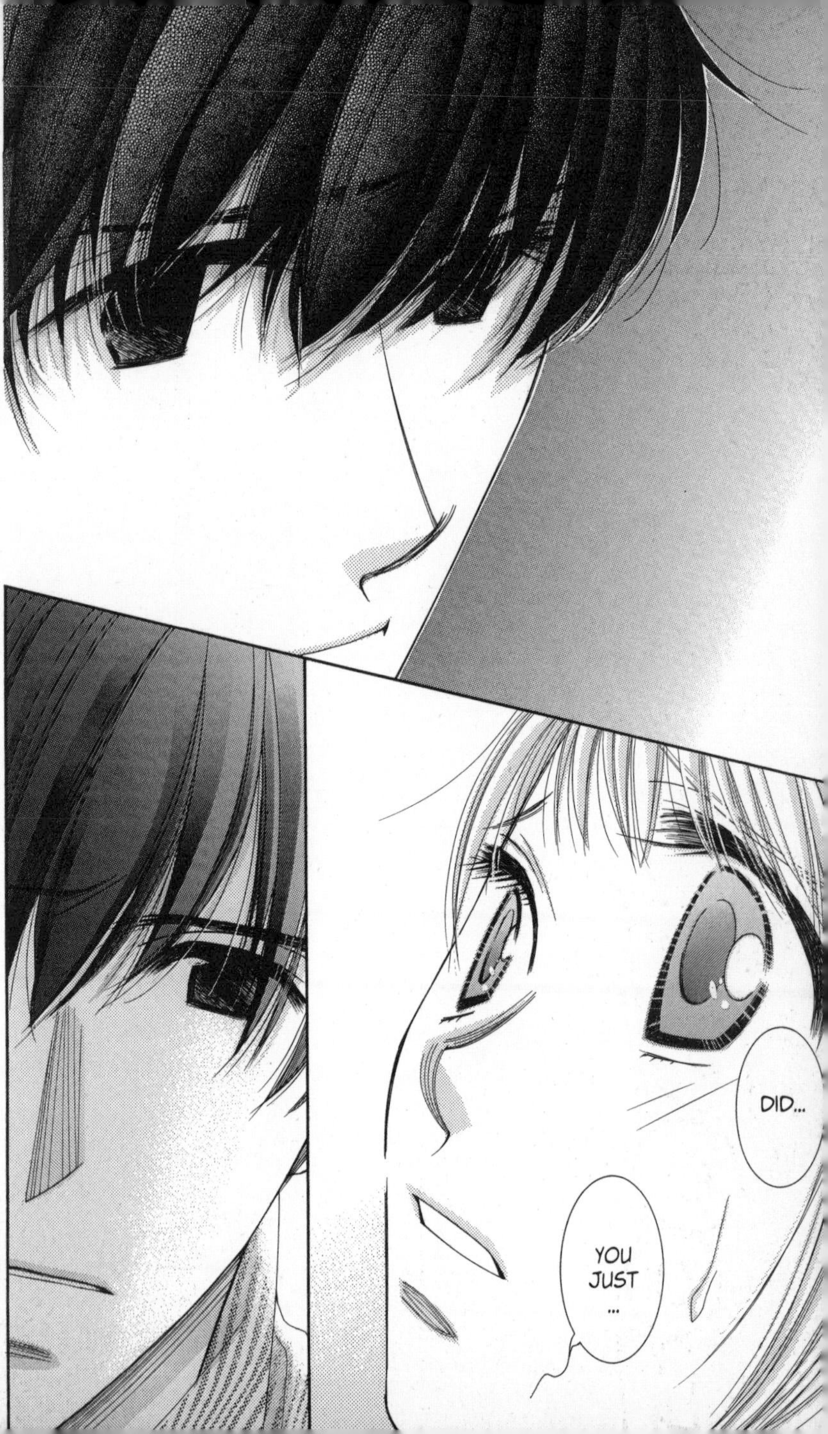
DID...
YOU JUST ...

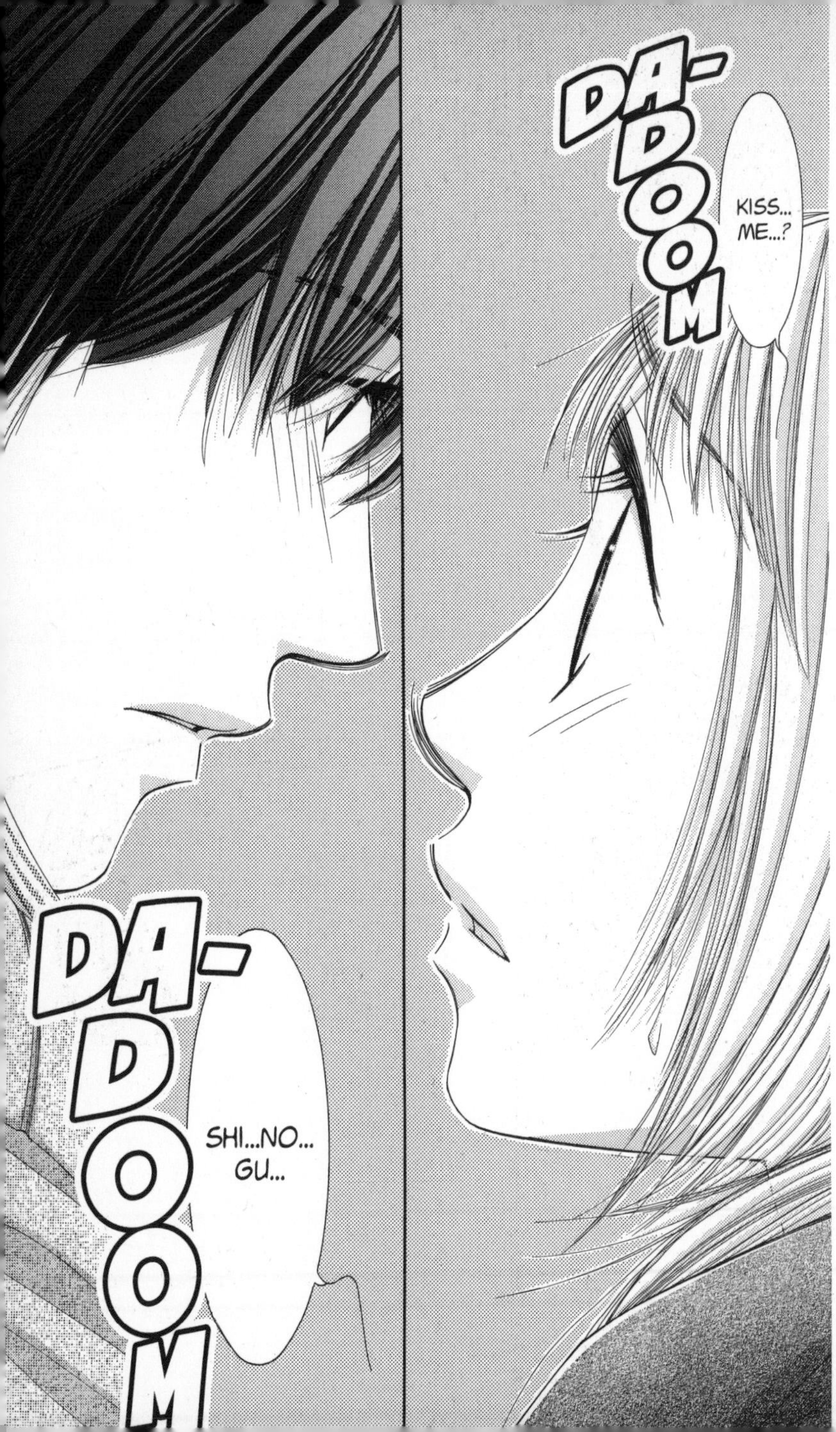
DA-DOOM
KISS... ME...?
DA-DOOM
SHI...NO... GU...

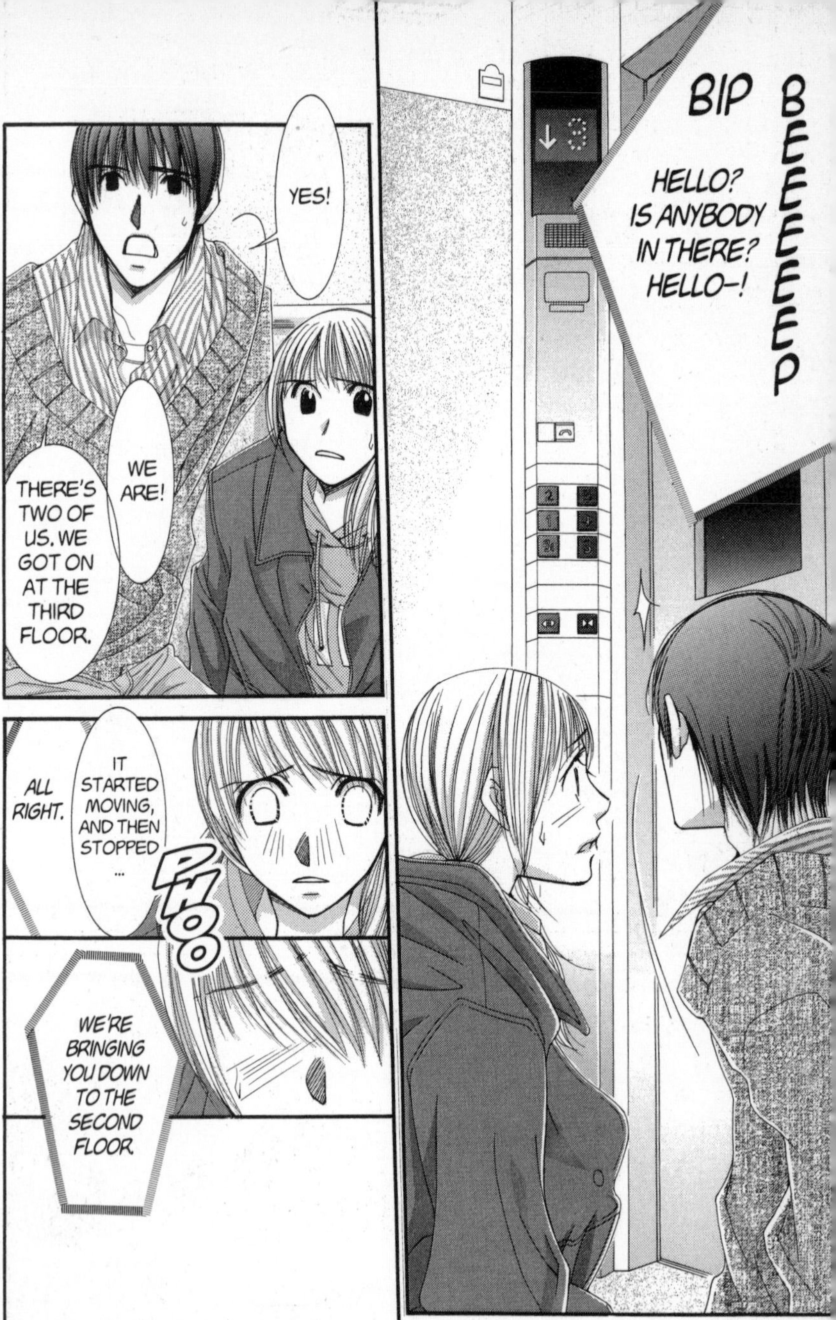
BIP
BEEEEEEP
HELLO? IS ANYBODY IN THERE? HELLO—!
YES!
WE ARE!
THERE'S TWO OF US. WE GOT ON AT THE THIRD FLOOR.
IT STARTED MOVING, AND THEN STOPPED ...
ALL RIGHT.
PHOO
WE'RE BRINGING YOU DOWN TO THE SECOND FLOOR.

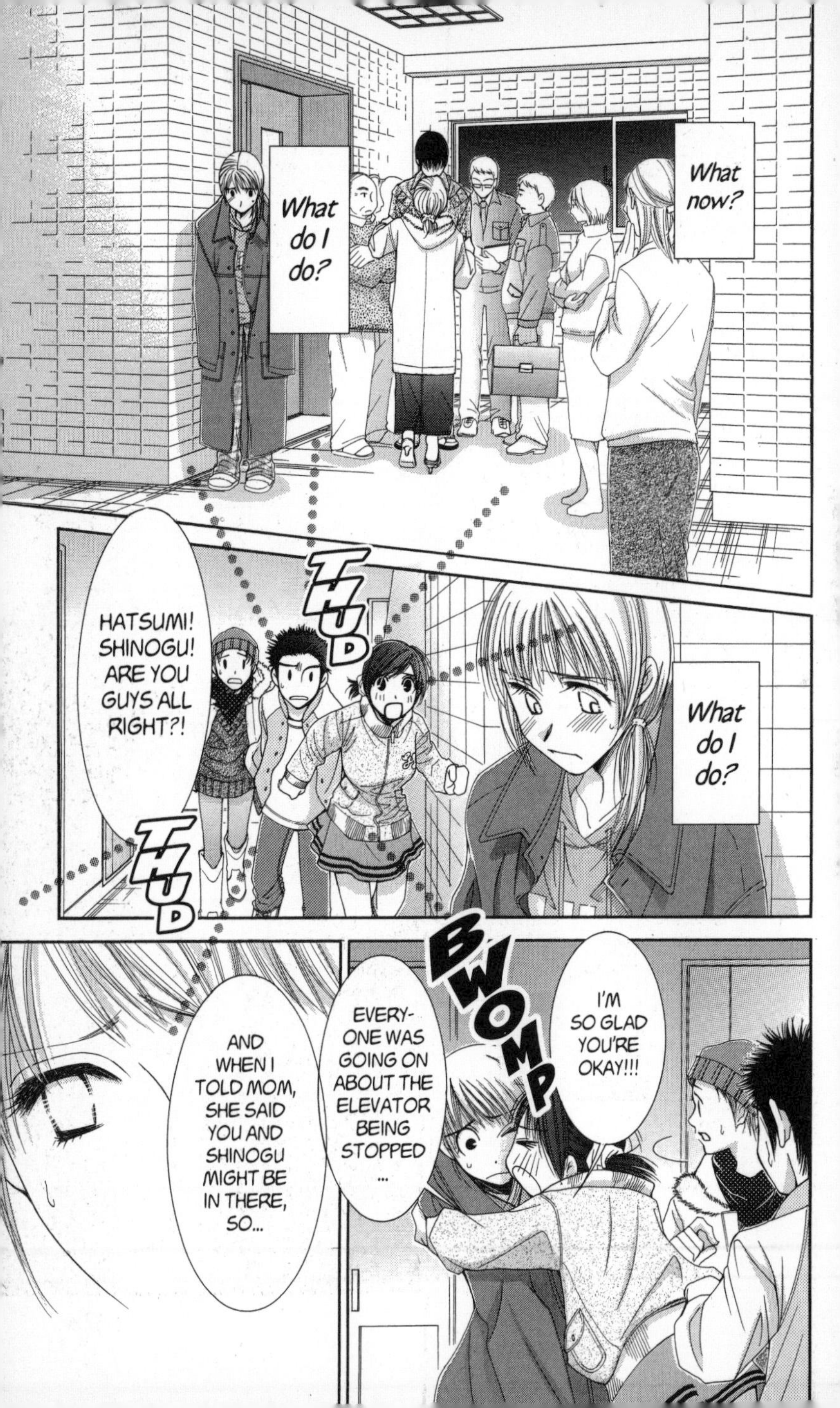
What now?
What do I do?
What do I do?
THUD
HATSUMI! SHINOGU! ARE YOU GUYS ALL RIGHT?!
THUD
BWOMP
I'M SO GLAD YOU'RE OKAY!!!
EVERY-ONE WAS GOING ON ABOUT THE ELEVATOR BEING STOPPED ...
AND WHEN I TOLD MOM, SHE SAID YOU AND SHINOGU MIGHT BE IN THERE, SO...

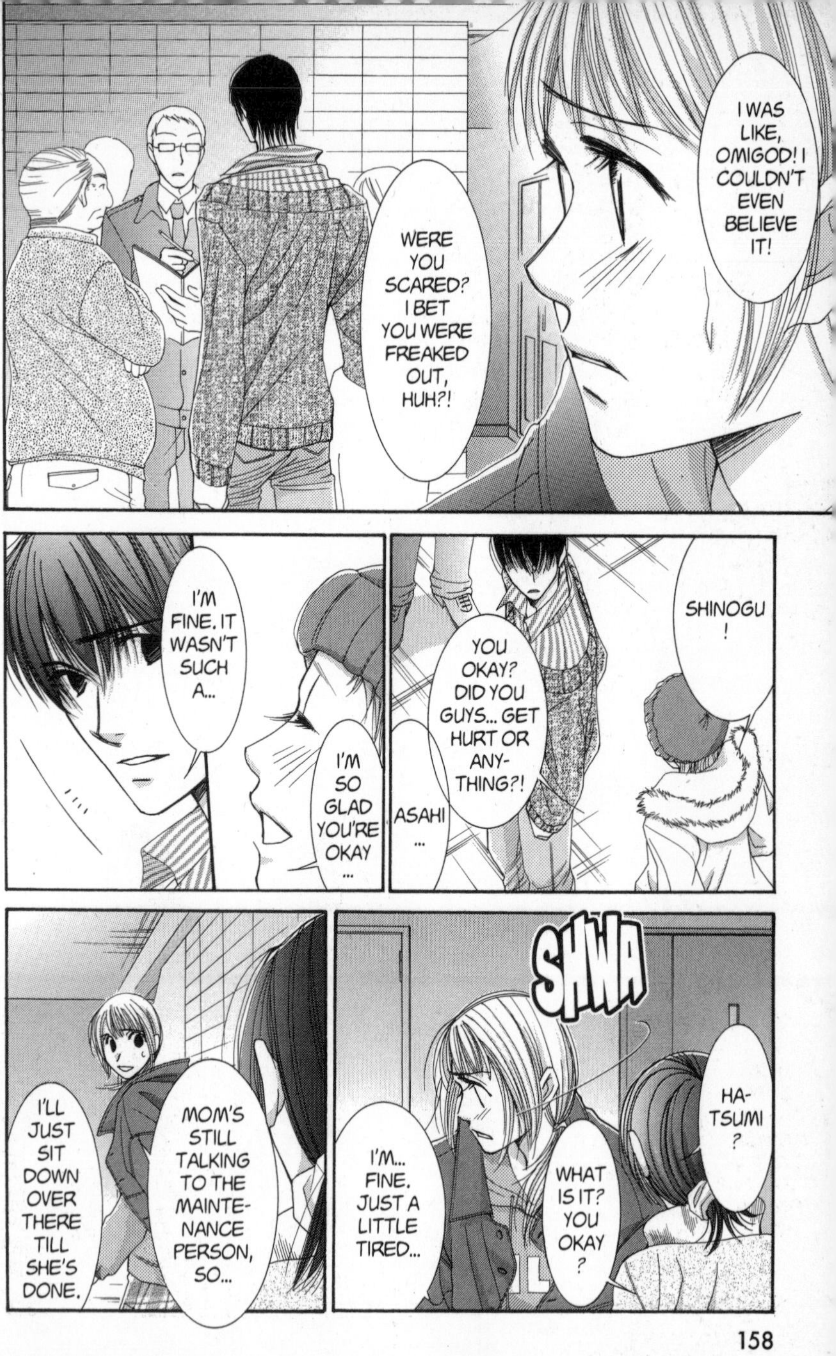
I WAS LIKE, OMIGOD! I COULDN'T EVEN BELIEVE IT!
WERE YOU SCARED? I BET YOU WERE FREAKED OUT, HUH?!
SHINOGU!
YOU OKAY? DID YOU GUYS... GET HURT OR ANY-THING?!
ASAHI...
I'M FINE. IT WASN'T SUCH A...
I'M SO GLAD YOU'RE OKAY...
SHWA
HA-TSUMI?
WHAT IS IT? YOU OKAY?
I'M... FINE. JUST A LITTLE TIRED...
MOM'S STILL TALKING TO THE MAINTE-NANCE PERSON, SO...
I'LL JUST SIT DOWN OVER THERE TILL SHE'S DONE.

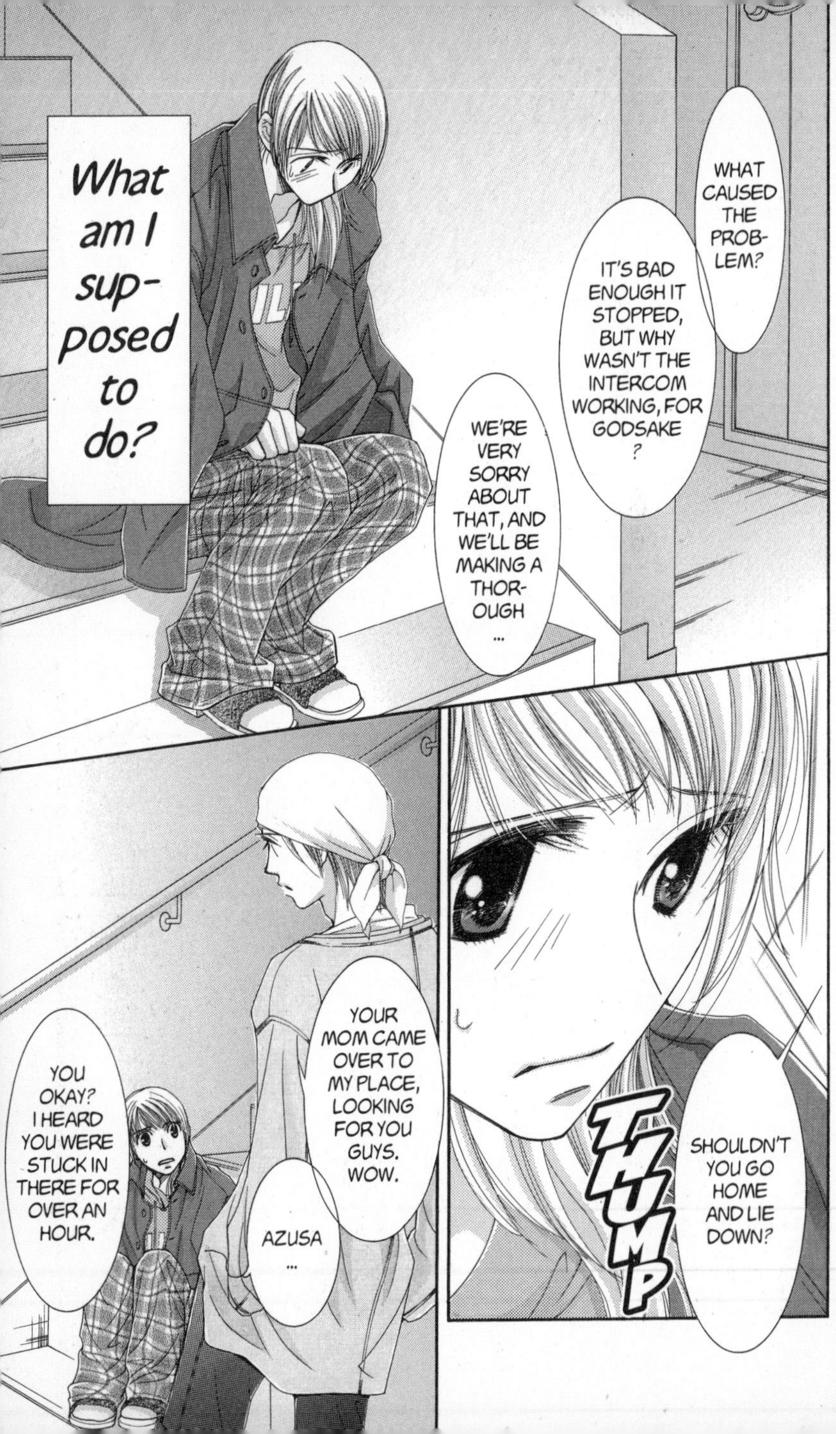
WHAT CAUSED THE PROB-LEM?
IT'S BAD ENOUGH IT STOPPED, BUT WHY WASN'T THE INTERCOM WORKING, FOR GODSAKE ?
WE'RE VERY SORRY ABOUT THAT, AND WE'LL BE MAKING A THOR-OUGH ...
What am I sup-posed to do?
THUMP
SHOULDN'T YOU GO HOME AND LIE DOWN?
YOUR MOM CAME OVER TO MY PLACE, LOOKING FOR YOU GUYS. WOW.
YOU OKAY? I HEARD YOU WERE STUCK IN THERE FOR OVER AN HOUR.
AZUSA ...

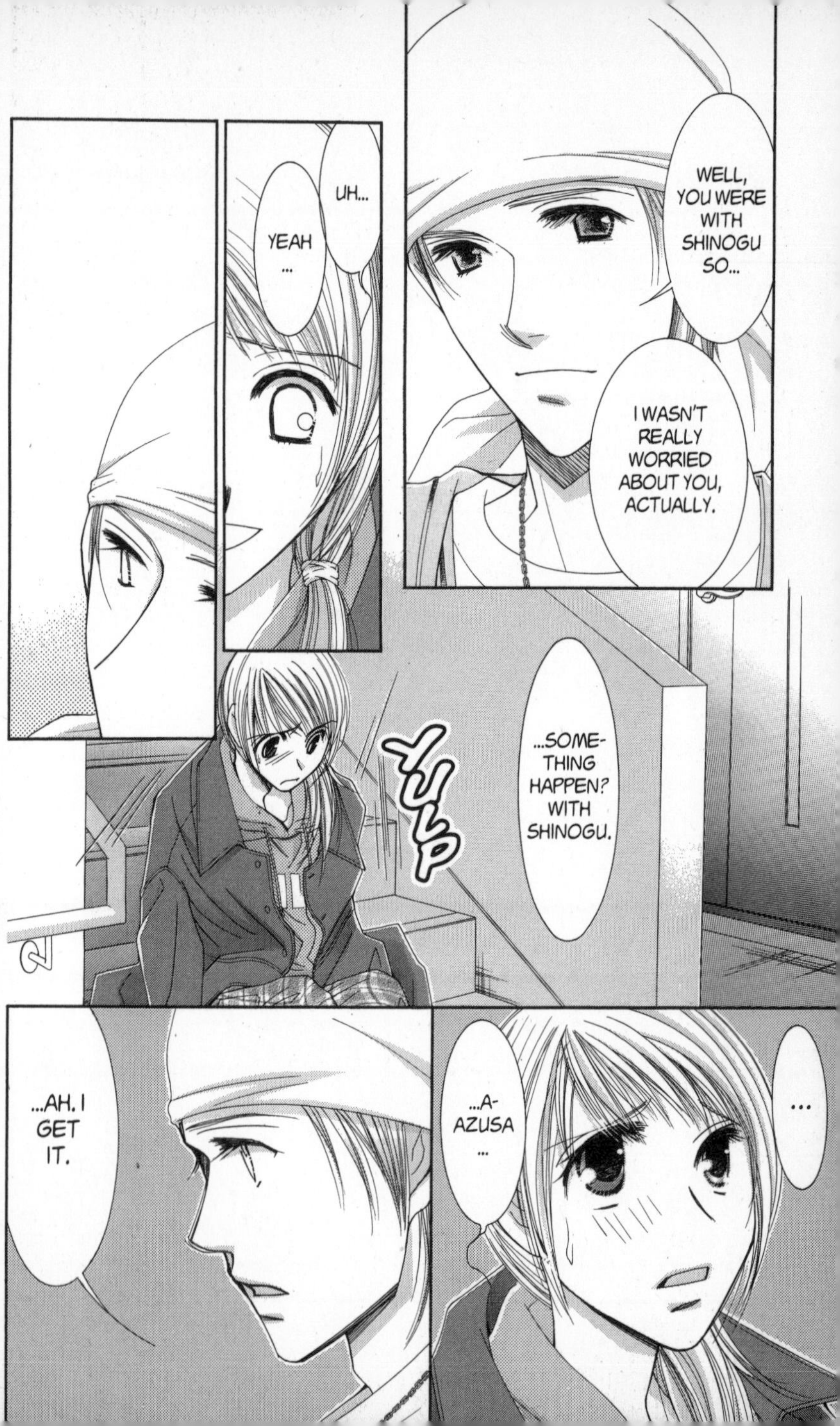
WELL, YOU WERE WITH SHINOGU SO...
I WASN'T REALLY WORRIED ABOUT YOU, ACTUALLY.
UH...
YEAH ...
...SOME-THING HAPPEN? WITH SHINOGU.
YUP
...
...A-AZUSA ...
...AH. I GET IT.

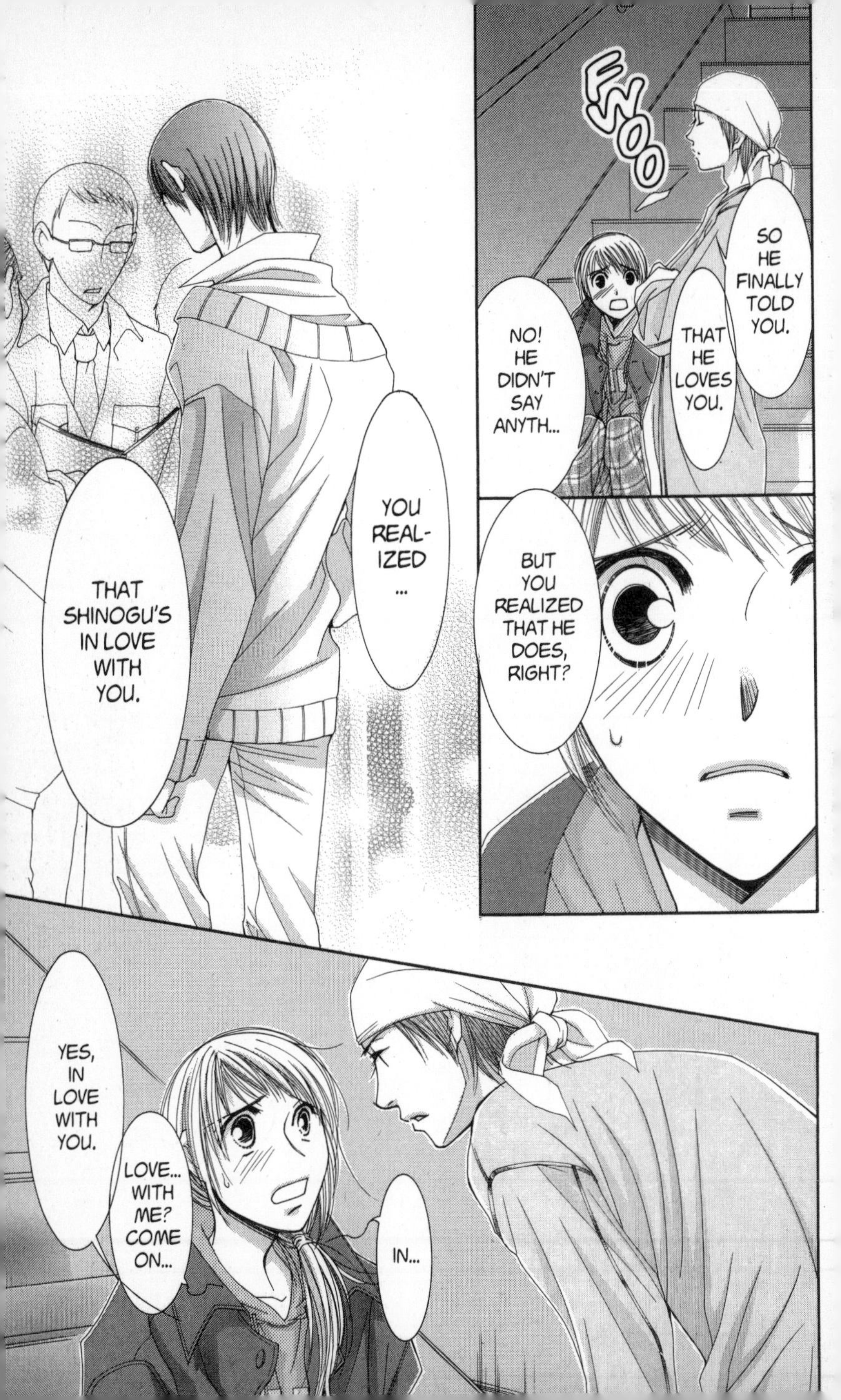
FWOO
SO HE FINALLY TOLD YOU.
THAT HE LOVES YOU.
NO! HE DIDN'T SAY ANYTH...
BUT YOU REALIZED THAT HE DOES, RIGHT?
YOU REAL-IZED...
THAT SHINOGU'S IN LOVE WITH YOU.
IN...
YES, IN LOVE WITH YOU.
LOVE... WITH ME? COME ON...

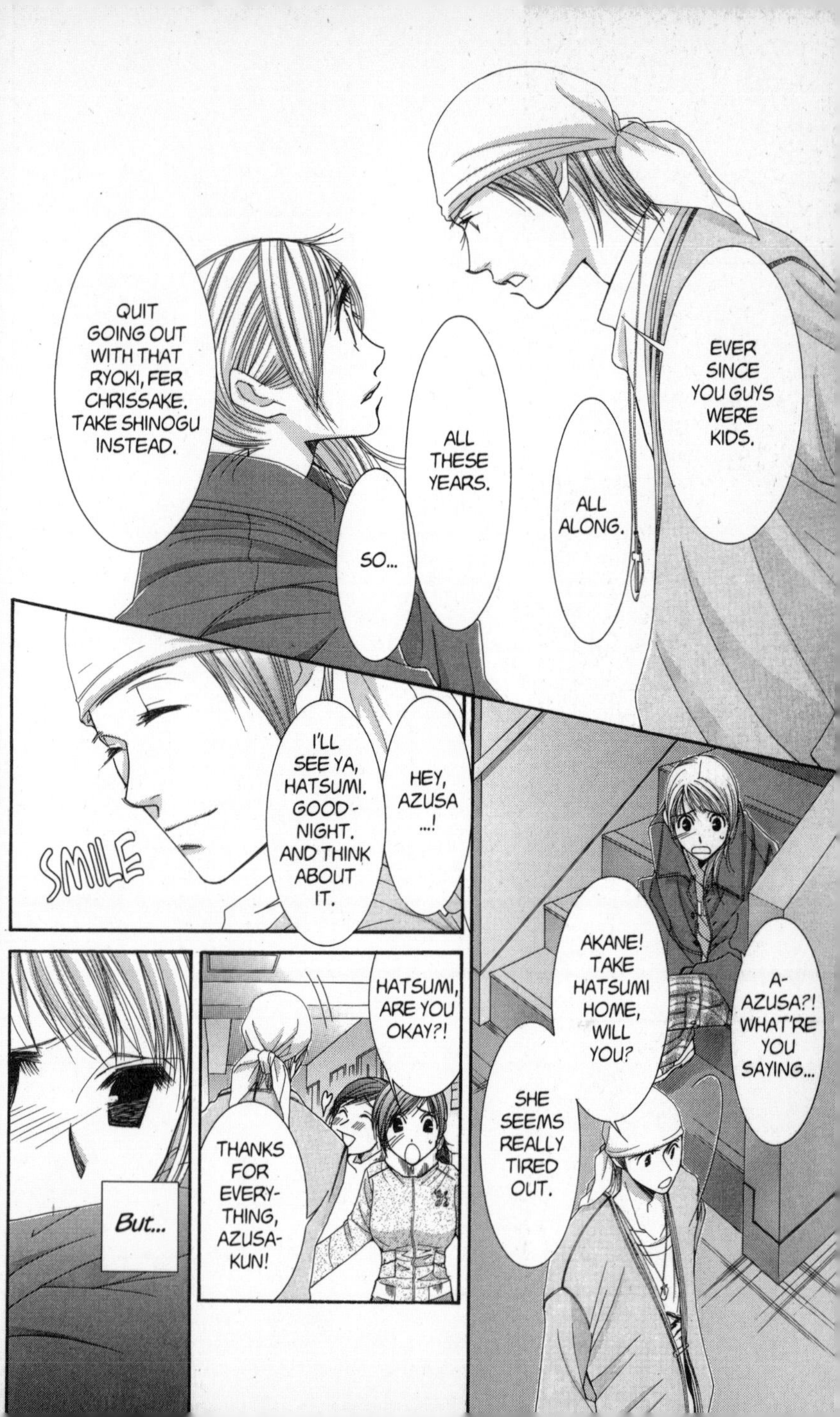
EVER SINCE YOU GUYS WERE KIDS.
ALL ALONG.
ALL THESE YEARS.
SO...
QUIT GOING OUT WITH THAT RYOKI, FER CHRISSAKE. TAKE SHINOGU INSTEAD.
A-AZUSA?! WHAT'RE YOU SAYING...
AKANE! TAKE HATSUMI HOME, WILL YOU?
SHE SEEMS REALLY TIRED OUT.
HEY, AZUSA...!
I'LL SEE YA, HATSUMI. GOOD-NIGHT. AND THINK ABOUT IT.
SMILE
HATSUMI, ARE YOU OKAY?!
THANKS FOR EVERY-THING, AZUSA-KUN!
But...

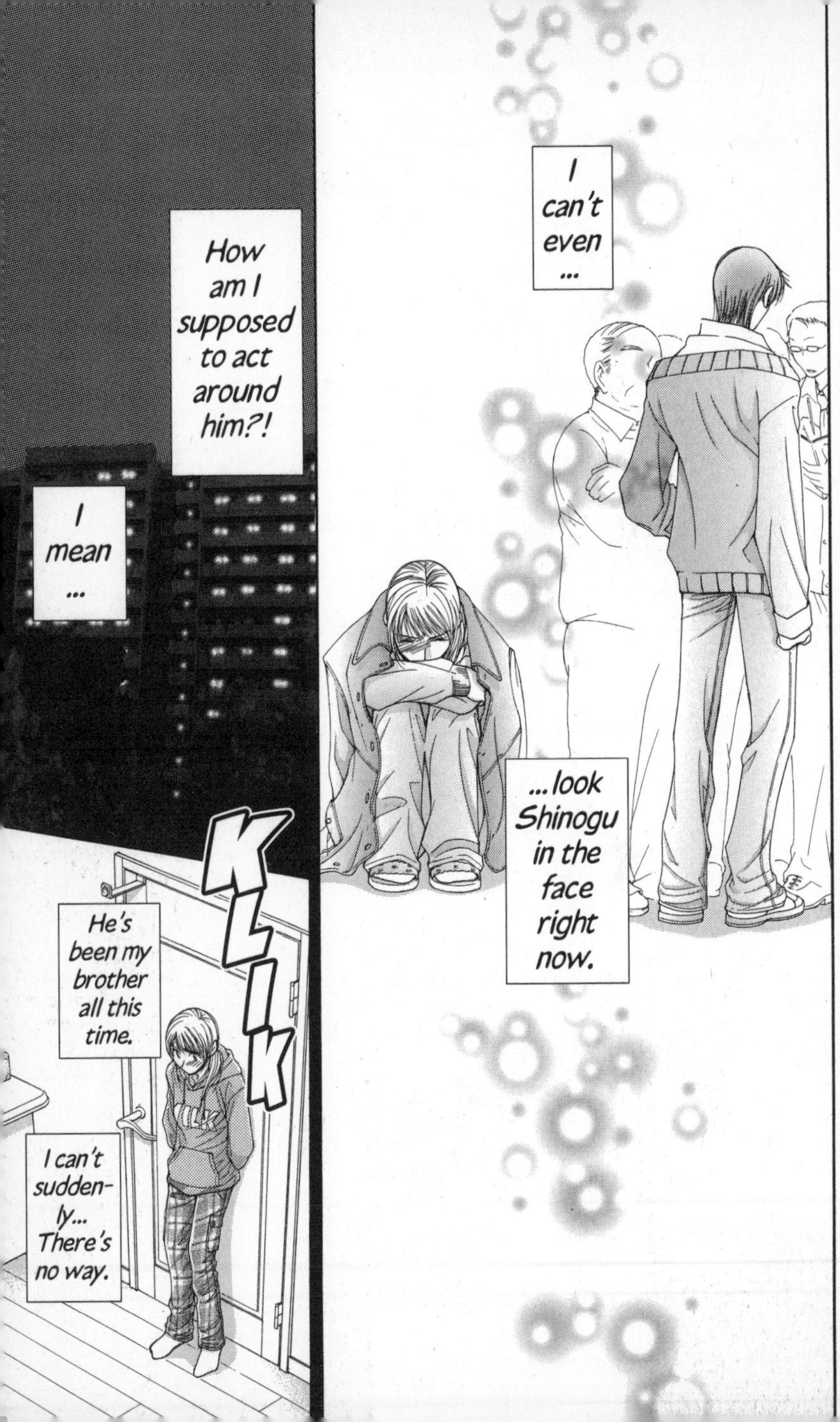
I can't even ...
...look Shinogu in the face right now.
How am I supposed to act around him?!
I mean ...
KLIK
He's been my brother all this time.
I can't sudden-ly... There's no way.

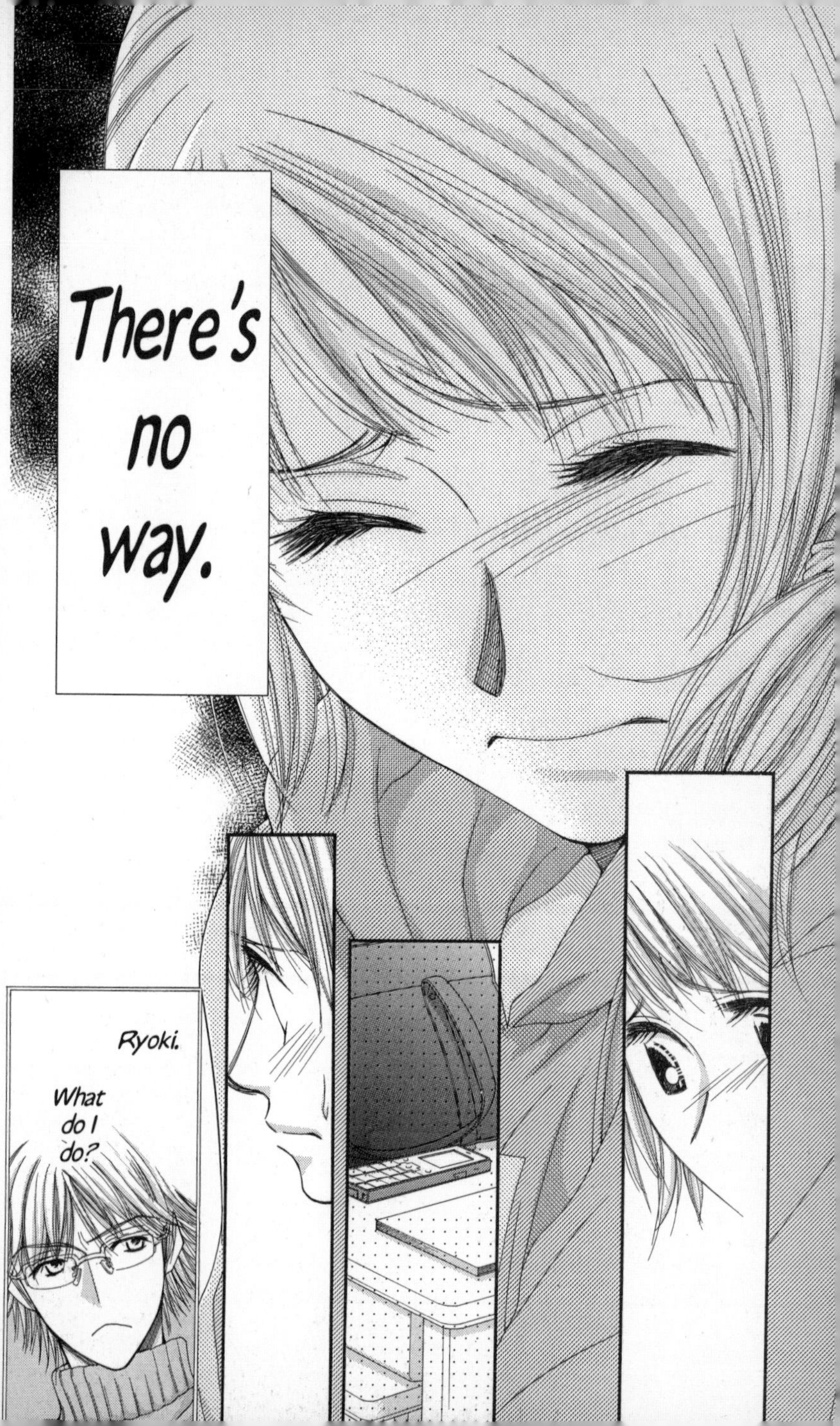
There's no way.
Ryoki.
What do I do?

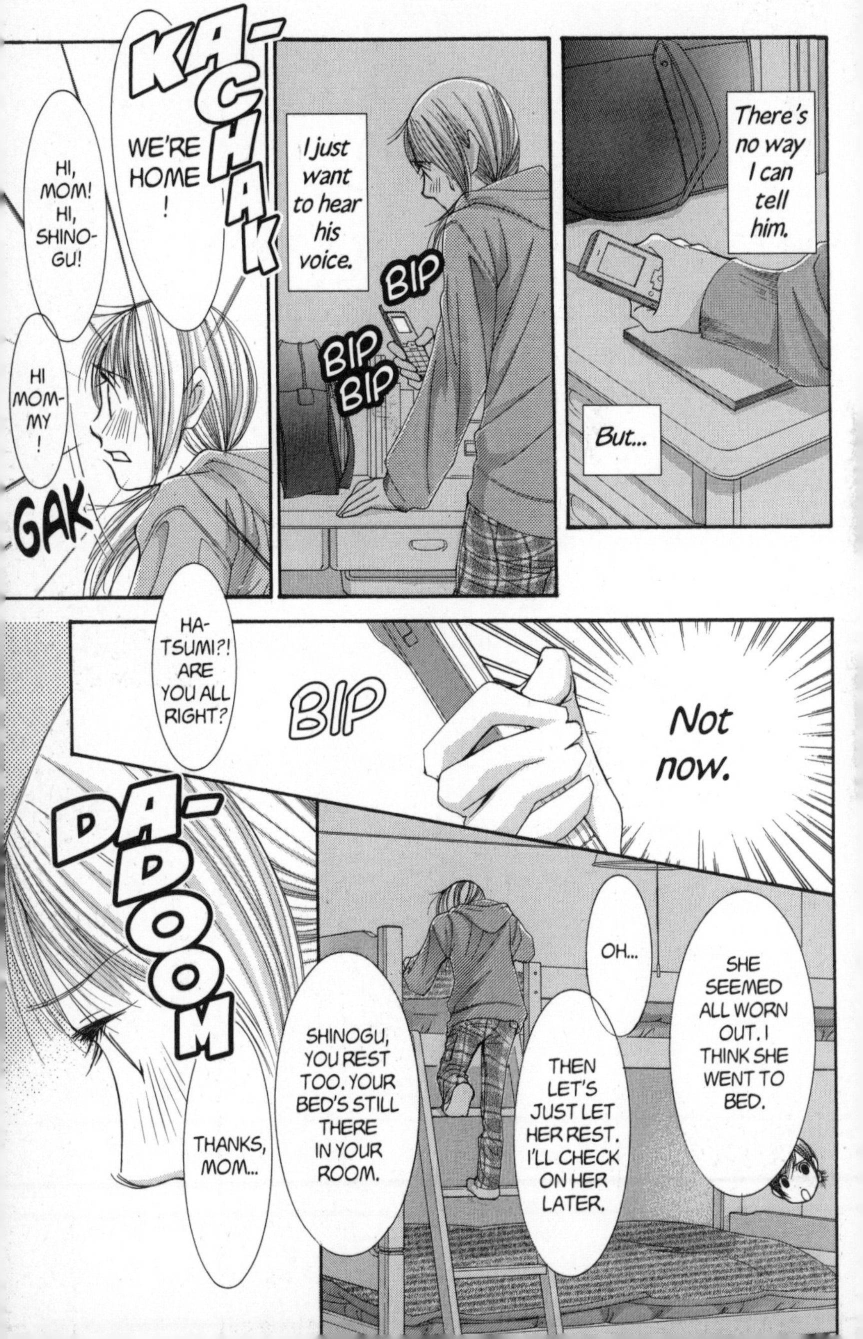
There's no way I can tell him.
But...
I just want to hear his voice.
BIP
BIP BIP
KA-CHAK
WE'RE HOME!
HI, MOM! HI, SHINOGU!
HI MOMMY!
GAK
Not now.
BIP
HATSUMI?! ARE YOU ALL RIGHT?
SHE SEEMED ALL WORN OUT. I THINK SHE WENT TO BED.
OH...
THEN LET'S JUST LET HER REST. I'LL CHECK ON HER LATER.
SHINOGU, YOU REST TOO. YOUR BED'S STILL THERE IN YOUR ROOM.
THANKS, MOM...
DA-DOOM

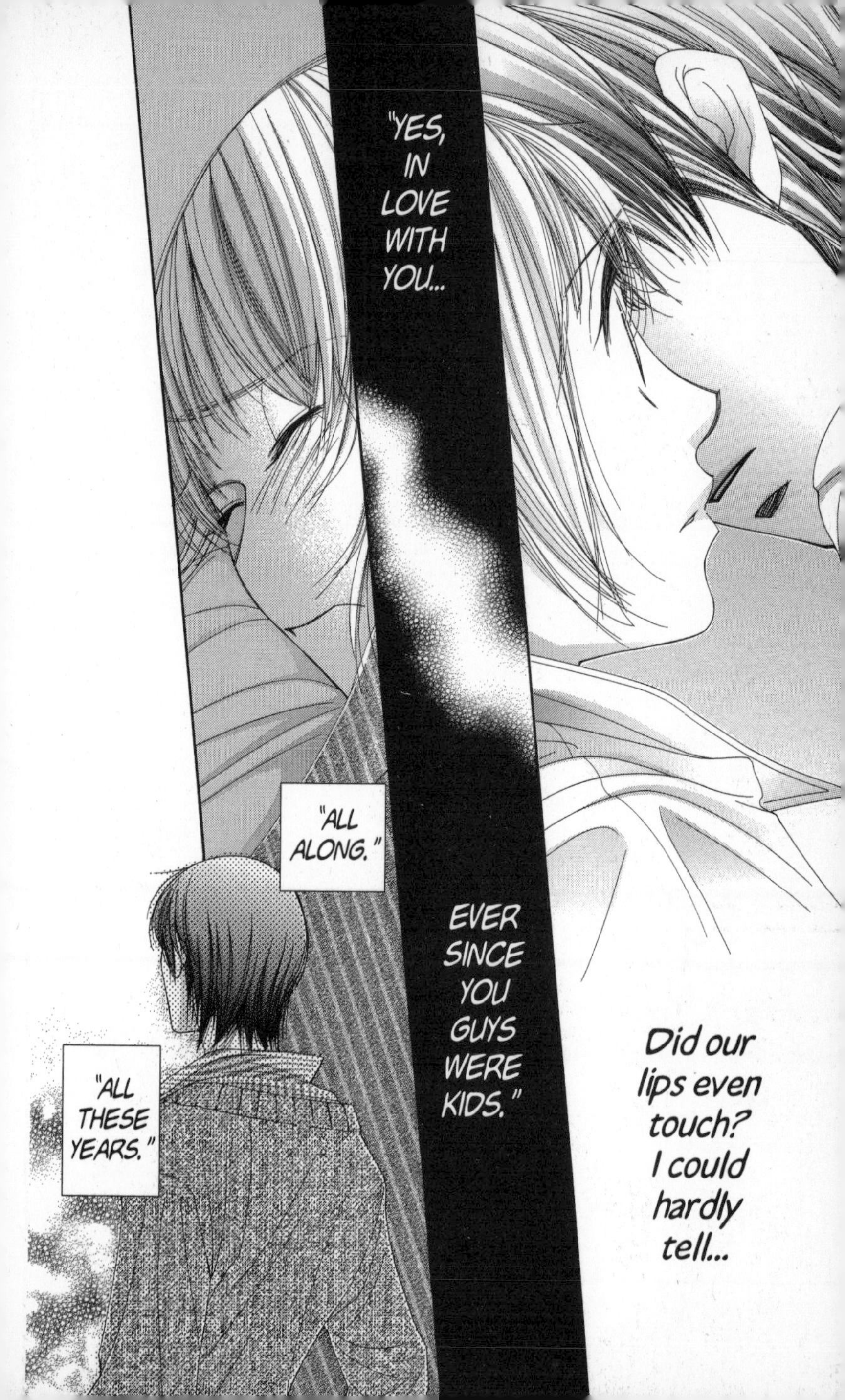
"YES, IN LOVE WITH YOU...
EVER SINCE YOU GUYS WERE KIDS."
"ALL ALONG."
"ALL THESE YEARS."
Did our lips even touch? I could hardly tell...

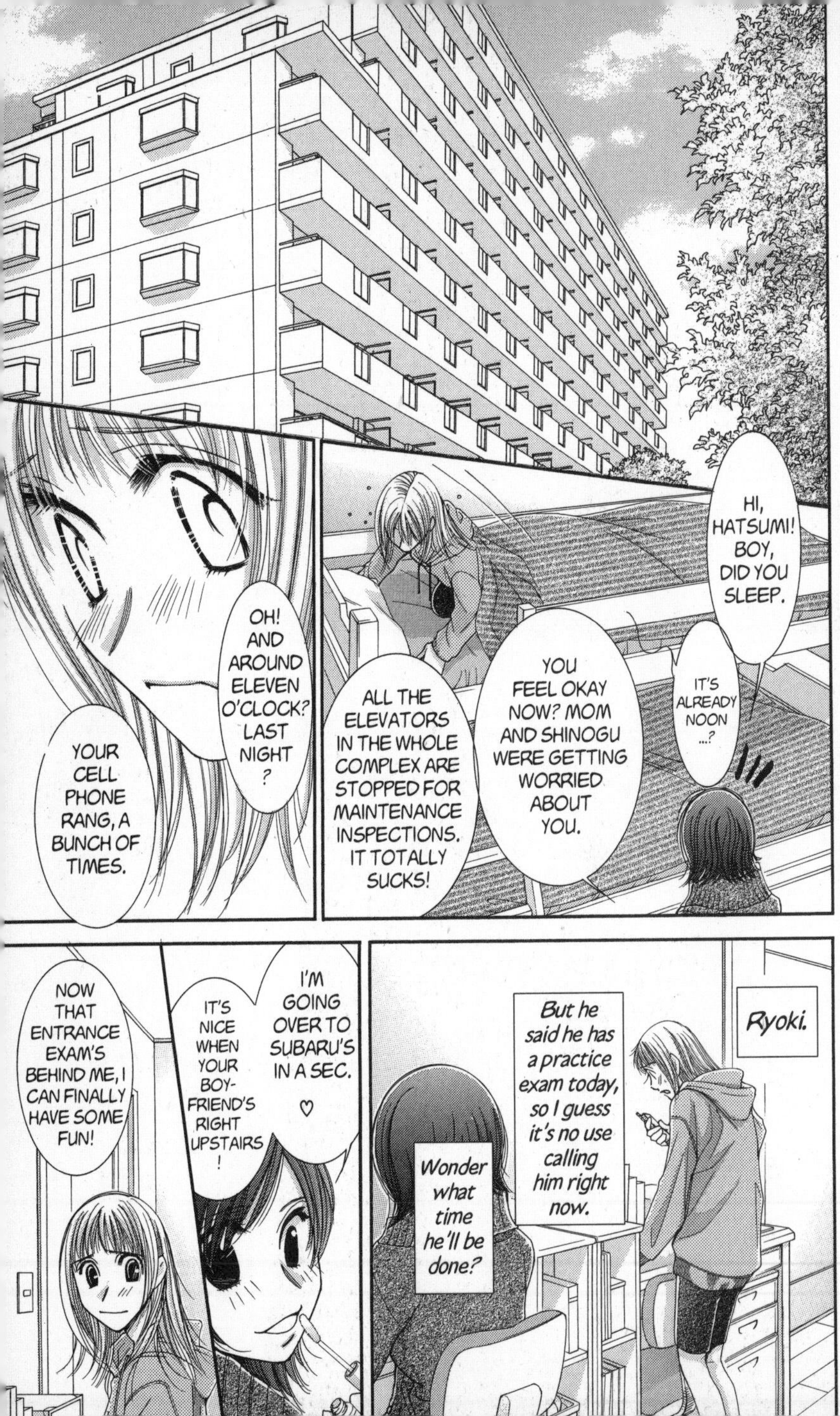
HI, HATSUMI! BOY, DID YOU SLEEP.
IT'S ALREADY NOON ...?
YOU FEEL OKAY NOW? MOM AND SHINOGU WERE GETTING WORRIED ABOUT YOU.
ALL THE ELEVATORS IN THE WHOLE COMPLEX ARE STOPPED FOR MAINTENANCE INSPECTIONS. IT TOTALLY SUCKS!
OH! AND AROUND ELEVEN O'CLOCK? LAST NIGHT?
YOUR CELL PHONE RANG, A BUNCH OF TIMES.
Ryoki.
But he said he has a practice exam today, so I guess it's no use calling him right now.
Wonder what time he'll be done?
I'M GOING OVER TO SUBARU'S IN A SEC. ♡
IT'S NICE WHEN YOUR BOY-FRIEND'S RIGHT UPSTAIRS!
NOW THAT ENTRANCE EXAM'S BEHIND ME, I CAN FINALLY HAVE SOME FUN!

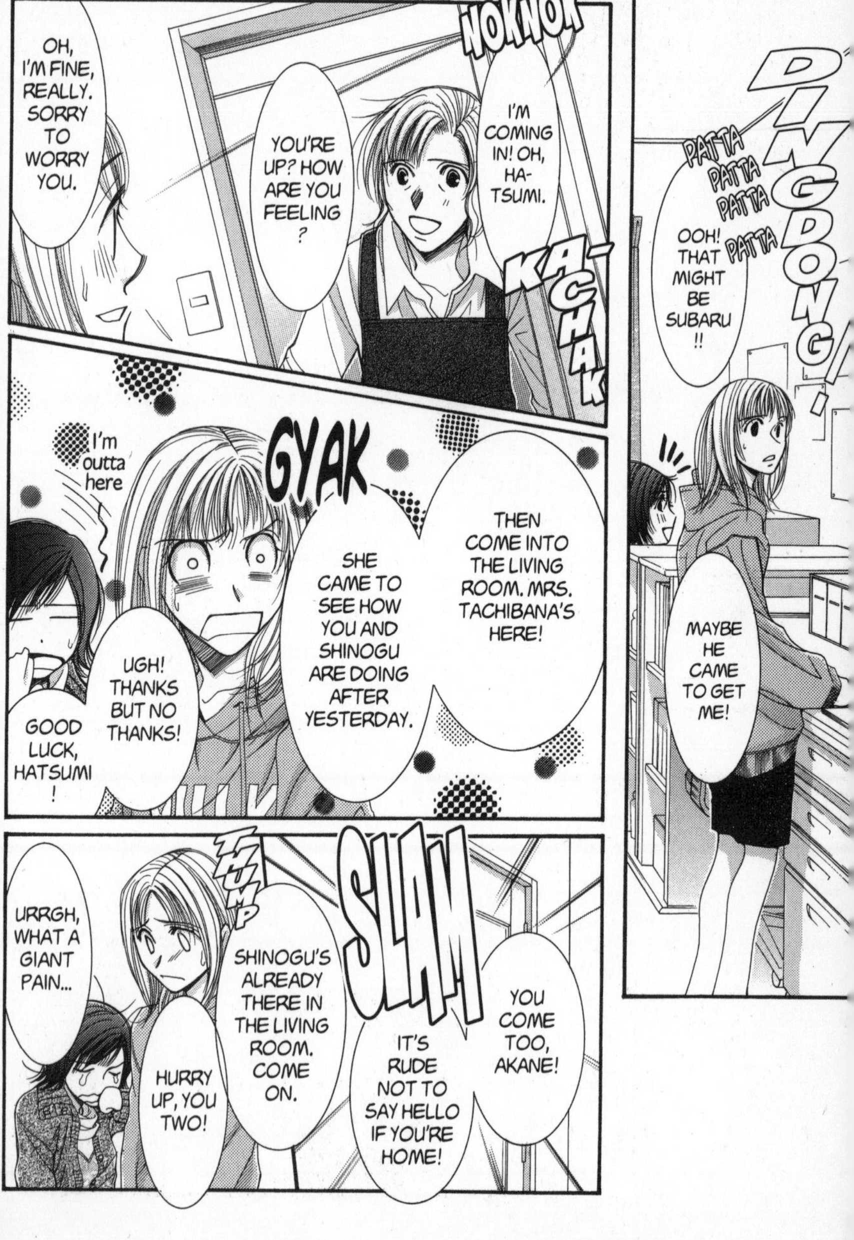
DING DONG!!
PATTA PATTA PATTA PATTA
OOH! THAT MIGHT BE SUBARU!!
MAYBE HE CAME TO GET ME!
NOKNOK
I'M COMING IN! OH, HATSUMI.
KA-CHAK
YOU'RE UP? HOW ARE YOU FEELING?
OH, I'M FINE, REALLY. SORRY TO WORRY YOU.
THEN COME INTO THE LIVING ROOM. MRS. TACHIBANA'S HERE!
SHE CAME TO SEE HOW YOU AND SHINOGU ARE DOING AFTER YESTERDAY.
GYAK
UGH! THANKS BUT NO THANKS!
I'm outta here
GOOD LUCK, HATSUMI!
SLAM
YOU COME TOO, AKANE!
IT'S RUDE NOT TO SAY HELLO IF YOU'RE HOME!
THUMP
SHINOGU'S ALREADY THERE IN THE LIVING ROOM. COME ON.
HURRY UP, YOU TWO!
URRGH, WHAT A GIANT PAIN...

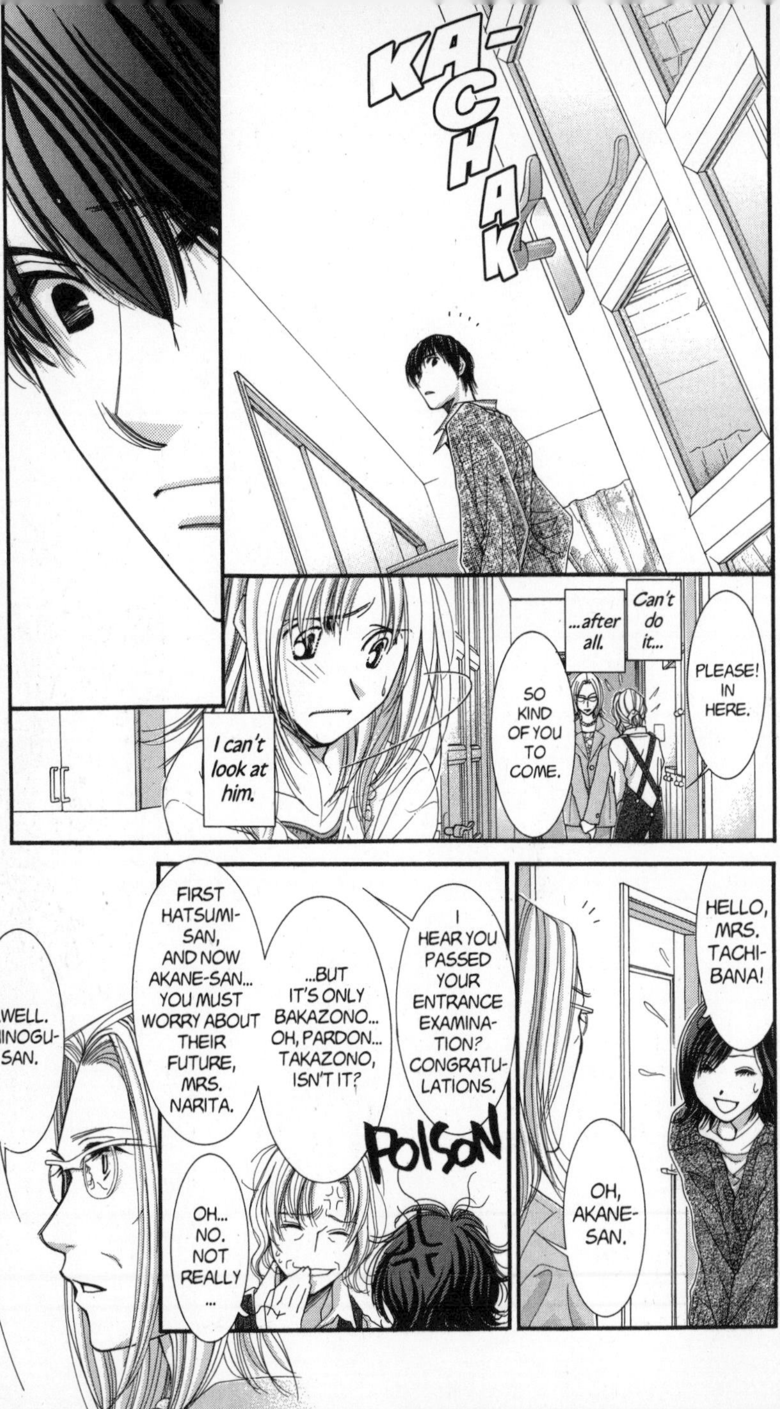
KA-CHAK
PLEASE! IN HERE.
Can't do it...
...after all.
SO KIND OF YOU TO COME.
I can't look at him.
HELLO, MRS. TACHIBANA!
OH, AKANE-SAN.
I HEAR YOU PASSED YOUR ENTRANCE EXAMINATION? CONGRATULATIONS.
...BUT IT'S ONLY BAKAZONO... OH, PARDON... TAKAZONO, ISN'T IT?
FIRST HATSUMI-SAN, AND NOW AKANE-SAN... YOU MUST WORRY ABOUT THEIR FUTURE, MRS. NARITA.
POISON
OH... NO. NOT REALLY...
...WELL. SHINOGU-SAN.

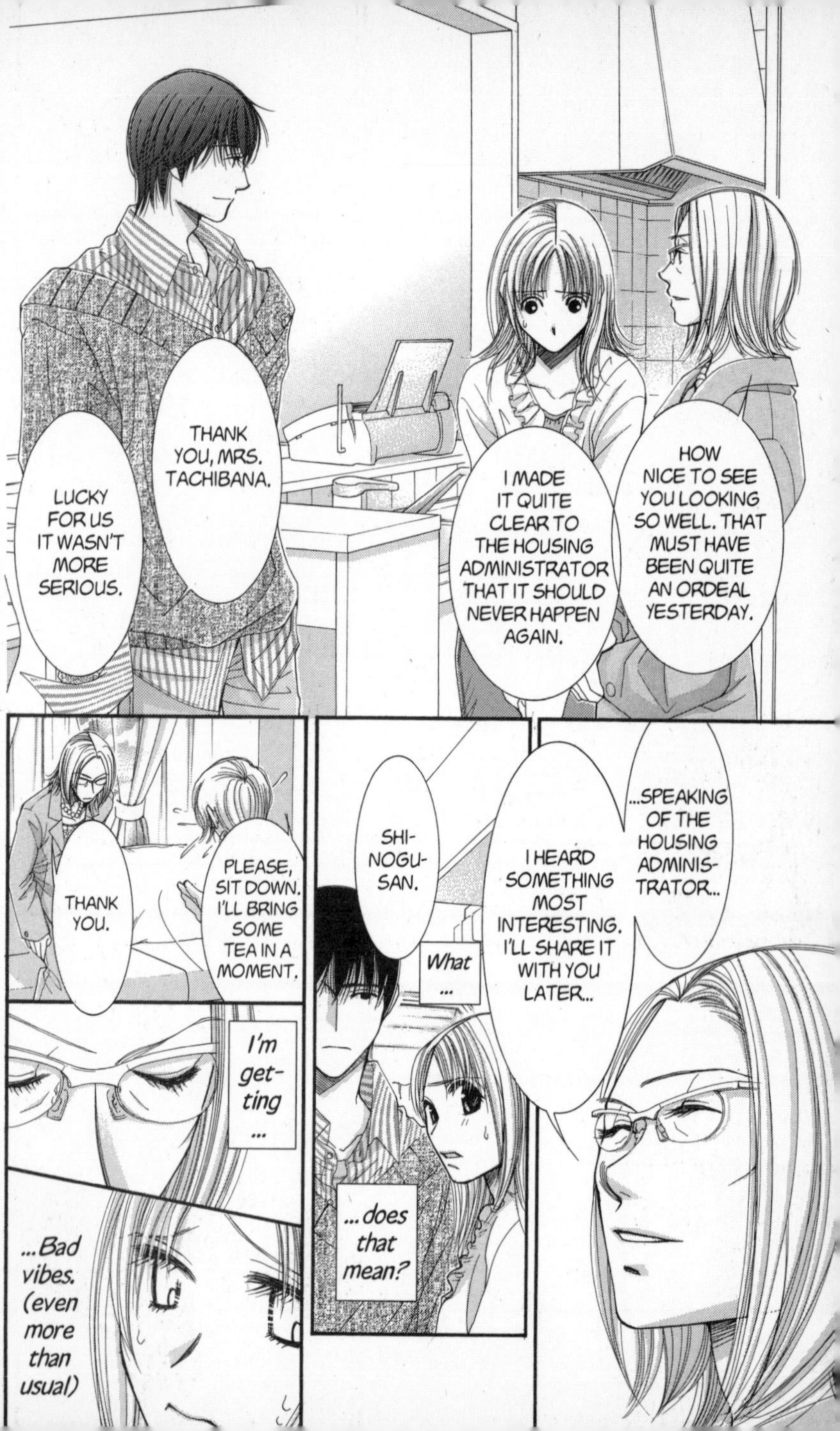
HOW NICE TO SEE YOU LOOKING SO WELL. THAT MUST HAVE BEEN QUITE AN ORDEAL YESTERDAY.
I MADE IT QUITE CLEAR TO THE HOUSING ADMINISTRATOR THAT IT SHOULD NEVER HAPPEN AGAIN.
THANK YOU, MRS. TACHIBANA.
LUCKY FOR US IT WASN'T MORE SERIOUS.
...SPEAKING OF THE HOUSING ADMINIS-TRATOR...
I HEARD SOMETHING MOST INTERESTING. I'LL SHARE IT WITH YOU LATER...
SHI-NOGU-SAN.
What ...
...does that mean?
PLEASE, SIT DOWN. I'LL BRING SOME TEA IN A MOMENT.
THANK YOU.
I'm get-ting ...
...Bad vibes. (even more than usual)

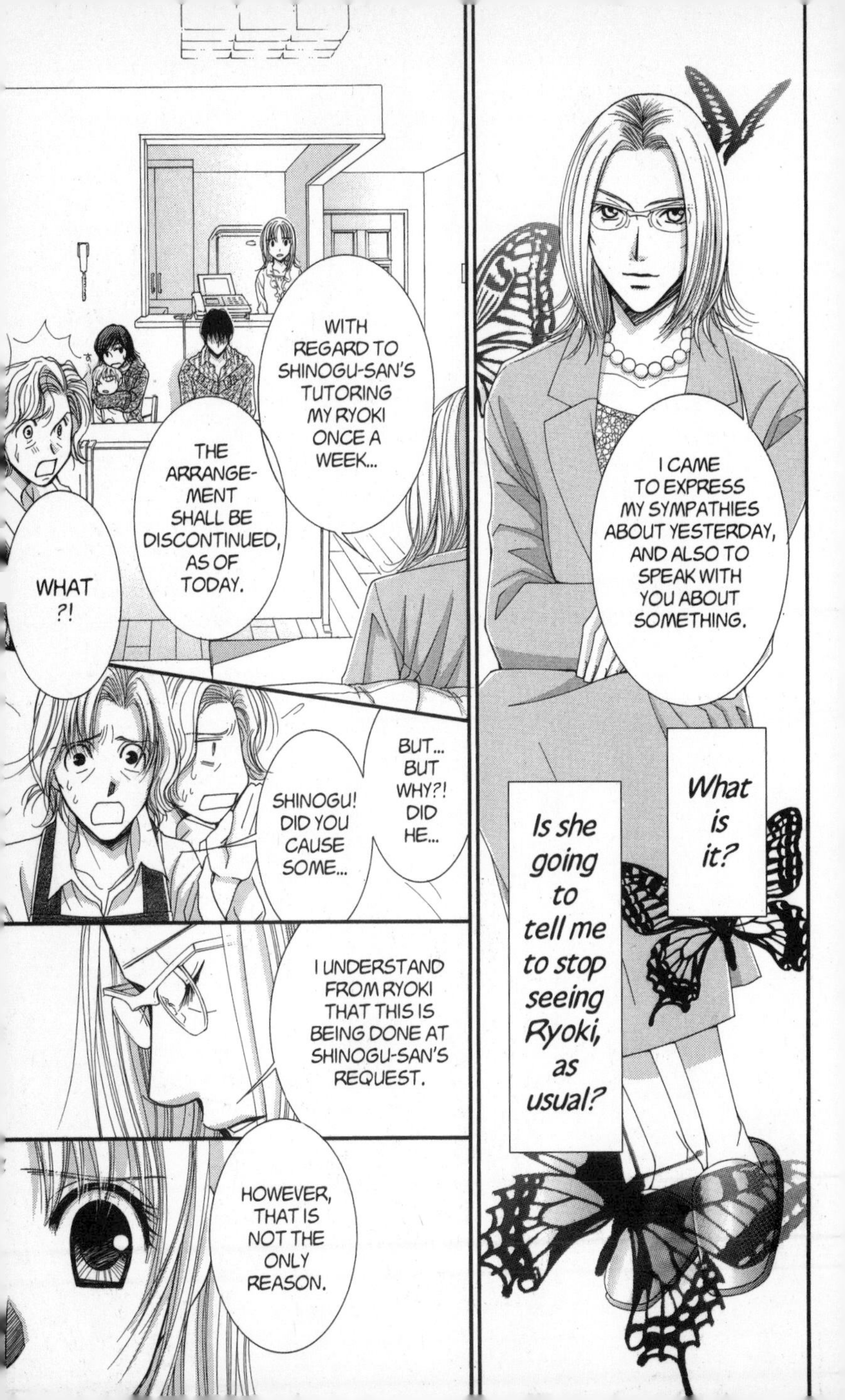
I CAME TO EXPRESS MY SYMPATHIES ABOUT YESTERDAY, AND ALSO TO SPEAK WITH YOU ABOUT SOMETHING.
What is it?
Is she going to tell me to stop seeing Ryoki, as usual?
WITH REGARD TO SHINOGU-SAN'S TUTORING MY RYOKI ONCE A WEEK...
THE ARRANGE-MENT SHALL BE DISCONTINUED, AS OF TODAY.
WHAT?!
BUT... BUT WHY?! DID HE...
SHINOGU! DID YOU CAUSE SOME...
I UNDERSTAND FROM RYOKI THAT THIS IS BEING DONE AT SHINOGU-SAN'S REQUEST.
HOWEVER, THAT IS NOT THE ONLY REASON.

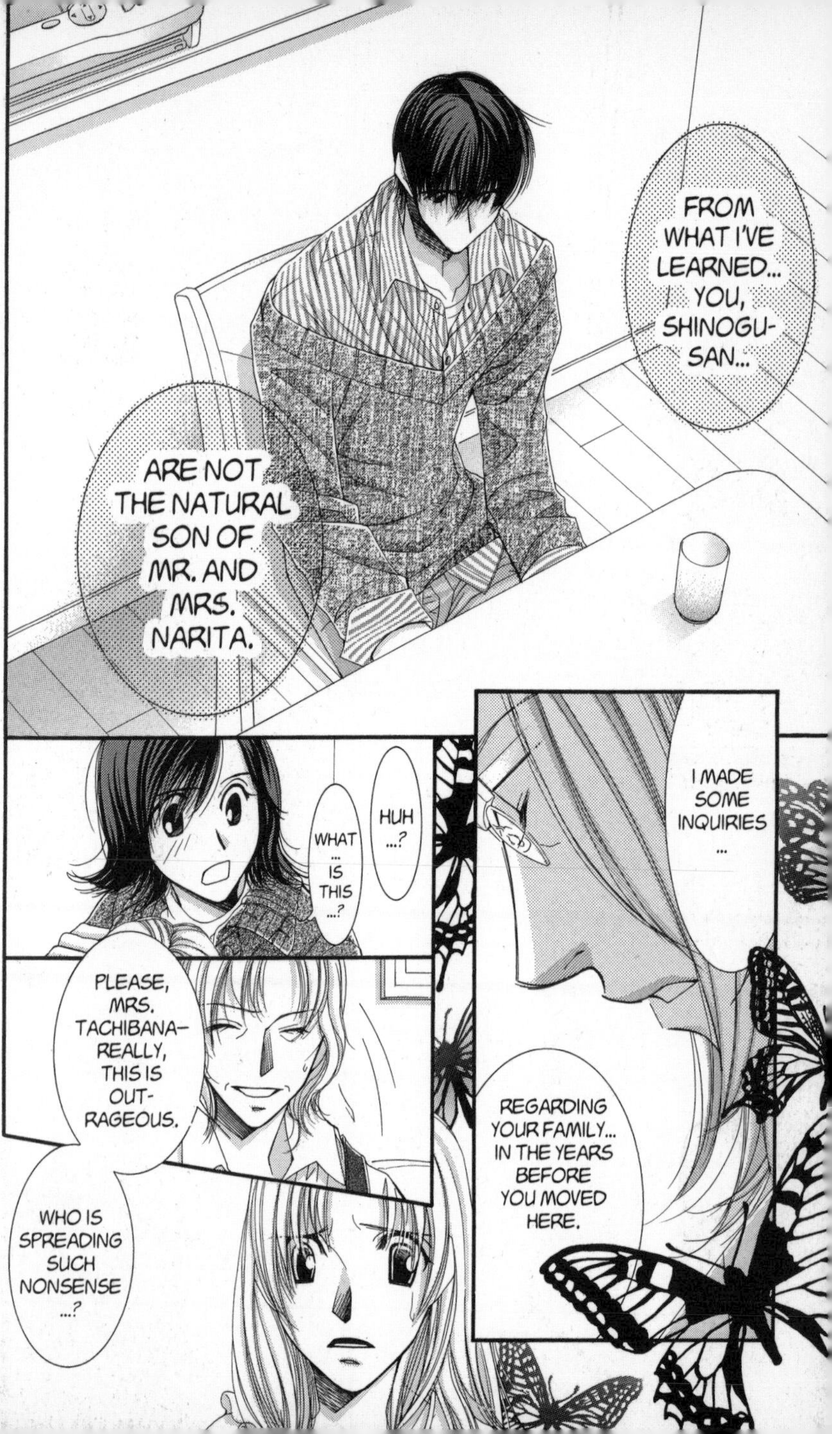
FROM WHAT I'VE LEARNED... YOU, SHINOGU-SAN...
ARE NOT THE NATURAL SON OF MR. AND MRS. NARITA.
I MADE SOME INQUIRIES ...
REGARDING YOUR FAMILY... IN THE YEARS BEFORE YOU MOVED HERE.
HUH ...?
WHAT ... IS THIS ...?
PLEASE, MRS. TACHIBANA-REALLY, THIS IS OUT-RAGEOUS.
WHO IS SPREADING SUCH NONSENSE ...?

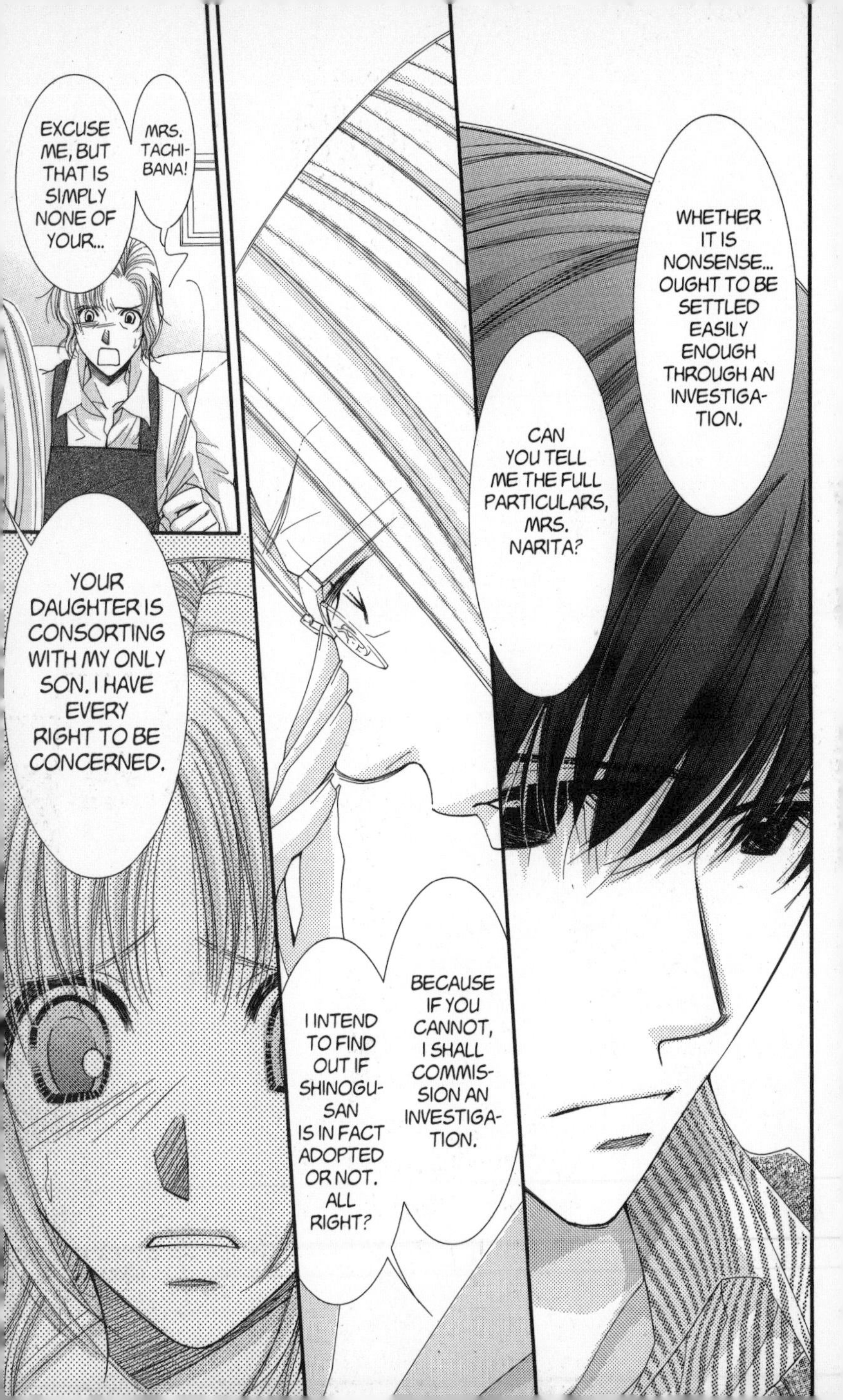
WHETHER IT IS NONSENSE... OUGHT TO BE SETTLED EASILY ENOUGH THROUGH AN INVESTIGATION.
CAN YOU TELL ME THE FULL PARTICULARS, MRS. NARITA?
BECAUSE IF YOU CANNOT, I SHALL COMMISSION AN INVESTIGATION.
I INTEND TO FIND OUT IF SHINOGU-SAN IS IN FACT ADOPTED OR NOT. ALL RIGHT?
MRS. TACHIBANA!
EXCUSE ME, BUT THAT IS SIMPLY NONE OF YOUR...
YOUR DAUGHTER IS CONSORTING WITH MY ONLY SON. I HAVE EVERY RIGHT TO BE CONCERNED.

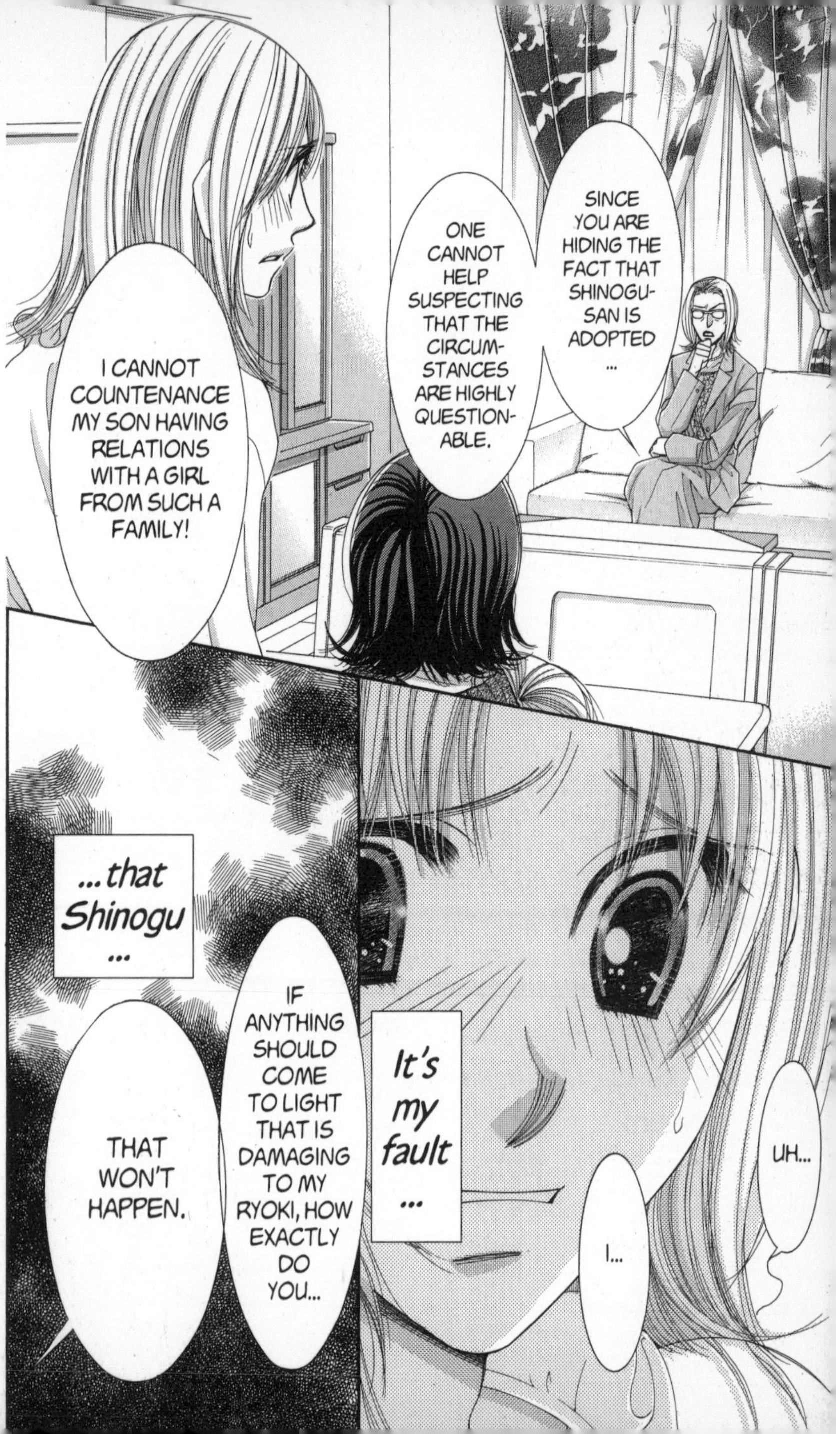
SINCE YOU ARE HIDING THE FACT THAT SHINOGU-SAN IS ADOPTED ...
ONE CANNOT HELP SUSPECTING THAT THE CIRCUM-STANCES ARE HIGHLY QUESTION-ABLE.
I CANNOT COUNTENANCE MY SON HAVING RELATIONS WITH A GIRL FROM SUCH A FAMILY!
UH...
I...
It's my fault ...
...that Shinogu ...
IF ANYTHING SHOULD COME TO LIGHT THAT IS DAMAGING TO MY RYOKI, HOW EXACTLY DO YOU...
THAT WON'T HAPPEN.

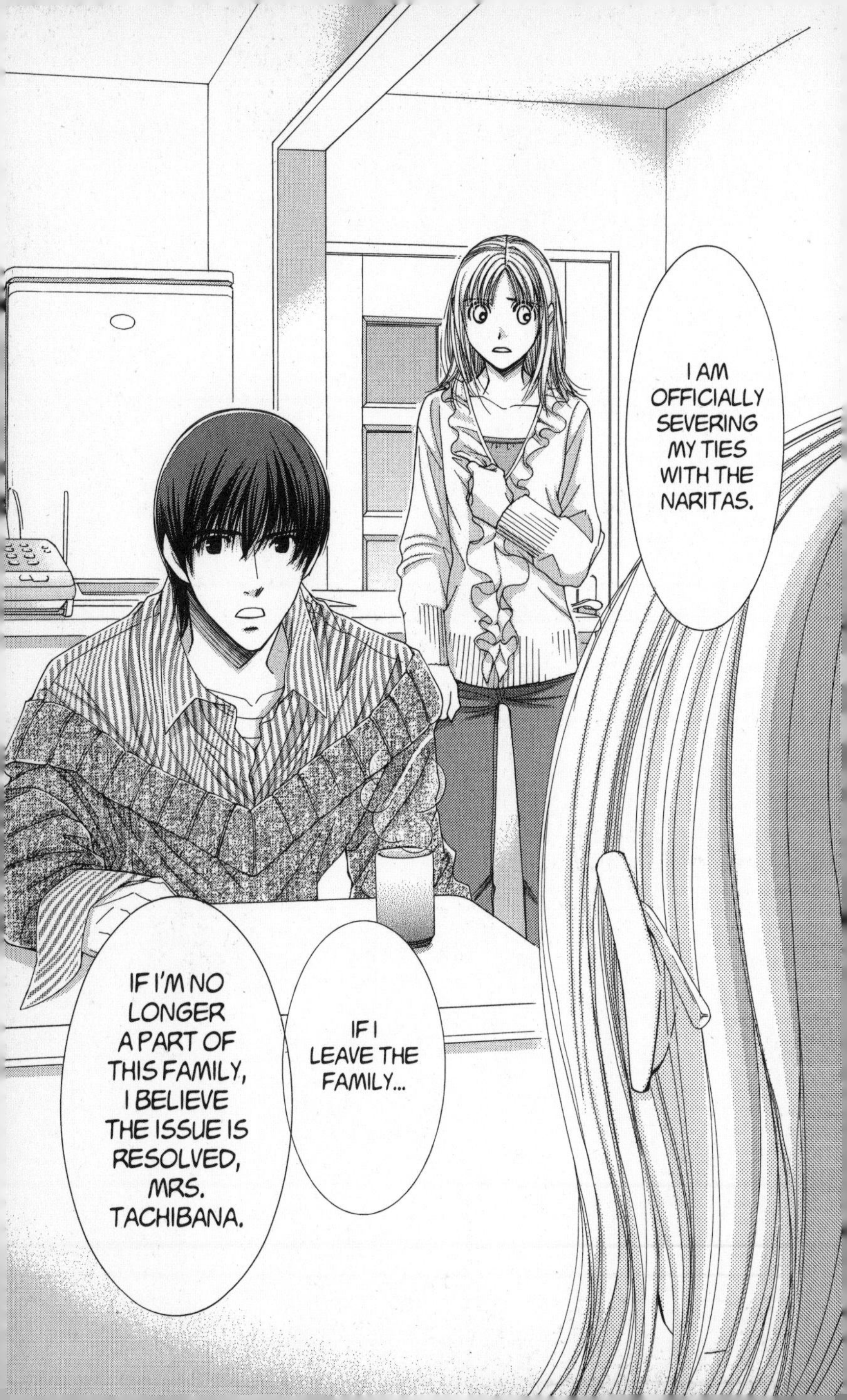
I AM OFFICIALLY SEVERING MY TIES WITH THE NARITAS.
IF I LEAVE THE FAMILY...
IF I'M NO LONGER A PART OF THIS FAMILY, I BELIEVE THE ISSUE IS RESOLVED, MRS. TACHIBANA.

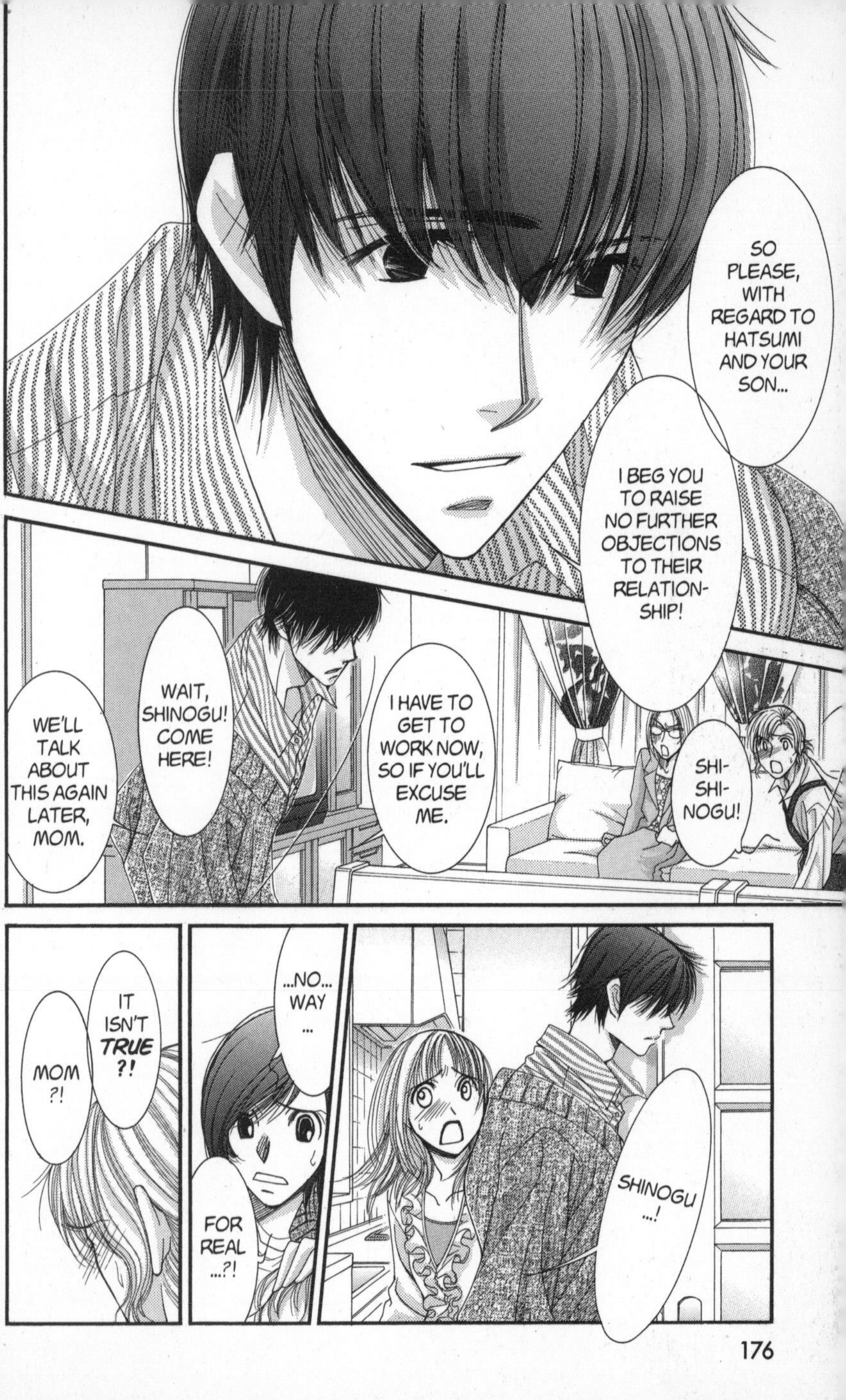
SO PLEASE, WITH REGARD TO HATSUMI AND YOUR SON...
I BEG YOU TO RAISE NO FURTHER OBJECTIONS TO THEIR RELATION-SHIP!
SHI-SHI-NOGU!
I HAVE TO GET TO WORK NOW, SO IF YOU'LL EXCUSE ME.
WAIT, SHINOGU! COME HERE!
WE'LL TALK ABOUT THIS AGAIN LATER, MOM.
SHINOGU ...!
...NO... WAY ...
FOR REAL ...?!
IT ISN'T **TRUE** ?!
MOM ?!

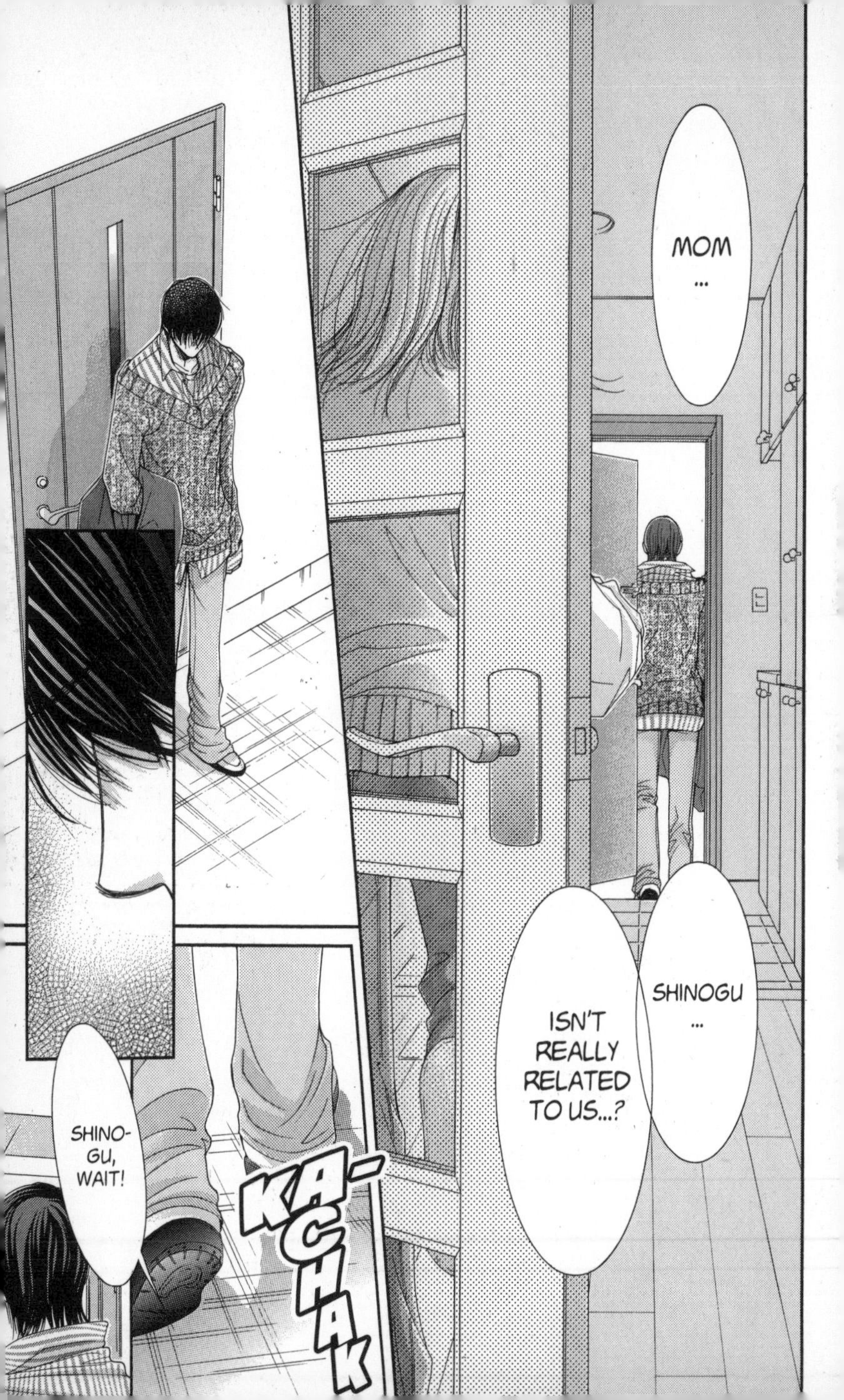
MOM ...
SHINOGU ...
ISN'T REALLY RELATED TO US...?
SHINO-GU, WAIT!
KA-CHAK

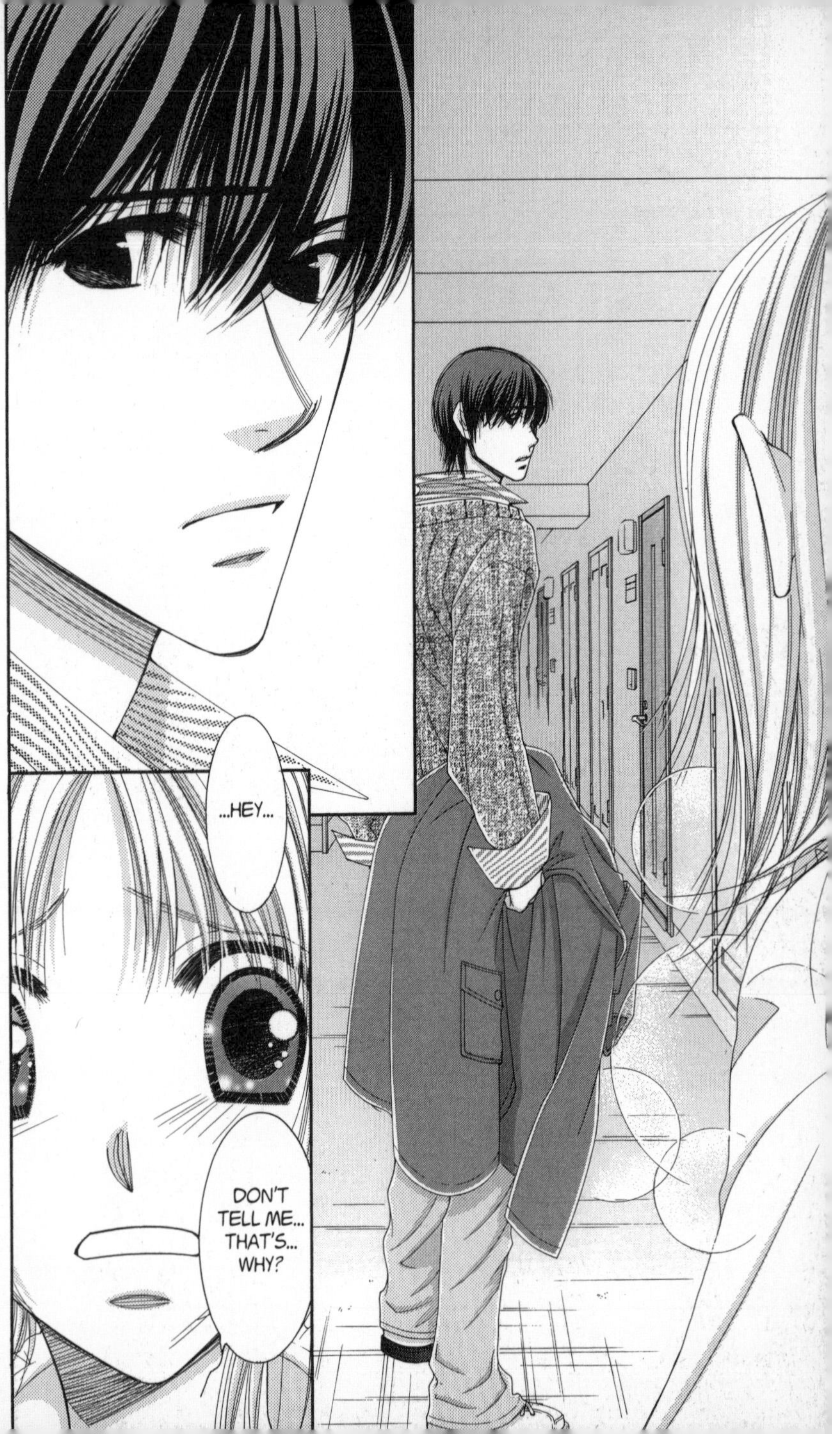
...HEY...
DON'T TELL ME... THAT'S... WHY?

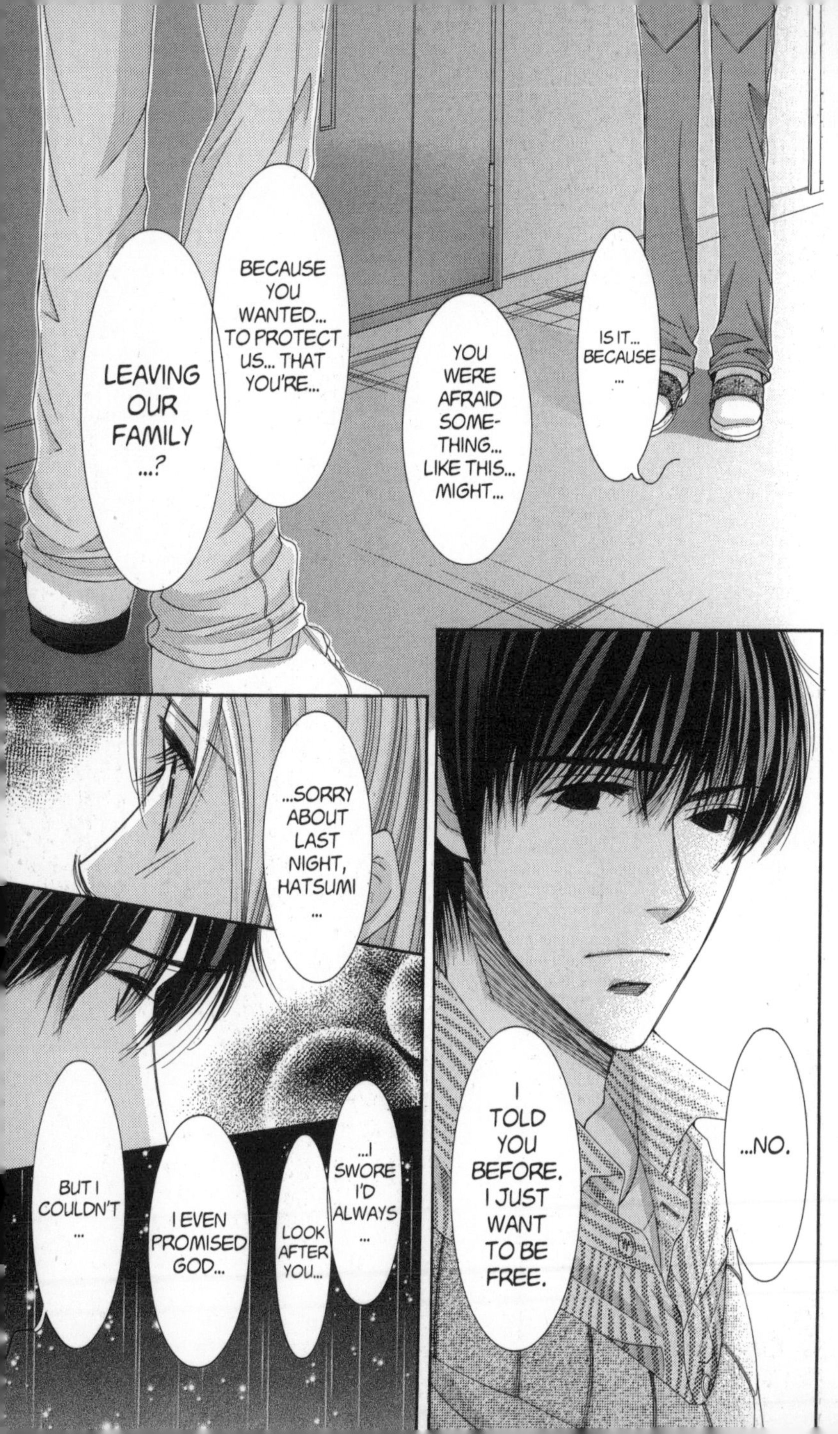
IS IT... BECAUSE ...
YOU WERE AFRAID SOME-THING... LIKE THIS... MIGHT...
BECAUSE YOU WANTED... TO PROTECT US... THAT YOU'RE...
LEAVING OUR FAMILY ...?
...NO.
I TOLD YOU BEFORE. I JUST WANT TO BE FREE.
...SORRY ABOUT LAST NIGHT, HATSUMI ...
...I SWORE I'D ALWAYS ...
LOOK AFTER YOU...
I EVEN PROMISED GOD...
BUT I COULDN'T ...

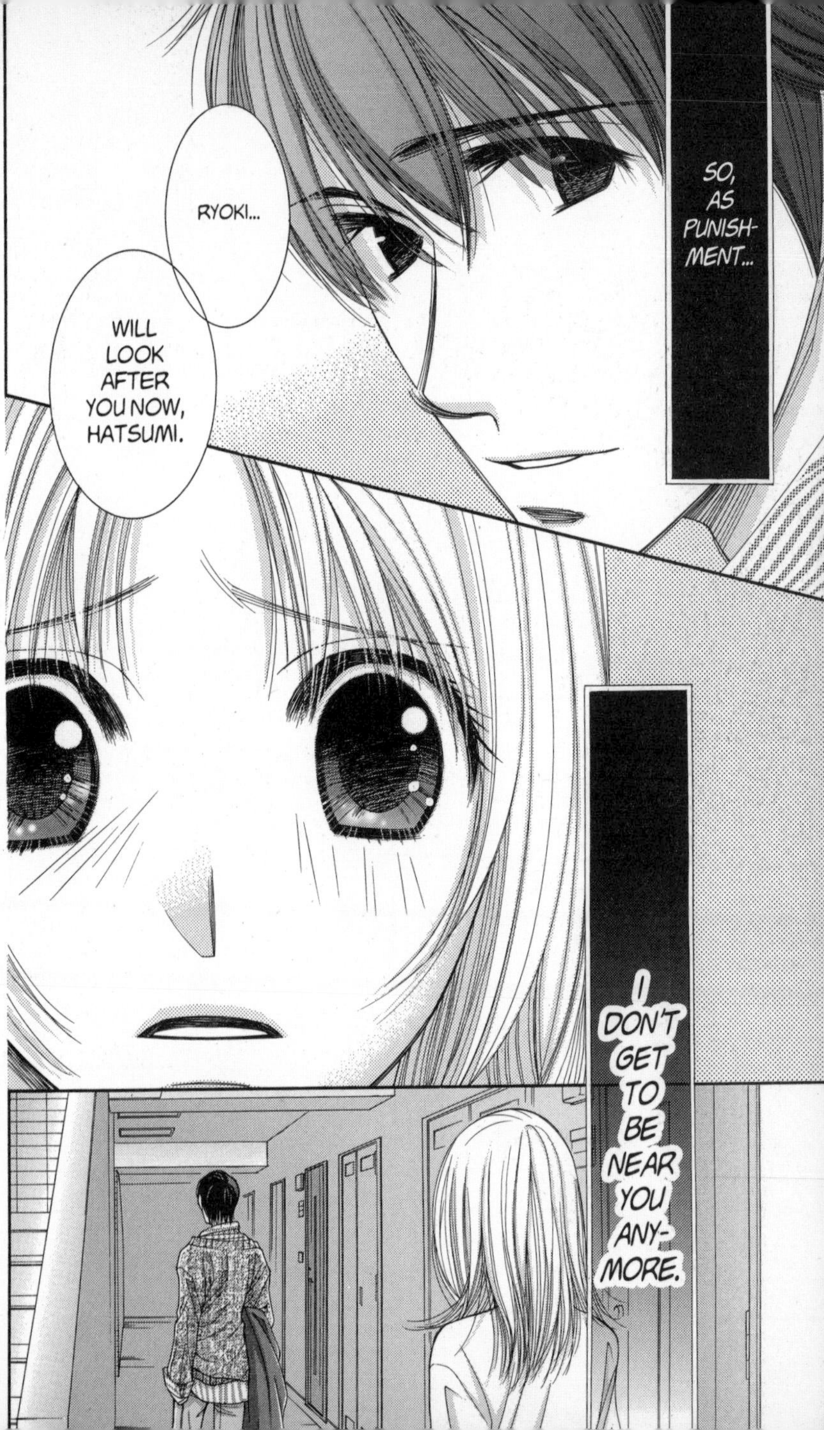
SO, AS PUNISH-MENT...
RYOKI...
WILL LOOK AFTER YOU NOW, HATSUMI.
I DON'T GET TO BE NEAR YOU ANY-MORE.

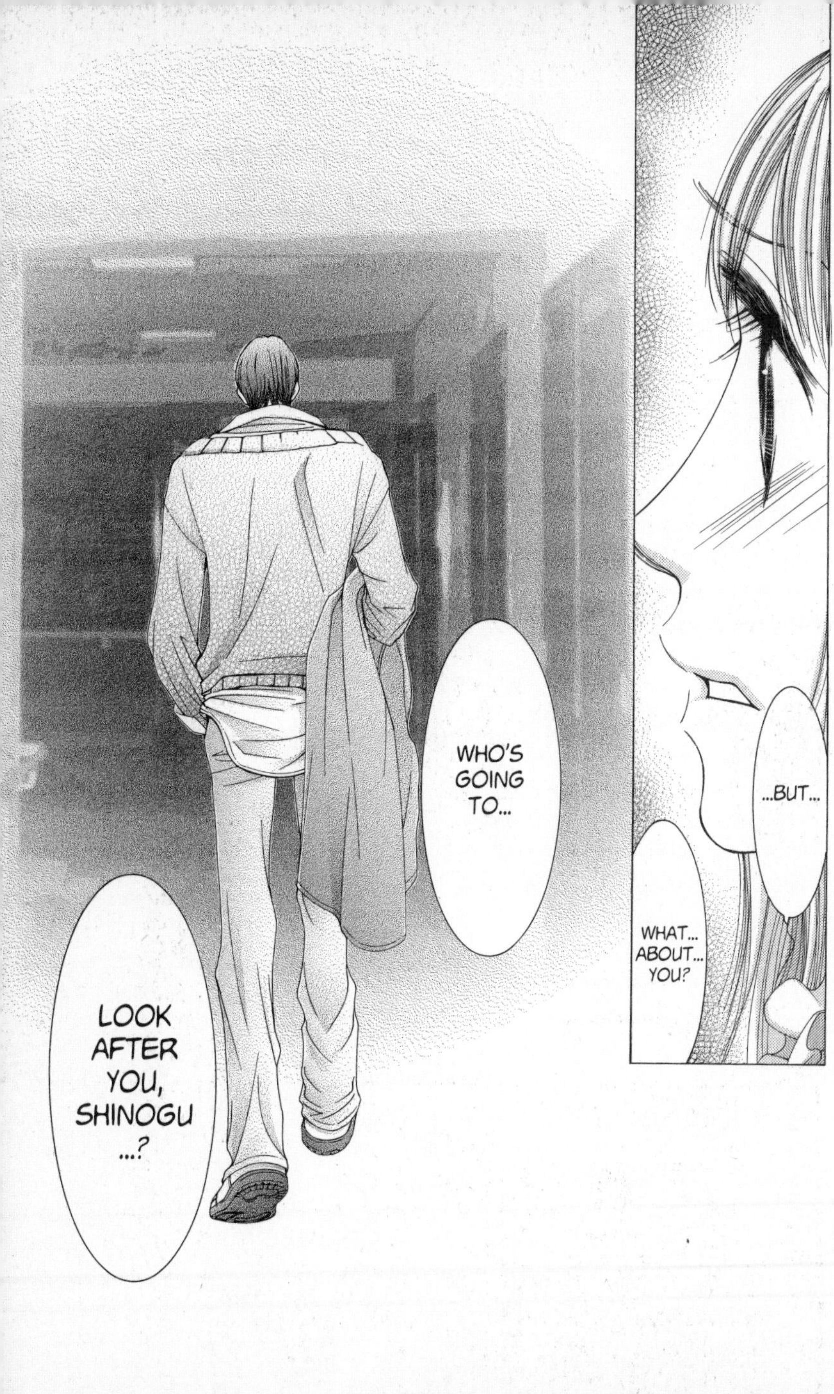
...BUT...
WHAT... ABOUT... YOU?
WHO'S GOING TO...
LOOK AFTER YOU, SHINOGU ...?

hot gimmick

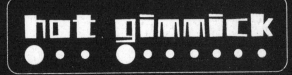

To be continued

HOT GIMMICK
Vol. 9

Shôjo Edition

STORY & ART BY MIKI AIHARA

ENGLISH ADAPTATION BY POOKIE ROLF

Touch-up Art & Lettering/Rina Mapa
Cover Design/Izumi Evers
Editor/Kit Fox

Managing Editor/Annette Roman
Director of Production/Noboru Watanabe
Vice President of Publishing/Alvin Lu
Sr. Director of Acquisitions/Rika Inouye
Vice President of Sales & Marketing/Liza Coppola
Publisher/Hyoe Narita

© 2001 Miki Aihara/Shogakukan, Inc. First published by Shogakukan, Inc. in Japan as "Hot Gimmick." New and adapted artwork and text © 2005 VIZ, LLC. The HOT GIMMICK logo is a trademark of VIZ, LLC. All rights reserved. The stories, characters and incidents mentioned in this publication are entirely fictional.

No portion of this book may be reproduced or transmitted in any form or by any means without written permission from the copyright holders.

Printed in Canada.

Published by VIZ, LLC
P.O. Box 77010
San Francisco, CA 94107

10 9 8 7 6 5 4 3 2 1
First printing, June 2005

PARENTAL ADVISORY
HOT GIMMICK is rated T+ for Older Teens.
Contains strong language and sexual themes.
Recommended for older teens (16 and up).

www.viz.com

Hot Gimmick

EDITOR'S RECOMMENDATIONS

**More manga!
More manga!**

**Did you like
Hot Gimmick?
Here's what VIZ
recommends you
try next:**

© 2002 Kaho Miyasaka/
Shogakukan, Inc.

KARE FIRST LOVE

Still feening for some more school time romantics? Look no further than Kaho Miyasaka's tale of a bashful gal coming into her own thanks to the affections of a super-cute photographer. If a picture is worth a thousand words, than Karin Karino's life is about to become an ordeal of Tolstoy-esque proportions.

© 2000 Kaneyoshi Izumi/
Shogakukan, Inc.

DOUBT!!

A wise man once said, "There are only two kinds of people: those that make wide, sweeping generalizations, and those that don't." Unfortunately, body-image-challenged Ai definitely falls into the former category for, as she sees it, there really only two kinds of girls: those who get noticed by boys, and those—like herself—who don't. Will an ultimate makeover change her luck with the fellas, or will she inevitably become just another vacuous slave to fashion?

© 2004 Rie Takada/
Shogakukan, Inc.

HAPPY HUSTLE HIGH

In a world fraught with conformity and lowered expectations, tough-as-she-wants-to-be Hanabi Ozora stands a head above the crowd. After her all-girls school is integrated with an all-boys school, Hanabi is appointed to the school council and clashes head-on with the shrewd (yet markedly hot) Vice President, Yasuaki. Can Hanabi win his heart and keep her pride?

A Beauty Who Feels Like a Beast!

To overcome an embarrassing past, teenage Ai gets a makeover and attends a new high school. Soon, the hottest guy at school is chatting her up! But beauty is only skin deep, and Ai learns that fresh makeup and new clothes can't hide her insecurities or doubts.

A tale of high school neurosis at its finest—start your graphic novel collection today!

doubt!!™

Only $9.99!

doubt!!™

DOUBT

vol 1

Story and art by Izumi Kaneyoshi

© 2000 Kaneyoshi Izumi/Shogakukan Inc.

VIZ

www.viz.com

VIZ

store.viz.com